Fodor's

UTAH

3rd Edition

**Where to Stay and Eat
for All Budgets**

**Must-See Sights
and Local Secrets**

Ratings You Can Trust

Fodor's Travel Publications   New York, Toronto, London, Sydney, Auckland
www.fodors.com

FODOR'S UTAH

Editor[s]: Eric B. Wechter & Carolyn B. Heller

Editorial Production: Evangelos Vasilakis

Editorial Contributors: John Blodgett, Janet Buckingham, Jane Gendron, Jenie Skoy, Kelley J.P. Lindberg, Denise Leto, Dana Doherty Menlove, Mark Menlove, Lucia Stewart, Jonathan Stumpf

Maps & Illustrations: Mark Stroud, Henry Colomb, David Lindroth, Inc., and Ed Jacobus, *cartographers*; William Wu; Bob Blake, Rebecca Baer, *map editors*

Design: Fabrizio LaRocca, *creative director*; Guido Caroti, Siobhan O'Hare, *art directors*; Tina Malaney, Chie Ushio, Ann McBride, *designers*; Melanie Marin, *senior picture editor*; Moon Sun Kim, *cover designer*

Cover Photo: ("Behind the Rocks" area, Moab): Whit Richardson/Aurora Photos

Production/Manufacturing: Angela L. McLean

COPYRIGHT

3rd Edition

ISBN 978-1-4000-0725-7

ISSN 1547-870X

SPECIAL SALES

This book is available at special discounts for bulk purchases for sales promotions or premiums. Special editions, including personalized covers, excerpts of existing books, and corporate imprints, can be created in large quantities for special needs. For more information, write to Special Markets/Premium Sales, 1745 Broadway, MD 6-2, New York, New York 10019, or e-mail specialmarkets@randomhouse.com.

AN IMPORTANT TIP & AN INVITATION

Although all prices, opening times, and other details in this book are based on information supplied to us at press time, changes occur all the time in the travel world, and Fodor's cannot accept responsibility for facts that become outdated or for inadvertent errors or omissions. So **always confirm information when it matters,** especially if you're making a detour to visit a specific place. Your experiences—positive and negative—matter to us. If we have missed or misstated something, **please write to us.** We follow up on all suggestions. Contact the Utah editor at editors@fodors.com or c/o Fodor's at 1745 Broadway, New York, NY 10019.

PRINTED IN THE UNITED STATES OF AMERICA
10 9 8 7 6 5 4 3 2 1

Be a Fodor's Correspondent

Your opinion matters. It matters to us. It matters to your fellow Fodor's travelers, too. And we'd like to hear it. In fact, we need to hear it.

When you share your experiences and opinions, you become an active member of the Fodor's community. That means we'll not only use your feedback to make our books better, but we'll publish your names and comments whenever possible. Throughout our guides, look for "Word of Mouth," excerpts of your unvarnished feedback.

Here's how you can help improve Fodor's for all of us.

Tell us when we're right. We rely on local writers to give you an insider's perspective. But our writers and staff editors—who are the best in the business—depend on you. Your positive feedback is a vote to renew our recommendations for the next edition.

Tell us when we're wrong. We're proud that we update most of our guides every year. But we're not perfect. Things change. Hotels cut services. Museums change hours. Charming cafés lose charm. If our writer didn't quite capture the essence of a place, tell us how you'd do it differently. If any of our descriptions are inaccurate or inadequate, we'll incorporate your changes in the next edition and will correct factual errors at fodors.com immediately.

Tell us what to include. You probably have had fantastic travel experiences that aren't yet in Fodor's. Why not share them with a community of like-minded travelers? Maybe you chanced upon a beach or bistro or B&B that you don't want to keep to yourself. Tell us why we should include it. And share your discoveries and experiences with everyone directly at fodors.com. Your input may lead us to add a new listing or highlight a place we cover with a "Highly Recommended" star or with our highest rating, "Fodor's Choice."

Give us your opinion instantly at our feedback center at www.fodors.com/feedback. You may also e-mail editors@fodors.com with the subject line "Utah Editor." Or send your nominations, comments, and complaints by mail to Utah Editor, Fodor's, 1745 Broadway, New York, NY 10019.

You and travelers like you are the heart of the Fodor's community. Make our community richer by sharing your experiences. Be a Fodor's correspondent.

Happy traveling!

Tim Jarrell, Publisher

CONTENTS

CLOSE UPS

MAPS

ABOUT THIS BOOK

Our Ratings

Sometimes you find terrific travel experiences and sometimes they just find you. But usually the burden is on you to select the right combination of experiences. That's where our ratings come in.

As travelers we've all discovered a place so wonderful that its worthiness is obvious. And sometimes that place is so unique that superlatives don't do it justice: you just have to be there to know. These sights, properties, and experiences get our highest rating, **Fodor's Choice**, indicated by orange stars throughout this book. Black stars highlight sights and properties we deem **Highly Recommended**, places that our writers, editors, and readers praise again and again for consistency and excellence. By default, there's another category: any place we include in this book is by definition worth your time, unless we say otherwise. And we will.

Disagree with any of our choices? Care to nominate a place or suggest that we rate one more highly? Visit our feedback center at www.fodors.com/feedback.

Budget Well

Hotel and restaurant price categories from ¢ to $$$$ are defined in the opening pages of each chapter. For attractions, we always give standard adult admission fees; reductions are usually available for children, students, and senior citizens. Want to pay with plastic? **AE, D, DC, MC, V** following restaurant and hotel listings indicate whether American Express, Discover, Diner's Club, MasterCard, and Visa are accepted.

Restaurants

Unless we state otherwise, restaurants are open for lunch and dinner daily. We mention dress only when there's a specific requirement and reservations only when they're essential or not accepted—it's always best to book ahead.

Hotels

Hotels have private bath, phone, TV, and air-conditioning and operate on the European Plan (aka EP, meaning without meals), unless we specify that they use the Continental Plan (CP, with a continental breakfast), Breakfast Plan (BP, with a full breakfast), or Modified American Plan (MAP, with breakfast and dinner) or are all-inclusive (including all meals and most activities). We always list facilities but not whether you'll be charged an extra fee to use them, so when pricing accommodations, find out what's included.

Many Listings

★	Fodor's Choice
★	Highly recommended
✉	Physical address
⊹	Directions
⌂	Mailing address
☎	Telephone
🖶	Fax
⊕	On the Web
✎	E-mail
✆	Admission fee
☉	Open/closed times
Ⓜ	Metro stations
▤	Credit cards

Hotels & Restaurants

🏨	Hotel
⇗	Number of rooms
⏷	Facilities
❍	Meal plans
✕	Restaurant
⇘	Reservations
⟍	Smoking
℗	BYOB
✕🏨	Hotel with restaurant that warrants a visit

Outdoors

⚐	Golf
⛺	Camping

Other

☾	Family-friendly
⇨	See also
✉	Branch address
☞	Take note

WHAT'S WHERE

SALT LAKE CITY 	Utah's capital city is cradled between the foothills of the Wasatch Range to the east and the Oquirrh Mountains and Great Salt Lake to the west. Since it's home to the state's only major airport, most visits to Utah begin here. Salt Lake City is in the middle of the Wasatch Front—Utah's urban corridor—which is home to about 80% of the state's population and stretches 175 mi from Brigham City in the north to Payson in the south. Interstate 15 runs north and south along the Wasatch Front and is the major route from Utah to Las Vegas and Los Angeles. The world headquarters of the conservative Church of Jesus Christ of Latter-day Saints (you can hardly visit Salt Lake City without at least passing by Temple Square), Salt Lake City is surprisingly cosmopolitan, with the state's most diverse population. Contrary to what you might have heard, Salt Lake City has a thriving nightlife scene and yes, you can get a drink. There's an active arts community and no dearth of good restaurants. And sports enthusiasts, take note: Salt Lake City is home to major basketball, hockey, baseball, and soccer clubs. Utah's largest newspapers and television stations originate here, and a significant feather in this city's cap was its terrific success as host to the world during the 2002 Winter Olympics.
PARK CITY & THE SOUTHERN WASATCH 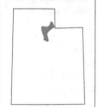	The Wasatch Mountains form a rugged divider from north to south, providing a spectacular staging ground for some of the finest ski resorts in the country, if not the world. With exceptional Wasatch Mountain terrain, and the lightest, driest, deepest powder around, the ski resorts of the southern Wasatch in and around Park City please even the most discriminating skiers and snowboarders. And, surprise-surprise, it's not just about the snow: this part of Utah is home to world-class fly-fishing streams, a variety of challenging golf courses, and loads of high adventure in the backcountry. And after all that recreating, you can enjoy a drink in a chichi club, move on to a delectable supper, and then, if you don't feel like going home to the hot tub just yet, you can cut loose with some live music on Main Street. Park City's rep of being Utah's "Sin City" is inextricably tied to its past: it, along with the towns of Alta and Brighton were birthed by raucous mining camps and a significant vein of that wild lifestyle continues to this day. In contrast the Heber City area is a classically Mormon pioneer-formed community, as is Provo, home to Brigham Young University. Recreation opportunities abound here, too, but the nightlife is decidedly toned-down.

NORTH OF SALT LAKE CITY	

Northern Utah has striking scenery but far fewer tourists than the more popular regions to the south. Heading north from Salt Lake City along the Wasatch Front you pass a number of bedroom communities that fuse Ogden, the largest city in northern Utah, with the greater Salt Lake City area. North beyond Ogden, Utah is still rough and rugged country, not so unlike the way it was when the Transcontinental Railroad builders met in lonely Promontory to drive their celebratory golden spike and link the two coasts for the first time, in 1869. A large part of the region is within boundaries of the Wasatch-Cache National Forest, with its breathtaking landscapes and countless miles of mostly undiscovered trails. In the northeastern part of the state is Logan, home to both Utah State University and the Utah Festival Opera. Logan is also a reliable base for hiking, biking, boating, and skiing excursions. Northern Utah is not necessarily the place for urban culture, but if you want genuine small-town charm you're likely to find a dose or two here. It doesn't get more down-home than the legendary fresh raspberry shakes made by locals in Bear Lake.

DINOSAURLAND & EASTERN UTAH

The Uinta Range of the Rocky Mountains is a land of craggy peaks whose foothills give way to the rural ranching country of the Uinta Basin, where fertile farm valleys and grazing lands mingle with red-rock deserts. The quickest access to the wild Uinta Mountains also happens to be highly scenic. Take the Mirror Lake Scenic Byway through canyons and over passes to Mirror Lake, an excellent base for hikes into the surrounding mountains. To the east, and named in 1869 by explorer John Wesley Powell for the way the sun reflects on the red rock, Flaming Gorge is indeed a sight to behold, with dramatic red rock mountains surrounding its reservoir. Visitors enjoy activities such as powerboating, waterskiing, camping, parasailing, rafting, swimming, and fishing for the lake's renowned trophy trout. Not unlike Powell, many folks today like to raft or canoe the Green River below the dam, famous also for its world-class trout fishing. And even if your children haven't already suggested a trip to the fascinating Dinosaur National Monument, consider it. Many folks like to strike out on a self-guided walk or auto tour here to orient themselves to the unique character of dinosaur habitat. Another classic idea is to enjoy the area's scenic beauty from a boat on a one- to multi-day river trip with one of the park's river concessionaires.

CAPITOL REEF NATIONAL PARK & ENVIRONS 	Formed by cataclysmic forces that have pushed and compressed the earth, Capitol Reef National Park is an otherworldly landscape with oversize, unique sandstone formations, some layered with plant and animal fossils. Though still pretty down-home by most standards, Loa, Teasdale, and Torrey have become hot spots for artists and a more progressive, cosmopolitan (if still small) population. If there is a place outside of downtown Salt Lake City, Park City, and Moab where a traveler might find a hint of hip urban culture, this would be it. So, grab whatever suits you—espresso or a bottle of water—and head out to Cassidy Arch to watch the sun work shadows across the rocks. The quietude and sheer visual experience of Capitol Reef National Park will set to soothing even the weariest soul.
ZION NATIONAL PARK 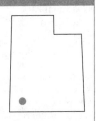	Known for its sheer 2,000-foot cliffs and river-carved canyons, Zion is located in the southwestern corner of the state. It's actually closer to Las Vegas–about 2 ½ hours' drive–than to Salt Lake City. At Zion, it's the character of the sandstone forms that defines the park's splendor. The domes, fins, and blocky massifs recall cathedrals and temples, prophets and angels. With world-class trails like Angels Landing and the Narrows, serious hikers can have a field day here. But you don't have to travel by foot to get a good sense of why the park is so special: the roadways leading through Zion provide ample viewing opportunities.
BRYCE CANYON NATIONAL PARK 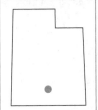	"It's a helluva a place to lose a cow." That's how pioneer cattleman Ebenezer Bryce summed up the terrain in what is now Bryce Canyon National Park, the area that came to bear his name. What made the landscape inhospitable to Bryce's bovine companions is what draws visitors today—the bizarrely-shaped, bright red-orange rocks that are this park's signature formation. Exploring these hoodoos, as these vivid limestone spires are known, is like wandering through a giant maze. If you can take to the trails at sunrise or sunset, your reward will be amazing colors; the sun's light at either end of the day intensifies the rocks' deep orange and crimson hues.

SOUTHWESTERN UTAH 	St. George is a regional hub for shopping, dining, sporting, and cultural events, but the best reason to visit this part of the state is not related to anything man-made. If you want to get out of your car and venture onto one of the many and varied trails, and if 2,500-foot red-and-white sandstone cliffs and intensely narrow canyons impress you, this entire region could be your paradise, including the mostly road-less, expansive Grand Staircase–Escalante National Monument. Another way to view the region's high-layered cliffs and smooth, colorful formations is by boat from Lake Powell. It is no wonder natural beauty attracts artists, many of whose work you'll find for sale in galleries in Springville, the gateway community to Zion National Park.
ARCHES NATIONAL PARK 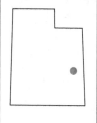	If your images of desert landscapes are painted in sandy beiges and browns, you'll have to repaint those mental pictures when you visit the region around Arches National Park. The desert here in southeastern Utah is adorned with a rich tapestry of colors, from reds, pinks, and oranges, to purples and deep chocolates. And it's not just the vibrant hues that draw visitors to this part of the state. Arches National Park has the largest collection of natural sandstone arches in the world—more than 2,000. Located near the town of Moab, about a four-hour drive from Salt Lake City, the park is easy to visit, particularly because you can see many of its dramatic rock formations without even getting out of your car. Yet it's worth taking to the trails, even briefly, to get up close and personal with this spectacular natural setting.
CANYONLANDS NATIONAL PARK 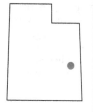	Compared to most national parks, Canyonlands is seldom crowded, making it a place where you can hike, mountain bike, raft, or drive through some of the wildest, most untouched country in the United States. Dramatic scenery is plentiful here, with mushroomlike rock formations rising randomly out of the ground, twisting into spires, pinnacles, buttes, and mesas, as bald eagles and red-tail hawks float above. Canyonlands is a large park, separated into three distinct districts that all begin south of Moab. With a little planning, you can find time for solitude and reflection, while having the adventure of a lifetime.

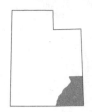

The vibrant red rock of the Colorado Plateau characterizes the southeastern part of Utah. With the evolution of Moab into a world-class mountain bike and river-running destination, the town has taken on something of a counter-culture feel, and it's a great base for an active outdoor trip. On the state's southern edge, stretching into Arizona, Monument Valley's iconic spires and buttes enchant and energize. Mile after mile of sage-brush flats may suddenly drop away into deep and narrow slot canyons. Mesas stretch, level and unbroken, or stacked one next to the other like giant step stools. Snow-capped mountains rise like a verdant mirage above the desert. Whether you're hiking through nearby Arches or Canyonlands National Parks, boating the Colorado River, or mountain biking the slickrock trail system, this landscape will grab hold of you in ways that you won't want to forget.

Utah

COLORADO
UTAH

Rock Springs

FLAMING GORGE NATIONAL REC. AREA

DINOSAUR NATIONAL MON.

Vernal

191

40

80

Manila

ASHLEY NATIONAL FOREST

Roosevelt

WYOMING
UTAH

Altamont

Duchesne

191

WASATCH NATIONAL FOREST

Helper

Price

UINTA NATIONAL FOREST

Randolph

Woodruff

Evanston

Kamas

150

31

Bear Lake

30

39

80

40

6

Springville

Fairview Spring

Logan

WASATCH NATIONAL FOREST

Park City

Heber City

Provo

Payson

89

Mt Pleasant

89

Smithfield

Ogden

84

Orem

UINTA NATIONAL FOREST

Brigham City

15

84

Clearfield

Layton

Bountiful

Utah Lake

Eureka

Nephi

Tremonton

Salt Lake City

Murray

Sandy

132

IDAHO
UTAH

30

Great Salt Lake

Tooele

73

36

6

SEVIER DESERT

Vernon

WASATCH NATIONAL FOREST

Rosette

SAWTOOTH NATIONAL FOREST

84

Evaporation Basin

80

GREAT SALT LAKE DESERT

GREAT SALT LAKE DESERT

Wendover

DEEP CREEK RANGE

NEVADA
UTAH

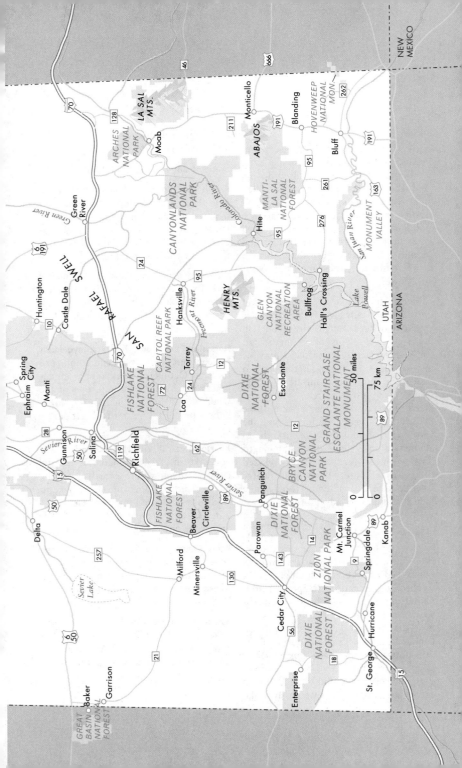

IF YOU LIKE

Hiking

Hiking is easily the least expensive and most accessible recreational pursuit. Sure, you could spend a few hundred dollars on high-tech hiking boots, a so-called "personal hydration system," and a collapsible walking staff made of space-age materials, but there's no need for such expenditure. All that's really essential are sturdy athletic shoes, water, and the desire to see the landscape under your own power.

Hiking in the Rockies is a three-season sport that basically lasts as long as you're willing to tromp through snow, though in the arid desert regions of Southern Utah and Southwestern Colorado it is possible to hike year-round without the need to attach snowshoes to your boots. (You could look at snowshoeing as winter hiking, for the trails are often the same.) One of the greatest aspects of this region is the wide range of hiking terrain, from high-alpine scrambles that require stamina, to flowered meadows that invite a relaxed pace, to confining slot canyons where flash floods are a real danger and can be fatal to the unwary adventurer.

There are few real hazards to hiking, but a little preparedness goes a long way. Know your limits, and make sure the terrain you are about to embark on does not exceed your abilities. It's a good idea to check the elevation change on a trail before you set out—a 1-mi trail might sound easy, until you realize how steep it is—and be careful not to get caught on exposed trails at elevation during afternoon thunderstorms in the summer. Dress appropriately, bringing layers to address changing weather conditions, and always carry enough drinking water. Also, make sure someone knows where you are going and when to expect your return.

Some of our favorite Utah hikes include:

Angels Landing Trail, Zion National Park. One of the park's most popular hikes also happens to be one of the most spectacular. Stop at Scout's Lookout for a breathtaking view. This isn't the trail to take, though, if you are afraid of heights.

Hickman Bridge Trail, Capitol Reef National Park. Just 2 mi long, this trail is a perfect introduction to Capital Reef. You'll walk past a great natural bridge as well as Fremont Indian ruins.

Horseshoe Canyon Trail, Canyonlands National Park: Every weekend from April through October, a park ranger guides hikers on this trail through one of the wilder section of Canyonlands. The highlight is one of the largest rock-art panels in North America.

The Narrows Trail, Zion National Park: When you take the trail through this narrow desert canyon, you're actually walking in the riverbed—and you might have to wade or even swim for part of the way—but you get to see parts of the park that are visible nowhere else.

Paria Canyon–Vermilion Cliffs Wilderness, Paria: The "Wave" may be the most sought-after hiking permit in all of Utah. These waves near Paria, in southwestern Utah, are made of sandstone, though.

Mount Timpanogas: One hour south of Salt Lake Valley, "Timp" is one of the tallest and most striking of the Wasatch Mountains. Trails rate moderate to difficult.

Biking

The Rockies are a favorite destination for bikers. Wide-open roads with great gains and losses in elevation test (and form) the stamina for road cyclists, while riders who prefer pedaling fat tires have plenty of mountain and desert trails to test their skills. Unmatched views often make it difficult to keep your eyes on the road.

Thanks to the popularity of the sport here, it's usually easy to find a place that rents bicycles if you'd prefer to leave yours at home. Shops often rent a variety of bikes from entry-level to high-end, though the latter come at a premium, and if you're in the market for a used bike, good deals can often be found when shops unload one season's rentals to make room for next year's models. Bike shops are also a good bet for information on local rides and group tours.

The rules of the road are the same here as elsewhere, though some areas are less biker-friendly than others. On the road, watch for trucks and stay as close as possible to the side of the road, in single file. On the trail, ride within your limits and keep your eyes peeled for hikers and horses (both of which have the right of way), as well as dogs. Always wear a helmet and carry plenty of water.

Some of our favorite areas in Utah for mountain biking include:

Antelope Island State Park: It's cheaper to enter Antelope on two wheels, and much more enjoyable. After crossing the 7-mi causeway, there are miles of rolling and empty trails to choose from. Watch out for bison and people on horseback.

Bonneville Shoreline Trail: Partway up and along the Wasatch Front on the Northeast side of Salt Lake City, this trail offers expansive views of the entire Salt Lake Valley, plus points west and south. It's easy to moderate in difficulty, with challenging stretches near the University of Utah Hospital.

Flaming Gorge National Recreation Area: Because it mixes high-desert vegetation—blooming sage, rabbit brush, cactus, and wildflowers—and red rock terrain with a cool climate, Flaming Gorge is an ideal destination for road and trail biking. The 3-mi round-trip Bear Canyon–Bootleg ride begins south of the dam off U.S. 191 at the Firefighters' Memorial Campground and runs west to an overlook of the reservoir.

Klondike Bluffs Trail, Moab: Though the trailhead is about 15 mi north of Moab, this trail offers the less-experienced mountain biker a relatively easy introduction to why Moab is esteemed with off-road cyclists. The climb to Klondike Bluffs is not difficult, and the reward is a fantastic view into Arches National Park. And how many bike rides can boast dinosaur footprints?

Skiing/Snowboarding

Utah's Greatest Snow on Earth can be a revelation for skiers and snowboarders familiar only with the slopes of other regions. Forget treacherous sheets of rock-hard ice, single-note hills where the bottom can be seen from the top, and mountains that offer only one kind of terrain from every angle. In Utah the snow builds up quickly, leaving a solid base at each resort that hangs tough all season, only to be layered upon by thick, fluffy powder that holds an edge, ready to be groomed into rippling corduroy or left in giddy stashes along the sides and through the trees. Moguls and half-pipe-studded terrain parks are the norm, not the special attractions, at Utah resorts.

Skiing Utah means preparing for all kinds of weather, because the high altitudes can start a day off sunny and bright but kick in a blizzard by afternoon. Layers help, as well as plenty of polypropylene to wick away sweat in the sun and a water-resistant outer layer to keep off the powdery wetness that's sure to accumulate, especially if you're a beginner snowboarder certain to spend time on the ground. Must-haves: Plenty of sunscreen, because the sun is closer than you think, and a helmet, because so are the trees.

The added bonus of Utah terrain is that there's something for everyone—often in the same ski resort, since so many of the areas have a wide variety of beginner, intermediate, advanced, and expert slopes. Turn yourself over to the rental shops, which are specialized enough at each resort to offer experts in helping you plan your day and the types of equipment you'll need.

Some of our favorite places in Utah to ski and snowboard include:

Alta Ski Resort/Snowbird Resort: These Little Cottonwood Canyon neighbors, within 40 minutes of downtown Salt Lake City, are regularly ranked the top ski resorts in the United States. Seasons with 500 to 600 and more inches of Utah's famous powder are at the root of the accolades. The AltaSnowbird pass lets you ski both mountains on one ticket, but snowboarders take heed: you're still not allowed at Alta.

Brian Head Ski Resort, Brian Head: The closest Utah ski resort to the Las Vegas airport, it's worth checking out for the novelty of skiing in Southern Utah. The red-orange rock formations of nearby Cedar Breaks National Monument form a backdrop to many trails, which tend to focus on beginner and intermediate skiers and snowboarders. Experts can ski off the 11,000 foot summit.

Deer Valley, Park City: This posh resort is known for its groomers, fine dining, and accommodations: the skiing is excellent, but for many it's the whole experience—including the midday feast at Silver Lake Lodge and suntanning on the snow-covered meadow—that keeps them coming back.

Utah Olympic Park, Park City: At the site of the 2002 Olympic bobsled, luge, and ski-jumping events, you can take recreational ski-jumping lessons or strap in behind a professional driver for a bobsled ride down the actual Olympic course.

Rafting

Rafting combines a sea of emotions ranging from the calming effects of flat waters surrounded by backcountry beauty and wildlife to the thrill and excitement of charging a raging torrent of foam.

For the inexperienced, the young, and the aged, dozens of tour companies throughout the West offer relatively mundane floats—ranging from one hour to one day and starting at just $20—that are ideal for anyone from 4 years old to 90. Others fulfill the needs of adventure tourists content only with chills, potential spills, and the occasional wall of water striking them smack-dab in the chest.

Seasoned outfitters know their routes and their waters as well as you know the road between home and work. Beginners and novices are encouraged to use guides, while more experienced rafters may rent watercraft. Many guides offer multi-day trips in which they do everything, including searing your steak in a beach barbecue, setting up your tent, and rolling out your sleeping bag.

If you go, wear a swimsuit or shorts and sandals and bring along sunscreen and sunglasses. Outfitters are required to supply a life jacket for each passenger, although most states don't require that it be worn. Mid-summer is the ideal time to raft in the West, although many outfitters will stretch the season, particularly on calmer routes.

Select an outfitter based on recommendations from the local chamber of commerce, experience-level, Web sites, and word of mouth. The International Scale of River Difficulty is a widely accepted rating system that ranges from Class I (the easiest) to Class VI (the most difficult— think Niagara Falls). When in doubt, ask your guide about the rating on your route before you book. Remember, ratings can vary greatly throughout the season due to run-off and weather events.

Numerous outfitters and guide services offer rafting trips in Utah, and the journey can vary from relaxing family outings to white-knuckled runs through raging waters. In all cases, you'll discover scenery, wildlife, and an off-the-road experience that you'll never get looking through a windshield.

Some of our favorite spots for rafting in Utah include:

Colorado River, Moab: The Grand Poobah of river rafting in Utah. There are numerous outfitters in the Moab area with a wide assortment of half-, full-, and multi-day trips of the river. Even in periods of low water, the infamous Cataract Canyon section still provides plenty of thrills and spills.

Green River: Before it meets up with the Colorado River in Canyonlands National Park, the Green River offers plenty of stunning scenery and fast water through canyons such as Desolation and Gray. Sign on with an outfitter in the town of Green River, about 45 minutes north and west of Moab.

Horseback Riding

Horseback riding options in Utah run the gamut, from hour-long rides on a well-worn trail to multi-day excursions out into the wilderness. A short trek is a great way to get acquainted with the landscape—and with horseback riding if you're a beginner. Longer horse-pack trips are great ways to visit the back-country, since horses can travel distances and carry supplies that would be impossible for hikers. Although horsemanship isn't required for most trips, it is helpful, and even an experienced rider can expect to be a little sore for the first few days. June through August is the peak period for horse-packing trips; before signing up with an outfitter, inquire about the skills they expect.

Since this is the West, jeans and cowboy boots are still the preferred attire for horseback, although hiking boots and Gore-Tex have long since become fashionable, especially in colder months and at higher altitudes. Long pants are a must either way. And as with most Utah activities, layering is key; plan to have some kind of fleece or heavier outer layer no matter what time of year since the mountains will be cooler the higher you go. Generally, outfitters provide most or all of the gear you'll need for extended trips, including a pack animal to carry it all for you and plenty of food for the sometimes surprisingly lavish dinners that they whip up in the middle of nowhere.

You can also find ranch-like resorts in Utah, that offer a wide range of activities in addition to horseback riding, including fishing, four-wheeling, spa services, and cooking classes. For winter, many ranches also have added such snow-oriented amenities as sleigh rides, snowshoeing, and cross-country skiing.

Some of our favorite places in Utah for horseback riding include:

Bryce Canyon National Park: The park's namesake claimed it was a "Hell of a place to lose a cow," but failed to say anything about how great a place it is to explore on horseback. Sign up for a guided tour at Ruby's Red Canyon Horseback Rides near the park entrance. Orange-pink spires and hoodoos offer a ride unmatched anywhere else.

Capitol Reef National Park: Much of this park is accessible only by foot or horseback, which promises an experience of wide-open western spaces that harken back to the time of cowboys. Indeed, some of the trails may have been used by herdsman and Native Americans. Sandstone, canyons, mesa, buttes—they're all here. Sign up with Hondoo Rivers & Trails or Wild Hare Expeditions for an unforgettable experience.

Zion Ponderosa Ranch Resort: Located just east of Zion National Park at the site of a former pioneer logging camp, this multi-pursuit resort offers plenty of things to do after time spent in the saddle meandering along the multitude of pioneer-era trails. Horseback riding options run from beginner to experienced (and even include a cattle round-up), and when you're not in the saddle you can ride an ATV, rent a Harley-Davidson motorcycle, or learn how to rappel and rock climb on the only man-made climbing wall in the Zion National Park area.

Fishing

Trout do not live in ugly places. And, so it is in the American West where you'll discover unbridled beauty, towering pines, rippling mountain streams, and bottomless pools. It is here that blue-ribbon trout streams remain much as they were when Native American tribes, French fur trappers, and a few thousand faceless miners, muleskinners, and sodbusters first placed a muddy footprint along their banks.

However, those early-day settlers had one advantage that you won't: time. If you're going to make best use of that limited vacation in which fishing is a preferred activity, you'll want to follow some basic observations.

Hire a guide. You could spend days locating a great fishing spot, learning the water currents and fish behavior, and determining what flies, lures, or bait the fish are following. A good guide will cut through the clutter, get you into fish, and turn your excursion into an adventure complete with a full creel.

If you're comfortable with your fishing gear, bring it along, though most guides loan or rent equipment. Bring a rod and reel, waders, vest, hat, sunglasses, net, tackle, hemostats, and sunscreen. Always buy a fishing license.

If you're not inclined to fork over the $250-plus that most quality guides charge per day for two fishermen and a boat, your best bet is a stop at a reputable fly shop. They'll shorten your learning curve, tell you where the fish are, what they're biting on, and whether you should be "skittering" your dry-fly on top of the water or "dead-drifting" a nymph.

Famed fisherman Lee Wolff wrote "catching fish is a sport. Eating fish is not a sport." Consequently, you'll find most fishermen practicing "catch and release" in an effort to maintain productive fisheries and protect native species.

Seasonality is always a concern when fishing. Spring run-offs can cloud the waters. Summer droughts may reduce stream flows. Fall weather can be unpredictable in the West. But, as many fishing guides will attest, the best time to come and wet a line is whenever you can make it.

Some of our favorite places in Utah to fish include:

Flaming Gorge: For some of the finest river fishing, try the Green River below Flaming Gorge Dam, where rainbow and brown trout are plentiful and big. Fed by cold water from the bottom of the lake, this stretch has been identified as one of the best trout fisheries in the world.

Lake Powell: Formed by the construction of Glen Canyon Dam, this popular recreational attraction in Southern Utah is home to a wide variety of fish, including striped, smallmouth, and largemouth bass; bluegill; and channel catfish. Ask the locals about night fishing for stripers.

Provo River: One of Utah's world-class fly fishing rivers, the Provo is divided into three sections, starting in the High Uintas Wilderness about 90 minutes east of Salt Lake City and ending in Utah Lake in Provo. Brown and rainbow trout are the big draw here, and Utah.com claims that in some sections upward of 7,500 fish per square mile can be sought.

UTAH CANYON COUNTRY DRIVING TOUR

ZION & BRYCE CANYON
Days 1 & 2

From Las Vegas, head up I–15, and take the Route 9 exit to ❶ **Zion National Park.** Spend your afternoon in the park—if it's April to October, take the National Park Service bus down Zion Canyon Scenic Drive (in fact, when the bus is "in season," cars are not allowed in the canyon). Overnight in Springdale, the bustling town right next to the park. The Best Western Zion Park Inn is your best bet for getting a room in the high season. Its Switchback Grille is excellent and open for breakfast, lunch, and dinner.

Spend the next morning in Zion. For a nice hike, try the short and easy (read: family-friendly) Canyon Overlook Trail, where you can gaze at the massive rock formations, such as East and West Temples. It won't take very long, even if you linger with your camera, so follow it with a stroll along the Emerald Pools Trail in Zion Canyon itself, where you might come across tame wild turkeys and ravens looking for handouts.

Depart the area via Route 9, the ❷ **Zion–Mount Carmel Highway.** You'll pass through a 1[1//10]-mi-long tunnel that is so narrow, RVs and towed vehicles must pay for an escort through. When you emerge, you are in slickrock country, where huge, petrified sandstone dunes are etched by ancient waters. Stay on Route 9 for 23 mi and then turn north onto U.S. 89. After 42 mi, you will reach Route 12, where you should turn east and drive 14 mi to the entrance of ❸ **Bryce Canyon National Park.** The overall trip from Zion to Bryce Canyon is about 90 minutes.

Central to your tour of Bryce Canyon is the 18-mi main park road, from which

THE PLAN	
Distance:	750–850 mi
Time:	9–10 days
Overnight in:	Springdale, Bryce, Torrey, Moab, Bluff, and Monument Valley

numerous scenic turnouts reveal vistas of bright red-orange rock (we recommend starting with the view at Sunrise Point). You'll notice that the air is a little cooler here than it was at Zion, so get out and enjoy it. Trails most worth checking out include the Bristlecone Loop Trail and the Navajo Loop Trail, both of which you can easily fit into a day trip and will get you into the heart of the park with minimum effort. Listen for peregrine falcons deep in the side canyons, and keep an eye out for the species of prairie dog that only lives in these parts. Overnight in the park or at Ruby's Inn, near the junction of routes 12 and 63.

CAPITOL REEF
Day 3

Head out this morning on the spectacular ❹ **Utah Scenic Byway–Route 12.** If the views don't take your breath away, the narrow, winding road with little margin for error will. Route 12 winds over and through ❺ **Grand Staircase–Escalante National Monument.** The views from the narrow hogback are nothing short of incredible. About 14 mi past the town of Escalante on Route 12 you can stop at ❻ **Calf Creek Recreation Area** to stretch your legs or make a 5½-mi round-trip hike to a gorgeous backcountry waterfall. Route 12 continues to gain elevation as you pass over Boulder Mountain.

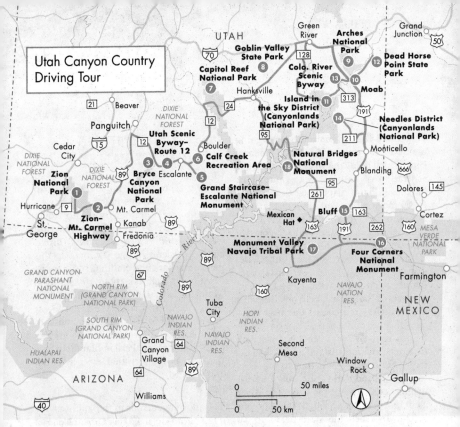

At the intersection of routes 12 and 24, turn east onto Route 24. You have traveled 112 mi from Bryce Canyon to reach ❼ **Capitol Reef National Park.** The crowds are smaller here than at other national parks in the state, and the scenery is stunning. Orchards in the small enclave of Fruita produce fruit—peaches, pears, and apples—in the late summer and early fall, and are close by ancient Indian rock art. If it's still daylight when you arrive, hike the 1-mi Hickman Bridge Trail if you want to explore a little, or stop in at the visitor center until 4:30 PM (later in the summer) and view pioneer and Native American exhibits, talk with rangers about geography or geology, or watch a film. Nearby Torrey is your best bet for lodging, and be sure to eat at the seasonal Cafe Diablo, serving some of Utah's finest Southwest cuisine from mid-April to mid-October. Enjoy freshly brewed coffee and baked goods at Robber's Roost Books and Beverages while perusing a selection of regionally themed books, viewing local artisan jewelry, or even browsing the Internet.

ARCHES & CANYONLANDS
Days 4–6

Explore Capitol Reef more the next morning. When you leave, travel east and north for 75 mi on Route 24. If you want a break after about an hour, stop at the small ❽ **Goblin Valley State Park,** 12 mi west off Route 24 on Goblin Valley Road. Youngsters love to run around the sandstone formations known as "goblins." Return to Route 24 and take it to I–70, turn east and continue your journey.

Take exit 182 south onto U.S. 191, going about 27 mi toward ❾ **Arches National Park,** which holds the world's largest concentration of natural rock windows or "arches." Plan on spending three nights in ❿ **Moab** while you explore the area. Adventurous types, note that the Colorado River runs near Moab. If you can squeeze in a raft trip on this legendary Western waterway, do it. Otherwise, dedicate Day 5 to Arches, perhaps including a guided hike in the Fiery Furnace, a maze of sandstone canyons and fins that is considered one of the most spectacular hikes in the park. Then on Day 6, launch your ⓫ **Canyonlands National Park** experience with the Island in the Sky District—but first take a detour to the mesa top at ⓬ **Dead Horse Point State Park** for magnificent views of the Colorado River as it goosenecks through the canyons below. To reach the state park, go 10 mi north of Moab on U.S. 191 to Route 313. Drive west for 15 mi, then turn right onto the unnamed road; continue for 6 mi to the Dead Horse fee station. To get from Dead Horse to Islands in the Sky, return to Route 313 and drive 7 mi past the Dead Horse turnoff to reach the park visitor center.

On your way back to Moab, enjoy the natural scenery on the ⓭ **Colorado River Scenic Byway (Route 128),** which runs for about 44 mi along the river, or view manmade art by traveling down Route 279 (Potash Road), where ancient Native American rock-art panels pop up after 4 ⁸/₁₀ mi from the U.S. 191 turnoff.

THE FOUR CORNERS & MONUMENT VALLEY

Day 7

On Day 7, travel 42 mi south of Moab on U.S. 191. At this point, you have a choice to make. Either turn onto Route 211 and drive 34 mi to ⓮ **Canyonlands' Needles District,** which is distinctly different from Island in the Sky, or skip this part of the park and continue south to the town of ⓯ **Bluff.** It's about 100 mi from Moab to Bluff, so if you want to break up the drive, stop en route for a bite to eat in **Monticello** or at the first-rate museum of the Ancestral Puebloan Indians in **Edge of the Cedars State Park** in **Blanding.** Stay the night in Bluff at the Desert Rose Inn and Cabins.

Day 8

This morning, detour to the southeast for a fun photo-op at ⓰ **Four Corners National Monument,** which straddles Colorado, New Mexico, Arizona, and Utah. The easiest route from Bluff is to take U.S. 191 for about 35 mi, to its junction with U.S. 160. (The U.S. 191–U.S. 160 junction is south of the Utah–Arizona border in the Navajo Nation.) Drive east on U.S. 160 for about 30 mi to Four Corners. When you've finished standing in four states at the same time, backtrack west along on U.S. 160 for the spectacular, deep-red desert of ⓱ **Monument Valley Navajo Tribal Park,** whose buttes and spires you will recognize from countless movie westerns and television commercials—if you want to do the 17-mi self-guided drive here, give yourself a couple of hours, or take a tram tour. Call it a night at Gouldings Lodge in Monument Valley.

Day 9

From Monument Valley, take U.S. 163 north about 25 mi toward Mexican Hat, then follow Route 261 north to Route 95 west and the ⑱ **Natural Bridges National Monument.** A scenic 9-mi drive takes you to all three of the large river-carved bridges here, or you can get out of the car for some hiking. Then it's time to begin wrapping up your driving tour, continuing northwest on Route 95 toward the town of Hanksville (back near Capitol Reef National Park). From there, the fastest way back to Las Vegas is to go north on Route 24 to I–70 west to I–15 south.

TIPS

U.S. 6, the most direct route from Southeastern Utah to Salt Lake City, is unfortunately one of the most accident-prone roads in the country, though improvements are being made. Drive with extreme caution and patience, especially through Price and Spanish Fork canyons.

Don't despair if it starts to rain in Southern Utah; showers rarely last long, and they always seem to be followed by spectacular sunsets.

Bring old sneakers or sandals to enjoy rafting or other water sports in the Moab area.

Gas isn't difficult to find, but it's always smart to top off the tank whenever you can just in case.

WHEN TO GO

Given the different elevations and climates in Utah, there's something to experience year-round, whether hiking the southern canyons in spring or fall, skiing in the mountains in winter, or golfing, biking, fishing, or swimming in summer. The national parks can become crowded in summer (and also hot). Early to mid-October is an ideal time to visit nearly any part of Utah, though the extreme high country can get chilly and even experience a surprise early snowstorm on occasion. Fall color displays can be found in nearly every canyon in the state. Cottonwood trees turning brilliant gold along river bottoms with a backdrop of red rock make particularly good photographs.

Climate

The Wasatch Front, including Salt Lake City, experiences four distinct seasons, and temperatures can vary wildly, reaching triple digits in summer and falling below zero occasionally in winter. Valleys experience winter inversions, when hot air above traps fog and smog below for days. When this happens, head to the mountains where the skies will be blue and the temperatures warmer. Expect afternoon thundershowers in the mountains, especially the High Uintas, in July and August.

Southern Utah's weather can be ideal any time of year, though heat in summer can be unpleasant. Spring break and Easter vacation bring some of the biggest crowds to places such as Moab, St. George, and Zion National Park. But always be prepared for the unpredictable. Be especially aware of the potential for flash floods in late summer in southern Utah parks, avoiding narrow canyons if there is any threat at all of a thunderstorm.

Forecasts **Weather Channel Connection** (⊕ www.weather.com).

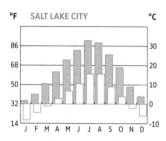

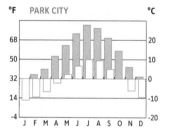

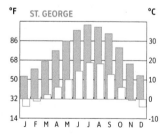

Salt Lake City

WORD OF MOUTH

"SLC has a facinating history. You can spend the entire day at Temple Square, if you care about history. . . . Go to Trolley Square for some fun shopping, or the State Capitol."

—clarassong

"Take some time to visit the Family History Library for info on your ancestors, the place will blow you away with information. They are open till 9 pm most weekdays."

—Norden1

Updated by
John Blodgett

SITTING AT THE FOOT OF the
rugged Wasatch Mountains and
extending to the south shore of
the Great Salt Lake, Salt Lake City
has some of the best scenery in the
country. The interface between city
and nature draws residents and visitors alike to the Salt Lake Valley.
There are few other places where
you can enjoy urban pleasures and,
within 20 minutes, hike a mountain
trail or rest by a rushing stream.

The city is emerging as a prominent economic center in the Rocky
Mountains. Since 2001 the number
of people living in the Salt Lake
Valley has climbed from 720,000
to more than 1 million. As a reflection of this growth, a dynamic
skyline has sprouted, along with
ever-widening rings of suburbia.

TOP REASONS TO GO

Temple Square. The floral, architectural, and other attractions at
the center of the Mormon universe can be enjoyed by all.

City-side Wilderness. The mountains of the Wasatch Front offer
four-season outdoor activity just
minutes from the urban bustle.

Inland Sea. The Great Salt Lake
is an unusual ecosystem that's
popular with cyclists, bird- and
bison-watchers.

Pow-pow-powder. Skiers with
just a weekend to spare have four
ski resorts within close proximity
to the airport

Smog occasionally bedevils the town, and some crime exists, but Salt
Lake is working hard to remain a small, personable city.

Brigham Young led the first party of Mormon pioneers to the Salt Lake
Valley in 1847. The valley appealed to him because, at the time, it was
under the control of Mexico rather than the U.S. government, which
the Mormons blamed for much of their persecution. Also, the area
had few permanent settlements and an adequate supply of water and
building materials, and it offered a protected location, with the high
Wasatch Mountains on the east side and a vast desert to the west. Still,
on July 24, 1847, when Young gazed across the vast and somewhat
desolate valley and reportedly announced "This is the right place," it
would have been understandable if his followers had some mixed feel-
ings. They saw no familiar green forests or lush grasslands, only a dry
valley and a salty lake.

Within hours of arriving, Young and his followers began planting
crops and diverting water for irrigation. They would build homes later;
their existence depended on being able to harvest crops before winter.
Within days Young drew up plans for Salt Lake City, which was to be
the hub of the Mormon's promised land, a vast empire stretching from
the Rocky Mountains to the southern California coast. Although the
area that eventually became the state of Utah was much smaller than
Young originally planned, Salt Lake City became much grander than
anything he could have imagined. Missionaries throughout Scandina-
via and the British Isles converted thousands who flocked to the city
from around the world to live near their church president—who is also
a living prophet according to Mormon doctrine—and to worship in
their newly built temple.

In the 1860s, income from railroads and mines created a wealthy class of industrialists who built mansions near downtown and whose businesses brought thousands of workers—mainly from Europe and most of whom were not Mormon—to Utah Territory. By the time Utah became a state in 1896, Salt Lake had become a diverse and thriving city. Although the majority of the city was Mormon, it claimed a healthy mix of Protestant, Catholic, and Jewish citizens.

Today the city is an important western center for business, medicine, education, and culture. The Church of Jesus Christ of Latter-day Saints (LDS), as the Mormon faith is officially called, still has its headquarters in Temple Square. Several high-rise hotels mark the skyline, restaurants serve up a whole world of tastes, fashionable retail enclaves are appearing all around town, and nightlife is hopping. Increased commitment to the arts from the public and private sectors has created a cultural scene as prodigious as you'd expect in a city twice Salt Lake's size. When it comes to sports, the community takes great pride in its NBA team, the Utah Jazz. And of course, no one can forget the hundreds of volunteers who gathered together to help Salt Lake City host the 2002 Olympic Winter Games.

Near Salt Lake City, Antelope Island has superb hiking, mountain biking, and wildlife watching. American history buffs might choose to travel one of the best-preserved sections of the original Pony Express Trail, the 133-mi section through the desert of west-central Utah.

EXPLORING SALT LAKE CITY

Despite its population of roughly 180,000, Salt Lake City feels like a small city. Wide streets and an efficient mass transit system make it easy to get around. The heart of Salt Lake's social, religious, and political institutions can be found within a few blocks of Temple Square downtown. Numerous museums and a state-of-the-art planetarium thrive here, and because many of the cultural institutions are supported by public funds you'll spend little money touring the city. In addition, the emphasis put on green spaces by past and present city planners means you won't experience the claustrophobic feeling found in many big cities.

Take time to stroll around the city center, shopping or visiting Temple Square. Choose a museum, theater, or historic building to explore, then branch out into the surrounding neighborhoods to capture more of the flavor of the city. Reminders of the 2002 Winter Olympics are scattered throughout.

Like most Utah municipalities, Salt Lake City is based on a grid plan that was devised by Brigham Young in the 19th century. Most street names have a directional and a numerical designation, which describes their location in relation to one of two axes. Streets with "East" or "West" in their names are east or west of (and parallel to) Main Street, which runs north–south; while "North" and "South" streets run parallel to South Temple street.

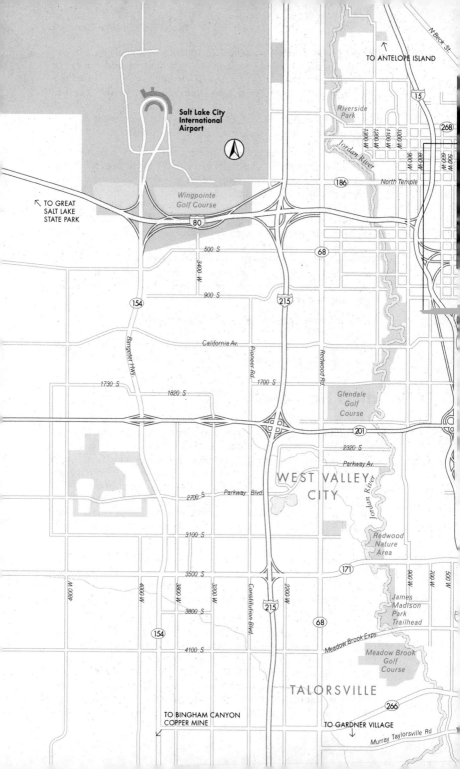

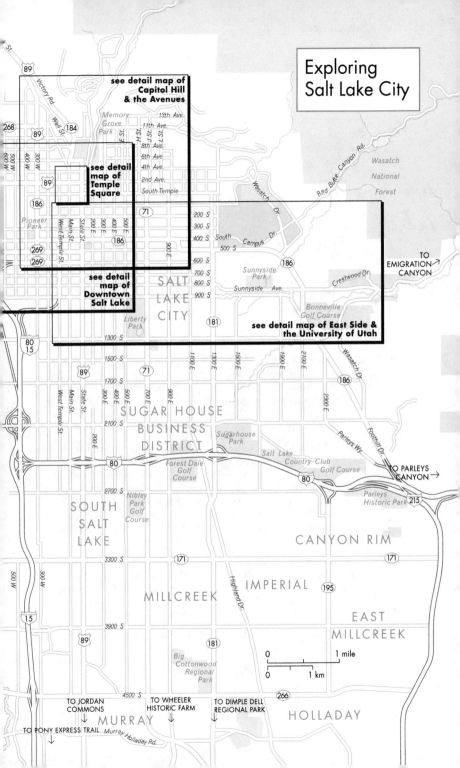

Exploring
Salt Lake City

see detail map of
**Capitol Hill
& the Avenues**

see detail
map of
**Temple
Square**

see detail
map of
**Downtown
Salt Lake**

see detail map of **East Side &
the University of Utah**

Wasatch
National
Forest

TO
EMIGRATION →
CANYON

13th Ave.
11th Ave.
8th Ave.
6th Ave.
4th Ave.
2nd Ave.
South Temple

Memory
Grove
Park

Victory Rd.
Wall St.

Red Butte Canyon Rd.

Wasatch Dr.

Crestwood Dr.

200 S
300 S
400 S
500 S
600 S
700 S
800 S
900 S

South
Campus Dr.

Sunnyside
Park

Sunnyside Ave.

Bonneville
Golf Course

Pioneer
Park

Liberty
Park

SALT
LAKE
CITY

West Temple St.
Main St.
State St.
200 E
300 E
400 E
500 E
900 E

1300 S
1500 S
1700 S
2100 S

TO PARLEYS
CANYON →

SUGAR HOUSE
BUSINESS
DISTRICT

Sugarhouse
Park

Salt Lake
Country Club
Golf Course

Parleys Wy.

Wasatch Dr.
Foothill Dr.
2700 E

West Temple St.
Main St.
State St.
300 E
400 E
500 E
700 E
900 E
1100 E
1300 E
1500 E
1900 E
2100 E

Forest Dale
Golf
Course

Parleys
Historic Park

SOUTH
SALT
LAKE

Nibley
Park
Golf
Course

2700 S
3300 S
3900 S
4500 S

200 E

CANYON RIM

MILLCREEK

IMPERIAL

Highland Dr.

Big
Cottonwood
Regional
Park

EAST
MILLCREEK

500 W
300 W

TO JORDAN
COMMONS
↓

TO WHEELER
HISTORIC FARM
↓

TO DIMPLE DELL
REGIONAL PARK
↓

MURRAY

HOLLADAY

TO PONY EXPRESS TRAIL
↓

Murray Holladay Rd.

St.
89
268
89
184
209 W
500 W
400 W
300 W
186
89
269
269
71
80
15
89
71
80
215
80
186
181
186
186
171
171
195
181
266

0   1 mile
0   1 km

The numbers tell how far the streets are from the axes. (For example, 200 East Street is two blocks east of Main Street.) Addresses typically include two directional references and two numerical references—320 East 200 South Street, for instance, is in the east 300 block of 200 South Street. Three of Salt Lake's most prominent streets are named after the Mormon Temple: North Temple, South Temple, and West Temple, indicating that the streets run parallel to the north, south, and west borders of Temple Square. Main Street borders the square's east side.

TEMPLE SQUARE

When Mormon pioneer leader Brigham Young first entered the Salt Lake Valley, he chose this spot at the mouth of City Creek Canyon for the headquarters of the Mormon Church, a role it maintains to this day. The buildings in Temple Square range in age from the Tabernacle constructed in the 1860s to the Conference Center constructed in 2000. Perhaps the most striking aspect of the square is the attention to landscaping, which makes the heart of downtown Salt Lake City into a year-round oasis.

WHAT TO SEE
Numbers correspond to the Temple Square map

★ ❶ **Beehive House.** Brigham Young's home, a national historic landmark, was constructed in 1854 and is topped with a replica of a beehive, symbolizing industry. Inside are many original furnishings; a tour of the interior will give you a fascinating glimpse of upper-class, 19th-century polygamous life. ⊠*67 E. South Temple, Temple Square* ☎*801/240–2671* ⊕*www.lds.org* ☑*Free* ⊙*Mon.–Sat. 9–9.*

❾ **Church of Jesus Christ of Latter-day Saints Conference Center.** The center features a 21,000-seat auditorium and an 850-seat theater. Equally impressive are the rooftop gardens landscaped with native plants and streams to mirror the surrounding mountains. Visitors must be accompanied by a guide. Tours are flexible but usually last 45 minutes. The Mormon Tabernacle Choir performs here regularly, and other concerts are scheduled on occasion. ⊠*60 W. North Temple, Temple Square* ☎*801/240–0075* ⊕*www.lds.org* ☑*Free* ⊙*Daily 9–9.*

★ ❻ **Family History Library.** Genealogy is important to Mormons. This library houses the world's largest collection of genealogical data. Mormons and non-Mormons alike come here to do research. ⊠*35 N. West Temple, Temple Square* ☎*801/240–2584 or 800/346–6044* ⊕*www.lds.org* ☑*Free* ⊙*Mon. 8–5, Tues.–Sat. 8 AM–9 PM.*

★ ❸ **Joseph Smith Memorial Building.** Once the Hotel Utah, this building on the National Register of Historic Places is owned and operated by the Mormon Church. You can use a computer program to learn how to do genealogical research at the FamilySearch Center here or watch an hour-long film about the Church's teaching of how Jesus Christ appeared in the western hemisphere after his resurrection. The center also has two restaurants and an elegantly restored lobby. The **FamilySe-**

CLOSE UP

The Mormon Influence

1

From its beginnings in 1830 with just six members, the Church of Jesus Christ of Latter-day Saints has evolved into one of the fastest-growing religions in the world. There are more than 10 million members in more than 160 countries and territories. The church was conceived and founded in New York by Joseph Smith, who said God the Father and his son, Jesus Christ, came to him in a vision when he was a young boy. Smith said he also saw a resurrected entity named Moroni, who led him to metal plates that were engraved with the religious history of an ancient American civilization. In 1827 Smith translated this record into the Book of Mormon.

Not long after the Church's creation, religious persecution forced Smith and his followers to flee New York, and they traveled first to Ohio and then to Missouri before settling in Nauvoo, Illinois, in 1839. But even here the fledgling church was ostracized, and Smith was killed by a mob in June 1844 in Carthage, Illinois. To escape the mounting oppression, Brigham Young, who ascended to the Church's leadership following Smith's death, led a pilgrimage to Utah, then a territory, with the first group arriving in the Salt Lake Valley on July 24, 1847. Here, under Young's guidance, the Church quickly grew and flourished.

In keeping with the Church's emphasis on proselytizing, Young laid plans to both colonize Utah and spread the Church's word. This work led to the founding of small towns not only throughout the territory but from southern Canada to Mexico. Today the Church continues that work through its young people, with most taking time out from college or careers to spend two years on a mission at home or abroad.

Latter-day Saints believe that they are guided by divine revelations received from God by the Church president, who is viewed as a modern-day prophet in the same sense as other biblical leaders. The Book of Mormon is viewed as divinely inspired scripture and is used side-by-side with the Holy Bible. Families are highly valued in the Church, and marriages performed in the Church's temples are thought to continue through eternity. Though Mormons were originally polygamists, the Church ended the practice in order to gain statehood for the territory in the 1890s. Excommunication is the consequence for those continuing polygamy. In 2001, after publicizing his five-wife family on national talk shows, Tom Green learned that Utah authorities could in fact be moved to prosecute polygamy. Since the 1950s, Utah law enforcement had held a "don't ask, don't tell" policy regarding polygamy. Green's 2001 trial was the state's first polygamy trial since the 1950s.

Under the Church's guidance, Utah has evolved into a conservative state where the good of the Church is placed above most other concerns. Despite most states' belief that church and government should be separate, Utah legislative leaders regularly consult with Church officials on key legislation. And the Church's opposition to alcoholic products has led to the state's peculiar liquor laws. To enter a bar that sells liquor, you first must purchase a "membership," usually $4 for three weeks. Beer bars, however, do not require such memberships, nor do restaurants that serve food with liquor.

A GOOD WALK

Temple Square is a good place to begin a walking tour of Salt Lake City. It covers only slightly more than three city blocks (be aware, however, that Salt Lake City blocks are larger than the average city block). For a loop tour, start at the foot of the Eagle Gate monument, at the corner of State Street and South Temple. Brigham Young's city home is here, divided into the **Beehive House** ❶ and the **Lion House** ❷. These houses mark the historic center of the city. Walk west along South Temple to the **Joseph Smith Memorial Building** ❸, and if time allows, check out your family history at the FamilySearch Center inside. In front of the Joseph Smith Memorial Building is the newest addition to Temple Square, Main Street Plaza. Stroll along the plaza on your way to the center of the square and the **Salt Lake Temple** ❹. West of the

Temple is the **Tabernacle** ❺, home to the famous Mormon Tabernacle Choir until 2000.

South of the Tabernacle is **Assembly Hall.** From Assembly Hall, cross the street to the **Family History Library** ❻ and the **Museum of Church History and Art** ❼. For a more detailed history of the Church of Jesus Christ of Latter-day Saints, cross West Temple to the east to visit the **North Visitors' Center** ❽. Across North Temple from the North Visitors' Center, the **Church of Jesus Christ of Latter-day Saints Conference Center** ❾ covers the entire block north of the temple. Walk along North Temple in front of the Conference Center. The sidewalk here is buffered from the street by trees and a brook babbling along past boulders quarried from the same canyon as the center and the temple.

arch Center, inside the Joseph Smith Memorial Building, has computers that allow you to search for ancestors using records compiled by the Mormon Church. Using the center costs nothing, and volunteers are on hand to help. Upstairs is the 1920 census and 70,000 volumes of personal histories of the faithful. ⊠*15 E. South Temple, Temple Square* ☎*801/240–1266* ⊕*www.lds.org* 🖃*Free* ⊙*Mon.–Sat. 9–9.*

❷ **Lion House.** Built two years after the Beehive House, the Lion House was also home to Brigham Young's family. Today it houses a restaurant, the Pantry, which serves good and simple old-fashioned home cooking. ⊠*63 E. South Temple, Temple Square* ☎*801/539–3258* ⊕*www. diningattemplesquare.com* 🖃*Free* ⊙*Mon.–Sat. 11–8.*

❼ **Museum of Church History and Art.** The museum houses a variety of artifacts and works of art relating to the history and doctrine of the Mormon faith, including personal belongings of church leaders Joseph Smith, Brigham Young, and others. There are also samples of Mormon coins and scrip used as standard currency in Utah during the 1800s, and beautiful examples of quilting, embroidery, and other handwork. Upstairs galleries exhibit religious and secular works by Mormon artists from all over the world. ⊠*45 N. West Temple, Temple Square* ☎*801/240–4615* ⊕*www.lds.org* 🖃*Free* ⊙*Weekdays 9–9, weekends 10–7.*

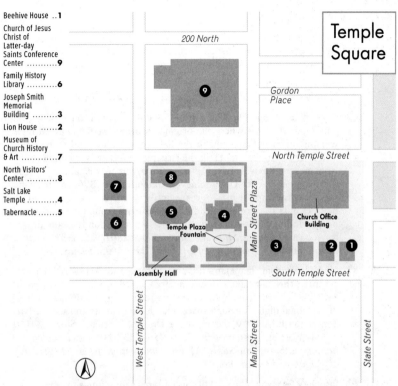

❽ North Visitors' Center. The history of the Mormon Church and the Mormon pioneers' trek to Utah is outlined in displays and a 53-minute film here. ⊠ *50 W. North Temple, Temple Square* ☎ *801/240–4872* ⊕ *www.lds.org* ☒ *Free* ⊙ *Daily 9–9.*

❹ Salt Lake Temple. Brigham Young chose this spot for a temple as soon as he arrived in the Salt Lake Valley in 1847, but work on the building didn't begin for another six years. Built of blocks of granite hauled by oxen and train from Little Cottonwood Canyon, the Mormon Temple took 40 years to the day to complete. Its walls are 16-feet thick at the base. Off-limits to all but faithful Mormons, the temple is used for marriages, baptisms, and other religious functions. ⊠ *South Temple and Main St., Temple Square* ☎ *No phone* ⊕ *www.lds.org* ⊙ *Not open to public.*

FodorsChoice ★

❺ Tabernacle. The Tabernacle is best known as the home of the famous Mormon Tabernacle Choir and its impressive organ. Visitors can tour the Tabernacle and hear organ recitals daily. From Memorial Day through Labor Day, organ recitals are held Monday through Saturday at noon and 2 and Sunday at 2. The rest of the year, recitals are held Monday through Saturday at noon and Sunday at 2. ⊠ *50 W. North Temple, Temple Square* ☎ *801/240–4872* ⊕ *www.lds.org* ☒ *Free.*

DOWNTOWN SALT LAKE

Although businesses and homes stretch in all directions, downtown's core is a compact, six-block area that includes three large malls, numerous historic buildings, and several entertainment venues.

WHAT TO SEE
Numbers correspond to the Downtown Salt Lake City map.

⓫ City and County Building. The seat of city government is on Washington Square, at the spot where the original Mormon settlers circled their wagons on their first night in the Salt Lake Valley. Said to be modeled after London's City Hall, the structure has details common to the Romanesque Revival style. Construction began in 1892 and continued for two years. After Utah achieved statehood in 1896, the building served as the capitol for 19 years until the current capitol could be built. Hundreds of trees, including species from around the world, and many winding paths and seating areas make the grounds a calm downtown oasis. ✉*451 S. State St., Downtown* ☎*801/535–6321* ⊕*www. slcgov.com/info/ccbuilding/default.htm* 🎟*Free* ⊘ *Weekdays 8–5.*

☾ ★ ❻ Clark Planetarium. The Hansen Dome Theatre and 3-D IMAX Theatre comprise this Salt Lake County facility located in The Gateway Mall. The Star Theatre uses state-of-the-art technology to simulate three-dimensional flights through space. Hands-on exhibits and science paraphernalia fill the "Wonders of the Universe" Science Store. ✉*110 S. 400 West St., Downtown* ☎*801/456–7827* ⊕*www.clarkplanetar ium.org* 🎟*Star Show $8, IMAX $8, combination tickets $14* ⊘ *Daily 10:30 AM–end of last show.*

☾ ❼ Discovery Gateway. The goal of this children's museum is to "create the love of learning through hands-on experience," and that's exactly what it does at its location in the Gateway Mall. Children can pilot a jetliner, draw with computers, dig for mammoth bones, or lose themselves in the many other interactive exhibits. ✉*444 W. 100 South St., Downtown* ☎*801/456–5437* ⊕*www.childmuseum.org* 🎟*$9.50* ⊘*Mon. and Fri. 10–9; Tues.–Thurs. and Sat. 10–6; Sun. noon–6.*

❸ EnergySolutions Arena. This arena, the home court for the NBA Utah Jazz, seats 20,000. Concerts, rodeos, ice shows, and other events are also held here. An information desk and a gift shop—with the city's best assortment of Utah Jazz paraphernalia—are open daily 9–5. ✉*300 W. South Temple, Downtown* ☎*801/325–2000* ⊕*www.energy solutionsarena.com.*

❾ Gallivan Center. This outdoor plaza hosts free lunchtime and evening concerts, farmers' markets, and unique arts-and-crafts activities for all ages. It also has an ice rink and a giant outdoor chessboard. ✉*36 E. 200 South St., Downtown* ☎*801/535–6110* ⊕*www.thegallivan center.com.*

★ ☾ ❺ The Gateway Mall. Thirty acres of shopping, entertainment, restaurants, offices, and housing cover the area called the Gateway. The Olympic Legacy Plaza stands in memory of the 2002 Winter Olympics, which

A GOOD WALK

Catch the mass transit train called TRAX at Salt Lake City's geographic center—the intersection of Main Street and South Temple. TRAX service is free in downtown. Get off at Symphony Hall and visit the **Salt Lake Art Center 1**. Adjacent to the Art Center is the **Salt Palace Convention & Visitor Center 2**, where you can find information about Salt Lake City and Utah. This is a good place to sign up for a tour of the Great Salt Lake or Bingham Copper Mine, located elsewhere in Salt Lake Valley. Return to TRAX. Take the train to the end of the line, the Arena stop, and get off to see the **EnergySolutions Arena 3**, formerly known as the Delta Center, and the **Union Pacific Building 4** (west of the arena on South Temple). Walk through the Union Pacific Building into the **Gateway Mall 5**, Salt Lake's newest shopping and entertainment center, with more than 90 shops and restaurants, as well as the **Discovery Gateway 7** children's museum. At the south end of the Gateway, adjacent to

the Megaplex 12, is **Clark Planetarium 6**, which houses a state-of-the-art IMAX theater. If history is your passion, walk south then west to the **Rio Grande Depot 8**, which holds the Utah History Research Center. Finish the loop by taking TRAX from the station outside back to visit the **Gallivan Center 9**, an outdoor gathering place with year-round activities. You can finish your tour with a snack at the wonderful **Salt Lake City Main Library 10** by going east on 400 South Street to 200 East Street. Or rest on the beautiful grounds of the **City and County Building 11**, which is one block south of the library.

TIMING

You can easily spend a day enjoying downtown, not because it's a big area (it's not) but because it's historic, interesting, and pretty in any season. A horse-drawn carriage ride around downtown is especially inviting in spring when the blossoming trees and flower beds of Temple Square burst with color.

were held in Salt Lake City. Entertainers perform regularly in the plaza and throughout the Gateway, which resembles shopping centers in Europe with its narrow streets and wide sidewalks. Two parking lots make access easy. Some of the stores and eateries here are part of national chains, but many are locally grown enterprises. The Clark Planetarium (see **Clark Planetarium**) and a large movie complex are also here. ⊠ *Between 200 South and 50 North Sts., and 400 West and 500 West Sts., Downtown* ☎ *801/456–0000* ⊕ *www.shopthegateway. com* ⊙ *Mon.–Sat. 10–9, Sun. noon–6.*

8 **Rio Grande Depot.** This 1910 depot was built to compete with the showy Union Pacific Railroad Depot three blocks north. It houses the **Utah History Research Center,** which has rotating exhibits on the history of Utah and the West. ⊠ *300 S. Rio Grande St., Downtown* ☎ *801/533–3535* ⊕ *www.history.utah.gov* ✉ *Free* ⊙ *Weekdays 8–5, Sat. 9–1.*

1 **Salt Lake Art Center.** You'll find art to challenge your senses and sensibilities at this art center where the mission is to explore contemporary

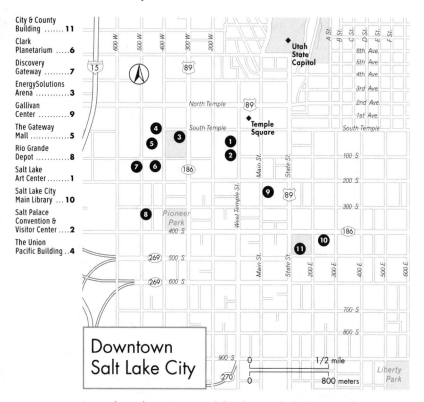

Downtown
Salt Lake City

issues through art. Recent exhibits have included "Scott Fife: Big Trouble, The Idaho Project," a series of 18 sculptures depicting the story of the 1905 assassination of Idaho Governor Frank Steunenberg. ✉*20 S. West Temple, Downtown* ☎*801/328–4201* ⊕*www.slartcenter.org* ✉*Free* ☺*Tues.–Thurs. and Sat. 11–6, Fri. 11–9.*

★ ☺ ❿ **Salt Lake City Main Library.** The library, constructed in 2003, has become a cultural center for the city. Inspired by the Roman Coliseum, architect Moshe Safdie designed the six-story walkable wall as both sculpture and functioning building. Activities are scheduled here all year, in the 300-seat auditorium, the plaza, or the spacious atrium. From the rooftop garden, you get a 360-degree view of the valley and mountains. The on-site coffee shop and deli mean you can stay here all day; other shops sell comic books and gifts, and there's also a film center. ✉*210 E. 400 South St., Downtown* ☎*801/524–8200* ⊕*www.slcpl.lib.ut.us* ✉*Free* ☺*Mon.–Thurs. 9–9, Fri. and Sat. 9–6, Sun. 1–5.*

❷ **Salt Palace Convention & Visitor Center.** The Convention Center is used for large conventions and trade shows. Volunteers are on hand at the visitor center to answer questions and dispense information on tourist sights in Salt Lake City and the state. A gift shop offers local books and gifts. ✉*90 S. West Temple, Downtown* ☎*801/534–4900* ⊕*www. visitsaltlake.com* 🏷*Free* ⊙*Daily 9–5.*

❹ **Union Pacific Building.** This depot, built in 1909 at a cost of $300,000, is a striking monument to the importance of railroads in the settling of the West. The slate-shingle mansard roof sets a distinctive French Second Empire tone for the exterior. Inside, Western-theme murals and stained-glass windows create a setting rich with color and texture. The station has been restored and now functions as the entrance to the Gateway Mall and as a special-events venue. ✉*400 W. 100 South St., Downtown* ☎*801/456–2852* ⊕*www.shopthegateway.com* 🏷*Free* ⊙*Mon.–Sat. 10–9, Sun. noon–6.*

CAPITOL HILL & THE AVENUES

The Capitol Hill and Avenues neighborhoods overlook the city from the foothills north of downtown. Two days after entering what would become Salt Lake City, Brigham Young brought his fellow religious leaders to the summit of the most prominent hill here, which he named Ensign Peak, to plan out their new home. After Temple Square was laid out, houses were constructed nearby. New arrivals built sod homes into the hillside of what is now known as the Avenues. Two-room log cabins and adobe houses dotted the area. With the coming of the railroad came Victorian homes.

The rich and prominent families of the city built mansions along South Temple. As the city has grown over the years, wealthy citizens have continued to live close to the city, but farther up the hill where the views of the valley are better. Since the early 1970s the lower Avenues have seen an influx of residents interested in restoring the older homes, making this area a diverse and evolving community.

The State Capitol, for which Capitol Hill is named, was completed in 1915. State offices surround the Capitol on three sides. City Creek Canyon forms its eastern boundary. The Avenues denotes the larger neighborhood along the foothills, north of South Temple, which extends from Capitol Hill on the west to the University of Utah to the east.

Getting around the Avenues is different than following the logic of the grid system of downtown. The Avenues start north of South Temple and increase in number as you head uphill, 1st Avenue being the beginning. From west to east, the streets are labeled alphabetically. Capitol Hill is a different story, obviously not planned by the master planner, Brigham Young.

WHAT TO SEE
Numbers correspond to the Capitol Hill & the Avenues map.

❺ **Cathedral of the Madeleine.** Catholics have been the largest religious minority in the Salt Lake area since soldiers and miners entered the city. The cathedral was dedicated in 1906. Its Romanesque exterior bristles with gargoyles, while its Gothic interior showcases bright frescoes and a large organ. The Madeleine Choir gives concerts regularly, and

A GOOD TOUR

A tour of Capitol Hill and the Avenues is a logical extension of a tour of downtown Salt Lake City. To begin the tour of this area, head north along State Street from South Temple to North Temple and turn right. Turn left on Canyon Road to the beginning of **Memory Grove ❶**. The road is blocked by a gate at the entrance to the grove. Park your car here, and continue walking past the gate and up toward the **Utah State Capitol ❷**. Visit the nearby **Pioneer Memorial Museum ❸** before returning east across East Capitol Boulevard to visit **Council Hall ❹**, home of the Utah Office of Tourism, for information on tourist destinations in Salt Lake City and the state. From Council Hall, return on East Capitol Boulevard to South Temple. Turn left on South Temple and stop to visit the **Cathedral of the Madeleine ❺**. Continue east on South Temple and finish your visit with a guided tour of the **Kearns Mansion ❻**.

TIMING

You can spend a half day or more touring the Capitol, Kearns Mansion, and the Pioneer Memorial Museum. If you include a picnic in the canyon, your tour could take all day. The views from Capitol Hill are impressive any time of year. The Kearns Mansion, as the official residence of Utah's governor, is most festive during the Christmas season.

tours of the cathedral are offered every Sunday at 12:30 PM. ⊠ *331 E. South Temple* ☎ *801/328–8941* ⊕ *www.saltlakecathedral.org* ✉ *Free* ⊗ *Mon.–Sat. 7 AM–9 PM, Sun. 7–7.*

NEED A BREAK?

For a sweet treat, stop at **Hatch Family Chocolates** (⊠ *390 E. 4th Ave., Temple Square* ☎ *801/532–4912* ⊗ *Closed Sun.*), a super-friendly and immaculate candy and ice-cream shop. Jerry Hatch uses his mother's secret recipe for creamy caramel, and each piece of chocolate is hand-dipped and sold by weight. Chocolate turtles here can weigh a full quarter-pound. They also serve espresso, Italian soda, ice cream, and the best hot chocolate in the city.

❹ **Council Hall.** Once a meeting place for politicians in the Utah Territory, Council Hall is now headquarters for the Utah Office of Tourism. You can pick up brochures and books on tourist destinations throughout the city and state, and ask questions of knowledgeable staff. A small gift store carries Utah books and gifts. ⊠ *300 N. State St., Capitol Hill* ☎ *801/538–1900* ✉ *Free* ⊗ *Mon.–Sat. 8–5.*

NEED A BREAK?

Take a break from your tours with a picnic from Cucina Deli (⊠ *1026 E. 2nd Ave., The Avenues* ☎ *801/322–3055*), an Italian deli specializing in gourmet lunches to eat in or take out. Choose a sandwich, like the Sicilian combo with capocolla ham, mortadella, salami, provolone, and tomatoes, and a side dish of one of many pasta salads. Bring your freshly packed lunch to Memory Grove or City Creek Canyon to relax and refuel amid beautiful surroundings.

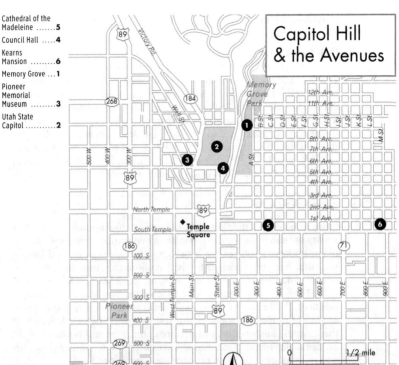

Capitol Hill
& the Avenues

★ ❻ **Kearns Mansion.** Built by silver-mining tycoon Thomas Kearns in 1902, this limestone structure—reminiscent of a French château with all its turrets and balconies—is now the official residence of Utah's governor. In its early days, the mansion was visited by President Theodore Roosevelt and other dignitaries from around the world. ✉*603 E. South Temple, The Avenues* ☎*801/538–1005* ⊕*www.utah.gov/governor/ mansion/index.html* ⌂*Free* ☉*Tours June–Aug. and Dec. 1–15, Tues. and Thurs. 2–4.*

❶ **Memory Grove.** Walk the quiet street, free from traffic, that runs through the park or take one of many trails near City Creek. Monuments to veterans of war are found throughout this grove. You can hike, jog, or bike part or all of the paved road along **City Creek Canyon** (closed to cars on odd-numbered days). Additional trails take off from the road, including the Bonneville Shoreline Trail, which takes you above the houses at the top of the Avenues.

❸ **Pioneer Memorial Museum.** The West's most extensive collection of settlement-era relics, many of which relate to Mormon pioneers, fills 38 rooms—plus a carriage house—on four floors. Displays include clothing, furniture, tools, wagons, and carriages. ✉*300 N. Main St., Capitol Hill* ☎*801/532–6479* ⊕*www.dupinternational.org* ⌂*Free,* *donations accepted* ☉ *June–Aug., Mon.–Sat. 9–5, Sun. 1–5; Sept.–May, Mon.–Sat. 9–5.*

★ ❷ **Utah State Capitol.** In 1912, after the state reaped $800,000 in inheritance taxes from the estate of Union Pacific Railroad president Edward Harriman, work began on the Renaissance Revival structure that tops Capitol Hill. From the exterior steps you get a marvelous view of the entire Salt Lake Valley. In the rotunda beneath the 165-foot-high dome a series of murals, commissioned as part of the WPA project during the Depression, depicts the state's history. Guided tours are offered weekdays on the hour between 9 AM and 4 PM. ✉ *400 N. State St., Capitol Hill* ☎ *801/538–1800* ⊕ *www.utahstatecapitol.utah.gov* ☉ *Tours weekdays 9–4, building weekdays 8–8, weekends 8–5.*

EAST SIDE & THE UNIVERSITY OF UTAH

Situated on one of the shorelines of ancient Lake Bonneville, the University of Utah is the state's largest higher-education institution and the oldest university west of the Mississippi. It contains a natural history museum, fine arts museum, football stadium that was the site of the opening and closing ceremonies during the 2002 Winter Olympics, and a 15,000-seat indoor stadium. The University Medical Center and its neighbor, the Primary Children's Medical Center, east of the campus, are active in medical training and research. Research Park, south of the campus, houses scores of private companies and portions of 30 academic departments in a cooperative enterprise to combine research and technology in order to produce marketable products.

As you leave the downtown and university area, there are opportunities to enjoy the outdoors. Hiking trails lead across the foothills above the university. Red Butte Garden and Arboretum is a treat for the eye and a great place to learn about plants that thrive in dry climates such as Utah's. And be sure to wander the boardwalks in This Is the Place Heritage Park.

Shop at one of the smaller neighborhood centers like Foothill Village or Trolley Square to find unique souvenirs of Utah.

WHAT TO SEE
Numbers correspond to East Side & the University of Utah map.

★ ☾ ❼ **Liberty Park.** Jog the outer path or stroll the inner sidewalk through Salt Lake's earliest and biggest city park. The Chase House, in the park's center, was built next to a mill and is now home to the Museum of Utah Folk Arts Council. Granite boulders from Little Cottonwood Canyon have been transported to the central sidewalk in Liberty Park to form a fountain that represents the major canyons of the Wasatch Front in Salt Lake City. Paddleboats ply the pond in summer, and there are playgrounds for children. ✉ *600 E. 900 South St., East Side.*

NEED A BREAK?	If you're getting hungry, make a pit stop at Emigration Market (✉ *1706 E. 1300 South St., East Side* ☎ *801/581–0138*), a small, beloved, and locally owned market that carries Utah products and food. Pack up your goodies

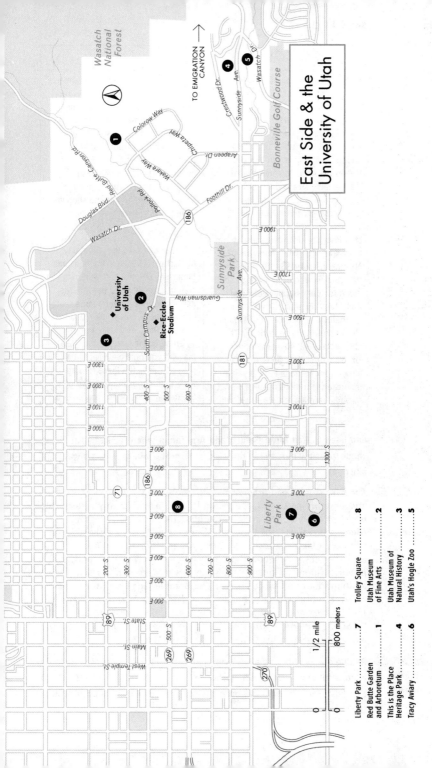

East Side & the University of Utah

Wasatch National Forest

TO EMIGRATION CANYON →

Bonneville Golf Course

University of Utah

Rice-Eccles Stadium

Sunnyside Park

Liberty Park

Liberty Park 7
Red Butte Garden and Arboretum 1
This is the Place Heritage Park 4
Tracy Aviary 6

Trolley Square 8
Utah Museum of Fine Arts 2
Utah Museum of Natural History 3
Utah's Hogle Zoo 5

1/2 mile

800 meters

A GOOD TOUR

Start your tour at the **Red Butte Garden and Arboretum ❶**, east of the University of Utah. Salt Lake is a high desert, yet these gardens in the foothills are surprisingly lush. From here, head back west along 500 South Street where you will see the Hoberman Arch. The arch spanned the medals plaza and the Olympic torch in this small park in front of Rice-Eccles Stadium during the 2002 Winter Olympics. At the University, stop in at the **Utah Museum of Fine Arts ❷** or the **Utah Museum of Natural History ❸**. When you've had your fill of museums, head south along the Lake Bonneville shoreline and spend an hour or two soaking up Utah's pioneer history at **This Is the Place Heritage Park ❹**. The child in you will enjoy exploring **Utah's Hogle Zoo ❺**, across the street from Heritage Park. If you're interested in a more detailed view of birds from around the world and

specifically Utah, make your way to the **Tracy Aviary ❻**, inside **Liberty Park ❼**. To end your tour, return to 700 East Street and head north toward downtown. Take a break by shopping and dining at **Trolley Square ❽**, one of the town's historic treasures, which has been converted from a 19th-century trolley garage into a high-end shopping, dining, and entertainment complex.

TIMING
This tour can take the whole day. Try to start early because the birds and butterflies are most active during the cool mornings in Red Butte Garden and Arboretum. Spend a large part of your day at This Is the Place Heritage Park, especially in summer when all of the living history takes place. If you only have half a day, start at This Is the Place Heritage Park, then choose one or two of the destinations depending on your interest.

and head to Red Butte Garden and Arboretum where you can eat in the shade, possibly next to the red sandstone grotto where there's a waterfall and pond.

★ ☾ ❶ **Red Butte Garden and Arboretum.** With more than 100 acres of gardens and undeveloped acres, the grounds here provide many pleasurable hours of strolling. Of special interest are the Perennial, Fragrance, and Medicinal gardens, the Daylily Collection, the Water Pavilion, and the Children's Garden. Lectures on everything from bugs to gardening in arid climates, workshops, and concerts are presented regularly. The popular Summer Concert Series attracts well-known musicians such as John Hiatt and Greg Brown. The Botanic Gift Shop offers books, soaps, sculptures, and fine gifts. ✉ *300 Wakara Way, east of Foothill Dr., University of Utah* ☎ *801/581–4747* ⊕ *www.redbuttegarden.org* 💲 *$6* ⏰ *May–Aug., Mon.–Sat. 9–9, Sun. 9–5; Sept. and Apr., Mon.–Sat. 9–7:30, Sun. 9–5; Oct.–Mar., daily 10–5.*

■ NEED A BREAK? **Rolling grassy hills with a few scattered trees provide plenty of room to fly a kite or throw a Frisbee at Sugarhouse Park (✉ *1300 East and 2100 South Sts., East Side*). The park was once a federal prison famous for incarcerating Utah polygamists.**

★ ☾ ❹ **This Is the Place Heritage Park.** Utah's premier historic park includes Heritage Village, a re-created 19th-century community, and This Is the Place Monument and visitor center. In summer almost 200 volunteers dressed in period clothing demonstrate what pioneer life was like. You can watch artisans at work in historic buildings, and take wagon rides around the compound. Watch a 20-minute movie depicting the pioneers' trek across America at the visitor center, or browse through the gift–book shop. ✉*2601 E. Sunnyside Ave., East Side* ☎*801/582–1847* ⊕*www.thisistheplace.org* ✉*Village $8; monument free* ☾*This Is the Place Monument, daily dawn–dusk; Heritage Village, Memorial Day–Labor Day, daily 9–5.*

☾ ❻ **Tracy Aviary.** Set on 7½ acres, this facility features some 135 species of birds from around the globe, including emus, bald eagles, flamingos, parrots, and several types of waterfowl. One of the aviary's missions is to educate the public about birds native to Utah and their corresponding ecosystems. There are two free-flight bird shows daily in summer. ✉*600 E. 900 South St., East Side* ☎*801/596–8500* ⊕*www.tracyaviary.org* ✉*$5* ☾*Late Oct.–Feb., daily 9–4:30; Mar.–mid-Oct., daily 9–6.*

❽ **Trolley Square.** From 1908 to 1945, this sprawling redbrick structure garaged nearly 150 trolleys and electric trains for the Utah Light and Railway Company. In the face of more contemporary modes of transport, however, the facility was closed. In the early 1970s the mission-style edifice was completely overhauled, and today it houses more than 90 boutiques and restaurants. ✉*600 S. 700 East St., East Side* ☎*801/521–9877* ☾*Mon.–Sat. 10–9, Sun. noon–5.*

★ ❷ **Utah Museum of Fine Arts.** Because it encompasses 74,000 square feet and more than 20 galleries, you'll be glad this facility has a café and a sculpture court—perfect places to rest. Special exhibits are mounted regularly, and the vast permanent collection includes Egyptian, Greek, and Roman relics; Italian Renaissance and other European paintings; Chinese ceramics and scrolls; Japanese screens; Thai and Cambodian sculptures; African and Latin American artworks; Navajo rugs; and American art from the 17th century to the present. ✉*410 Campus Center Dr., University of Utah* ☎*801/581–7332* ⊕*www.utah.edu/umfa* ✉*$5* ☾*Tues.–Fri. 10–5, Wed. 10–8, weekends 11–5.*

☾ ❸ **Utah Museum of Natural History.** Exhibits focus on the prehistoric inhabitants of the Colorado Plateau, the Great Basin, and other Southwestern locations. Utah's dry climate preserved for centuries not only the structures of these peoples, but also their clothing, foodstuffs, toys, weapons, and ceremonial objects. In the basement are thousands of dinosaur fossils, dominated by creatures from the late Jurassic period, many from the Cleveland-Lloyd quarry in central Utah. Collections of rocks, minerals, wildlife, and other fossils round out the museum. ✉*1390 E. Presidents Cir.University of Utah* ☎*801/581–6927* ⊕*www.umnh.utah.edu* ✉*$6* ☾*Mon.–Sat. 9:30–5:30, Sun. noon–5.*

☾ ❺ **Utah's Hogle Zoo.** The zoo houses more than 1,400 animals from all over the world. Exhibits present animals in their representative habitats. A children's zoo, interactive exhibits, and special presentations make visits informative and engaging for both adults and children. In summer, youngsters can tour the zoo aboard a miniature train. ✉ *2600 E. Sunnyside Ave., East Side* ☎ *801/582–1631* ⊕ *www.hoglezoo.org* ✑ *$8* ⊙ *Mar.–Oct., daily 9–5; Nov.–Feb., daily 9–4.*

OFF THE BEATEN PATH

Bingham Canyon Copper Mine. Depending on your point of view, the Bingham Copper Mine is either a marvel of human engineering or simply a great big eyesore. This enormous open-pit mine measures nearly 2½ mi across and ¾ mi deep—the result of removing 5 billion tons of rock. Since operations began in the early 1900s by the Kennecott Utah Copper company, about 17 million tons of copper have been produced. At the visitor center, exhibits and multimedia presentations explain the history and present-day operation of the mine. Outside, trucks the size of dinosaurs and cranes as tall as apartment buildings continue to reshape the mountain. ✉ *Rte. 48, Copperton* ☎ *801/252–3234* ⊕ *www.kennecott.com* ✑ *$5 per vehicle* ⊙ *Apr.–Oct., daily 8–8.*

THE GREAT SALT LAKE

No visit to Utah is quite complete without a trip to the Great Salt Lake. This wonder of the world is actually more popular with tourists than locals. This was not always the case, but drastic changes in lake levels keep the state and private developers from cashing in on this unique site so close to a major city. Because the lake is so shallow, an inch or two of change in the lake's depth translates into yards of sticky mud between the sandy beach and water deep enough to float in. This shouldn't keep anyone from taking a cruise on the lake or visiting Antelope Island, where the shore dynamics are much different.

WHAT TO SEE

Great Salt Lake State Park. The Great Salt Lake is eight times saltier than the ocean and second only to the Dead Sea in salinity. What makes it so briny? There's no outlet to the ocean, so salts and other minerals carried by rivers and streams become concentrated in this enormous evaporation pond. Ready access to this wonder is possible at Great Salt Lake State Park, 16 mi west of Salt Lake City, on the lake's south shore.

The fickle nature of the Great Salt Lake is evident here. From the marina you will see a large, Moorish-style pavilion to the north. This pavilion was built to re-create the glory days of the lake from the 1890s to the 1950s when first the train, then automobiles, brought thousands of people here for entertainment. Floating in the lake was the biggest draw, but ballroom dancing and an amusement park made for a day's recreation. In addition, three resorts made this a popular place, despite varying lake levels. It was the decline of ballroom dancing together with a severe drop in the lake level that spelled the end of the pavilion's run in the 1960s. In 1981 the present pavilion, souvenir shop, and a dance floor were built. Two years later, record flooding made an island of the pavilion. It sits on dry land today, but its current owners have been unable to recreate its former stature.

The Legendary Great Salt Lake

Legends of an enormous body of water with an outlet to the Pacific Ocean drew explorers north from Mexico as early as the 1500s. By the 1700s, other legends—about piles of gold and mines full of jewels—had been proven false by Spanish explorers, but the lake legend endured. Following a source of water through the West's harsh desert, and traveling along a flat river bank instead of struggling over mountains, would make trade easier between New Mexico and the settlements springing up along California's coast. Perhaps goods could be shipped to the coast rather than hauled by mules, a trip the Spanish guessed (and they were right) would take months.

Franciscan fathers Francisco Atanasio Dominguez and Francisco Silvestre Velez de Escalante came close to finding Great Salt Lake in 1776, but they cut through the Wasatch Mountains too far to the south. They did blaze a major trade route through Utah, but there is no record of any travelers wandering far enough off the route to see the lake of legend. In 1804–05, Lewis and Clark searched for a water route to the West Coast, but their focus on the Columbia River gave them no reason to travel south of Idaho. They, too, missed the lake.

Mountain men had heard of the lake. Legend has it that an argument about the lake broke out at the alcohol-soaked 1824 rendezvous in northern Utah—the trappers couldn't agree whether the nearby Bear River flowed into the lake. Jim Bridger was chosen to settle the argument, some say because he was the youngest. For whatever reason, he was set adrift on the Bear River in a rickety bull boat and told to report his findings at a future rendezvous—if he survived.

Jim Bridger did survive, and he was able to report that the Bear River did flow into the Great Salt Lake. However, his travels and those of fellow mountain man Jedediah Smith indicated that the lake was landlocked. Plus it was no good for drinking. (With no rivers to drain the lake, water that flows in has no way out but to evaporate, leaving behind a highly concentrated solution of salts and minerals.) Even worse, the explorers found that travel around the lake was hampered by vast expanses of marshland, a muddy shoreline, and hundreds of square miles of salt flats that looked solid but were often little more than a thin crust over layers of muck.

With dreams of a freshwater oasis and an easy route to the coast crushed, the legends of the lake changed. The lake became a place where monsters lurked in the water, giants rode elephantlike creatures on the islands, and the bottom periodically opened, swallowing everything nearby. The area became a place to avoid, or to pass by quickly, until 1847, when Brigham Young and the Mormon pioneers crossed the plains to settle on its shore.

The state park used to manage the beaches north of the pavilion, but the lake is too shallow here for convenient floating. The picnic beaches on Antelope Island State Park are the best places to float. If you can't take the time to get to Antelope Island, however, you can walk down the boat ramp at the Great Salt Lake State Marina and stick your legs in the water to experience the unique sensation of floating on water that won't let you sink. Your feet will bob to the surface and you will see tiny orange brine shrimp floating with you. Shower off at the marina. At the marina, you can make arrangements for group or charter sails. Trips take from one to six hours, and there's a range of reasonable prices to match; some include meals. **Salt Island Adventures** (☎ *801/252–9336* ⊕ *www.gslcruises.com*)runs cruises year-round. ✉ *Frontage Rd., 2 mi east of I–80 Exit 104, Salt Lake City* ☎ *801/250–1898* 🖼 *$2* ⊗ *Daily 7* AM*–10* PM.

WHERE TO EAT

ON THE MENU

Utah's traditional local cuisine was the brunt of many jokes during the 2002 Winter Olympics. The fact that Utahns consume more green Jell-O than any state in the union and love a dish called funeral potatoes (a casserole made from frozen hash browns and cream of mushroom soup covered with crushed cornflakes and butter) led to countless chuckles and a few souvenir pins. Although it's true these dishes are common at potluck family and church dinners, when it comes to eating out, Salt Lakers have a much broader palate and many more choices. Salt Lake is home to nationally recognized bastions of New American cuisine, as well as original "Rocky Mountain" cuisine that embraces fresh fish and game along with locally grown organic produce, wild mushrooms, bumper crops of local fresh berries, cherries, peaches, heirloom tomatoes, and artisan products such as goat cheese. The city and resort areas boast some savvy northern Italian restaurants, French bistros, countless sushi bars, delis, and at least one or two restaurants for every exotic cuisine—from Afghan to Peruvian. You'll also find creative wine lists and knowledgeable service. Bakers here are rivaling San Francisco's bread-makers with their own rustic sourdough and Tuscan loaves. The weekly summer farmers' market is thriving, and chefs are building more and more of a food community. All in all, Salt Lake's culinary scene has finally grown up and offers something for every taste, from simple to sophisticated.

WHAT IT COSTS					
	¢	$	$$	$$$	$$$$
AT DINNER	under $8	$8–$12	$13–$18	$19–$25	over $25

Restaurant prices are per person for a main course at dinner, excluding sales tax of 7.6%.

DOWNTOWN SALT LAKE

AMERICAN

$$-$$$ ✕**Lamb's Grill Café.** With its long marble counter, deco-style trim, and cozy mahogany booths, one of the city's oldest dining establishments has aged well. It's a white-tablecloth kind of place where you can still indulge in an old-fashioned barbecued lamb shank or blackened salmon at a reasonable price. The longtime Greek owners have added a few Mediterranean touches to the big menu. Newspaper, business, and political types often gather here for breakfast or lunch. ✉ *169 S. Main St., Downtown* ☎ *801/364–7166* ▭ *AE, D, MC, V* ⊙ *Closed Sun.*

$-$$$ ✕**Red Rock Brewing Company.** Head to this contemporary brewpub for creative whole-meal salads, thin-crust wood-fired pizzas, and perfectly beer-battered fish-and-chips. An on-site brewery (try the crowd-favorite Amber Ale), house-brewed sodas, a full bar, and an overall sense of style add up to a lively lunch and dinner spot near the EnergySolutions Arena. ✉ *254 S. 200 West St., Downtown* ☎ *801/521–7446* ▭ *AE, D, DC, MC, V.*

★ **$-$$** ✕**Squatters Pub Brewery.** A glass wall separates gleaming fermentation tanks from the bar at this casual, high-energy brewpub in the 1906 Boston Hotel building. It's a happening spot on summer days and nights when the patio with its cooling mist system is in full swing and the chef fires up the outdoor grill. Featuring plenty of organic and locally sourced ingredients, the menu veers from locally made bratwurst to curry specials, fish tacos, and big, juicy buffalo burgers. ✉ *147 W. Broadway, Downtown* ☎ *801/363–2739* ⚶ *Reservations not accepted* ▭ *AE, D, DC, MC, V.*

$-$$ ✕**Stoneground Pizza, Pasta & Pool.** On the top floor of a glass-fronted building across the street from the city's architecturally spectacular main public library, this is a casual pizza, pasta, beer, and pool hangout. The menu offers better-than-average pub food and pizzas at reasonable prices. Note the $12 "all you can eat" pizza-and-salad on Sunday, when servers circulate with fresh-from-the-oven pies sliced small enough for sampling. ✉ *249 E. 400 South St., Downtown* ☎ *801/364–1368* ▭ *AE, D, MC, V* ⊙ *No lunch Sun.*

CHINESE

$-$$ ✕**Hong Kong Tea House.** Lacquered wood-and-marble tables, comfortable chairs, and warm colors give the Tea House's three small dining rooms a welcoming look and feel. At lunch, ask for a dim sum menu and simply mark your choices, or wait until servers walk by with small dishes or bamboo baskets of all the Cantonese-style classics, from steamed pork buns to crunchy chicken feet. Dinner menus are more formal, offering traditional Peking duck, spicy Szechuan-style chicken with green beans, and other authentic, regional Chinese favorites. Don't miss the steamed sea bass with ginger. ✉ *565 W. 200 South St., Downtown* ☎ *801/531–7010* ▭ *D, DC, MC, V* ⊙ *Closed Mon.*

CONTEMPORARY

★ **$$$-$$$$** ✕**Bambara.** Seasonal menus reflect regional American and international influences at this artfully designed destination restaurant. The setting, formerly an ornate bank lobby adjacent to the swank Hotel Monaco,

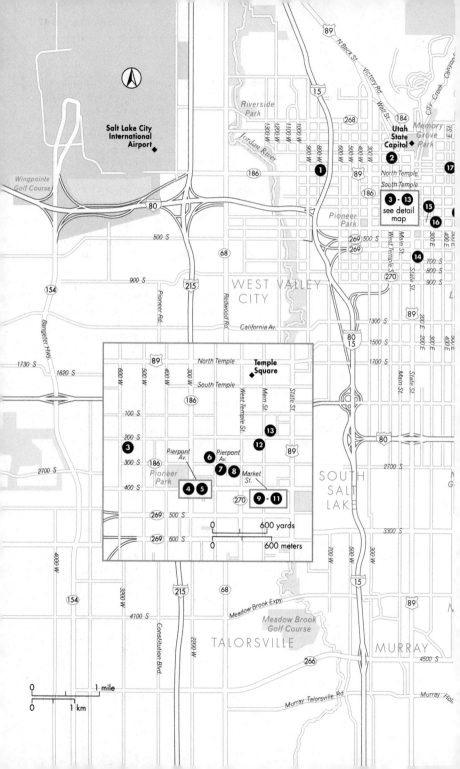

Where to Eat in Salt Lake City

1

is as much of a draw as the food. An open marble-fronted kitchen, big windows framed in fanciful hammered metal swirls, and a definite "buzz" make Bambara a popular gathering spot. You can also dine in the adjoining private club, or simply enjoy a cocktail while snuggled in a velvet-lined booth. ⊠*202 S. Main St., Downtown* ☎*801/363–5454* ▱*AE, D, DC, MC, V.*

$$$–$$$$ × **Metropolitan.** From its inventive cuisine to its minimalist design, owner
Fodor'sChoice Karen Olson's restaurant is chic in every way. Menus veer from Asian-
★ fusion to regional Rocky Mountain fare. You can usually walk in and get a seat at the curved bar or a bar table and order from a small bistro menu. But for the full experience, reserve a table and put yourself in the culinary team's capable hands with the daily tasting menu. Service here borders on choreography—synchronized, yet unobtrusive. The wine list is the best in the city. ⊠*173 W. Broadway, Downtown84101* ☎*801/364–3472* ▱*AE, D, MC, V* ☉*Closed Sun. No lunch.*

CONTINENTAL

$$–$$$$ × **The New Yorker and the Café at the New Yorker.** This subterranean, clubby bar, café, and restaurant with its modern Continental menu, starched white tablecloths, stained-glass ceilings, and rounded banquette seating offers great people-watching potential. If you feel like indulging, try the filet mignon or the veal chop with morel mushrooms and brandy cream sauce. The café–bar area has a lower-price, more casual menu. You'll usually find a crowd of loyal locals, including power-lunchers mingling and having a good time. ⊠*60 W. Market St., Downtown* ☎*801/363–0166* ▱*AE, D, DC, MC, V* ☉*Closed Sun. No lunch Sat. No lunch Fri. (Café).*

DELICATESSEN

★ ¢–$ × **Tony Caputo's Market and Deli.** The people who line up out the door at lunch hour are usually salivating in anticipation of a generous, authentic deli sandwich at this stocked-to-the-rafters Italian deli and market. Whether you fancy a juicy, sauce-drenched meatball concoction, buffalo mozzarella with basil and fresh tomatoes, salami with roasted red peppers, or a hot daily special such as lasagna, it's a great value and a convivial, casual place. Lunch and early dinner are available to eat in or take away. ⊠*308 W. 300 South St., Downtown* ☎*801/531–8669* ▱*AE, D, MC, V.*

ECLECTIC

★ $–$$ × **The Bayou.** You'll find more than 200 microbrews, both bottled and on tap, at chef-owner Mark Alston's lively, often crowded bar and restaurant. There's also a full bar and wine list. The menu offers everything from Cajun specialties such as jambalaya and étouffée to blackened seafood and a terrific, garlicky hamburger with sweet-potato fries. Live jazz, pool tables, and a clean design create a casual, high-energy atmosphere. It's a private club, so visitors must pay $4 for a temporary membership. ⊠*645 S. State St., Downtown* ☎*801/961–8400* ▱*AE, D, MC, V* ☉*No lunch weekends.*

$–$$ × **Oasis Cafe.** From morning to well into the evening, a selection of fine teas and espresso drinks, big breakfasts, and fresh, innovative entrées draw regulars to this café and its serene patio courtyard. The menu leans toward vegetarian and seafood selections, and there are plenty of rich, house-made pastries available, as well as a nice wine list. The café is a popular gathering spot and shares space with The Golden Braid, a shop that sells books and gifts. ⊠*151 S. 500 East St., Downtown* ☏*801/322–0404* ⊟*AE, D, DC, MC, V.*

ITALIAN

★ **$$–$$$$** ✕**Cucina Toscana.** One of the city's most bustling trattorias is tucked into the corner of a former Firestone Tire shop. The menu of house-made pastas includes handmade gnocchi and spinach- and ricotta-filled ravioli. Tiramisù is a favorite dessert. The deco-style pressed-tin ceiling, open kitchen, bas-relief trim, and banquette seating create an urban, artsy atmosphere, which complements the top-notch service, food, and wines. ⊠*307 W. Pierpont Ave., Downtown* ☏*801/328–3463* ⊟*AE, D, MC, V* ☉*Closed Sun. No lunch.*

JAPANESE

$–$$$ ✕**Ichiban.** This is one of the most interesting dining destinations in town. It's set in a former church, complete with exquisite stained-glass windows, vaulted ceilings, and a modernized, feng-shui–inspired interior. The specialties include both classic sushi as well as multilayered Americanized interpretations, some with hot chilis, or with esoteric, locally inspired combinations. You can order some fine cold sakes, and there's a full bar. ⊠*336 S. 400 East St., Downtown* ☏*801/532–7522* ☉*No lunch* ⌣*Reservations not accepted* ⊟*AE, MC, V.*

$–$$$ ✕**Takashi.** One of Salt Lake's most popular Japanese restaurants is hip ★ and lively and has the city's finest sushi, including *uni nigiri* (sea-urchin sushi) that defines melt-in-your-mouth. The calamari is a must-try, too, and on many days owner–chef Takashi Gibo can be seen behind the sushi bar. The full-service bar serves up crisp sake and fine martinis. ⊠*18 W. Market St., Downtown* ☏*801/519–9595* ⊟*AE, D, DC, MC, V* ☉*Closed Sun. No lunch Sat.*

MEXICAN

$–$$ ✕**Red Iguana.** This lively Mexican restaurant is staffed with a warm
Fodor'sChoice and accommodating crew, serving the best house-made moles and
★ chile verde in town. They pour premium margaritas and good Mexican beers, and always keep the salsa and chips coming. Expect a wait almost always. This is a great place to stop on your way to or from the airport if you don't want to take the freeway. ⊠*736 W. North Temple, Downtown* ☏*801/322–1489* ⊟*AE, D, DC, MC, V.*

SEAFOOD

$$–$$$$ ✕**Market Street Grill.** Seafood's the focus in this Salt Lake standby located
★ in a beautifully restored 1906 building. It's a popular breakfast, lunch, and dinner destination where the selections range from daily fresh seafood entrées to certified Angus beef. Portions are large and include all the side dishes. The atmosphere is usually lively. ⊠*48 Market St., Downtown* ☏*801/322–4668* ⌣*Reservations not accepted (dinner)* ⊟*AE, D, DC, MC, V.*

$$-$$$$ ✕ **Market Street Oyster Bar.** Some would call this popular bar–restaurant more of a "meet market," but it's a fun and upbeat place. Popular items include the clam chowder, crab and shrimp cocktails, and more expensive seafood entrées. The decor features original hand-painted pillars, rounded booths that face the action, and televisions on at all hours. The Market Street Oyster Bar is a private club (which means you have to buy a temporary membership for $4) adjoining the Market Street Grill. ✉ *54 Market St., Downtown* ☎ *801/531–6044* ⚄ *Reservations not accepted* ☰ *AE, D, DC, MC, V.*

CAPITOL HILL & THE AVENUES

ECLECTIC

$$-$$$ ✕ **Em's.** Fresh, flavorful, creative, and artsy—chef Emily Gassmann's small café combines it all in a renovated brick storefront in the Marmalade District, west of the Capitol. The café has an urban feel with its modern art and polished wood floors. Sit at the counter, at wooden tables, or on the patio and enjoy the varied menu of salads, soups, savory crepes, meat, and vegetarian entrées. Brunch is served on Sunday. ✉ *271 N. Center St., Capitol Hill* ☎ *801/596–0566* ☰ *AE, MC, V* ⊗ *Closed Mon. No dinner Tues. No lunch weekends.*

TIBETAN

¢–$ ✕ **Cafe Shambala.** Go for savory Tibetan food at bargain prices in this small, clean restaurant decorated with brightly colored Tibetan flags. You can indulge in hearty entrées such as spicy potatoes, chicken curry, and versions of chow mein, and specials such as beef chili, all washed down with pots of tea. The lunchtime buffet is the best deal. ✉ *382 4th Ave.* ☎ *801/364–8558* ☰ *AE, MC, V* ⊗ *Closed Sun.*

EAST SIDE & THE UNIVERSITY OF UTAH

CONTEMPORARY

$–$$ ✕ **Desert Edge Brewery.** This lively microbrewery has brass-top tables, loft seating, a sheltered patio, and lots of music and noise. It also offers a great view of the sunset through floor-to-ceiling windows. The menu offers basic pub food, but goes beyond with creative sandwiches such as salmon with pickled ginger-cucumber slaw, whole-meal salads, and Mexican-inspired fare. ✉ *273 Trolley Sq., East Side* ☎ *801/521–8917* ☰ *AE, D, MC, V.*

INDIAN

★ $–$$ ✕ **Bombay House.** You're enveloped in exotic aromas the minute you step into this dark, intimate restaurant in a small strip mall above busy Foothill Boulevard. Enjoy good Indian standards, including the softest naan and spiciest of curries, tandoori dishes, and lots of vegetarian options. There's a selection of domestic and imported beers as well as traditional teas and tea-based drinks. ✉ *2731 E. Parleys Way, East Side* ☎ *801/581–0222* ☰ *AE, D, MC, V* ⊗ *Closed Sun. No lunch.*

ITALIAN

$$$–$$$$ ✕**Fresco Italian Cafe.** This intimate restaurant is tucked back from the street in a clapboard house that adjoins an independent bookstore. Items like maple-brined pork chops, the daily risotto, and beef short-rib cannelloni take center stage as the season dictates. In summer seating is available on the small patio. ⊠*1513 S. 1500 East St., East Side* ☎*801/486–1300* ⊟*AE, D, DC, MC, V* ⊘*Closed Mon. No lunch.*

MIDDLE EASTERN

$$–$$$ ✕**Mazza Middle Eastern Cuisine.** Authentic and affordable Middle Eastern food in a casual order-at-the-counter setting is what Mazza is all about. The homemade falafel, stuffed grape leaves, lamb, chicken and beef kebabs, and an assortment of side dishes are all fresh and tasty. So are the sweets, such as the honey-drenched baklava. ⊠*1515 S. 1500 East St., East Side* ☎*801/484–9259* ⊟*AE, D, MC, V* ⊘*Closed Sun.*

SEAFOOD

$$–$$$$ ✕**Market Street Grill University.** Formerly a firehouse, circa 1930, this popular restaurant is casual, with a focus on seafood. You can sit at the counter, in the shaded sidewalk café area, or upstairs where the decor is nautical and designed to feel like a luxury yacht. Menu highlights include crab cakes, daily fish specials, a great Cobb salad, and some pricey steak and seafood combinations. There's also an on-site fish market. ⊠*260 S. 1300 East St., University of Utah* ☎*801/583–8808* ⊟*AE, D, DC, MC, V.*

FARTHER AFIELD

CONTEMPORARY

$$–$$$$ ✕**Log Haven.** This elegant mountain retreat was put on the map with
Fodor'sChoice inventive takes on American cuisine laced with everything from Asian
★ ingredients to pure Rocky Mountain style. It excels with fresh fish, game, and seasonal local ingredients, creating such dishes as rabbit with white corn polenta or ahi tuna served with lime sticky rice and baby bok choy. The knowledgeable staff can help you pair wines with the menu's multilayered flavors. With its romantic setting in a beautifully renovated log home amid pine trees, waterfalls, and wildflowers, and its summertime patio seating, this is definitely a restaurant to remember. ⊠*6451 E. Millcreek Canyon Rd., Millcreek Canyon* ⊕*From I–15, take I–80 E to I–215 S; exit at 39th South; turn left at end of ramp, and left onto Wasatch Blvd., then turn right at 3800 South. Continue 4 mi up canyon* ☎*801/272–8255* ⊟*AE, D, MC, V.*

ECLECTIC

$–$$$ ✕**Porcupine Pub and Grille.** Above a ski- and board-rental shop at the mouth of Big and Little Cottonwood canyons sits one of the Valley's most lively pubs. Inside the large A-frame chaletlike building you'll find bright polished wood floors and trim, and a friendly vibe. The menu offers more than 40 variations on standard pub food, including buffalo wings, rock shrimp pizza, burgers, ribs, burritos, and ahi tuna. The full-service bar features spirits, microbrews on tap, and a wine list. ⊠*3698 E. Fort Union Blvd., Cottonwood* ☎*801/942–5555* ▭*AE, D, MC, V.*

MEXICAN

¢　✕**Lone Star Taqueria.** This place is hard to miss. Look for the lime-green building surrounded by a fence topped with old cowboy boots, and fronted by an old sticker-covered car that looks as though it crashed through the fence. Amid the concrete floors, metal tables, and bright umbrellas, there's some excellent, cheap Mexican food to be had— including house special fish tacos, handmade tamales, burritos of all types, and plenty of chilled Mexican beer. There's a drive-through window for takeout, too. ⊠*2265 E. Fort Union Blvd., Cottonwood* ☎*801/944–2300* ⌦*Reservations not accepted* ▭*No credit cards* ☉*Closed Sun.*

WHERE TO STAY

Luxury grand hotels, intimate bed-and-breakfasts, reliable national "all suites" chains—Salt Lake City has plenty of options when it comes to resting your head at night. Unlike in most cities, hotels, motels, and even bed-and-breakfasts here are all tuned into serving visiting skiers in winter months. Many offer ski packages, transportation, and equipment rental options, as well as knowledgeable staff who are probably on the slopes when they're not at work. Most of the hotels are concentrated in the downtown area and west of the airport, but there are also numerous options to the south of Salt Lake proper and closer to the canyon areas, where several high-tech companies and corporate headquarters are located.

WHAT IT COSTS				
	¢	$	$$	$$$	$$$$
FOR 2 PEOPLE	under $70	$70–$110	$111–$150	$151–$200	over $200

Hotel prices are for two people in a standard double room in high season, excluding taxes of 10.1% to 11.2%.

DOWNTOWN SALT LAKE

$$$$　**The Grand America Hotel.** With its white Bethel-granite exterior, this Fodor'sChoice 24-story luxury hotel dominates the skyline a few blocks south of ★ downtown. Inside the beveled-glass and brass doors, you step into a world of Italian marble floors and walls and pure old-world style— think English wool carpets, French furniture and tapestries, and colorful Murano-glass chandeliers. The posh guest rooms average 700 square feet. Most have views and small balconies. This is a great place to sit back with room service and revel in some pampering. The big outdoor pool and indoor spa are among the best in the city. **Pro:** As stately and grand as its name suggests. **Con:** Airport shuttle no longer provided. ⊠*555 S. Main St., Downtown, 84111* ☎*801/258–6000 or 800/621–4505* 🖷*801/258–6911* ⊕*www.grandamerica.com* ⇄*386*

rooms, 389 suites ♿ In-room: safe, kitchen (some), refrigerator (some), DVD (on request), VCR (on request), Ethernet. In-hotel: restaurant, room service, 2 bars, 2 pools, gym, spa, laundry service, concierge, executive floor, public Internet, public Wi-Fi, parking (fee), no-smoking rooms ⊟AE, D, DC, MC, V ⏐⏐EP.

$$$$ 🖥 **Salt Lake Marriott City Center.** If you want to be in the heart of the city, this hotel's location is superb. It's right next to Gallivan Center, site of all kinds of concerts in summer and ice-skating in the winter. Inside, the lobby and public areas are clean and contemporary, with a fresh, upscale feeling. Rooms are furnished with king-size beds and comfortable seating. You have all the conveniences here, including a Starbucks, an indoor pool, and a fitness center. **Pros:** Newest hotel in the heart of downtown. Large fitness room. **Con:** On-site parking fees can add up. ✉220 S. State St., Downtown, 84111 ☎801/961–8700 📠801/961–8704 ⊕www.marriott.com ⬅342 rooms, 17 suites ♿ In-room: safe, kitchen (some), refrigerator (some), Ethernet. In-hotel: restaurant, room service, bar, pool, gym, laundry service, concierge, executive floor, public Wi-Fi, airport shuttle, parking (fee), no-smoking rooms ⊟AE, D, DC, MC, V ⏐⏐EP.

$$$–$$$$ 🖥 **Hotel Monaco Salt Lake City.** This swank hotel is ensconced in a former
FodorsChoice bank, distinguished by an exterior decorated with classical cornices
★ and cartouches. Inside, the look and feel are sophisticated, eclectic, and upbeat. Rooms offer extras such as big fringed ottomans, oversize framed mirrors and beds, and lots of pillows. And, there are special rooms for especially tall folks, with extra-long beds. Bambara Restaurant, on the ground level (under separate management), is one of the city's most celebrated dining spots. **Pros:** A distinctive hotel in the heart of downtown. Restaurant has impeccable service and innovative food. **Con:** Service in the bar does not match that in the dining room. ✉15 W. 200 South St., Downtown, 84101 ☎801/595–0000 or 800/805–1801 📠801/532–8500 ⊕www.monaco-saltlakecity.com ⬅187 rooms, 38 suites ♿ In-room: safe, refrigerator, Ethernet, Wi-Fi. In-hotel: restaurant, room service, bar, gym, laundry service, concierge, public Wi-Fi, parking (fee), some pets allowed ⊟AE, D, DC, MC, V.

$$$–$$$$ 🖥 **Hilton–Salt Lake City Center.** This Hilton is one of the city's largest and best-appointed places to stay, and it's within walking distance of all downtown attractions and many great restaurants. Its on-site restaurants and bars are so good they're destinations for locals. Like many Salt Lake hotels, it also caters to skiers by offering complimentary ski storage. Knowledgeable staff can usually fill visitors in on the various ski resorts and rental shops. Some room packages include breakfast. **Pro:** Walking distance to Temple Square and other downtown sights. **Con:** Some might find the size—500+ rooms—somewhat overwhelming. ✉255 S. West Temple, Downtown, 84101 ☎801/328–2000 or 800/445–8667 📠801/238–4888 ⊕www.hilton.com ⬅499 rooms, 20 suites ♿ In-room: safe, Ethernet, dial-up, Wi-Fi. In-hotel: 2 restaurants, room service, 2 bars, pool, gym, spa, laundry service, concierge, executive floor, public Internet, public Wi-Fi, airport shuttle, parking (fee), some pets allowed, no-smoking rooms ⊟AE, DC, MC, V.

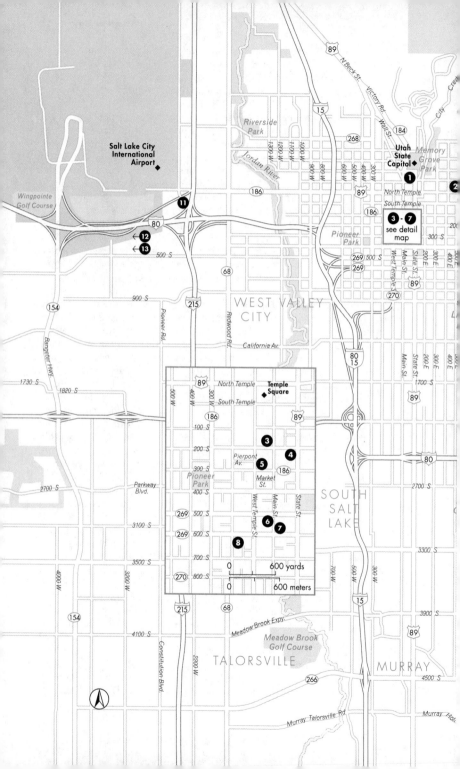

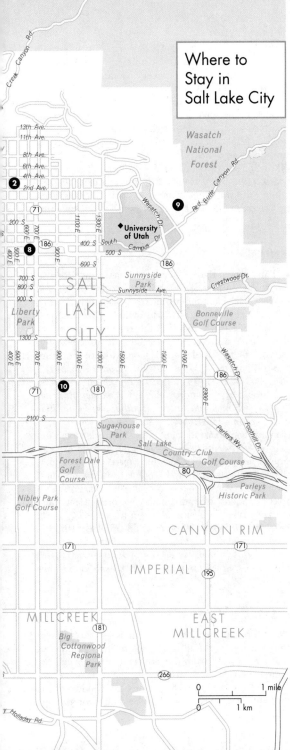

Where to Stay in Salt Lake City

$–$$$ ▢**Little America Hotel.** Located on the TRAX light-rail line and inside
★ the "free ride zone," this reliably comfortable hotel has a loyal follow-ing. You can choose between spacious "tower" rooms inside the 17-story building, or garden rooms with private entrances. There's a large indoor–outdoor pool, a lobby fireplace, and elegant details such as brass railings, chandeliers, and marble tubs. The spacious guest rooms are conservatively furnished, but with richly textured fabrics and plush seating. **Pros:** Large rooms. Trees make the courtyard an oasis. **Con:** Airport shuttle no longer provided. ⊠*500 S. Main St., Downtown, 84101* ☎*801/363–6781 or 800/453–9450* 🖷*801/596–5911* ⊕*www.littleamerica.com* 🛏*850 rooms* △*In-room: safe, Ethernet, DVD (some). In-hotel: 2 restaurants, room service, bar, 2 pools, gym, conciergelaundry service, public Wi-Fi, parking (no fee), no-smoking rooms.* ▤*AE, D, DC, MC, V.*

CAPITOL HILL & THE AVENUES

$$–$$$ ▢**Inn on the Hill.** This turn-of-the-20th-century Renaissance Revival
★ mansion makes a striking impression with its red rock exterior and bold painted trim. Inside, it's like stepping into the just-polished parlor and living rooms of a private home, replete with stained-glass windows. Rooms are eclectic in style, with historic Utah themes. All are very cushy, with big bathtubs and fireplaces. **Pros:** Elegant stone mansion on Capitol Hill. Short walk to Temple Square. **Con:** Modern rooms are a little short on period charm. ⊠*225 N. State St., Capitol Hill, 84103* ☎*801/328–1466* 🖷*801/328–0590* ⊕*www.inn-on-the-hill.com* 🛏*6 rooms, 6 suites* △*In-room: refrigerator (some), VCR (some), Ethernet (some). In-hotel: no elevator, public Internet, public Wi-Fi, no kids under 14, no-smoking rooms* ▤*AE, MC, V* ⎷◉*BP.*

$$ ▢**Ellerbeck Mansion Bed and Breakfast.** Stay in this Victorian mansion to get a feel for why city residents flock to live in the historic Avenues district. Temple Square and other points downtown are a short 10-minute walk away. Each theme room is bright. Some feature a fireplace, private balcony, or hand-carved wood furniture and fixtures. **Pros:** It's a pleasant walk to Temple Square from this stately Victorian home. **Con:** Expect room surcharges when conventions are in town. ⊠*140 B St., Capitol Hill, 84103* ☎*801/355–2500 or 800/966–8364* 🖷*801/530–0938* ⊕*www.ellerbeckbedandbreakfast.com* 🛏*6 rooms* △*In-room: kitchen (some), refrigerator (some), Wi-Fi. In-hotel: no elevator, public Wi-Fi, parking (no fee), no children under 10, no-smoking rooms* ▤*AE, D, MC, V* ⎷◉*BP.*

EAST SIDE & THE UNIVERSITY OF UTAH

$–$$$ ▢**Anton Boxrud Bed & Breakfast Inn.** Quirky furnishings—some of them antiques—from all over the world fill the rooms of this eclectic Victorian manor a 15-minute stroll from the city center and around the corner from the stately Governor's mansion. The complimentary evening snacks and beverages served near the parlor's bay window are as delicious as the bountiful breakfasts served in the dining room. **Pros:**

1

Chocolates and fresh flowers in the rooms. Convenient to the Avenues district. **Con:** Some may find it a long walk to downtown. ⊠*57 S. 600 East St., East Side, 84102* ☎*801/363–8035 or 800/524–5511* 🖷*801/596–1316* ⊕*www.antonboxrud.com* ⟿*7 rooms* ♿*In-room: no phone, safe, no TV, Wi-Fi. In-hotel: DVD, VCR, no elevator, concierge, public Internet, public Wi-Fi, no kids under 10, no-smoking rooms* ☰*AE, D, DC, MC, V* ⊙|*BP.*

$–$$$ 🏨**Salt Lake City Marriott University Park.** This mid-size but spacious hotel is airy and inviting, with mountain views, and offers easy access to nearby canyons. It's in Salt Lake's Research Park, home to biotech giants and University of Utah–affiliated research facilities. One of the city's major attractions, Red Butte Garden, is nearby. **Pro:** Close to hiking and biking trails. **Con:** Inconvenient to downtown. ⊠*480 Wakara Way, University of Utah, 84108* ☎*801/581–1000* 🖷*801/584–3321* ⊕*www. marriott.com* ⟿*189 rooms, 29 suites* ♿*In-room: Ethernet. In-hotel: restaurant, bar, room service, pool, gym, laundry service, concierge, executive floor, airport shuttle, parking (no fee)* ☰*AE, D, MC, V.*

$–$$ 🏨**Wildflowers Bed & Breakfast.** An elegant "painted lady" with a private yard full of larkspur, columbine, and foxglove, this Victorian inn was built as a private home in 1891. The interior has been renovated to provide more light, but the rooms are furnished in keeping with the period. If you're traveling with a group, or just want more space, you can reserve the full-floor "bird's nest" suite with a full kitchen and dining room. **Pro:** Listed on National Register of Historic Places. **Con:** A bit of a walk to downtown. ⊠*936 E. 1700 South St., East Side, 84105* ☎*801/466–0600, 800/569–0009 reservations* 🖷*801/466–4728* ⊕*www.wildflowersbb.com* ⟿*4 rooms, 1 suite* ♿*In-room: refrigerator (some), no TV. In-hotel: no elevator, parking (no fee), no-smoking rooms* ☰*AE, D, MC, V* ⊙|*BP.*

WEST SIDE & THE AIRPORT

$–$$$$ 🏨**Hilton Salt Lake City Airport.** A self-contained world on a man-made lake, 2 mi from the airport, this big hotel meets business travelers' needs with plenty of business and personal services, shuttles, and proximity to downtown. **Pros:** Modern building. Large weight room. **Con:** No attractions within walking distance. ⊠*5151 Wiley Post Way, Airport, 84116* ☎*801/539–1515 or 800/999–3736* 🖷*801/539–1113* ⊕*www. hilton.com* ⟿*276 rooms, 12 suites* ♿*In-room: Wi-Fi. In-hotel: restaurant, room service, bar, pool, gym, laundry facilities, laundry service, executive floor, public Wi-Fi, airport shuttle, parking (no fee), some pets allowed, no-smoking rooms* ☰*AE, D, MC, V* ⊙|*EP.*

$$$ 🏨**Radisson Hotel Airport.** This very comfortable hotel is a good bet near the airport. There's no need to leave the premises, as you have access to an on-site pool and gym, and you're literally five minutes from airport check-in. Breakfast isn't included, though it is served in the restaurant. **Pro:** Closer to downtown than other airport hotels. **Con:** Still too far to walk to downtown attractions. ⊠*2177 W. North Temple, Airport, 84116* ☎*801/364–5800 or 800/333–3333* 🖷*801/364–5823* ⊕*www. radisson.com* ⟿*126 rooms* ♿*In-room: refrigerator, Ethernet, Wi-Fi.*

In-hotel: restaurant, room service, pool, gym, laundry facilities, laundry service, public Internet, public Wi-Fi, airport shuttle, parking (no fee), no-smoking rooms ☐*AE, D, DC, MC, V.*

$$–$$$ ☐**Comfort Inn Airport.** Spacious, modern, and fully decked out with amenities, this is a good value for a stay near the airport, with easy access to downtown. The furnishings and separate work spaces in guest rooms make this facility a more upscale property than many in this chain. **Pro:** Caters to business travelers. **Con:** Downtown seems far away. ⊠*200 N. Admiral Byrd Rd., Airport, 84116* ☎*801/746–5200 or 800/535–8742* 🖷*801/532–4721* ⊕*www.slccomfortinn.com* 🛏*153 rooms, 2 suites* ⚲*In-room: refrigerator, VCR, Ethernet, dial-up. In-hotel: restaurant, room service, pool, gym, spa, laundry facilities, laundry service, executive floor, airport shuttle, parking (no fee), some pets allowed* ☐*AE, D, DC, MC, V* ⍣*BP.*

NIGHTLIFE & THE ARTS

For information on what's happening around town, pick up a *City Weekly* news and entertainment weekly, available at stands outside restaurants and stores in town.

THE ARTS

Salt Lake City's arts tradition officially started in 1847 with the Deseret Musical and Dramatic Society, founded by Brigham Young. The city has continued to give strong support for the arts, even voting for a special tax to support cultural organizations like the opera and symphony. Ballet West and the Utah Symphony have kept Utah on the nation's cultural map. The Capitol and Rose Wagner theaters host Broadway touring companies. The Pioneer Theatre Company is a well-regarded professional troupe. Lesser known and locally written plays are presented in small theaters throughout the valley.

FESTIVALS & EVENTS ★ If you're in town in late June, check out the **Utah Arts Festival** (⊕*www.uaf.org*). Look for original art at the Marketplace, create your own at the Art Yard, sample eclectic food, and swing to the beat of live music. Local artists and art galleries enjoy one evening each month (usually the third Friday of the month) sharing their artwork with the public in the **Gallery Stroll.** A possible starting point is **Phillips Gallery** (⊠*444 E. 200 South St.* ☎*801/364–8284*). Stop at any gallery on the stroll to obtain a self-guiding map. Artists and art lovers chat over wine and snacks at each stop.

Fodor'sChoice ★ Rub shoulders with the "beautiful people" in Park City during Robert Redford's **Sundance Film Festival** (✉*Box 684429, Park City 84068* ☎*435/658–3456* ⊕*www.sundance.org*) or come to three venues in downtown Salt Lake City. The festival has more than 100 screenings in Salt Lake City at the Tower Theatre, Broadway Center Theatre, and Rose Wagner Performing Arts Center. Buy tickets ahead online, or purchase day-of-show tickets, if available, at the theaters.

TICKETS For tickets to cultural events, contact **ArtTix** (☎*801/355–2787 or 888/451–2787* ⊕*www.arttix.org*). **Smiths Tix** (☎*801/467–8499 or 800/888–8499* ⊕*www.smithstix.com*)sells tickets to sporting events and concerts.For tickets to events at the EnergySolutions Arena, contact **Ticketmaster** (☎*801/325–7328* ⊕*www.ticketmaster.com*).

MAJOR PERFORMANCE VENUES

There are three main performance spaces in Salt Lake City. Ballet West and the Utah Opera perform at the **Capitol Theatre** (⊠*50 W. 200 South St., Downtown* ☎*801/355–2787*) , which also hosts Broadway touring companies.The Utah Symphony plays at **Abravanel Hall** (⊠*123 W. South Temple St., Downtown* ☎*801/355–2787*). **The Rose Wagner Center** (⊠*138 W. 300 South St., Downtown* ☎*801/355–2787*)is comprised of the Black Box Theatre, the Jeanné Wagner Theatre, and the Studio Theatre. It's home to the Ririe-Woodbury Dance Company and the Repertory Dance Theatre, as well as providing performance space for many of the city's smaller theater and dance companies.

DANCE

Ballet West (☎*801/323–6900* ⊕*www.balletwest.org*) is a respected professional ballet company, performing both classic and original works. **Repertory Dance Theatre** (☎*801/534–1000* ⊕*www.xmission.com/~rdt/*)
★ presents modern-dance performances. **Ririe-Woodbury Dance Company** (☎*801/297–4241* ⊕*www.ririewoodbury.com*)is Salt Lake's premier modern-dance troupe, recognized for its innovation and commitment to community education.

FILM

Art and independent films are shown at **Brewvies** (⊠*676 S. 200 West St., Downtown* ☎*801/355–5500* ⊕*www.brewvies.com*)on their second run. You can have a beer and dinner with the show.The Salt Lake
★ Film Society shows independent and foreign films at **Broadway Centre Theatre** (⊠*111 E. 300 South St., Downtown* ☎*801/321–0310* ⊕*www.saltlakefilmsociety.org*). Independent, cult, and foreign films,
★ often shown at midnight on weekends, are standard at **Tower Theatre** (⊠*876 E. 900 South St., East Side* ☎*801/321–0310* ⊕*www.saltlake filmsoci ety.org*), a historic art deco theater.

MUSIC

★ The **Mormon Tabernacle Choir** (⊠*Temple Sq.* ☎*801/240–4150* ⊕*www. mormontabernaclechoir.org*), which includes men and women of all ages from around the Intermountain region, performs sacred music, with some secular—classical and patriotic—works. You can hear the Choir during their weekly broadcast, "Music and the Spoken Word," Sunday mornings from 9:30–10 in the Tabernacle on Temple Square, except for June, July, August, and December, when the broadcasts are held in the Conference Center. The Choir's weekly rehearsal, also open to the public, is held Thursday evenings from 8–9:30 in the Tabernacle.

The **Utah Symphony** (⊠*Abravanel Hall, 123 W. South Temple, Downtown* ☎*801/533–6683* ⊕*www.utahsymphony.org*) performs more than 250 concerts annually, both at home in the acoustically acclaimed

Maurice Abravanel Concert Hall, and in cities across the nation and abroad.

OPERA
The **Utah Opera Company** (⊠*123 W. South Temple, Downtown* ☎*801/533–6683* ⊕*www.utahopera.org*) produces five operas a year, often featuring nationally recognized stars.

THEATER
Off Broadway Theatre (⊠*272 S. Main St., Downtown* ☎*801/355–4628* ⊕*www.theobt.com*) puts on musicals, plays, and improvisational comedy events. **Pioneer Theatre Company** (⊠*300 S. 1400 East St., East Side* ☎*801/581–6961* ⊕*www.pioneertheatre.org*)stages classic and contemporary musicals and plays. **Salt Lake Acting Company** (⊠*168 W. 500 North St., Downtown* ☎*801/363–7522* ⊕*www.saltlakeacting company.org*) is recognized for its development of new regionally and locally written plays. Performances run year-round.

NIGHTLIFE

An increasingly cosmopolitan atmosphere is spreading through downtown Salt Lake City. Bars and clubs serve up cocktails and live music to meet diverse tastes. The state's quirky liquor laws make for a few surprises to newcomers, however. First of all, don't expect to spend the night barhopping along a single street. Only two private clubs, requiring a membership to be purchased for admission, are allowed per block. Last call is 1 AM, and some bars call it earlier. Cabs are not on hand at every bar or club, so you will probably have to call for one.

BARS & LOUNGES
Catch the game on the giant screen at **Cassadys** (⊠*1037 E. 3300 South St., The Suburbs* ☎*801/486–3008*), or take a turn at karaoke on Tuesday and Thursday nights.

Hard Rock Cafe (⊠*505 S. 600 East St., East Side* ☎*801/532–7625*) has pretty good burgers, rock and roll memories, and touring national bands. A good place for spotting Utah Jazz basketball players and their ★ visiting competitors is **Port O' Call** (⊠*78 W. 400 South St., Downtown* ☎*801/521–0589*), a sports bar with 18 satellite dishes and 50 TVs. Expect to wait for a table here on weekends.

★ For beer brewed on the premises, head to **Squatters Pub Brewery** (⊠*147 W. Broadway, Downtown* ☎*801/363–2739*). Sandwiches and pasta dishes are on the menu.Try a martini at **The Red Door** (⊠*57 W. 200 South St., Downtown* ☎*801/363–6030*), a trendy bar with a cosmopolitan accent, where an eclectic crowd of T-shirt-and-jeans meets suit-and-tie hangs out. **The Tavernacle Social Club** (⊠*201 E. Broadway, Downtown* ☎*801/519–8900*) features dueling pianos and is smoke-free.

NIGHTCLUBS
★ Jazz bands play on a draped circular stage at **Circle Lounge** (⊠*328 S. State St., Downtown* ☎*801/531–5400*), where you can also enjoy late-night sushi and cocktails. **Green Street Social Club** (⊠*602 E. 500 South*

St., East Side ☎*801/532–4200)* is a fine spot to meet or make friends while enjoying light food, live music, and dancing. Known as one of the city's premier pick-up joints, it's also a fine place for a game of pool with your friends. At **Kristauf's Martini Bar** (✉*16 W. Market St., Downtown* ☎*801/366–9490)* you'll have a hard time choosing which martini to try from among the more than 80 varieties. Service is sometimes slow, but the collegiate crowd doesn't seem to mind.

SPORTS & THE OUTDOORS

Salt Lake City's magic lies not in its skyline, but its backdrops. The Great Salt Lake and Wasatch Mountains are more than pretty pictures, however. Rich outdoors experiences await you within minutes of downtown, from a quiet stroll up City Creek Canyon to a peaceful cruise on the Great Salt Lake. The weather usually cooperates with these pursuits—the city's average 10 inches of precipitation comes mainly in the form of snow. Even on the hottest summer day you can find a shady canyon with a stream passing through.

Salt Lake City is a gateway to the excellent ski resorts strung along the Wasatch Range. There are also a handful of nearby golf courses. In town you can readily bicycle or jog along the wide streets and through the many parks.

Smiths Tix (☎*801/467–8499 or 800/888–8499* ⊕*www.smithstix.com*) sells tickets to sporting events and concerts. For tickets to events at the EnergySolutions Arena, contact **Ticketmaster** (☎*801/325–7328* ⊕*www.ticketmaster.com*).

BASKETBALL

★ The **Utah Jazz** (✉*EnergySolutions Arena, 301 W. South Temple, Downtown* ☎*801/355–3865* ⊕*www.nba.com/jazz*) is Salt Lake's NBA team and a real crowd-pleaser. Home games are played at EnergySolutions Arena.

BICYCLING

★ Salt Lake City is a comparatively easy city to tour by bicycle, thanks in part to its extra-wide streets. Look for white striping on certain streets indicating a bike lane. An especially good route is **City Creek Canyon,** east of the capitol, particularly on odd-number days from Memorial Day through Labor Day and daily between Labor Day and Memorial Day, when the road is closed to vehicles. Liberty Park and Sugarhouse Park also have good cycling and running paths.

GOLF

If you're near the east side of the city, try the **Bonneville Golf Course** (✉*954 S. Connor St., East Side* ☎*801/583–9513).* Less than five minutes from downtown you can tee off at the 18-hole **Rose Park Golf Course** (✉*1386 N. Redwood Rd., West Side* ☎*801/596–5030).* A championship course and spectacular scenery await you 20 minutes away at the **South Mountain Golf Club** (✉*1247 E. Rambling Rd., Draper* ☎*801/495–0500).* **Stonebridge Golf Club** (✉*4415 Links Dr., West Valley City*

☎801/957–9000) is a five-minute drive from Salt Lake International Airport, and it offers a Johnny Miller signature design course.

ICE-SKATING

Classic Fun Center (⊠9151 S. 255 West St., The Suburbs ☎801/561–1791)offers ice-skating along with roller-skating, a waterslide park, laser tag, and Rollerblade rentals. Choose to swim, jog, lift weights, play tennis, or ice skate at the **Cottonwood Heights Recreation Center** (⊠7500 S. 2700 East St., The Suburbs ☎801/943–3160).The 2002 Winter Olympics started an ice-skating boom. Find time on the ice at **The Salt Lake City Sports Complex** (⊠645 Guardsman Way, University of Utah ☎801/583–9713) near the University of Utah. Use the same ice as the 2002 Winter Olympians at the **Utah Olympic Oval** (⊠5662 S. 4800 West St., The Suburbs ☎801/968–6825). The **West Valley Accord Ice Center** (⊠5353 W. 3100 South St., The Suburbs ☎801/966–0223) was the 2002 Winter Olympics practice hockey and skating rink. Call the center for public ice-skating times.

PARKS

Most neighborhoods have a small park, usually with a children's playground. **Salt Lake City Parks Division** (☎801/972–7800 ⊕www.slcgov. com/publicservices/parks/)operates several pools and maintains many parks, including the Raging Waters Waterslide park. Parks not under the city's jurisdiction are operated by **Salt Lake County Parks & Recreation** (☎801/468–2299 ⊕www.parks-recreation.org).

☾ Take the kids to **Fairmont Park** (⊠1044 Sugarmont Dr., East Side), a smaller park with a children's play area, duck pond, and large indoor
☾ swimming pool. **Liberty Park** (⊠900 S. 700 East St., East Side) has a jogging path, tennis courts, picnic areas, and children's playgrounds,
★ ☾ including a state-of-the-art playground for children with disabilities. **Sugarhouse Park** (⊠2100 S. 1300 East St., East Side)is primarily open space where you can jog, bicycle, fly a kite, throw a Frisbee, or soak up some rays.

SKIING

If you are heading out to some of Utah's fine ski resorts, advance equipment and clothing rental reservations are available from **Utah Ski & Golf** (⊠134 W. 600 South St., Downtown ☎801/355–9088 or 800/858–5221 ⊕www.utahskigolf.com). The company has locations downtown and in Park City. It also offers free shuttle service from downtown hotels to their stores.

SOCCER

Major League Soccer came to Utah when **Real Salt Lake** (⊠400 S. 1400 East St., Downtown ☎866/976–2237 ⊕realsaltlake.com) started its first season in 2005. Home games are held at Rice-Eccles Stadium until the team's new stadium in Sandy is completed, slated for late 2008.

SHOPPING

Salt Lake's shopping is concentrated downtown as well as in several malls. Good bets for souvenirs include books, Mormon crafts, and Western collectibles. The vicinity of 300 South and 300 East streets has several shops that specialize in antique jewelry, furnishings, art, and knickknacks.

PLAZAS & MALLS

Crossroads Plaza (⊠*50 S. Main St., Downtown* ☎*801/531–1799*) is an all-inclusive downtown shopping experience; among its 140 stores and restaurants are Nordstrom and Mervyn's.

Foothill Village (⊠*1300 S. Foothill Dr., East Side* ☎*801/487–6670*)has a wide range of shops—from apparel, gifts, and jewelry to health and wellness—and dining opportunities from fast food to fine dining.

★ **The Gateway Mall** (⊠*18 N. Rio Grande St., Downtown* ☎*801/456–0000*)is a combination shopping mall, restaurant district, and business and residential center, all accessible by TRAX, Salt Lake's mass transit.

The **Sugar House Business District** (⊠*Between 1700 South and 2700 South Sts., from 700 East to 1300 East Sts., East Side*)is a funky mix of locally owned shops and restaurants, including a large thrift store.

★ The wares at **Trolley Square** (⊠*600 S. 700 East St., East Side* ☎*801/521–9877*) run the gamut from estate jewelry and designer clothes to bath products, baskets, and saltwater taffy. Stores include Laura Ashley, Gap, Williams-Sonoma, Banana Republic, and an assortment of restaurants including a Hard Rock Cafe.

OUTDOOR MARKETS

Farmers bring produce, flowers, and other goodies to the popular Downtown Farmers' Market at Pioneer Park, at 300 West and 300 South streets, each Saturday from June through mid-October. Local bakeries and restaurants also sell tasty treats ranging from fresh salsa to cinnamon rolls, and there is live music, too.

SPECIALTY STORES

ANTIQUES **Elementé** (⊠*353 W. Pierpont Ave., Downtown* ☎*801/355–7400*)specializes in unique and unusual period pieces; look for bargains in the basement.Just a short walk from downtown is **Moriarty's Antiques & Curiosities** (⊠*959 S. West Temple, Downtown* ☎*801/521–7207*), which specializes in furnishings for the home and garden. The staff will ship gifts nationwide.Visit **R. M. Kennard Antiques** (⊠*215 E. 300 South St., Downtown* ☎*801/328–9796*) for fine American and European art, furniture, and dishes.

ART GALLERIES The **Glendinning Gallery** (⊠*617 E. South Temple, Downtown* ☎*801/533–3581*) is housed in the historic Glendinning mansion that is also home to the Utah Arts Council. Find the best of Utah's artists' work at **Phillips Gallery** (⊠*444 E. 200 South St., Downtown* ☎*801/364–8284*).

BOOKS **Ken Sanders Rare Books** (✉*268 S. 200 East St., Downtown* ☎*801/521–* ★ *3819*) specializes in literature about Utah, Mormons, and Western explo- ★ ration. In a rambling house with room after room packed with books, **The King's English** (✉*1511 S. 1500 East St., East Side* ☎*801/484–9100*) is a great place to browse. Ask about the owner's book on being an ★ independent bookseller—it's a great read. **Sam Weller's Zion Bookstore** (✉*254 S. Main St., Downtown* ☎*801/328–2586*) stocks more than half a million new and used books.

CRAFTS **Mormon Handicraft** (✉*7200 S. 1100 East St., The Suburbs* ☎*801/561–* *8777 or 800/843–1480*) sells exquisite children's clothing as well as quilts and other crafts—all made by Utah residents. **The Quilted Bear** (✉*145 W. 7200 South St., The Suburbs* ☎*801/566–9382*) is a co-op with gifts, home accessories, and collectibles created by more than 600 craftspeople.

SPORTING Locally-owned **Kirkham's Outdoor Products** (✉*3125 S. State St., The Sub-*
GOODS *urbs* ☎*801/486–4161 or 800/453–7756*), carries a wide spectrum of outdoors gear.

SIDE TRIPS FROM SALT LAKE CITY

ANTELOPE ISLAND STATE PARK

25 mi north of Salt Lake City via I–15 and the Antelope Island Causeway.

In the 19th century, settlers grazed sheep and horses on Antelope Island, ferrying them back and forth from the mainland across the waters of the Great Salt Lake.

★ **Antelope Island State Park** is today the most developed and scenic spot in which to experience the Great Salt Lake. Hiking and biking trails criss-cross the island, and the lack of cover—cottonwood trees provide some of the only shade—gives the place a wide-open feeling and makes for some blistering hot days. You can go saltwater bathing at several beach areas. Since the salinity level of the lake is always greater than that of the ocean, the water is extremely buoyant (and briny-smelling)—simply sit down in the water and bob to the surface like a rubber duck. Hot showers at the marina remove the chill and the salt afterward.

The island has historic sites, as well as desert wildlife and birds in their natural habitat. The island's most popular inhabitants are the mem-bers of a herd of more than 500 bison descended from 12 brought here in 1893. Each October at the **Buffalo Round-Up,** more than 250 volunteers on horseback round up the free-roaming animals and herd them to the island's north end to be counted. The island's **Fielding-Garr House,** built in 1848 and now owned by the state, was the oldest continuously inhabited home in Utah until the last resident moved out in 1981. The house displays assorted ranching artifacts, and guided horseback riding is available from the stables next to the house. Be sure to check out the modern visitor center, and sample a bison burger

CLOSE UP

Ride on the Pony Express Trail

1

Imagine a young man racing over the dusty trail on the back of a foaming mustang. A cloud of dust rises to announce him to the station manager, who waits with a new mount, some beef jerky, and water. The rider has galloped 11 mi since breakfast and will cover another 49 before he sleeps. That was the daily life of a courier with the Pony Express.

A rider had to weigh less than 120 pounds. He was allowed only 25 pounds in gear, which included four leather mail pouches, a light rifle, a pistol, and a Bible. The standard uniform consisted of a bright red shirt and blue pants. Hostile Indians, bandits, and rattlesnakes were handled with the guns. The blazing heat of the desert in the summer and blinding blizzards in the winter were his constant foes.

There are few places in the United States where the original trail and stations of the Pony Express exist in such pristine condition as they do in Utah. One of the best-preserved sections of the original Pony Express Trail, which was in operation for 19 months in the mid-19th century, is the 133-mi section through the desert of west-central Utah. You'll see territory that remains much as it was during the existence of the Pony Express, and many of the sights you'll see along the way haven't changed perceptibly since that time. The desert has preserved them.

If you want to traverse the route, the logical starting point is Camp Floyd–Stagecoach Inn State Park in Fairfield. The end is in Ibapah, 133 mi away on the Utah–Nevada border. Stone pillars with metal plaques mark the route that starts and ends on pavement,

then becomes a dirt road for 126 mi that is passable when dry. The Bureau of Land Management maintains a campground at Simpson Springs, one of the area's most dependable water sources. Some interesting ruins are still visible at Faust, Boyd, and Canyon stations. A brochure describing the major stops along the trail is available from the U.S. Bureau of Land Management's Salt Lake Field Office.

It takes a certain breed of romantic to appreciate the beauty of the land and life lived by those who kept the mail moving during the short time that the Pony Express existed. For those with a similar sense of adventure as the wiry young riders, who included "Buffalo Bill" Cody, traveling this trail is a chance to relive history. Historians say the enterprise enabled communications between Washington, D.C., and California, keeping the state in the union and helping to secure the North's eventual success in the Civil War.

Stagecoaches, freight wagons, the Transcontinental Railroad, and the Lincoln Highway all followed the route pioneered by the Pony Express. The labor-intensive system of communicating cross-country ended with the invention of the telegraph. But before the Pony Express, it took mail six to eight weeks to travel from Missouri to California. By Pony Express, the mail took 10 days to arrive. But by the time the telegraph was invented and put into wide use, messages went across the continent in a mere four hours.

at the stand that overlooks the lake to the north. If you're lucky, you'll hear coyotes howling in the distance. Access to the island is via a 7½-mi causeway. ⊠ *4528 W. 1700 South St., Syracuse* ☏ *801/773–2941* ✉ *$9 per vehicle, $6 per bicycle including causeway toll* ⊘ *May–Sept., daily 7 AM–10 PM; Oct., daily 7 AM–8 PM; Nov–Feb., daily 7–6; Mar., daily 7–7; Apr., daily 7 AM–9 PM.*

SPORTS & THE OUTDOORS

HIKING Antelope Island State Park offers plenty of space for the avid hiker to explore, but keep a few things in mind. All trails are also shared by mountain bikers and horseback riders, so keep an eye out for your fellow recreationists—not to mention the occasional bison. Trees are few and far between on the island, making for high exposure to the elements, so bring (and drink) plenty of water and dress appropriately. In the spring, biting insects make bug repellent a must-have. Pick up a trail map at the visitor center.

Once prepared, hiking Antelope Island can be a very enjoyable experience. Trails are fairly level except for a few places, where the hot summer sun makes the climb even more strenuous. Mountain ranges, including the Wasatch Front to the east and the Stansbury Mountains directly to the west, provide beautiful background in every direction, though haze sometimes obscures the view. Aromatic sage plants offer shelter for a variety of wildlife, so don't be startled if your next step flushes a chukar partridge, horned lark, or jackrabbit. A bobcat is a rarely seen island resident that will likely keep its distance.

MOUNTAIN & Road bikers race along the causeway to Antelope Island, then ride
ROAD BIKING through the park, which also offers superb mountain-bike trails. **Bountiful Bicycle Center** (⊠ *2482 S. Hwy. 89, Woods Cross* ☏ *801/295–6711*)rents mountain and road bikes and offers great advice on trails.

WHERE TO CAMP

⚠ **Antelope Island State Park.** The abundant wildlife—it's not uncommon for free-roaming buffalo to wander through campsites—excellent bird-watching, and well-maintained facilities more than make up for lack of shade at this quiet state-run campground. The $12 camping fee is in addition to the $9 park entrance fee. ♿ *Flush toilets, dump station, drinking water, showers, picnic tables, food service, public telephone, swimming (lake)* ⛺ *26 campsites without hookups* ⊠ *4528 W. 1700 South St., 25 mi north of Salt Lake City via I–15, Exit 335 to Syracuse, then west 7½ mi on causeway across Great Salt Lake, Syracuse, 84075* ☏ *801/773–2941, 800/322–3770 reservations* ⊕ *www.state parks.utah.gov* ▤ *MC, V.*

THANKSGIVING POINT

⏱ *28 mi south of Salt Lake City via I–15 South*

Initially purchased in 1995 by a local family as a small farm for their children, Thanksgiving Point is now home to an ever-evolving project for all visitors to enjoy. Wander through the world's largest dinosaur museum, the Museum of Ancient life; play golf on an 18-hole Johnny

Miller–designed course; or take in a Western musical review. There are greenhouses, gardens, a hands-on barnyard animal park, two restaurants, and a movie theater. Two large gift shops sell home-decor items, jewelry, and unique children's learning toys. ⊠*3003 N. Thanksgiving Way,* ☎*801/768–2300 or 888/672–6040* ⊕*www.thanksgivingpoint. com* ☜*$9.50 museum; $8 gardens; $3.50 farm country* ☉*Mon.–Sat., daily 10–8.*

TIMPANOGOS CAVE NATIONAL MONUMENT

36 mi from Salt Lake City via I-15 south and Rte. 92 east.

Soaring to 11,750 feet, Mount Timpanogos is the centerpiece of a wilderness area of the same name and towers over Timpanogos Cave National Monument along Route 92 within American Fork Canyon. After a strenuous hike up the paved 1½-mi trail to the entrance, you can explore three caves connected by two man-made tunnels. Stalactites, stalagmites, and other formations make the three-hour round-trip hike and tour worth the effort. No refreshments are available on the trail or at the cave, and the cave temperature is 45°F throughout the year, so bring water and warm clothes. Although there's some lighting inside the caves, a flashlight will make your explorations more interesting; it will also come in handy should you have to head back down the trail at dusk. These popular tours are often sold out; to guarantee your place on Saturdays and holidays, purchase tickets in advance. ⊠*Rt. 92, 3 mi from American Fork,* ☎*801/756–5239 cave info; 801/756–5238 advance tickets* ⊕*www.nps.gov/tica* ☜*Tours $7* ☉*Early May–Oct., daily 7–5:30.*

OFF THE BEATEN PATH

Alpine Loop Scenic Byway. Beyond Timpanogos Cave, Route 92 continues up American Fork Canyon before branching off to climb behind Mount Timpanogos itself. Designated the Alpine Loop Scenic Byway, this twisting road reveals stunning scenery before dropping into Provo Canyon to the south. The 9-mi Timpooneke Trail and the 8-mi Aspen Trail, both off the byway, reach the summit of Mount Timpanogos. Closed in winter, the Alpine Loop isn't recommended for motor homes and trucks pulling trailers. This is the roundabout way to get to scenic Provo Canyon from I–15; the more direct route is U.S. 189 east from Orem.

SALT LAKE CITY ESSENTIALS

AIRPORTS & TRANSFERS

Salt Lake City International Airport is 7 mi northwest of downtown. It's served by American, Continental, Delta, Northwest, Southwest, JetBlue, Frontier, Skywest, US Airways, and United.

All the major car-rental agencies have desks at the airport. To drive downtown, take I-80 east to North Temple, which leads directly to the city center. A taxi ride from the airport into town will cost about $15. The Utah Transit Authority (UTA) runs buses between the airport and the city center. Most downtown hotels offer guests free shuttle service.

Information **Salt Lake City International Airport** (☎ *801/575–2400 or 800/595–2442* ⊕ *www.slcairport.com*).

Taxis & Shuttles **City Cab Company** (☎ *801/363–8400*).**Utah Transit Authority (UTA)** (☎ *801/743–3882 or 888/743–3882* ⊕ *www.rideuta.com*). **Ute Cab Company** (☎ *801/359–7788*).**Yellow Cab** (☎ *801/521–2100*).

BUS TRAVEL TO & FROM SALT LAKE CITY

Greyhound Lines runs several buses each day to the terminal at 160 West South Temple.

Bus Information **Greyhound Lines** (☎ *801/355–9579 or 800/231–2222* ⊕ *www. greyhound.com*).

BUSINESS HOURS

Most retail stores are open daily 9 AM or 9:30 AM to 6 PM or 7 PM in downtown locations, and until 9 PM or 10 PM in suburban shopping malls. Downtown stores sometimes stay open later Thursday and Friday nights, and many shops close their doors on Sunday. Normal banking hours are weekdays 9–5; some branches are also open on Saturday morning. Museums are generally open weekdays and Saturday 10–6; some have shorter hours on weekends, and still others are closed Sunday and/or Monday.

CAR TRAVEL

Highway travel around Salt Lake is usually quick and easy, though construction can sometimes throw you for a loop. From I–80, take I–15 north to 600 South Street to reach the city center. Salt Lake City's streets are extra wide and typically not congested. Most are two-way. Expect heavy traffic weekdays between 6 AM and 10 AM and again between 4 PM and 7 PM. To encourage carpooling, some freeways have special lanes for so-called high-occupancy vehicles (HOV)—cars carrying more than one passenger.

EMERGENCIES

Hospitals **Columbia St. Mark's Hospital** (✉ *1200 E. 3900 South St., The Suburbs* ☎ *801/268–7111*). **LDS Hospital** (✉ *8th Ave. and C St., Temple Square* ☎ *801/408–1100*). **Primary Children's Medical Center** (✉ *100 N. Medical Dr., University of Utah* ☎ *801/662–1000*). **Salt Lake Regional Medical Center** (✉ *1050 E. South Temple, Downtown* ☎ *801/350–4111*). **University Hospital and Clinics** (✉ *50 N. Medical Dr., University of Utah* ☎ *801/581–2121*).

Pharmacies **Harmon's Supermarket** (✉ *3270 S. 1300 East St., The Suburbs* ☎ *801/487–5461*). **Rite Aid** (✉ *72 S. Main St., Downtown* ☎ *801/531–0583*) **Walgreens** (✉ *531 E. 400 South St., Downtown* ☎ *801/478–0703*).

PUBLIC TRANSPORTATION

Finding your way around Salt Lake City is easy, largely because early Mormon settlers laid out the town in grids. However, the city blocks are longer than in many other cities, so distances can be deceiving. Salt Lake has a very workable public transportation system. A Free Fare Zone for travel by bus covers a roughly 36-square-block area downtown and on Capitol Hill. A light rail system, called TRAX, moves passengers quickly around the city and to the suburbs south of Salt Lake.

The north–south light-rail route begins at the EnergySolutions Arena (formerly the Delta Center) and ends at 10000 South Street; there are 18 stations altogether, and 11 have free park-and-ride lots. The east–west route begins at the University of Utah and ends at Main Street. For $4.50 you can buy an all-day ticket good for unlimited rides on buses and TRAX. For trips that begin on a bus, you must purchase the day pass at selected UTA Pass outlets. For trips beginning on TRAX, day passes must be purchased at a ticket vending machine.

Information **Utah Transit Authority (UTA)** (☎ *801/743–3882 or 888/743–3882* ⊕ *www.rideuta.com*).

TAXIS

Though taxi fares are low, cabs can be hard to find on the street. If walking and public transportation aren't your thing, it's best to rent a car or plan to call for taxis. Yellow Cab provides 24-hour service throughout the Salt Lake Valley; other reliable companies are Ute Cab and City Cab.

Information **City Cab Company** (☎ *801/363–8400*). **Ute Cab Company** (☎ *801/359–7788*). **Yellow Cab** (☎ *801/521–2100*).

TOURS

Most excursions run by Salt Lake City Tours include lunch at Brigham Young's historic living quarters. Utah Heritage Foundation offers the most authoritative tours of Salt Lake's historic sights.

Contacts **Salt Lake City Tours** (⊠ *3359 S. Main St., Downtown* ☎ *801/534–1001* ⊕ *www.saltlakecitytours.org*). **Utah Heritage Foundation** (⊠ *485 Canyon Rd., Temple Square* ☎ *801/533–0858* ⊕ *www.utahheritagefoundation.com*).

TRAIN TRAVEL

Amtrak serves the area daily out of the Amtrak Passenger Station.

Information **Amtrak Passenger Station** (⊠ *340 S. 600 West St., Downtown* ☎ *801/322–3510 or 800/872–7245 reservations* ⊕ *www.amtrak.com*).

VISITOR INFORMATION

In downtown, the Salt Lake Convention and Visitors Bureau is open weekdays 9–6 and weekends 9–5. The Utah Office of Tourism, located in Council Hall on Capitol Hill, has information as well as books on travel and related topics throughout the city and state.

Information **Salt Lake Convention and Visitors Bureau** (⊠ *90 S. West Temple, Downtown, 84101* ☎ *801/534–4900, 800/541–4955* ⊕ *www.saltlake.org*). **Utah Office of Tourism** (⊠ *300 N. State St., Capitol Hill, 84114* ☎ *801/538–1030 or 800/200–1160* ⊕ *www.utah.com*).

Park City & the Southern Wasatch

WORD OF MOUTH

"Park City is paradise in the summer. SHHHH, don't tell anyone. . . . There are almost too many activities, concerts, festivals, etc. to list. Mtn biking, hiking, water skiing, alpine slides and zip lines, Olympic Park, golf, hot air balloons, horseback riding."

—Dayle

"There are great hiking trails all around Park City, and I personally love to do the one-hour drive to Mirror Lake Highway and hike around there. The lakes are gorgeous and there are some nice waterfalls to see along the way."

—ncounty

Updated by
Jane Gendron

ALTHOUGH THE WASATCH RANGE SHARES the same desert climate as the Great Basin, which it rims, these craggy peaks rising to more than 11,000 feet cause storms moving in from the Pacific to stall and drop more than twice the precipitation they drop on the rest of the Great Basin. The result is a 160-mi stretch of verdure that is home to three-fourths of all Utahns. Although its landscape is crisscrossed by freeways and dappled by towns large and small, the vast Wasatch still beckons adventurers with its alpine forests and windswept canyons. Those who visit follow in the footsteps of Native Americans and in the wagon-wheel ruts of Mormon pioneers and miners.

TOP REASONS TO GO

Sundance Resort for its beautiful hiking and food.

Deer Valley Resort—there's a reason this place keeps getting a No. 1 ranking.

Mirror Lake Highway for its stunning scenery.

Utah Olympic Park's Flying Ace All-Star Show, a glimpse of that 2002 spirit.

Park City's Main Street is both historical and vibrant (great for strolling, dining, and checking out art).

As the meeting place of three geologically distinct regions—the Rocky Mountain Province, the Colorado Plateau Province, and the Basin and Range Province—the Wasatch Range combines characteristics of each. Within this one compact range you'll find broad glacial canyons with towering granite walls, stream-cut gorges through purple, tan, and green shale, and rounded red rock bluffs and valleys.

Uppermost in many people's minds is the legendary skiing found at resorts such as Snowbird, Alta, and Park City. But this region is truly a year-round destination. Bright-blue lakes afford fantastic boating, sailing, windsurfing, and waterskiing opportunities. Some of the West's best trout streams flow from the high country. Add to this picturesque mountain communities, miles of hiking and biking trails, and truly spectacular alpine scenery, and you have a vacation that's hard to beat.

The snow stops falling in April or May, and a month later the temperatures are in the 80s. (Locals joke that if you don't like the weather in spring, wait a minute and it will change.) Spring may be the shortest season, but it's one of the most interesting. You can ski in the morning, play 18 holes of golf or hike through fields of wildflowers in the afternoon, and take a dinner cruise on the Great Salt Lake at sunset.

In summer water-sports enthusiasts of all stripes flock to the region's reservoirs, alpine lakes, rivers, and streams to fish, waterski, windsurf, sail, and canoe. The Wasatch Mountains also draw people on foot, bike, and horseback seeking respite from the heat of the valley.

Fall's colors rival those of New England. On a walk through a forest or drive along a scenic route, you'll see the yellows, reds, oranges, and golds of aspens, maples, and oaks against the deep evergreen of fir and spruce. Fall drives along the Alpine Loop east of Provo or up Pine Canyon out of the Heber Valley are autumn traditions.

Regardless of the season, you can find cultural activities and entertainment at every turn. The Sundance Film Festival, hosted by actor–director Robert Redford, attracts movie stars and independent filmmakers from all over and seems to get bigger every January. Major recording artists of all types play both indoor and outdoor venues along the Wasatch Range. The number of nightclubs is increasing, featuring everything from blues and jazz to folk and rock; and Park City offers an ample variety of nightlife possibilities.

EXPLORING THE WASATCH

Each canyon of the Wasatch is different in topography and scenery. The back side of the range is rural with high-mountain pastures, farms, and small towns while the front side is a long stretch of cosmopolitan metropolis. This is not an area that lends itself to checking off points along a straight line. You'll enjoy the area more if you let it unfold in a series of loops and meanders, using the larger canyons to move back and forth between the two sides of the range.

ABOUT THE RESTAURANTS

American cuisine dominates the Wasatch dining scene with great steaks, barbecue, and traditional Western fare. There's also an abundance of good seafood, which the busier eateries fly in daily from the West Coast. Resort towns like Park City cater to discriminating clientele with upscale Continental restaurants and ethnic food ranging from Chinese and Mexican to Iranian and Vietnamese. At most resort-town restaurants, hours of operation vary seasonally, so it's a good idea to call ahead.

ABOUT THE HOTELS

Chain hotels and motels dot I–15 all along the Wasatch Front and nearly always have availability. Every small town on the back side of the range has at least one good bed-and-breakfast, and most towns have both independent and chain motels. The ski resorts of Big and Little Cottonwood offer hotels from quaint to ultramodern. Condominiums dominate Park City lodging, but you also find high-end hotels, luxurious lodges, and well-run bed-and-breakfast inns. All this luxury means prices here tend to be higher than other areas in the state. Make reservations well in advance for busy ski holidays like Christmas, Presidents' Day, and Martin Luther King Day, and during January's Sundance Film Festival. As the mountain country is often on the cool side, lodging facilities at higher elevations do not need air-conditioning.

WHAT IT COSTS					
	¢	$	$$	$$$	$$$$
RESTAURANTS	under $8	$8–$12	$13–$18	$19–$25	over $25
HOTELS	under $100	$100–$170	$171–$240	$241–$310	over $310

Restaurant prices are for a main course at dinner, excluding sales tax of 8.25%. Hotel prices are for two people in a standard double room in high season, excluding service charges and 10.35% tax.

TIMING

One of the best reasons to vacation in the Wasatch is that a short drive from the valleys to the mountains will make you feel like you're getting two seasons in a single day. Winter is long in the mountains, but surprisingly short in the valleys. In March, when snow is still piling up at the ski resorts, you can golf, hike, bike, or fish in any of the Wasatch valleys or foothills. Hikers crowd the backcountry from June through Labor Day. Ski resorts buzz from December to early April. If you don't mind sometimes capricious weather, spring and fall are opportune seasons to visit. Rates drop and crowds are nonexistent. Spring is a good time for fishing, rafting on rivers swollen with snowmelt, birding, and wildlife-viewing. In fall, trees splash the mountainsides with golds and reds, the fish are spawning, and the angling is excellent.

Summer begins in the mountains in late June or early July. Fall begins in September, often with a week of unsettled weather around mid-month, followed by four to six gorgeous weeks of Indian summer—frosty nights and warm days. Winter creeps in during November, and deep snows arrive in the mountains by December. Temperatures usually hover near freezing by day, thanks to the surprisingly warm mountain sun, dropping considerably overnight. Winter tapers off in March, though snow lingers into April on valley bottoms and into July on some mountain passes.

PARK CITY & ENVIRONS

The best known areas of the Wasatch lie east of Salt Lake City. Up and over Parley's Canyon via I–80 you'll find the sophisticated mountain town of Park City with its three ski resorts and myriad summer attractions. The neighboring canyons of Big Cottonwood and Little Cottonwood are home to Brighton, Solitude, Alta, and Snowbird resorts. A network of hiking and mountain biking trails leads past pristine mountain lakes and connects all three canyons.

After silver was discovered in Park City in 1868, it quickly became a rip-roaring mining town with more than two dozen saloons and a thriving red-light district. In the process it earned the nickname Sin City. A fire destroyed many of the town's buildings in 1898; this, combined with declining mining fortunes in the early 1900s, caused most of the residents to pack up and leave. It wasn't until 1946 that its current livelihood began to take shape in the form of the small Snow Park ski hill, which opened where Deer Valley Resort now sits.

Park City once again profited from the generosity of the mountains as skiing became popular. In 1963 Treasure Mountain Resort began operations with its skier's subway—an underground train and hoist system that ferried skiers to the mountain's summit via old mining tunnels. Facilities were upgraded over time, and Treasure Mountain became the Park City Mountain Resort. Although it has a mind-numbing collection of condominiums, at Park City's heart is a historic downtown

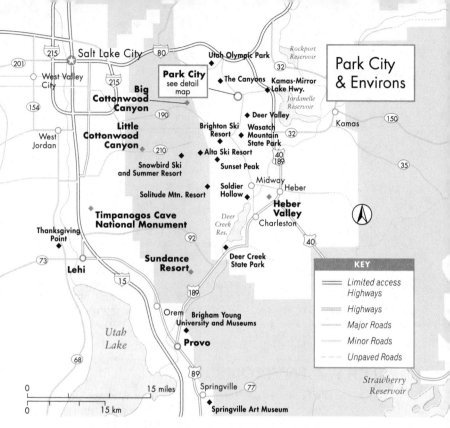

district that rings with authenticity and reminds you that this is a real town with real roots.

EXPLORING PARK CITY

Numbers in the margin correspond to the Park City map.

Park City and the surrounding area hosted the lion's share of skiing and sliding events during the 2002 Winter Olympic Games, and the excited spirit of the Games is still evident around town. Visitors often enjoy activities at the Utah Olympic Park or simply taking candid photos at various memorable skiing venues.

Park City also serves as an excellent base camp for summer activities. Hiking trails are plentiful. A scenic drive over Guardsman Pass (via a gravel road that's passable for most vehicles) provides incredible mountain vistas. There are some acclaimed golf greens, hot-air ballooning is available, and mountain bikers find the ski slopes and old mining roads truly exceptional pedaling. With so much to offer both summer and winter visitors, the town now has three resorts, each with its own special qualities.

GREAT ITINERARIES

IF YOU HAVE 3 DAYS

In three days you'll be hard-pressed to see all of this region so your best bet is to stick to the central Wasatch. Start with a day and a night in **Park City**, skiing one of its three resorts in winter or taking advantage of lift-served mountain biking in summer, then enjoying a night out on historic Main Street. The next day drive west on I–80, south along Salt Lake City's eastern bench on I–215, and east again on Route 210 up **Little Cottonwood Canyon**. In winter spend a day skiing at Alta or Snowbird. In summer hike the Catherine Pass trail into neighboring **Big Cottonwood Canyon**. On your final day head south again on I–15, then east on Route 92 on the Alpine Loop scenic drive to **Sundance Resort**, where you can pamper yourself with a massage at the Spa and a quiet meal at the Tree Room or the Foundry Grill. In winter the Alpine Loop will be closed to traffic, so instead of driving east on Route 92 continue south on I–15 and spend some time exploring **Provo** before driving east on U.S. 189 to Sundance.

IF YOU HAVE 5 DAYS

Start your five-day trip by following the suggested three-day itinerary above and then tack on the following: on Day 4 leave Sundance, heading east on Route 189 up Provo Canyon to the **Heber Valley**. In winter spend the day cross-country skiing or snowshoeing before your late-afternoon sleigh ride, and in summer go hiking, golfing, or horseback riding in Wasatch Mountain State Park. The point is to take in the beauty of the Wasatch at a slower pace than downhill skiing or snowboarding allows. Treat yourself to supper at Snake Creek Grill before retiring to the overnight comforts of the Homestead Resort. Strike out on Day 5 using River Road to connect to U.S. 40 and back to **Park City** where, even though you started your trip here, something new awaits. Ski and/or snowboard until you're worn out and then nestle into an après-ski lounge for a hot toddy before suppertime and your pre-sleep hot tub. In warmer months spend your day fly-fishing with one of the guides from Trout Bum 2 or hiking some of Park City's extensive trail system and cap it off with supper on the patio of one of Park City's fine restaurants.

The emphasis at the original Park City Mountain Resort is on skiing and socializing in town. In a somewhat secluded area on the edge of Park City you can revel in the peace and creature comforts of Deer Valley. The Canyons is a rapidly growing destination resort north of town; it ranks in the top five resorts in America in terms of overall ski area, and it combines luxury with a casual atmosphere. A free shuttle-bus system serves the town of Park City, the three resorts, and the surrounding hotels and shops. Although the shuttle is efficient, the region is fairly spread out, so a car can be helpful.

Small-town celebrations unofficially mark the beginning and end of summer in Park City.

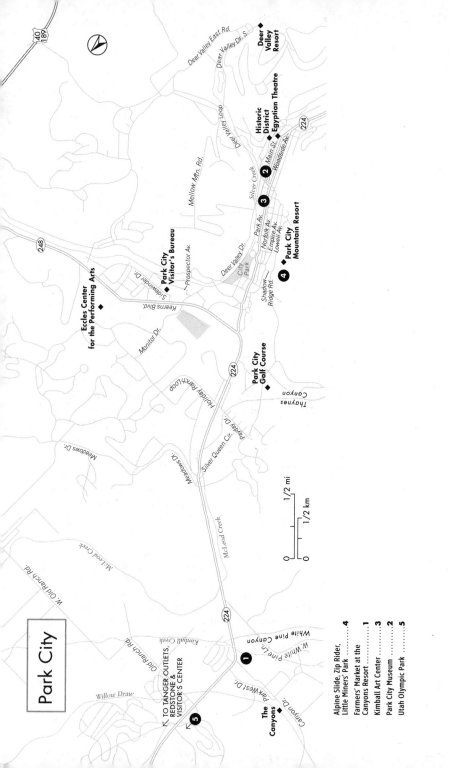

Park City

Alpine Slide, Zip Rider,
Little Miners' Park **4**

Farmers' Market at the
Canyons Resort **1**

Kimball Art Center **3**

Park City Museum **2**

Utah Olympic Park **5**

IF YOU LIKE

FALL FOLIAGE

Few places in the world are as beautiful as the Wasatch Mountains in September and October. Seize the day to luxuriate in the bright colors and crisp temperatures. Pack a picnic lunch and head out on the Alpine Loop Scenic Byway, Route 92, from American Fork Canyon to Provo Canyon. Or take a ride on the Heber Valley Historic Railroad, which runs twice a day from Heber City. It snakes along the shore of Deer Creek Reservoir and parallels the Provo River as it plunges down narrow Provo Canyon. If you don't mind driving on a rough, sometimes washboard, dirt road, take the drive out of Midway up Pine Canyon through Wasatch Mountain State Park.

SUMMER SPORTS

Many transplanted locals in towns like Park City and Alta will tell you they first visited the Wasatch for the winters, but they moved here for the summers. It's hard to find a more comfortable climate than a Wasatch summer. The air is dry and temperatures range from 10 to 15 degrees cooler than in the Salt Lake Valley. Plus, the area becomes a summer recreation mecca. Well-maintained hiking and mountain biking trails lead between Big and Little Cottonwood canyons and the Park City area; local canyons offer excellent rock climbing; state parks on area reservoirs provide facilities for an array of water sports; and you'll find excellent trout fishing on Wasatch streams and lakes.

WINTER SPORTS

There's more than local bragging behind the claim that Utah resorts have the best snow in the world. There's science behind it, too. The secret to Utah's famous powder is in the unique combination of atmospheric conditions and geography. Storms move from the Pacific across the Great Basin desert, pick up extra moisture over the Great Salt Lake, and then stall when they hit the high Wasatch Mountains. Large quantities of snowflakes called dendrites are formed under these conditions and fall to earth in layers with lots of air between them. Skiing through such light powder feels like floating through clouds. Although the area's downhill skiing receives most of the attention, snowmobiling, cross-country skiing, and snowshoeing are other popular powder-snow pursuits. You can also head for the Utah Olympic Park to catch a U.S. Bobsled Team practice. Or, take a ride yourself while team members steer.

⟳ A traditional **Independence Day Celebration** (☎ 435/649–6100 ⊕ *www. parkcityinfo.com*), complete with parade, fireworks, and all-day activities in City Park, is a sure sign that summer has arrived.

⟳ **Miner's Day** (☎ 435/649–6100 ⊕ *www.parkcityinfo.com*), Park City's name for Labor Day, ends the summer season with a slightly campy parade down Main Street, the Rotary Club's "Running of the Balls"— with tennis balls rather than Pamplona's bulls—followed by miners' competitions of mucking and drilling at Library Park.

❶ Two outdoor markets make a weekly appearance in Park City from June through early autumn. The long-running **Farmers' Market at the**

Canyons Resort, held each Wednesday, is a good spot to pick up fresh bread, fruits and veggies, handmade wares, and flowers. ⊠ *The Canyons Resort* ☎ *435/649–5400* ⊕ *www.thecanyons.com.*

Every Sunday, at the **Park Silly Sunday Market,** a funky and constantly changing assortment of artisans, entertainers, and culinary vendors transform Old Town into an environmentally friendly street festival, complete with wandering opera singers and crêpe stands. ⊠ *Lower Main Street, Park City* ☎ *435/655–0994* ⊕ *www.parksillysundaymarket.com.*

❷ The **Park City Museum,** one of the best small museums in Utah, is housed in Park City's old Territorial Jail. Though exhibits are closed for the museum's expansion until spring 2009, the **Park City Historical Society** offers one-hour guided walking tours on Main Street from June through September. The temporary location for the museum until the renovations are complete is 333 Main Street, Suite 24. The tours start at 2 PM Monday through Friday, weather permitting. Other tours include historian-led daylong hikes and ski tours around Park City and the Wasatch Mountains that combine recreation and mining lore. Most of the tours, which focus on mining, railroad, or architectural history, begin in town; some include transportation to more distant locations. Call ahead for meeting locations. You must be a member to participate in the tours, but it's easy to join in advance over the Internet: membership is $25 for one person or $50 for a family. Each June the Park City Historical Society sponsors the **Historic Home Tour,** when many homeowners open their restored 19th-century homes in the historic section of Park City to the public. Food and drink receptions are provided by some of the best eateries in this resort area. The tour is self-guided. ⊠ *528 Main St., Box 555, 84060* ☎ *435/649–7457* ⊕ *www.parkcityhistory.org* ⊠ *Call for tour prices* ☉ *Call for museum hours.*

❸ One of more than two dozen art galleries in Park City, the **Kimball Art Center** is the town's nonprofit community art center. It hosts national exhibitions as well as community art classes and workshops. ⊠ *638 Park Ave.* ☎ *435/649–8882* ⊕ *www.kimball-art.org* ⊠ *Exhibits free; fees for classes* ☉ *Mon. and Wed.–Fri. 10–5, weekends noon–5.*

☾ ❹ In summer Park City Mountain Resort transforms itself into a mountain amusement park including attractions such as the **Alpine Slide, Zip Rider, Alpine Coaster, and Little Miners' Park.** The Alpine Slide begins with a chairlift ride up the mountain, then special sleds carry sliders down 3,000 feet of winding concrete and fiberglass track at speeds controlled by each rider. The Zip Rider is 60 seconds of adrenaline rush as riders strap into a harness suspended from a cable for a 500-foot vertical drop spanning 3,000 feet of track. The gravity-propelled Alpine Coaster (which operates year-round) lacks the inversion of traditional roller coasters, but zooms through mountainous twists and turns at speeds up to 35 mph. The Little Miners' Park has children's rides. There's also a miniature golf course, climbing wall, horseback riding, trampolines, a human maze, and lift-served mountain biking and hiking. ⊠ *1310 Lowell Ave.* ☎ *435/649–8111* ⊕ *www.parkcitymountain.com.*

CLOSE UP

2002 Winter Olympics Legacies

Though the 2002 Winter Olympics are a distant but pleasant memory, their legacy lives on. Thanks to the healthy profit the Games produced, main venues have been able to remain open to host world-class competitions and provide recreation and training.

The best place to enjoy the legacy of 2002 is at the Utah Olympic Park near Park City, the site of the bobsled, luge, skeleton, and ski jumping. In addition to touring the facility, you can ride the bobsled—wheeled in summer and on ice in winter—or try freestyle skiing. The interactive Alf Engen Ski Museum offers a chance for a virtual reality trip down the Olympic ski courses.

At the nearby Soldier Hollow facility in Midway, site of the cross-country skiing and biathlon events, you can ski on groomed expert or beginner trails, snowshoe, tube, or use the trail system to hike or mountain bike in summer.

A tent-shape structure made of steel and glass covers the speed-skating oval in West Valley City. It provides year-round ice for speed skating, figure skating, hockey, and curling. To get a feel for how fast Olympic speed skaters go, just try to skate the 400-meter track. A running track goes around the outside of the skating oval.

The Olympic torch still stands at Rice-Eccles Stadium on the University of Utah campus. A park—including the Hoberman Arch used during the medal ceremonies, a fountain, and historical information—surrounds the torch.

On hot days kids of all ages gather at the Olympic Legacy Snowflake Fountain at the Gateway Mall in downtown Salt Lake City where they dodge shooting sprays of water, often set to music. An Olympic Hall of Fame is east of the fountain.

2

At the **Utah Olympic Park**—site of the 2002 Olympic bobsled, skeleton, luge, and ski-jumping events—you can take recreational ski-jumping lessons or strap in behind a professional driver for a bobsled ride down the actual Olympic course. The 389-acre park also serves as a year-round officially sanctioned training site for members of the U.S. Ski Team and other athletes. In summer, check out the freestyle ski jumpers doing flips and spins into a splash pool and Nordic jumpers soaring to soft landings on a synthetic outrun. Ride one of two zip lines—the extreme version parallels the K-120 jump—or zoom down the steel track of the Quicksliver Alpine Slide. There's also an interactive ski museum and an exhibit on the 2002 Winter Olympics; guided tours are offered year-round, or you can take a self-guided tour. ⊠*3419 Olympic Pkwy., Park City* ☎*435/658–4200* ⊕*www.olyparks.com* ⊠*Museum and self-guided tours free; guided tours $7; rides from $15.*

FodorsChoice
★

SPORTS & THE OUTDOORS

CROSS-COUNTRY SKIING

On the edge of town, **White Pine Touring** (⊠*On Park City Golf Course, Rte. 224* ☎*435/649–6249* ⊕*www.whitepinetouring.com*) offers 20 km (12 mi) of set track, cross-country ski instruction, equipment rent-

EQUIPMENT RENTALS

Many shops in Park City rent equipment for skiing and other sports. You can reserve your equipment in advance with **Breeze Winter Sports Rentals** (✉ *1284 Lowell St., near Pay Day lift* ☎ *435/649–2736 or 888/427–3393* ✉ *1415 Lowell St., near ice rink* ☎ *435/649–1902* ✉ *4343 N. Rte. 224, The Canyons* ☎ *435/655–7066* ⊕ *www. breezeski.com* ☉ *Closed May–Nov.*), which also rents clothing and helmets.For winter ski, snowboard, snowshoe, and clothing rental and summer bike rental, **Cole Sport** (✉ *1615 Park Ave.* ☎ *435/649–4800 or 800/345–2938* ✉ *Park City Mountain Resort* ☎ *435/649–4600* ✉ *Silver Lake Village at Deer Valley* ☎ *435/649–4601* ⊕ *www.cole sport.com*)offers expert fitting and advice with a broad range of equipment.**Jans Mountain Outfitters** (✉ *1600 Park Ave.* ☎ *435/649–4949 or 800/745–1020* ⊕ *www.jans. com* ✉ *Park City Resort Center* ☎ *435/649–2500* ✉ *The Lodges at Deer Valley* ☎ *435/649–8770*)rents ski and snowboard equipment packages and clothing in winter and bikes in summer. Jans "test program" allows you to rent high-end gear and apply the rental fee toward equipment purchase.

At the base of Park City Mountain Resort, **Park City Sport** (✉ *1335 Lowell Ave.* ☎ *435/645–7777 or 800/523–3922* ☉ *Closed May–Oct.*)is a convenient place to rent ski and snowboard equipment. You can drop off your personal gear at the end of a ski day and they'll have it tuned and ready for you the next morning. **Utah Ski & Golf** (✉ *698 Park Ave.* ☎ *435/649–3020* ⊕ *www.utahs kigolf.com* ✉ *50 Shadow Ridge Rd., in Shadow Ridge Hotel* ☎ *435/655–8367*)offers downhill and cross-country equipment, snowshoes, clothing, and golf club rental.**White Pine Touring** (✉ *1790 Bonanza Dr.* ☎ *435/649–8710* ⊕ *www.whitepi netouring.com*)has a good selection of telemark and alpine touring gear as well as mountain bikes and climbing shoes.

als, and a well-stocked cross-country ski shop. The fee to use the track is $18 or $10 after 3 PM. Reservations are required for their guided backcountry ski and snowshoe tours in the surrounding mountains.

DOWNHILL SKIING & SNOWBOARDING

Fodor'sChoice ★ Strong intermediate and advanced skiers can hook up with the **Ski Utah Interconnect Adventure Tour** (☎ *801/534–1907* ⊕ *www.skiutah.com*)for a guided alpine ski tour that takes you to as many as six resorts (Deer Valley, Park City, Brighton, Solitude, Alta, and Snowbird) in a single day, all connected by backcountry ski routes with unparalleled views of the Wasatch Mountains. Guides test your ski ability before departure. The tour includes guide service, lift tickets, lunch, and transportation back to the point of origin and costs $195. You'll even walk away with a finisher's pin. The Deer Valley Departure Tour operates Sunday, Monday, Wednesday, and Friday; the Snowbird Departure Tour operates Tuesday, Thursday, and Saturday. Reservations are required.

The Canyons Resort has similar mountain terrain to that of neighboring Park City Mountain Resort, but intermediates will find somewhat longer

2

cruising runs here. Above-tree-line bowls feed into some fine tree-skiing for experts, and first-time skiers and boarders have 7 acres designated just for them. Don't be deceived when you pull into the parking lot—most of the terrain is not visible from the base. The resort has 3,700 acres of skiable terrain with 155 runs and is building a year-round base. As the first Park City mountain to allow snowboarding, this resort is popular with younger crowds. The Perfect Turn program bills itself as a "coaching" program, rather than an instructional program, for skiers and snowboarders of all ages. In addition to the advanced terrain park, The Canyons has a beginners' terrain park for first-time skiers and riders. ✉ *4000 The Canyons Resort Dr., Park City, 84098* 🕾 *435/649–5400, 888/226–9667 central lodging reservations, 435/615–3456 snow reports* 🖷 *435/649–7374* ⊕ *www.thecanyons.com* ☞ *3,190-ft vertical drop; 3,700 skiable acres; 10% beginner, 44% intermediate, 46% advanced; 1 8-passenger gondola, 1 6-passenger high-speed chair, 1 open-air gondola, 4 high-speed quad chairs, 4 quad chairs, 2 triple chairs, 2 double chairs, 1 surface lift and 1 magic carpet* 🎟️ *Lift tickets $76.*

With 106 trails and 750 acres of open bowls, the **Park City Mountain Resort** is one of Utah's largest complexes. Roughly half the terrain is rated as intermediate, but the slopes that line Jupiter Peak are revered by experts. The east face of Jupiter has some particularly hairy, rock-lined chutes. Portuguese Gap is an elevator shaft lined by trees, and a "six-pack" (six-passenger) chair in McConkey's Bowl provides access to additional steeps. Motherlode Meadows is a gentler approach to tree skiing and has glade-free options as well. Snowmaking covers 500 acres, and night skiers will delight in Pay Day, the longest lighted run in the Rockies. Park City's main drawback is lack of length. Despite a vertical drop of 3,100 feet, it's hard putting together a run of more than about 1,400 vertical feet. The area is made up of a series of ridges and peaks rather than a single mountain face. That said, Park City probably has the best overall terrain mix of any area in Utah—enough to keep skiers of all abilities happy for days. The Eagle Superpipe, with 22-foot walls, is one of the largest in North America and, combined with the half-pipe and four terrain parks with state-of-the-art rails and funboxes, makes this resort an important destination for snowboarders, too. The Kids Signature 5 programs limit lesson groups to only five students. There are also excellent programs for skiers with disabilities. ✉ *1310 Lowell Ave., 84060* 🕾 *435/649–8111, 800/222–7275 central lodging reservations and snow reports* 🖷 *435/647–5374* ⊕ *www.park citymountain.com* ☞ *3,100-foot vertical drop; 3,300 skiable acres; 17% beginner, 50% intermediate, 33% advanced; 4 high-speed 6-passenger chairs, 2 high-speed quad chairs, 5 triple chairs, 4 double chairs* 🎟️ *Lift tickets $79.*

🕭
Fodor'sChoice
★

One mile south of downtown Park City, **Deer Valley Resort** set new standards in the ski industry by providing such amenities as ski valets, grooming fit for a king, and slope-side dining of the highest caliber. For such pampering, the resort has drawn rave reviews from virtually every ski and travel magazine. The careful layout of runs—all taking advantage of the best possible fall line—and the quality of the grooming leads to skiing's version of ballroom dancing. With the Empire Canyon and Lady Morgan areas, the resort also offers bona fide expert terrain. For many, part of the ski experience here includes a two- to three-hour mid-day interlude of feasting at the Silver Lake Lodge buffet and catching major rays on the snow-covered meadow in front of the lodge—an area known appropriately as McHenry's Beach. The ski experience, in other words, fits right in with the resort's overall image. With lessons for kids from preschool through teens, Deer Valley's acclaimed children's ski school is sure to please both children and parents. ⊠*2250 Deer Valley Dr., 84060* ☏*435/649–1000, 800/558–3337 central lodging reservations, 435/649–2000 snow reports* ☎*435/645–6939* ⊕*www.deervalley.com* ⚲*3,000-ft vertical drop; 2,026 skiable acres; 27% beginner, 41% intermediate, 32% advanced; 1 high-speed gondola, 11 high-speed quad chairs, 2 quad chairs, 6 triple chairs, 2 double chairs* ⛷*Lift tickets $79.*

FLY-FISHING

The mountain-fed waters of the Provo and Weber rivers and several smaller streams near Park City are prime trout habitat. See Chris Kunkel, owner of the **Park City Fly Shop** (⊠*2065 Sidewinder Dr.* ☏*435/645–8382 or 800/324–6778* ⊕*www.pcflyshop.com*), for good advice, guide service, and a modest selection of fly-fishing necessities. Jon "Harley" Jackson and the rest of the fly-fishing experts at **Trout Bum 2** (⊠*4343 N. Rte. 224* ☏*435/658–1166 or 877/878–2862* ⊕*www.troutbum2.com*), Park City's full-service fly shop, can outfit you with everything you need, then guide you to where the fish are. George "Squid" Sideris knows fishing gear at **Jans Mountain Outfitters** (⊠*1600 Park Ave.* ☏*435/649–4949* ⊕*www.jans.com*), and a team of guides, led by Jeremy Rogers, helps reveal the best spots for making the most of those rods and reels.

FRISBEE GOLF

Frisbee fans can try a high-altitude round of "nine holes" at **Alpine Disc Golf** at The Canyons (⊠*4000 The Canyons Resort Dr., Park City 84098* ☏*435/649–5400* ⊕*www.thecanyons.com* ⛷*$12 for the gondola ride, free to play, disc rental available* ⊙*Mid-June–early Sept., Thurs.–Sun. 10–4*)

GOLF

Within 20 minutes of Park City are 10 golf courses: five public and five private. The **Park City Municipal Golf Course** (⊠*1541 Thaynes Canyon Dr.* ☏*435/615–5800*) has 18 holes right in the heart of town with views of the ski runs and surrounding peaks.

The only swanky private club in the area to make tee times available to the general public, **Promontory-The Ranch Club** (⊠*8758 Promontory Ranch Rd.* ☏*435/333–4218* ⊕*www.promontoryclub.com*) offers limited tee times to nonmembers on its challenging and sometimes windy Pete Dye-designed course. The club is renowned for extraordinary views and exemplary service. Greens fees are $200 per person (with cart).

HIKING

The Wasatch mountains surrounding Park City offer hundreds of miles of hiking trails, ranging from easy, meandering meadow strolls to strenuous climbs up wind-blown peaks. With 350 miles of trails, getting away from civilization and into the aspens is easy, and lucky hikers might spy fox, coyotes, moose, elk, deer, and red-tailed hawks. Many of the trails take off from the resort areas, but some of the trailheads are right near Main Street. For beginners, or for those acclimating to the elevation, the Rail Trail is a good place to start. Another alternative is to take the McLeod Creek Trail from behind Park City Market all the way to the Redstone Center. Round Valley and Lost Prospector Trails are still mellow but slightly more challenging. To really get the blood pumping, head up Spiro or Iron Canyon.

For up-to-date information about trail conditions and answers to your trails questions, contact **Mountain Trails Foundation** (*Box 754, Park City, 84060* 🖃*435/649–6839* ⊕*www.mountaintrails.org*), whose mission is to promote, preserve, advocate for, and maintain Park City's local trail system. Maps detailing trail locations are available at most local gear shops.

HORSEBACK RIDING

Red Pine Adventures (⊠*2050 W. White Pine Canyon Rd.* 🖃*435/649–9445 or 800/417-7669* ⊕*www.redpinetours.com*) leads trail rides through thousands of acres of private land.Saddle up for a taste and feel of the Old West with **Rocky Mountain Recreation** (⊠*Rte. 224, Deer Valley, Park City* 🖃*435/645-7256* ⊕*www.rockymtnrec.com*). Guided mountain trail rides are offered from several locations in the Park City area, complete with fantastic Wasatch scenery and good cowboy grub. **Wind In Your Hair Riding** (🖃*435/336–4795 or 435/901–4644* ⊕*www.windinyourhair.com*)is for experienced riders who are looking for a get-up-and-go kind of mountain riding adventure on Paso Fino horses, noted for their smooth ride. Lessons are available for beginners as well.

HOT-AIR BALLOONING

Park City Balloon Adventures (🖃*435/645–8787 or 800/396–8787* ⊕*www. pcballoonadventures.com*)offers half-hour and one-hour scenic flights daily, weather permitting. Fliers meet at a local hotel and are shuttled to the take-off site, which varies from day to day. A champagne or nonalcoholic toast is offered on touchdown. Reservations are required.

ICE-SKATING

The Olympic-size rink at the **Park City Ice Arena** (⊠*600 Gillmor Way* 🖃*435/615–5700* ⊕*www.pcice.org* 🖃*$5.75* ⊙*July–Apr., call for public skate times*)provides plenty of space for testing out that triple-toe loop or slap shot. The hill outside the building is popular sledding terrain.

MOUNTAIN & ROAD BIKING

With more than 350 mi of public trails and smooth blacktop roads stretching in every direction, it's no wonder Park City is home to a number of internationally elite mountain and road bikers. You can join local road or mountain bikers three evenings a week for free group rides sponsored by Park City bike shops. Pick up a free map of area trails at any local bike shop or get details online from **Mountain Trails Foundation** (☎435/649–6839 ⊕*www.mountaintrails.org*).

Road bikers can ride with a pack each Monday and Thursday evening from mid-May through mid-September from **Cole Sport** (✉*1615 Park Ave.* ☎*435/649–4800 or 800/345–2938* ⊕*www.colesport.com*). You can rent mountain and road bikes from Cole; be ready to ride from the shop at 6 PM.If you're looking to learn to mountain bike or improve your skills, **Deer Valley Mountain Bike School** (✉*Silver Lake Village at Deer Valley* ☎*435/649–6648 or 888/754–8477* ⊕*www. deervalley.com*) offers clinics and guided tours in myriad packages; a half-day group clinic is $40. For a little help getting uphill, **Deer Valley Resort** (✉*Silver Lake Village and Snow Park Lodge at Deer Valley* ☎*435/649–1000 or 888/754–8477* ⊕*www.deervalley.com*) offers lift-assisted mountain biking or hiking daily mid-June through mid-September; it's $24 for a lift ticket. Bike rentals are available. On Tuesday evenings from May through September, the bike experts at **Jans Mountain Outfitters** (✉*1600 Park Ave.* ☎*435/649–4949 or 800/745–1020* ⊕*www.jans.com*) lead groups of mountain bikers up and down local trails. Meet at the shop at 6 PM for this free group ride, where you can also rent equipment. Mountain bikers and hikers can ride the chairs at **Park City Mountain Resort** (✉*1310 Lowell Ave.* ☎*435/649–8111 or 800/222–7275* ⊕*www.parkcitymountain.com*)to access the on-mountain trail complex. An all-day lift pass is $18. Equipment rentals are available.Thursday evenings from May through September, mountain bikers of all levels get together for a free employee-led tour at **White Pine Touring** (✉*1790 Bonanza Dr.* ☎*435/649–8710* ⊕*www.whitepinetouring.com*). Employees lead a women-only ride on Tuesdays. For both rides, meet at the shop at 6 PM, and rent equipment there.

ROCK CLIMBING

If you're looking for some hang time on the local rocks but don't know the area, **White Pine Touring** (✉*1790 Bonanza Dr.* ☎*435/649–8710* ⊕*www.whitepinetouring.com*)offers guided climbing tours, equipment rental, and private and group lessons.

SNOWMOBILING

For a winter speed thrill of the machine-powered variety, hop on a snowmobile with **Red Pine Adventures** (✉*2050 W. White Pine Canyon Rd.* ☎*435/649–9445 or 800/417–7669* ⊕*www.redpinetours.com*), and follow your guide along private groomed trails adjacent to The Canyons resort. **Thousand Peaks Snowmobile Adventures** (☎*435/645–9292 or 888/304–7669* ⊕*www.thousandpeaks.com*)operates backcountry snowmobile tours on one of Utah's largest private mountain ranches just minutes from Park City, where you can catch a free shuttle. Clothing, such as snowsuits, gloves, and boots, are available to rent.

SNOW TUBING

⟳ Park City Mountain Resort's **Gorgoza Park** (✉*3863 W. Kilby Rd.* ☎*435/658–2648* ⊕*www.gorgoza.com*), off I–80 near Parley's Summit, offers lift-served snow tubing for the whole family and mini-snowmobile rentals for kids ages 5–12.

WHERE TO EAT

★ \$\$\$\$ ✕**Grappa Italian Restaurant.** At the top of Main Street, this restaurant specializes in northern Italian cuisine with impeccable presentation. Heavy floor tiles, bricks, and timbers lend a rustic, warm, farmhouse feel. Tables on the wraparound balcony overlook those on the first floor. The menus, which change seasonally, offer appetizers such as a grapes and gorgonzola salad with roasted walnuts and innovative entrées like horseradish-encrusted salmon. ✉*151 Main St.* ☎*435/645–0636* ⚑*Reservations essential* ⊟*AE, D, MC, V* ⊗*Open daily Dec.–Apr.; call ahead June–Oct. Closed May and Nov. No lunch.*

\$\$\$\$ ✕**Riverhorse on Main.** With two upper-level warehouse loft rooms, exposed beams, black-and-white furnishings, and walls adorned with original art, this café feels like an ultramodern big-city supper club. Piano or jazz entertainment adds to the metropolitan atmosphere. For a lively evening, ask for a seat near the music, but for quiet conversation, sit in the booth-lined dining room. Choose from entrées such as ahi tuna, the surf-and-turf-style Caribbean lobster tail and filet of beef, or the signature macadamia-crusted Alaskan halibut. Don't miss out on the mashed potatoes—they're famous. ✉*540 Main St.* ☎*435/649–3536* ⚑*Reservations essential* ⊟*AE, D, MC, V* ⊗*June–Sept., closed Mon.–Tues. Closed May, Oct., and Nov. No lunch.*

\$\$\$\$ ✕**Shabu.** Hip "freestyle" Asian cuisine matches the chic interior of a restaurant that draws visiting Hollywood types and locals alike. The red-hued dining room, accented with contemporary art and strains of an acoustic guitar, epitomizes "cool," which makes sucking down a Peach Ball sake martini perfectly acceptable here. The firecracker shrimp, orange crunch sushi roll, black angus ribeye, and namesake Shabu Shabu, a Japanese hot pot, are all favorites. Dress is casual, but jeans that cost more than a suit aren't uncommon. ✉*333 Main St.* ☎*435/645–7253* ⊟*AE, D, MC, V* ⊗*No lunch.*

★ \$\$\$\$ ✕**350 Main Brasserie.** Chef Michael LeClerc is known for innovative entrées like black pepper-encrusted venison medallions with blackberry-shiitake jus, roasted beets, and cranberry-orange marmalade. This Old Town restaurant has verdigris-toned furniture and a rust-tint ceiling. It's warm and inviting after a day on the slopes. ✉*350 Main St.* ☎*435/649–3140* ⊟*AE, D, DC, MC, V* ⊗*Closed May.*

\$\$\$\$ ✕**The Viking Yurt.** Don your Scandinavian sweater for the sleigh ride up to this gentrified Nordic hut. After a hot drink, tuck into a four- or five-course feast that might feature Kobe beef, salmon, or duck. Warmed by a wood-burning stove and the soft light of solar-powered lanterns, you may find yourself raising a pewter goblet to toast your fellow diners and the musician tickling the ivories. ✉*Meet at The Forum of The Can-*

yons Resort ☎435/615–9878 △Reservations essential ☐AE, MC, V ⊙Closed Apr.–Nov.

$$$$
Fodor'sChoice
★
✕**Wahso.** Warm finger towels, deep jade table settings, curtained booths, and attentive service call back the Jazz-era Orient. Start your evening with a sake martini shaken table-side, then ask your server about the appetizer-and-soup sampler plate. Though it's not on the menu, if the kitchen isn't too slammed, the chef will prepare an artistic selection of appetizers such as crispy salt-and-pepper calamari, Malaysian cur-ried-chicken pot stickers, and a couple of shot-glass-size soup tast-ers. The dynamite salmon and the Szechuan filet mignon are favorite entrées. ✉577 Main St. ☎435/615–0300 △Reservations essential ☐AE, D, MC, V ⊙No lunch.

> ### NOT SO DRY
>
> It's a desert climate, but there's nothing dry about Park City when it comes to tipping back a drink or two. A cocktail contest each fall gets the creative bartending juices flowing and the momentum keeps up until summer, when a slew of festivals feature beer gardens and wine tastings. Breweries, wine bars, and martini joints pick up where the restaurant wine lists end. Keep in mind that altitude and dehydration go hand in hand. So, don't forget to drink water along with that blueberry mojito!

$$$–$$$$
★
✕**Adolph's.** This longtime local favorite is the beloved stomping ground of athletes from around the globe. Chef Adolph Imboden's food is European with strong ties to his Swiss roots. Start off with raclette or escargots, move to the chateaubriand, then finish with a flambé. Signed photos and posters of skiing greats through the years line the walls. ✉1500 Kearns Blvd. ☎435/649–7177 △Reservations essen-tial ☐AE, MC, V.

$$$–$$$$
✕**Blind Dog.** Look carefully for the paw prints on the ceiling. Inspired by the owner's black lab Rigger, this establishment manages to get away with adding wagging-tongue dog clocks to wood-paneled finery. The owners ship in fresh seafood daily, which is perhaps why their crab cakes are in such high demand. The New York steak with blue cheese is equally popular. Arrive a little early to order cheese fondue and a glass of merlot at the bar. ✉1781 Sidewinder Dr. ☎435/655–0800 ☐AE, D, MC, V ⊙No lunch. Call ahead Apr.–Nov.

$$$–$$$$
✕**Café Terigo.** This airy café with the best patio in town serves several well-prepared pasta and seafood dishes using only fresh ingredients. Good picks include almond-crusted salmon or smoked chicken with sun-dried tomatoes over fettuccine. An order of bread pudding or mud pie perfectly tops off a meal. ✉424 Main St. ☎435/645–9555 ☐AE, D, MC, V ⊙Closed Sun. Apr.–Nov.

$$$–$$$$
Fodor'sChoice
★
✕**Glitretind.** Wood trim, cranberry tablecloths, crystal glasses, hand-painted china, and fresh-cut flowers set the scene for executive chef Zane Holmquist's creative dishes like tea-and-Szechuan pepper-crusted duck breast at this European-style restaurant. Every major wine-grow-ing region is represented among the 800-plus wine selections, and artistic desserts provide a perfect finish. You'll be tempted to make an all-day affair out of the Jazz Sunday brunch. It's open for breakfast,

lunch, and dinner daily. ⊠ *7700 Stein Way, Deer Valley* ☎ *435/645–6455* ⚐ *Reservations essential* ▤ *AE, D, DC, MC, V.*

$–$$$$ ✗ **Zoom.** Owned by Robert Redford, this "Western chic" eatery is housed in an old train depot and still sports the worn wooden plank floors and floor scale. When the weather is warm, the sunken patio is a perfect place to enjoy pumpkin seed-crusted trout fillet, jerk-marinated pork tenderloin, or the beefed-up, but totally meatless, portobello mushroom sandwich. Leave room for warm chocolate torte with crisp almond brittle or homemade vanilla ice cream. ⊠ *660 Main St.* ☎ *435/649–9108* ▤ *AE, D, DC, MC, V.*

$–$$$ ✗ **Wasatch Brew Pub.** A down-to-earth respite from the fancy establishments lining the rest of Main Street, this brew pub's been concocting irreverent stories and delicious brew for a couple of decades. Sidle up to the bar for a mug of Polygamy Porter and a burger or cozy up with the entire family in a booth. Start with the wings, move on to the fish-and-chips, trout, or ribs, and top it all off with an ice cream sandwich. On warm days, grab an outside table for good people watching. ⊠ *250 Main St.* ☎ *435/645–9500* ⚐ *Reservations not accepted* ▤ *AE, D, MC, V.*

★ $–$$ ✗ **Windy Ridge Café.** You'll think you're at one of Park City's high-end eateries—with the columns, chandeliers, rustic wood furniture, attentive service, and creative menu selections—until you see the prices. It's well worth a short trip away from Main Street and the resorts for the homemade soups and breads, and fresh salads and sandwiches here. In summer, take advantage of the patio's umbrella-covered seclusion. Be sure to sample a pastry or two from the neighboring Bakery at Windy Ridge. ⊠ *1250 Iron Horse Dr.* ☎ *435/647–0880* ▤ *AE, D, DC, MC, V.*

☼ ¢–$$ ✗ **Nacho Mama's.** In Prospector Square, a few minutes from Main Street, Nacho Mama's features Southwestern dishes that will test your taste buds' heat tolerance. The chiles rellenos, which come with chicken, beef, or shrimp, push the upper limits of spicy, while the beef chipotle, with its thinly sliced meat and tangy sauce, sates any carnivore's appetite. ⊠ *1821 Sidewinder Dr.* ☎ *435/645–8226* ▤ *AE, D, MC, V* ☾ *No lunch.*

★ ¢ ✗ **El Chubasco.** For a quick and hearty meal of traditional Mexican food, this popular place is perfect. Favorites are camarones a la diabla, chile rellenos, and fish tacos. The burritos are large enough to feed two. The low-key atmosphere is part of the charm. ⊠ *1890 Bonanza Dr.* ☎ *435/645–9114* ▤ *AE, D, DC, MC, V.*

WHERE TO STAY

$$$$ ▦ **The Chateaux at Silver Lake.** Just steps away from the Deer Valley lifts ★ at Silver Lake Village, this modern interpretation of a luxury French château incorporates designer furnishings, heated towel racks, wet bars in hotel rooms, full kitchens in suites, gas fireplaces, and numerous windows to take advantage of the spectacular mountain views. The service is exemplary and the on-site restaurant, Bistro Toujours, and bar, Buvez, offer eclectic French food and drink in a warm and relaxing space. **Pros:** Luxury digs without stuffy atmosphere. Close

to the Deer Valley slopes. **Cons:** Not within walking distance of bustling Old Town. Evenings tend to be quiet and meals expensive in Silver Lake area. ⊠*7815 Royal St. E, 84060* ☎*435/658–9500 or 800/453–3833* 🖷*435/658–9513* ⊕*www.chateaux-deervalley.com* ↪*114 rooms, 46 suites* ⇩*In-room: kitchen (some), refrigerator, DVD (some), VCR, Ethernet, dial-up, Wi-Fi. In-hotel: restaurant, bar, pool, concierge, laundry facilities, laundry service, public Wi-Fi, airport shuttle, parking, no-smoking* ▭*AE, D, DC, MC, V.*

WORD OF MOUTH

"If you want to be at the base of Park City Mtn Resort, try the Marriott Mountainside. Very nice condo-hotel right at the base. You can walk to Main Street from there, or if it's really cold and you have little ones with, take the free shuttle. Extremely simple."

–Dayle

$$$$ 🏨 **Grand Summit Resort Hotel and Conference Center.** The Grand Summit hosted Katie and Matt and NBC's *Today* show during the 2002 Olympic Winter Games, so if you tuned into the games you've probably seen this luxury hotel at the base of the Canyons Resort. Nearly every room opens to a view of the mountains, and you can walk out of the upper lobby right onto the Flight of the Canyons Gondola. During ski season ask about the "ski free" package when you stay here. **Pros:** Legions of employees help you navigate this large resort. Luxury accommodations with mountain views. **Cons:** Ongoing construction in the area can be disruptive. ⊠*4000 The Canyons Resort Dr., 84098* ☎*435/615–8040 or 866/604–4170* 🖷*435/615–8041* ⊕*www.thecanyons.com* ↪*326 units* ⇩*In-room: safe, kitchen (some), DVD, dial-up, Wi-Fi. In-hotel: restaurant, room service, bar, pool, gym, spa, laundry service, concierge, public Wi-Fi, children's programs (ages 6 wks–6), parking, no-smoking* ▭*AE, D, DC, MC, V.*

★ $$$$ 🏨 **Hotel Park City.** On the Park City golf course, this all-suites hotel is built in the tradition of the grand old lodges of the West and furnished with leather furniture, marble bathrooms, and rustic luxury in all the details. Each room has a private balcony or patio, fireplace, and jetted tub, and the cottages have hot tubs. The 8,500-square-foot spa includes everything you'd expect with extras like a yoga room and a candlelit couples treatment room. **Pros:** Location close to town and the ski hills. Grand lodge-style rooms with views. Bulgari bath products. **Cons:** Though front desk staff is friendly, there's a whiff of pretension here. ⊠*2001 Park Ave., 84068* ☎*435/940–5000* 🖷*435/940–5001* ⊕*www.hotelparkcity.com* ↪*54 in-hotel suites and 46 cottage suites* ⇩*In-room: kitchen, DVD, Ethernet, Wi-Fi. In-hotel: restaurant, room service, bar, pool, gym, spa, laundry facilities, public Wi-Fi, parking, no smoking* ▭*AE, D, DC, MC, V.*

$$$$ 🏨 **Marriott Mountainside Resort.** Gabled roofs, stonework, and heavy beams re-create the look of Park City's mining era buildings at this resort on the plaza at Park City Mountain Resort, steps away from the ski lifts. The rooms and indoor common areas have more traditional decor than the rustic exterior. **Pros:** Ski-in ski-out convenience. Heated outdoor pool and hot tubs. Helpful, pleasant staff. **Cons:** Be prepared

2

for a sales pitch at this vacation ownership property. ✉*1305 Lowell Ave., 84060* ☎*435/940–2000 or 800/845–5279* 🖷*435/940–2010* ⊕*www.mvci.com* 🛏*182 rooms* ♿*In-room: safe, kitchen, DVD, dial-up, Wi-Fi. In-hotel: pool, gym, laundry facilities, concierge, children's programs (ages 3–12), parking, no smoking* ▤*AE, D, MC, V.*

$$$$
Fodor's Choice
★

🖥 **Stein Eriksen Lodge.** Like the legendary Norwegian ski hero it's named after, this slope-side lodge is perfectly groomed, timelessly gracious, and uniquely charming. Massive stone fireplaces, vaulted ceilings, and natural woodwork in the main lodge combine with in-room fireplaces, imported European fabrics, and heavy wood furniture to create an old-world Norwegian atmosphere. The service and facilities are impeccable, right down to the heated sidewalks and bell staff who light your in-room fire for you. All rooms have oversize whirlpool baths and many have deck hot tubs and in-room steam showers. A full-service Norwegian spa will pamper you after a hard day on the slopes. **Pros:** It's where the rich and famous stay without fear of being mobbed by fans. **Cons:** Expect to spend a pretty penny here. ✉*7700 Stein Way, Deer Valley, 84060* ☎*435/649–3700 or 800/453–1302* 🖷*435/649–5825* ⊕*www.steinlodge.com* 🛏*112 rooms, 73 suites* ♿*In-room: kitchen (some), DVD, VCR, dial-up, Wi-Fi. In-hotel: restaurant, room service, bar, pool, gym, spa, bicycles, laundry service, concierge, public Wi-Fi, parking, no smoking* ▤*AE, D, DC, MC, V.*

$$$–$$$$

🖥 **Holiday Inn Express Hotel and Suites.** With fireplaces and log furniture, this hotel near I–80 conveys the feel of a rustic cabin. Free shuttle service gets you to and from the Park City area resorts in winter. Continental breakfast is included. **Pros:** Basic, affordable home base for on-the-go families. **Cons:** Location outside town center means relying on shuttle for transportation. ✉*1501 W. Ute Blvd., 84098* ☎*435/658–1600 or 800/465–4329* 🖷*435/658–5059* ⊕*www.hieparkcity.com* 🛏*76 rooms* ♿*In-room: dial-up, Wi-Fi. In-hotel: pool, gym, laundry facilities, public Wi-Fi, parking, some pets allowed, no smoking* ▤*AE, D, DC, MC, V* ⦿*CP.*

$$$–$$$$
★

🖥 **Washington School Inn.** Originally an 1880s schoolhouse, the inn has high, vaulted ceilings, cherry wainscoting, and a stunning center staircase leading to the bell tower. The large rooms and suites have Victorian-era furnishings with country-style wall coverings, handwoven area rugs, tile-and-stone flooring, claw-foot tubs, and, in some rooms, four-poster canopy beds. **Pros:** Excellent breakfast quiche (some guests demand the recipe). Located just steps from Main Street. **Cons:** The occasional squeaky floorboard or noisy pipe. ✉*543 Park Ave., Box 536, 84060* ☎*435/649–3800 or 800/824–1672* 🖷*435/649–3802* ⊕*www.washingtonschoolinn.com* 🛏*12 rooms, 3 suites* ♿*In-room: refrigerator (some), DVD (some), VCR (some), dial-up, Wi-Fi. In-hotel: no elevator, public Wi-Fi, no kids under age 18* ▤*AE, MC, V* ⦿*BP.*

$$–$$$$

🖥 **Yarrow Resort Hotel & Conference Center.** Easy access to all three Park City resorts and the city golf course via shuttles is the principal attraction here. The high ceilings with exposed beams and flagstone entry to the lobby lend a mountain lodge feel to this otherwise standard hotel. Some rooms have fireplaces, jetted tubs, and kitchenettes. **Pros:** Clean, basic rooms suit the clientele (primarily cost-conscious tourists and conference attendees). **Cons:** No-frills accommodations. Traffic can clog Park Avenue during peak season. ✉*1800 Park Ave., 84060* ☎*435/649–7000 or 800/927–7694* 🖷*435/645–7007* ⊕*www.yarrow resort.com* ⟳*173 rooms, 8 suites* ⟁*In-room: safe, kitchen (some), refrigerator, Ethernet, Wi-Fi. In-hotel: restaurant, room service, bar, pool, gym, laundry facilities, concierge, public Wi-Fi, parking, no smoking* ☰*AE, D, DC, MC, V.*

$–$$$

Fodor's Choice

★

🏨**Old Town Guest House.** The country-style decor and lodgepole pine furniture make this inn, which is listed on the National Register of Historic Places, warm and cozy. Innkeeper Deb Lovci, a backcountry ski guide, triathlete, and mountain-bike racer, is an engaging host as well as a wealth of information on outdoor activities in the area. **Pros:** If the location—steps from the slopes and trails—doesn't motivate you to get outdoors, the energetic innkeeper will. **Cons:** Couch potatoes may feel out-of-place. Rooms and common areas are cozy but petite. ✉*1011 Empire Ave., 84060* ☎*435/649–2642 or 800/290–6423 Ext. 3710* 🖷*435/649–3320* ⊕*www.oldtownguesthouse.com* ⟳*4 rooms* ⟁*In-room: no a/c, safe, DVD, VCR, Wi-Fi. In-hotel: no elevator, laundry facilities, public Wi-Fi, some pets allowed, parking, no-smoking rooms* ☰*AE, MC, V* ⦿*BP.*

$

🏨**Chateau Après.** Just 150 yards from Park City Mountain Resort, this classic skiers' lodge has been run by the Hosenfeld family since 1963. The rooms aren't fancy, but they're clean and the service is as friendly as you'll find anywhere. You can choose one queen or a double and a twin. Or, if privacy isn't a must, you can rent a bed in the dorm room for $35 a night, which also includes the Continental breakfast. **Pros:** Comfortable, inexpensive place for outdoor enthusiasts to crash. Long-time local owners. **Cons:** If you're looking for cushy pampering or fancy eggs-benedict breakfasts, look elsewhere. ✉*1299 Norfolk Ave., 84060* ☎*435/649–9372 or 800/357–3556* 🖷*435/649–5963* ⊕*www. chateauapres.com* ⟳*32 rooms* ⟁*In-room: no a/c. In-hotel: no elevator, public Wi-Fi, no-smoking rooms* ☰*AE, D, MC, V* ⦿*CP.*

CONDOS The reservationists at **Deer Valley Lodging** (✉*1375 Deer Valley Dr. S, 84060* ☎*435/649–4040 or 800/453–3833* 🖷*435/645–8419* ⊕*www. deervalleylodging.com*) are knowledgeable and the service efficient at this high-end property-management company. They can book distinctive hotel rooms, condominiums, or private homes throughout Deer Valley and Park City.

WHERE TO CAMP ⛺**Hailstone: Jordanelle State Park.** Shade is at a premium at this lakeside campground on the west side of Jordanelle Reservoir. The views of surrounding mountains are stunning and the facilities clean and modern. Reservations are essential. ⟁*Laundry facilities, flush toilets, partial hookups, dump station, drinking water, showers, fire grates, picnic tables, food service, public telephone, swimming (lake)* ⟳*177 sites* ✉*U.S. 40 between Park City and Heber City, Mayflower Exit 8, Hwy. 319, 84032* ☎*435/649–9540 or 800/322–3770 reservations* 🖷*435/655–9058* ⊕*www.stateparks.utah.gov* ☰*AE, MC, V.*

⛺**Park City RV Resort.** Just off I–80, this four-acre RV resort has a hot tub, swimming pool, and easy access to Kimball Junction's shops, restaurants, and trails. ☼ *Wi-Fi, gym, laundry facilities, flush toilets, full hookups, dump station, drinking water, showers, picnic tables, public telephone, general store, play area* ➥*88 full hookups* ⊠*2200 Rasmussen Rd., 84098* ☎*435/649–2535* ☎*435/649–2536* ⊕*www.parkcity rvresort.com* ☐*AE, D, MC, V.*

NIGHTLIFE & THE ARTS

NIGHTLIFE

★ In a state where nearly every town was founded by Mormon pioneers who eschewed alcohol and anything associated with it, Park City has always been an exception. Founded by miners with healthy appetites for whiskey, gambling, and ladies of the night, Park City has been known since its mining heyday as the Sin City of Utah. The miners are gone, but their legacy lives on in this town that boasts far more bars per capita than any other place in Utah. **Cisero's** (⊠*306 Main St.* ☎*435/649–5044*) offers live music some evenings and also serves good Italian and American food.On lower Main, **Mulligan's** (⊠*804 Main St.* ☎*435/658–0717*)lives up to its name with Guinness on tap, occasional live music, and a congenial pub atmosphere with a couple of pool tables.The name has changed, or rather, disappeared, but the **No Name Saloon** (⊠*447 Main St.* ☎*435/649–6667*) is still the anchor of Main Street's nightlife: a classic wood-backed bar, lots of memorabilia, and a regular local clientele.If you're looking for a tasty garlic burger or hot wings, a favorite of local ski bums is **O'Shucks** (⊠*427 Main St.* ☎*435/645–3999*). No frills, no attitude, just the saltiest peanuts—throw the shells on the floor—and the coldest beer around.

★ **Sidecar** (⊠*333 Main St.* ☎*435/645–7468* ⊕*www.sidecarbar.com*)has live music most nights, quiet spots for conversation, cocktails for the sipping crowd as well as great pizza.Well worth the sleuthing it takes to find it (you walk through an alley next to 350 Main Restaurant), **The Spur** (⊠*352 Main St.* ☎*435/615–1618*) is an upscale, smoke-free club with good cowboy-style food and live music nightly. Belly up to the bar on one of the leather bar stools and choose from eight different tequilas to order one of their famous margaritas.Six miles from Main Street at Kimball Junction, **Playground** (⊠*1612 Ute Blvd.* ☎*435/658–2665*) has lots of room for nationally prominent live music leaning toward the eclectic and draws crowds from the Salt Lake Valley as well as Park City. If quiet conversation and a good single malt scotch in front of a fire is your idea of nightlife, try the **Troll Hallen Lounge** (⊠*7700 Stein Way* ☎*435/645–6455*), at Stein Eriksen Lodge.

THE ARTS

Main Street is packed with great art galleries, and the best way to see them all is the **Park City Gallery Stroll** (⊠*638 Park Ave.* ☎*435/649–8882* ⊕*www.kimball-art.org*), presented by the Kimball Art Center, where you can pick up tickets and a map. You can sample fine art and hors d'oeuvres at 23 local galleries and restaurants on the last Friday of each month, except January.

★ The **Eccles Center for Performing Arts** (✉ *1750 Kearns Blvd.* ☎ *435/655–3114* ⊕ *www.ecclescenter.org*) hosts dance, avant-garde theater, wide-ranging concerts, family shows, and other performances in a state-of-the-art auditorium that also hosts the biggest premieres during the Sundance Film Festival.

Theater has been a Park City tradition since its mining days in the 1880s. In 1922 the **Egyptian Theatre** (✉ *328 Main St.* ☎ *435/649–9371* ⊕ *www.egyptiantheatrecompany.org*) was constructed on the site of the original Dewey Theatre that collapsed under record-breaking snow. Patrons enjoy many different off-Broadway–style plays by local groups as well as national touring companies.

☾ **Mountain Town Stages** (☎ *435/901–7664* ⊕ *www.mountaintownstages. com*), a nonprofit organization fostering a nationally recognized musical community in the Park City area, uses seven different venues from ski resort plazas to Main Street. No matter what show you go to, you're likely to see every age group represented and enjoying the music.

Held in July, the **Park City Food & Wine Classic** (☎ *877/328–2783* ⊕ *www. parkcityfoodandwineclassic.com*) includes food and wine pairings, educational seminars, and gourmet dinners at various locations around town. It culminates in a grand tasting at The Canyons.

★ The **Park City Jazz Festival** (☎ *435/940–1362* ⊕ *www.parkcityjazz.org*) is a major summer event. Each August, artists like George Benson, Stanley Clarke, Bela Fleck, and the Ramsey Lewis Trio have performed at this annual three-day festival dedicated to jazz. Daily workshops and clinics for jazz musicians are held, and the nightly performances feature various kinds of jazz groups and styles.

☾ Celebrating visual and culinary art, the **Park City Kimball Arts Festival** (✉ *Main St.* ☎ *435/649–8882* ⊕ *www.kimball-art.org*), held the first weekend in August, is the biggest summer event in town. More than 200 artists from all over North America exhibit and offer their work to 40,000 festival attendees. Live music, upscale food, and three beer and wine gardens are featured.

☾ Rock, reggae, and country bands draw fans of all ages to The Canyons' free **Summer Concert Series** (✉ *4000 The Canyons Resort Dr., Park City84098* ☎ *435/649–5400* ⊕ *www.thecanyons.com*) on Saturdays in July and August.

Deer Valley Resort's **Summer Concert Series** (☎ *435/649–1000* ⊕ *www. deervalley.com*) includes everything from Utah Symphony performances to country music. Big names like Willie Nelson, Bonnie Raitt, Chris Isaak, and Judy Collins have graced the outdoor amphitheater.

For 11 days each January, Park City morphs into a mountain version of Hollywood as movie stars and film executives gather for the internationally recognized **Sundance Film Festival** (☎ *435/658–3456* ⊕ *www. sundance.org*), hosted by Robert Redford's Sundance Institute. In addition to panels, tributes, premieres, and screenings of independent films at various venues in Park City, Sundance, Ogden, and Salt Lake

City, the festival's Music Café hosts daily performances by emerging and established musicians.

SHOPPING

Within the colorful structures that line Park City's Main Street are a number of clothing boutiques, sporting-goods stores, and gift shops. **Bunya Bunya** (⊠*511 Main St.* ☎*435/649–1256*)might be a small retail space, but it's neatly packed with unique and stylish women's clothing and accessories.**Chloe Lane** (⊠*558 Main St.* ☎*435/645–9888*)has three different, but interconnected, storefronts: one for high-fashion denim for women, one for high-quality, contemporary American and European clothing and accessories for women, and one combining all of the above for men.

★ ☺ For many returning visitors, the first stop in town is **Dolly's Bookstore** (⊠*510 Main St.* ☎*435/649–8062*), to check on the cats, Dolly and Che Guevara, and to browse a great selection of Utah and regional books as well as national best-sellers. Dolly's also has a uniquely complete selection of children's books and toys.Jam-packed with classic toys and modern fun, **J.W. Allen & Sons** (⊠*1675 W. Redstone Center* ☎*435/575–8697* ⊕*www.parkcitytoystore.com*) has everything a kid could want. Scary dinosaurs, giant stuffed bears, dolls, techie toys, sleds, scooters, and kites are as irresistible as the candy.

★ ☺ Classical music and the aroma of fresh-roasted coffee greet you at **La Niche** (⊠*401 Main St.* ☎*435/649–2372*). Owner Jane Schaffner brings together a cozy collection of linens, home decorations, quilts, cooking and decorating books, and an intimate espresso and gelato bar in the back. **Mary Jane's** (⊠*613 Main St.* ☎*435/645–7463*)has an eclectic selection of locally handmade and independently designed shoes and clothing, accessories, and handbags for women, men, and children. And then there are the items the owner–buyer just couldn't pass up. If you like shoes, this shop is a must.You'll find a quick fix for your sweet tooth at either location of **Rocky Mountain Chocolate Factory** (⊠*510 Main St. or 1385 Lowell Ave.* ☎*435/649–0997 or 435/649–2235*), where you can watch them make homemade fudge, caramel apples, and other scrumptious treats. If you like Christmas, you'll love **Rocky Mountain Christmas** (⊠*355 Main St.* ☎*435/649–9169*), where Christmas ornaments and decorations crowd the tightly spaced shelves. Toys are upstairs as well.

A few miles north of Park City, next to I–80, are the **Tanger Outlets** (⊠*6699 N. Landmark Dr.* ☎*435/645–7078*). Represented in this collection of 60 outlets are Banana Republic, Nike, Gap, Ralph Lauren, Eddie Bauer, and Mikasa.Take a swing at **Wolf Summit Golf,** (⊠*1675 Redstone Center Dr.* ☎*435/575–0597* ⊕*www.wolfsummitgolf.com*), where testing out clubs is not only allowed, but encouraged by the unpretentious sales crew. Balls, spikes, clubs, and duds are all pro quality.

BIG COTTONWOOD CANYON

44 mi from Park City via I–80 west, I–215 west, and Rte. 190 south.

The history of mining and skiing in Utah often go hand in hand, and that's certainly true of Big Cottonwood Canyon with its adjacent ski resorts of **Brighton** and **Solitude.** In the mid-1800s, 2,500 miners lived at the top of this canyon in a rowdy tent city. The old mining roads make great hiking, mountain biking, and backcountry ski trails. Rock climbers congregate in the lower canyon for excellent sport and traditional climbing.

Opened in 1936, Brighton is the second-oldest ski resort in Utah and one of the oldest in North America. Just down the canyon, Solitude has undergone several incarnations since it opened in 1957, and has invested heavily in overnight accommodations and new base facilities since the early 1990s. As an area, Big Cottonwood is quieter than Park City or neighboring Little Cottonwood Canyon, home of Alta and Snowbird resorts.

SPORTS & THE OUTDOORS

CROSS-COUNTRY SKIING
Accessible from Solitude Village, the **Solitude Nordic Center** (⊠ *Big Cottonwood Canyon Rd.* ☎*801/536–5774*) has 20 km (12 mi) of groomed cross-country trails, 10 km (6 mi) of snowshoe trails, and a small shop offering rentals, lessons, food, and guided tours. For $12 you can use the trails all day; for $45 you receive an all-day trail pass and a one-hour private lesson.

DOWNHILL SKIING
With the perfect combination of all the fluffy powder of Alta and Snowbird and all the quiet charm many large resorts have left behind, **Brighton Ski Resort** is a favorite among serious snowboarders and out-on-the-edge skiers. If you're looking for excitement, more than one-third of the runs are for advanced skiers, and lifts provide access to extensive backcountry areas for the real experts. Photos taken in the Brighton backcountry are regular fodder for the extreme skiing and snowboarding magazines. Its expert terrain and renegade image notwithstanding, this is still a great place for families, with ideal beginner and intermediate terrain. It was the first in Utah to offer a kids-ski-free program, and it has received many awards for its service to children and parents. ⊠*12601 Big Cottonwood Rd., Brighton, 84121* ☎*801/532–4731, 800/873–5512, 800/873–5512 snow report* 🖷*435/649–1787* ⊕*www. brightonresort.com* ☞*1,745-ft vertical drop; 1050 skiable acres; 21% beginner, 40% intermediate, 39% advanced/expert; 4 high-speed quad chairs, 1 fixed grip quad, 1 triple chair* 🎿*Lift tickets $53.*

Since the early 1990s the base of **Solitude Mountain Resort** has grown into a European-style village with lodges, condominiums, a luxury hotel, and award-winning restaurants, but downhill skiing and snowboarding are still the main attractions. Day guests will enjoy relaxing after a hard day on the slopes at the comfortable 12,000-square-foot Moonbeam Day Lodge. Honeycomb Canyon has pristine expert terrain along with a good mix of intermediate cruising runs and beginner-friendly slopes. Skiers and boarders can access the slopes directly from the parking lot *on the fixed-grip quad lift.* ✉*12000 Big Cottonwood Canyon, Solitude, 84121* ☎*801/534–1400, 800/748–4754, 801/536–5774 Nordic Center, 801/536–5777 snow report* 🖷*435/649–5276* ⊕*www.skisolitude.com* ✆*2,047-ft vertical drop; 1,200 skiable acres; 20% beginner, 50% intermediate, 30% advanced; 1 high-speed quad chair, 2 quad chairs, 1 triple chair, 4 double chairs* ✆*Lift tickets $55.*

2

The upper section of Big Cottonwood Canyon is a glacier-carved valley with many side drainages that lead to picturesque alpine lakes. In the Brighton area you can access beautiful mountain lakes just a short jaunt from the highway. The elevation at Brighton's parking lot is 8,700 feet, so take it easy, rest often, and drink plenty of water. A beautiful

HIKING

★

hike is along the **Brighton Lakes Trail** past four alpine lakes and then ascending to Catherine Pass. At Catherine Pass you have the option of continuing up to **Sunset Peak,** which, at 10,648 feet, is one of the most accessible summits in the Wasatch Range. It's another short grunt to the top but well worth the effort for the unsurpassed, nearly 360-degree views. The breathtaking vistas include the Heber Valley, Park City, Mt. Timpanogos, Big and Little Cottonwood Canyons, and even a portion of the Salt Lake Valley. From here you can choose to descend into Little Cottonwood's Albion Basin near Alta (but remember, you'll need a shuttle for the 45-minute ride back to Brighton), or back along the Brighton lakes trail to Brighton.

ICE-SKATING

Open mid-December through April, from 3 PM to 8 PM, **Solitude Ice-Skating Rink** (✉*Solitude Village* ☎*801/534–1400*), in the heart of Solitude Village, provides skate rentals and a rink-side fire for family fun or a romantic outing.

MOUNTAIN
BIKING

There are great single-track trails within Big Cottonwood Canyon as well as routes that connect neighboring canyons. **Solitude Mountain Resort** (✉*12000 Big Cottonwood Canyon Rd.* ☎*801/534–1400*) offers lift-served mountain biking with rentals available at the Powderhorn Adventure Center in Solitude Village.

WHERE TO EAT

⟳ $$–$$$$ ✕ **Creekside Restaurant.** Excellent pizzas and calzones from a wood-fired oven and creative pastas make this Solitude Village restaurant a good choice for families. In summer the patio is a great outdoor retreat from the Salt Lake Valley heat, but bring a sweater because when the sun goes down you'll need it. It's open seven days a week for lunch and dinner during ski season and for dinner (Thursday–Sunday) and Sunday brunch in summer. Call ahead during May and October. ✉*12000 Big Cottonwood Canyon Rd.* ☎*801/536–5787* ▭*AE, D, DC, MC, V.*

WHERE TO STAY

$$$$ 🏠 **Powderhorn Lodge.** The clock tower on this Tyrolean-style lodge chimes hourly and is the centerpiece of Solitude Village. Many of these elegantly furnished one- to three-bedroom condos have private balconies and all have fireplaces. **Pros:** Handsome furnishings and full kitchens. Convenient to slopes and Solitude's village. **Cons:** This is an early-to-bed spot, so if you want to yodel, do so before dark. ✉*12000 Big Cottonwood Canyon Rd., 84121* ☎*801/534–1400 or 800/748–*

4754 ☎801/517–7705 ⊕*www.skisolitude.com* ➪*60 units* ♿*In-room: no a/c, kitchen, DVD, VCR (some), Ethernet. In-hotel: laundry facilities, parking, no smoking* ▤*AE, D, DC, MC, V.*

$$$–$$$$ 🏨**The Inn at Solitude.** You get ski-in ski-out luxury and VIP treatment at this well-appointed hotel with comfortable and spacious rooms. After a strenuous day on the slopes, enjoy a hot toddy at St. Bernard's bar, get a massage at the full-service spa, then relax under the stars in the outdoor heated pool or hot tub. **Pros:** White glove service. No big-city hustle and bustle. **Cons:** "Solitude" equals "quiet." ✉*12000 Big Cottonwood Canyon Rd., 84121* ☎*801/534–1400 or 800/748–4754* 📠*801/517–7705* ⊕*www.skisolitude.com* ➪*42 rooms, 4 suites* ♿*In-room: no a/c, DVD. In-hotel: restaurant, pool, gym, spa, laundry facilities, no smoking* ▤*AE, D, DC, MC, V* ⊗*Closed May–Nov.*

★ $–$$ 🏨**Silver Fork Lodge.** Any day of the week, any time of the year, you'll find people driving up from the Salt Lake Valley for the consistently delicious food ($–$$$) and friendly service in this rustic lodge a mile down the road from Solitude Mountain Resort. In warm months breakfast on the patio is delightful. Log furniture, wood paneling, and country decor make the rooms warm and inviting, and the views are unbeatable. Service is attentive, but not overbearing. **Pros:** Renowned dining (hearty breakfasts included). No in-room phones or TVs to disrupt the peace and quiet. **Cons:** Nightlife is lacking. Some may find it a little *too* quiet. ✉*11332 Big Cottonwood Canyon Rd., 84121* ☎*801/533–9977 or 888/649–9551* 📠*435/649–3428* ⊕*www.silverforklodge.com* ➪*6 rooms, 1 suite* ♿*In-room: no a/c, no phone, no TV, Wi-Fi. In-hotel: restaurant, bar, no elevator, public Wi-Fi, parking, no smoking* ▤*AE, D, MC, V* ⍾*BP.*

¢–$$ 🏨**Brighton Lodge.** Brighton Ski Resort's emphasis on value extends to this lodge, which is quiet, comfortable, and so reasonably priced (keep in mind that children 10 and under stay free) that you might be able to stretch your ski weekend into a full week. Situated right on the slopes, the lodge has a tradition of friendliness. Rooms have few frills but are still comfortable. **Pros:** Unpretentious in every way. A good deal for families. **Cons:** If you don't have kids, the family atmosphere may not appeal. ✉*12601 Big Cottonwood Canyon Rd., 84121* ☎*801/532–4731 Ext. 120 or 800/873–5512 Ext. 120* 📠*435/649–1787* ⊕*www.brightonresort.com* ➪*18 rooms (5 share bath), 2 suites* ♿*In-room: no a/c, refrigerator, no TV. In-hotel: parking, no smoking* ▤*AE, D, MC, V* ⍾*CP.*

WHERE TO ⛺**Spruces Campground.** As the name implies, this campground is in the
CAMP middle of a grove of spruce pines that provide plenty of shade. This is the trailhead for several good hiking routes and Big Cottonwood Creek runs next to the campground. Reservations are essential. ♿*Flush toilets, drinking water, fire grates, picnic tables* ➪*100 sites* ✉*10 mi up Big Cottonwood Canyon on Rte. 190* ☎*801/733–2660 or 877/444–6777* ⊕*www.recreation.gov* ▤*AE, D, MC, V* ⊗*Mid-May–mid-Oct.*

CLOSE UP

This Lake Is for the Birds

Although it's too salty for fish, the Great Salt Lake teems with algae and bacteria. These provide food for brine shrimp and brine flies, which seem like caviar to the millions of shore birds that stop here during their migrations. The following is a list of some of the more than 250 species that you can spot at natural saltwater marshes, man-made freshwater marshes, and wetland refuges around the lake: Avocet, Bald Eagle, Black-Necked Stilt, California Gull, Common Snipe, Cormorant, Egret (Great and Snowy varieties), Grebe (Eared and Western), Heron (Great Blue and Black-Crowned Night), Killdeer, Long-Billed Curlew, Long-Billed Dowitcher, Marbled Godwit, Merganser, Northern Phalarope, Plover (Black-Bellied, Lesser, Golden, Snowy, Semipalmated), Red Knot, Sanderling, Sandpiper (Baird's, Least, Pectoral, Semipalmated, Solitary, Spotted, Stilt, Western), Tern (Caspian and Forster's), White-Faced Ibis, Willet, and the Yellowlegs (Greater and Lesser).

It's a bird-watchers paradise, so bring your binoculars!

NIGHTLIFE

NIGHTLIFE   Old-time ski bums and younger snowboarders come together to shoot pool and tip back a few at **Molly Green's** (⊠ *Brighton Ski Resort* ☎ *435/649–7909* ⊙ *Closed Mon.–Wed. May–Nov.*), a smoky bar with a laid-back attitude at the base of Brighton Ski Resort. A good place to unwind after skiing is the **Thirsty Squirrel** (⊠ *Powderhorn Bldg., Solitude Village* ☎ *801/536–5797* ⊙ *Closed May–Oct.*); it's pretty quiet once the après-ski crowd leaves.

LITTLE COTTONWOOD CANYON

25 mi from Brighton and Solitude via Rte. 190 west, Rte. 210 south; 20 mi from Salt Lake City via I–15 south, I–215 east, Rte. 210 south.

Skiers have been singing the praises of Little Cottonwood Canyon since 1938 when the Alta Lifts Company pieced together a ski lift using parts from an old mine tram to become the **Alta Ski Resort,** the second ski resort in North America. With its 500 inches per year of dry, light snow and unparalleled terrain, this canyon is legendary among diehard snow enthusiasts. A mile down the canyon from Alta, **Snowbird Ski and Summer Resort,** which opened in 1971, shares the same mythical snow and terrain quality. Since 2001 Alta and Snowbird have been connected via the Mineral Basin area. You can purchase an Alta Snowbird One Pass that allows you on the lifts at both areas, making this a huge skiing complex.

But skiing isn't all there is to do here. Many mountain biking and hiking trails access the higher reaches of the Wasatch–Cache National Forest, and the trails over Catherine Pass will put you at the head of Big Cottonwood Canyon at the Brighton Ski Area. The hike to Catherine Pass is relatively easy and quite scenic. Formed by the tireless path of an ancient glacier, Little Cottonwood Canyon cuts a swath through the

Wasatch–Cache National Forest. Canyon walls are composed mostly of striated granite, and traditional climbing routes of varied difficulty abound. Down the canyon from Alta and Snowbird is the trailhead for the Red Pine Lake and White Pine Lake trails. Some 3½ mi and 5 mi in, respectively, these mountain lakes make for great day hikes.

"If it ain't broke, don't fix it," could be the motto at Alta Ski Resort. There's an old-world charm here that many regulars call magic. Most of the lodges have been here since the '40s or '50s, and the emphasis is on efficiency and quality rather than the latest fads.

At Snowbird's base area, modern structures house guest rooms, restaurants, and nightclubs. The largest of these buildings, the Cliff Lodge, is an entire ski village under one roof. The resort mounts a variety of entertainment throughout the year, including live jazz shows; rock, blues, folk, and bluegrass concerts; and an Oktoberfest in fall. As a guest, you receive free membership to the Club at Snowbird and can enjoy a drink at any of several base-area lounges.

All year long, Snowbird's tram takes sightseers to the top, and in summer, hikers can ride up to hike atop Hidden Peak. Mountain bikers are discovering that the slopes make for some excellent, if strenuous, riding. The resort also has a competition-class outdoor climbing wall.

SPORTS & THE OUTDOORS

SKIING You'll find 5 km (3 mi) of groomed track for skating and classic skiing plus a good selection of rental equipment and even an espresso bar at the **Alta Nordic Shop** (⊠ *Wildcat Ticket Office Bldg.* ☎*801/799–2293*).

Fodor'sChoice When it comes to skiing, **Alta Ski Area** is widely acclaimed for both
★ what it has and what it doesn't have. What it has is perhaps the best snow anywhere in the world—up to 500 inches a year, and terrain to match it. What it doesn't have is glitz and pomp. Neither does it have snowboarders. Alta is one of the few resorts left in the country that doesn't allow snowboarding. Sprawling across two large basins, Albion and Wildcat, Alta has a good mixture of expert, intermediate, and beginner terrain. Much of the best skiing (for advanced or expert skiers) requires either finding obscure traverses or doing some hiking: it takes some time to get to know this mountain so if you can find a local to show you around you'll be ahead of the game. Albion Basin's lower slopes have a terrific expanse of novice and lower-intermediate terrain. Rolling meadows, wide trails, and light dry snow create one of the best places in the country for less-skilled skiers to learn to ski powder. Two-hour lessons start at $45. Half-day group lessons for adults and children are available. ⌂*Box 8007, 84092* ☎*801/359–1078, 801/572–3939 snow report* ⊕*www.alta.com* ⌒*2,020-ft vertical drop; 2,200 skiable acres; 25% novice, 40% intermediate, 35% advanced; 2 high speed quads, 3 triple chairs, 3 double chairs* ⊟*Lift tickets $59; Alta Snowbird One Pass $79.*

Like its up-canyon neighbor, **Snowbird Ski and Summer Resort** has plenty of powder-filled chutes, bowls, and meadow areas with an even longer vertical drop. Snowbird's signature 125-passenger tram takes you from the base all the way to the top in one fell swoop for a leg-burning top to bottom run of more than 3,000 vertical feet. The terrain here is weighted more toward experts—35% of Snowbird is rated black-diamond—and if there is a drawback to this resort it's a lack of beginner terrain. The open bowls, such as Little Cloud and Regulator Johnson, are challenging; the Upper Cirque and the Gad Chutes are hair-raising. On deep-powder days—not uncommon at the Bird—these chutes are exhilarating for skiers who like that sense of a cushioned free fall with every turn. With a nod to intermediate skiers, Snowbird opened North America's first skier tunnel in 2007, reducing the trek to Mineral Basin's terrain. If you're looking for intermediate cruising runs, there's the long, meandering Chips Run. After a day of powder turns, visitors can lounge on the 3,000-square-foot deck of Creekside Lodge at the base of Gad Valley. Of note is Snowbird's Dean Cummings Big Mountain Experience, a combination of guidance and instruction for expert skiers or snowboarders in challenging, off-slope terrain and variable snow conditions. Full-day workshops for skiers and boarders of all levels start at $100. ⊠*Hwy. 210, Box 929000, Snowbird, 84092* ☎*801/933–2222, 800/232–9542 lodging reservations, 801/933–2110 special events, 801/933–2100 snow report* 🖷*801/947–8227* ⊕*www.snowbird.com* ↝*3,240-ft vertical drop; 4,700 skiable acres; 27% novice, 38% intermediate, 35% advanced; 125-passenger tram, 4 quad lifts, 6 double chairs, and a skier tunnel with surface lift* 🎟*Lift tickets $69 tram and chairs, $59 chairlift only; Alta Snowbird One Pass $79.*

If you don't mind paying for it, the best way to find untracked Utah powder is with **Wasatch Powderbird Guides** (⊠*Snowbird* ☎*801/742–2800* ⊕*www.powderbird.com*). A helicopter drops you on the top of the mountain and a guide leads you back down. A full day costs $840 in low season and $980 in high season.

Fodor'sChoice Strong intermediate and advanced skiers can hook up with the **Ski Utah**
★ **Interconnect Adventure Tour** (☎*801/534–1907* ⊕*www.skiutah.com*) for a guided alpine ski tour that takes you to as many as six resorts (Deer Valley, Park City, Brighton, Solitude, Alta, and Snowbird) in a single day, all connected by backcountry ski routes with unparalleled views of the Wasatch Mountains. Guides test your ski ability before departure. The tour includes guide service, lift tickets, lunch, and transportation back to the point of origin and costs $195. You'll even walk away with a finisher's pin. The Deer Valley Departure Tour operates Sunday, Monday, Wednesday, and Friday; the Snowbird Departure Tour operates Tuesday, Thursday, and Saturday. Reservations are required.

HIKING The upper canyons provide a cool haven during the hot summer months. Wildflowers and wildlife are plentiful and most trails provide a good balance of shade and sun. Due to high altitude, even fit hikers often become fatigued and dehydrated faster than they would otherwise, so remember to take it easy, rest often, and drink plenty of water. **White Pine Trailhead,** 0.7 mi below Snowbird on the south side of the road, accesses some excellent easy hikes to overlooks. If you want to keep going on more intermediate trails, continue up the trail to the lakes in White Pine Canyon, Red Pine Canyon, and Maybird Gulch. All of these hikes share a common path for the first mile.

★ The trailhead for the 4-mi out-and-back hike to **Sunset Peak** starts high in Little Cottonwood Canyon, above Alta Ski Resort, in Albion Basin. This is a popular area for finding wildflowers in July and August. After an initial steep incline, the trail wanders through flat meadows before it climbs again to Catherine Pass at 10,240 feet. From here intermediate hikes continue along the ridge in both directions. Continue up the trail to the summit of Sunset Peak for breathtaking views of the Heber Valley, Park City, Mt. Timpanogos, Big and Little Cottonwood Canyons, and even a part of the Salt Lake Valley. You can alter your route by starting in Little Cottonwood Canyon and ending your hike in neighboring Big Cottonwood Canyon: from Catherine Pass descend into Big Cottonwood Canyon passing four lakes and finally ending up at Brighton Ski Resort.

MOUNTAIN BIKING The steep, rocky terrain here is not recommended for beginners, but advanced mountain bikers can ride the tram at **Snowbird Ski and Summer Resort** (⊠ *Hwy. 210* ☎ *801/933–2222*) to the top of the mountain and access a network of trails. Summer tram tickets are $12 per ride or $18 all day. Bike rentals are available.

ROCK CLIMBING Whether you're an experienced climber or have never climbed but want to learn, **Snowbird Ski and Summer Resort** (⊠ *Hwy. 210* ☎ *801/933–2222*) offers instruction and equipment rental with climbing on the man-made, 120-foot-tall International Climbing Competition Wall on the Cliff Lodge. The fee of $10 per climb includes instruction and climbing shoes. Reservations are recommended.

WHERE TO EAT

$$$–$$$$ ✕ **The Aerie Restaurant, Lounge and Sushi Bar.** Spectacular panoramic views through 15-foot windows, white-linen tablecloths, and dark Oriental rugs set a romantic mood at Little Cottonwood's most elegant dining alternative on the 10th floor of the Cliff Lodge. Entrées like tenderloin of venison with butternut squash gnocchi or roast chicken served with tomato risotto are the fare in the restaurant, while the menu and mood are more casual at the sushi bar and lounge. ⊠ *Cliff Lodge, 10th fl., Snowbird Ski and Summer Resort, Snowbird* ☎ *801/933–2160* ⊟ *AE, D, DC, MC, V* ⊗ *Closed Sun. and Mon. No lunch May–Nov.*

★ $$$–$$$$ ✕ **Shallow Shaft.** For fine Angus beef, wild game, seafood, poultry, and pasta dishes, Alta's only sit-down restaurant that's not part of a hotel is the place to go. The small interior is cozy, with a sandy color scheme and walls adorned with 19th-century mining tools found on the mountain. The cuisine has a regional focus, with dishes like smoked Utah trout cakes or bison tenderloin. The restaurant makes its own ice cream daily. ⊠ *Rte. 210, across from Alta Lodge, Alta* ☎ *801/742–2177* ⌂ *Reservations essential* ⊟ *AE, D, MC, V* ⊗ *Closed May; closed Tues. and Wed. June–Nov. No lunch.*

$$$–$$$$ ✕ **Steak Pit.** Views and food take precedence over interior design at Snowbird's oldest restaurant, where some of the original wait staff are still serving. The dining room is warm and unpretentious, with some

wood paneling and an expanse of glass. The menu is full of well-prepared steak and seafood choices. Whether you opt for the oven-baked scallops or filet mignon, you can't go wrong. And be sure to save room for their famous mud pie. ⊠ *Snowbird Plaza Center, Hwy. 210, Snowbird* ☎ *801/933–2181* ▭ *AE, D, DC, MC, V* ⊘ *No lunch.*

WHERE TO STAY

★ $$$$ 🏨 **Alta Lodge.** Built in 1939, this is the original lodge at Alta Ski Area. Wings were added later with wall-to-wall windows for excellent views. This is a homey place where many families have been booking the same week each year for several generations. Upstairs, the Sitzmark Club is a casual, quiet place for an après-ski cocktail. For price-conscientious guests, the Alta Lodge offers a bed in a dorm room for $138. The dining room is open daily for breakfast, lunch, and dinner in winter and for Saturday lunch and Sunday brunch in summer. Breakfast and dinner are included in the winter lodging price, even for dorm room guests. **Pros:** Located close to Alta's steep-and-deep slopes. Views of the Wasatch Mountains. Pleasant staff. **Cons:** Cinderblock hallways recall college dorms. ⊠ *10230 Little Cottonwood Canyon Rd., Alta, 84092* ☎ *801/742–3500 or 800/707–2582* ▤ *801/742–3504* ⊕ *www.altalodge.com* ⟳ *53 rooms, 4 dorms, 4 share bath* ⚬ *In-room: no a/c, no TV. In-hotel: restaurant, bar, no elevator, laundry facilities, no smoking* ⊘ *Closed mid-Apr.–May and early Oct.–mid-Nov.* ▭ *D, MC, V* ❑ *MAP.*

$$$$ 🏨 **Cliff Lodge.** The stark concrete walls of this 10-story structure are meant to complement the surrounding granite cliffs. Inside you'll find a self-contained village with restaurants, bars, shops, a high-end spa, and North America's foremost Oriental rug collection as decor. Every window has a scenic view, and rooms are decorated in hues matching the mountain landscape. Spa-level rooms have flat-screen TVs and Tempur-Pedic beds. In addition to the two heated pools and four hot tubs, the luxurious Cliff Spa has a rooftop lap pool and 20 treatment rooms. Camp Snowbird offers summer and winter day camps for children. **Pros:** Ten stories of windows facing the Wasatch Range. The rooftop spa. Several eateries and bars on-site. **Cons:** Looking down from the top floor may induce some vertigo. ⊠ *Little Cottonwood Canyon Rd., Snowbird Ski and Summer Resort, Snowbird, 84092* ☎ *801/933–2222 or 800/232–9542* ▤ *801/947–8227* ⊕ *www.snowbird.com* ⟳ *511 rooms* ⚬ *In-room: safe, refrigerator, Wi-Fi. In-hotel: 4 restaurants, 2 bars, pools, gym, spa, children's programs (ages 6 wks–12), laundry facilities, laundry service, parking, no smoking* ▭ *AE, D, DC, MC, V.*

$$$$ 🏨 **Rustler Lodge.** Alta's fanciest lodge resembles a traditional full-service hotel. The interior is decidedly upscale; common areas have dark-wood paneling, burgundy chairs and couches, and handsome wooden backgammon tables. Guest quarters are warmly decorated with dark woods, white brick walls, and richly colored fabrics. Larger rooms have sofas and seating areas. All but three units have private baths. As at all of Alta's lodges, breakfast and dinner are included in the price. **Pros:** Mountain views. On the slopes of Alta Ski Resort. **Cons:** "Fancy" at down-to-earth Alta is a relative term; don't expect the Ritz. ⊠ *10380 E. Hwy. 210 Box 8030, Alta, 84092* ☎ *801/742–2200*

or 888/532–2582 🖶*801/742–3832* ⊕*www.rustlerlodge.com* ⮐*85 rooms, 4 dorms* ♿*In-room: no a/c, Wi-Fi. In-hotel: restaurant, bar, pool, spa, laundry facilities, parking, no smoking* ⊘*Closed May and Oct.–mid Nov.* ▤*AE, D, MC, V* ⍩*MAP.*

$$$–$$$$ 🏨 **Iron Blosam Lodge.** This Snowbird condominium lodging has accommodations and amenities to suit most any traveler's needs, including studios, bedrooms with lofts, and one-bedroom suites. Many have fireplaces and balconies. **Pros:** Comfortable accommodations close to the slopes. **Cons:** There's not much happening on-site in the evenings. ⊠*Hwy. 210, Resort Entry 2, Snowbird, 84092* 🖶*801/933–2222 or 800/453–3000* 🖶*801/933–2148* ⊕*www.snowbird.com* ⮐*159 rooms* ♿*In-room: no a/c, kitchen (some). In-hotel: restaurant, bar, tennis courts, pools, gym, laundry facilities, public Internet, public Wi-Fi, parking, no smoking* ▤*AE, D, DC, MC, V* ⊘*Closed 1 wk Nov., 1 wk May.*

NIGHTLIFE & THE ARTS

NIGHTLIFE   Almost all of the lodges in Little Cottonwood have their own bar or lounge and tend to be on the quiet side, centering around the après-ski scene.

★   Lots of couches and a fireplace give the **Aerie Lounge** (⊠*Cliff Lodge, 10th fl., Snowbird* 🖶*801/933–2222*) a relaxed feel. You can hear live jazz here every Wednesday and Saturday night. Upstairs at the Alta Lodge, **The Sitzmark Club** (⊠*Alta Lodge, Alta* 🖶*801/742–3500*) is a small, comfortable, retro bar that is a favorite with many of the free skiers who call Little Cottonwood home. Thick glass windows looking into the gears of the Snowbird tram give the **Tram Club** (⊠*Snowbird Center, Snowbird* 🖶*801/933–2222*) an industrial feel. Live music most nights, pool, and video games draw a younger crowd.

THE ARTS   When the snow melts, **Snowbird Ski and Summer Resort** (⊠*Hwy. 210, Snowbird* 🖶*801/933–2110*) hosts a number of events including a Rock and Blues Festival, a Folk and Bluegrass Festival, a month-long Oktoberfest, as well as free outdoor music of every genre on the plaza.

SOUTH OF SALT LAKE CITY

The Utah Valley was a busy place long before the Mormons settled here in 1851. With Utah Lake teeming with fish and game plentiful in the surrounding mountains, several bands of Native Americans lived in the area, and Spanish explorers passed through in 1775. Traders from several countries used the explorers' trail to bring goods here and to capture slaves to sell in Mexico, and fur trappers spent winter seasons in the surrounding mountains. With so many groups competing for the area's resources, conflicts were inevitable. The conflicts became more intense when Mormons settled Provo in 1851 and then began claiming land in other parts of the valley, land that had always been used by Native Americans. Several battles were fought here between Mormon settlers and Native American groups during the Walker and Black Hawk wars.

Between Salt Lake City and Provo you'll find chain motels and fast food off most of the I–80 exits. There are also a couple of great scenic and historic excursions, such as **Thanksgiving Point, Timpanogos Cave,** and the **Alpine Loop Scenic Byway** (⇨ *Chapter 1, Side Trips from Salt Lake City),* if you don't mind getting off the beaten path.

PROVO

45 mi south of Salt Lake City via I–15; 14 mi south of Lehi via I–15.

With Mount Timpanogos to the east and Utah Lake to the west, Provo and the adjacent city of Orem make up one of the prettiest communities in the West. With a combined population of 200,000, this two-city community is also one of the fastest-growing. Provo's historic downtown includes many small shops and family restaurants; in the newer sections you'll find malls, factory outlet stores, a variety of eateries, and the headquarters for several large corporations. The presence of Brigham Young University and the LDS Missionary Training Center imbue the community with a wholesome quality.

Each June, the month-long **America's Freedom Festival** (☎ *801/818–1776* ⊕ *www.freedomfestival.org*) combines a series of patriotic activities and contests. The event peaks with a hot-air balloon festival and the state's biggest Independence Day parade. A gathering in 65,000-seat Cougar Stadium on the Brigham Young University campus closes the festival with live entertainment and an enormous fireworks display.

Provo and the entire region are probably best known as the home of **Brigham Young University.** The university was established by the Mormon church as the Brigham Young Academy in 1875, with a mandate to combine teaching about the sacred and the secular. It has grown into one of the world's largest church-affiliated universities, and still reflects the conservative nature of the Mormon Church. Students must adhere to a strict dress and honor code and refrain from alcohol, tobacco, coffee, and tea. BYU is known for its large variety of quality undergraduate and graduate programs, is a considerable force in regional athletics, and serves as a cultural center for the southern Wasatch area. Heading up BYU attractions is a quartet of museums. A free guided university tour is offered Monday through Friday on the hour by appointment. ⊠ *BYU visitor center, Campus Dr.* ☎ *801/422–4678* ⊕ *www.byu.edu.*

★ The permanent collection of more than 17,000 works at the **Museum of Art at Brigham Young University** includes primarily American artists such as Maynard Dixon, Dorothea Lange, Albert Bierstadt, Minerva Teichert, and Robert Henri, and emphasizes the Hudson River School and the American impressionists. Utah artists are represented with works from the Mormon pioneer era to the present. Rembrandt, Monet, and Rubens also turn up, along with some fine Far Eastern pieces. The museum's café overlooks the sculpture garden. ⊠ *N. Campus Dr., southeast of Cougar Stadium* ☎ *801/422–8287* ⊕ *http://moa.byu.edu* ⌨ *Free* ☉ *Weekdays 10–9, Sat. noon–5.*

☾ BYU's **Monte L. Bean Life Science Museum** has extensive collections of birds, mammals, fish, reptiles, insects, plants, shells, and eggs from around the world as well as revolving nature-art exhibits. ⊠*645 E. 1430 North St., north of bell tower* ☎*801/422–5051* ⊕*http://mlbean. byu.edu* ⊠*Free* ☉ *Weekdays 10–9, Sat. 10–5.*

☾ The **BYU Earth Science Museum** features dinosaur bones, fossils, and tours for adults and children. Kids love the hands-on activities, which include a table of touchable artifacts. ⊠*1683 N. Canyon Rd., across from Cougar Stadium* ☎*801/378–3680* ⊕*http://cpms.byu.edu/ESM* ⊠*Free* ☉ *Weekdays 9–5.*

The **BYU Museum of Peoples and Cultures** is an interesting student-curated collection of artifacts relating to cultures from all over the world. Clothing, pottery, rugs, weapons, and agricultural tools of Utah's Native American cultures are often on display. ⊠*700 N. 100 East St.* ☎*801/422–0020* ⊕*http://mpc.byu.edu* ⊠*Free* ☉ *Weekdays 9–5.*

Pioneer Village and Museum recreates what life was like for the first settlers in the mid-19th century. Original cabins and shops furnished with period antiques are staffed by volunteer history buffs. ⊠*500 W. 600 North St.* ☎*801/852–6609* ⊕*www.provo.org/parks.pioneer_main. html* ⊠*Free* ☉ *June–Aug., village open Tues.–Sat. noon–4, weather permitting; museum hrs vary.*

☾ **Seven Peaks Water Park** has 26 acres of waterborne fun with plenty of play areas and a wave pool. When you splash down from a waterslide or rope swing, there won't be a temperature shock because the water is heated. ⊠*1330 E. 300 North St.* ☎*801/377–4386* ⊕*www.seven-peaks.com* ⊠*$21.95* ☉ *Memorial Day–Labor Day, Mon.–Sat. 11–8.*

Fishing is popular at **Utah Lake State Park,** which, at 96,600 acres, is the state's largest freshwater lake. In spring and fall the lake gets some of the best wind in Utah for windsurfing and sailing. You can also come here for boating—power boats to canoes. ⊠*4400 W. Center St.* ☎*801/375–0731 or 801/375–0733* ⊕*www.stateparks.utah.gov* ⊠*$9* ☉ *Daily.*

OFF THE BEATEN PATH

Springville Museum of Art. Springville, 10 mi south of Provo on I–15 or U.S. 89, is known for its support of the arts, and its museum is a must-stop for fine-arts fans. Built in 1937 to accommodate works by John Hasen and Cyrus Dallin, the museum now features mostly Utah artists, among them Gary Lee Price, Richard Van Wagoner, and James T. Harwood. It also has a collection of Soviet working-class impressionism. ⊠*126 E. 400 South St., Springville* ☎*801/489–2727* ⊕*www. sma.nebo.edu* ⊠*Free* ☉ *Tues., Thurs., Fri., and Sat. 10–5, Wed. 10–9, Sun. 3–6.*

SPORTS & THE OUTDOORS

BICYCLING In the Provo area, road cyclists may make a 100-mi circumnavigation of Utah Lake or tackle U.S. 189 through Provo Canyon or the Alpine Loop Scenic Byway. Mountain bikers can choose from a large selection of trails, varying in degrees of difficulty.

For information about biking in the area, bicycle sales, and world-class service, go to **Racer's Cycle Service** (⊠ *159 W. 500 North St., Provo* ☎ *801/375–5873* ⊕ *www.racerscycleservice.com*) and talk to owner "Racer" Jared Gibson.

GOLF You'll find 11 public courses within Utah Valley ranging from canyon or mountain settings to relatively flat and easy-to-walk terrain. Tee times are usually easy to get and greens fees are reasonable.

★ The canyon setting at **Hobble Creek Golf Course** (⊠ *Hobble Creek Canyon Rd. east of Springville* ☎ *801/489–6297*) makes for a beautiful day no matter how you play, particularly in fall when the hills explode with color. The 18 holes at the **Reserve at East Bay** (⊠ *1860 S. East Bay Blvd.* ☎ *801/373–6262*), near Utah Lake, give golfers a chance to meander along ponds and wetlands and to spot birds.

HIKING Visitors to the southern part of the Wasatch find many trails from which to choose. The easy, paved **Provo Parkway** meanders along the Provo River from the mouth of Provo Canyon and provides a good mix of shade and sun. The trailhead to **Bridal Veil Falls** is 2½ mi up Provo Canyon; after the moderate climb, hikers are rewarded with a cold mountain waterfall shower. The 100-mi **Bonneville Shoreline Trail** from Brigham City to Nephi spans the foothills of the Wasatch Front following the eastern shoreline of ancient Lake Bonneville. The section near Provo begins at the Rock Creek trailhead and continues south along the foothills, past the Y trailhead, to the Hobble Creek Parkway trailhead.

ICE-SKATING A 2002 Olympic Hockey venue, **Peaks Ice Arena** (⊠ *100 N. 7 Peaks Blvd.* ☎ *801/377–8777* ⊕ *www.peaksarena.com* ⊠ *$4*) includes two ice sheets and is open throughout the year for figure skating, hockey, and parties.

ROCK **American Fork Canyon,** 10 mi north of Provo in the Uinta National CLIMBING Forest, has northern Utah's best sport climbing, with dozens of fixed routes. The steep walls also offer face, slab, and crack climbs.

WATER Although Utah Lake, the state's largest freshwater lake, is 11 mi wide SPORTS and 24 mi long, it averages a scant 9 feet deep. Boating, sailing, windsurfing, and fishing are popular, but the cloudy water makes swimming questionable. On the east shore, **Utah Lake State Park** (⊠ *4400 W. Center St.* ☎ *801/375–0731*) is the best access point. In addition to three boat ramps, campgrounds, picnic areas, and a marina, the park has a wheelchair-accessible fishing area.

WHERE TO EAT

$$–$$$$ ✕ **The Chef's Table.** Owner-Chef Kent Andersen serves freshly made pastas, meat dishes, and seafood. The macadamia nut–crusted halibut and duck in tart cherry reduction sauce are popular choices, and the large wine list is impressive. An intimate atmosphere, and views of the Utah Valley and Wasatch Mountains through French windows, make this *the* place for a romantic meal in Orem. ⊠ *2005 S. State St., Orem* ☎ *801/235–9111* 🝢 *AE, D, DC, MC, V* ☺ *Closed Sun.*

$$$ ✕ **Tucanos.** Servers in this festive Brazilian grill come to your table with skewers of beef, poultry, pork, vegetables, and grilled pineapple, and they keep coming back until you can't eat any more. The atmosphere is more conducive to a party than to quiet, intimate dining. ⊠*4801 N. University Ave.* ☎*801/224–4774* ▭*AE, D, MC, V* ⊘*Closed Sun.*

¢–$$ ✕ **Los Hermanos.** In an old downtown Provo building, this long-standing Utah Valley favorite serves great Mexican food in a mazelike space with separate rooms and cubby tables. Favorites are the halibut Vera Cruz, grilled with a secret blend of spices and extra-virgin olive oil, and the spicy fajitas. ⊠*16 W. Center St.* ☎*801/375–5732* ▭*AE, D, DC, MC, V* ⊘*Closed Sun.*

¢–$ ✕ **Guru's.** An art-deco portrait of Gandhi decorates one wall of this downtown hippie refuge. Metal sculptures and blue skyscapes urbanize the good karma along with veggie-friendly fare. Try the Marco Polo pasta, any rice bowl, or a veggie burrito with a side of sweet potato fries. ⊠*45 E. Center St.* ☎*801/375–4878* ▭*AE, D, MC, V.*

¢ ✕ **Gandolfo's New York Deli.** In a basement location, just odd enough to
★ be interesting, Gandolfo's serves a good variety of thick sandwiches like the Bronx Barbecue or Brooklyn Bridge, all named after New York City spots. Gandolfo's is now a franchise, but this location is the original. ⊠*18 N. University Ave.* ☎*801/375–3354* ▭*AE, D, MC, V* ⊘*Closed Sun.*

WHERE TO STAY

$–$$ ▦ **Hines Mansion Bed & Breakfast.** Much of the original woodwork, brick, and stained glass has been left intact in this 1896 mansion, originally owned by one of the wealthiest residents of Provo. The well-lit rooms are decorated with period furniture and antique household items, and have two-person whirlpool tubs. **Pros:** Close to BYU. Antique furnishings. Welcome bottles of sparkling cider. **Cons:** Welcome bottles of sparkling cider (champagne isn't big in conservative Provo). ⊠*383 W. 100 South St., 84601* ☎*801/374–8400 or 800/428–5636* ▦*801/374–0823* ⊕*www.hinesmansion.com* ➿*9 rooms* ♿*In-room: no phone, DVD (some), VCR, Wi-Fi. In-hotel: no elevator, public Wi-Fi, parking, no kids under 18, no-smoking* ▭*AE, D, DC, MC, V* ⦿*BP.*

$ ▦ **Provo Marriott Hotel.** Close to downtown, this large hotel offers clean, upscale rooms and attentive service. Rooms and common areas have more sophisticated furnishings than many properties in this price range. The Seasons Lounge, one of Provo's few private clubs, is a great place to go for drinks and music. **Pros:** In the center of Provo. Standard chain amenities draw everyone from visiting athletic teams to business execs. **Cons:** Provo essentially shuts down on Sundays. ⊠*101 W. 100 North St., 84601* ☎*801/377–4700 or 800/777–7144* ▦*801/377–4708* ⊕*www.marriott.com* ➿*330 rooms, 6 suites* ♿*In-room: safe, kitchen (some), refrigerator (some), DVD (some), Ethernet, Wi-Fi. In-hotel: restaurant, room service, bar, pools, gym, laundry facilities, laundry service, concierge, executive floor, public Wi-Fi, parking, no smoking* ▭*AE, D, DC, MC, V.*

¢–$ ▦ **Provo Courtyard by Marriott.** This hotel faces the Wasatch Range near
★ BYU, so some of its rooms have mountain views. Friendly service, comfortable common areas, and touches like fresh fruit and warm cookies

in the evening give this chain a personal feel. **Pros:** All the standard necessities. Helpful staff. **Cons:** Location is convenient, but not as quaint as Provo's historic district. ✉*1600 N. Freedom Blvd., 84604* ☎*801/373–2222* 🖷*801/374–2207* ⊕*www.marriott.com* ⇖*94 rooms, 6 suites* &*In-room: Wi-Fi. In-hotel: restaurant, room service, bar, pool, gym, laundry facilities, public Wi-Fi, parking, no smoking* ▭*AE, D, DC, MC, V.*

NIGHTLIFE & THE ARTS

NIGHTLIFE Although Provo isn't completely "dry," the standards of BYU are evident in the city's dearth of nightlife options. Local bands, DJs, and karaoke keep things hopping at **Atchafalaya** (✉*210 W. Center St., off I–15 at the Center St. exit* ☎*801/373–9014*). The **Seasons Lounge** (✉*101 W. 100 North St.* ☎*801/377–4700*), in the Provo Marriott Hotel, is a casual gathering spot. The music is generally soft, making this a good place for quiet conversation.

THE ARTS Because **BYU** (☎*801/422–4322*) has a considerable interest in the arts, Provo is a great place to catch a play, dance performance, or musical production. BYU has a dozen performing groups in all. The BYU International Folk Dancers and Ballroom Dancers travel extensively, but also perform at home. The Deseret Chamber Music Festival takes place each May. Most performances are held in the **Harris Fine Arts Center,** which houses a concert hall, recital hall, and three theaters.

SHOPPING

Shopping in the Provo–Orem area centers around four primary areas. In addition to the malls, visitors find shopping opportunities at boutiques and galleries in downtown Provo, especially along Center Street.

★ The **Shops at Riverwoods** (✉*North University Ave. at the eastern extension of Orem's Center St.* ☎*801/802–8430*) is home to upscale retailers like Ann Taylor, Banana Republic, Eddie Bauer, and Williams-Sonoma. On the south end of Provo, the **Provo Towne Centre Mall** (✉*1200 S. University Ave.* ☎*801/852–2400*) has mainstream retailers like Dillard's and Sears, and specialty shops like Hallmark and Victoria's Secret. **University Mall** (✉*575 E. University Pkwy., Orem* ☎*801/224–0694*) caters to the needs of BYU students and departing missionaries with stores like Deseret Book and Mr. Mac, as well as standard retailers like Nordstrom, Macy's, and Mervyns.

SUNDANCE RESORT

Fodor'sChoice *12 mi northeast of Provo (51 mi south of Salt Lake City), off Rte. 92.*
★
Sundance Resort, set on the eastern slopes of the breathtaking 11,750-foot Mount Timpanogos, came into being when Robert Redford purchased the land in 1969. In concept and practice, the 5,000-acre mountain community reflects Redford's commitment to the natural environment, outdoor exploration, and artistic expression. All resort facilities—constructed from local materials such as indigenous cedar, fir, and pine, and locally quarried stone—blend well with the natural landscape. No matter the season, you'll find plenty of recreational

opportunities including hiking, biking, fly-fishing, horseback riding, alpine and cross-country skiing, snowboarding, and snowshoeing. If you're looking for a more indulgent experience, relax with a body treatment in The Spa at Sundance or take one of many creative classes at The Art Shack. The Sundance Film Festival, based in nearby Park City each January, is an internationally recognized showcase for independent films. Festival screenings and summer workshops are held at the resort. ✉ *North Fork Provo Canyon, Sundance* ☎ *801/225–4107 or 800/892–1600* 🖷 *801/226–1937* 🌐 *www.sundanceresort.com* ☞ *2150-ft vertical drop; 450 skiable acres; 20% novice, 40% intermediate, 40% advanced; 1 quad lift, 2 triple chairs, 1 surface lift* 🎫 *Lift tickets $45.*

SPORTS & THE OUTDOORS

CROSS-COUNTRY SKIING
Enjoy terrain suitable for all skill levels while cross-country skiing Sundance Resort's 24 km (15 mi) of groomed trails. Ten km (6 mi) of dedicated snowshoeing trails wind through mature aspen groves and pines. Lessons and equipment rentals, including telemark gear, are available for all techniques of cross-country skiing and snowshoeing.

SKIING
Skiers and snowboarders at Sundance Resort will find 450 acres of varied terrain. The mountain isn't big, but it does offer something for everyone and you'll almost never find a lift line here. The focus on a total experience, rather than just on skiing or snowboarding, makes this a delightful destination. Services include specialized ski workshops (including ladies' day clinics and personal coaching), a PSIA-certified ski school, and a ski school just for children with programs that include all-day supervision, lunch, and ski instruction. Children younger than four may enroll in private lessons; children older than four are eligible for group lessons. Rentals are available for all skill levels.

FLY-FISHING
The Provo River, minutes from Sundance Resort, is a fly-fishing catch-and-release waterway. Access to the rainbow and German brown trout found in the river is year-round. You can purchase the required fishing license in the general store at the resort; if you opt for a tour, equipment is provided.

HIKING
Hiking trails in the Sundance area vary from the easy 1.25-mi Nature Trail and the popular lift-accessed Stewart Falls Trail (3.1 mi), to the 7.4-mi Big Baldy Trail, which leads past a series of waterfalls up steep, rugged terrain. You can access moderate- to expert-level trails from the

resort base or chairlift. Select from three routes to summit the 11,000-foot Mount Timpanogos. Guided naturalist hikes are available.

MOUNTAIN
BIKING

You'll find more than 25 mi of ski-lift accessed mountain biking trails at Sundance Resort, extending from the base of Mount Timpanogos to Ray's Summit at 7,250 feet. High-tech gear rentals are available for full or half days, as is individual or group instruction. **Sundance Mountain Outfitters** (☎801/223–4849) has answers to your mountain biking questions.

WHERE TO STAY & EAT

$$$–$$$$
Fodor's Choice
★

✕ **Tree Room.** It's easy to imagine you're a personal guest of Robert Redford at this intimate, rustic restaurant with its exquisite collection of Native American art and Western memorabilia, and servers who look like they double as Sundance catalog models. Try the roasted Utah elk with celery root purée, baby beets, and wild mushroom jus or the seared tuna with Napa cabbage in a curried carrot broth. Or, let executive chef Mark Shoup put together a tasting menu for your whole table. ⊠*Sundance Resort, N. Fork Provo Canyon* ☎*801/223–4200* ▤*AE, D, DC, MC, V* ⊗*No lunch.*

★ $$–$$$$

✕ **Foundry Grill.** Wood-oven–baked pizzas, rotisserie rack of pork with sweet potato purée, and spit-roasted chicken are among the hearty staples served up at this restaurant. Like the rest of Sundance, everything here, from the food presentation to the decor to the staff, is natural, beautiful, and pleasant. They're open for breakfast, lunch, and dinner, and if you're here on the weekend, don't miss Sunday brunch. ⊠*Sundance Resort, N. Fork Provo Canyon* ☎*801/223–4220* ▤*AE, D, DC, MC, V.*

$$$$
Fodor's Choice
★

🖫 **Sundance Cottages.** All the cottages are connected by paths winding through old-growth pines, groves of aspen, and along clear mountain streams. Ranging in size from one to three bedrooms, the cottages reflect their woodland setting with rough-sawn beams, natural-wood trim, and richly textured, colorful fabrics; suites have a stone fireplace or woodstove, deck, and either full kitchen and dining area or kitchenette. There are also two- to five-bedroom mountain homes suitable for families or groups who want more space and privacy. Many rooms have large private baths, and some of the mountain homes have private hot tubs. All Sundance properties have the commercial-free Sundance Channel, showing award-winning feature films, documentaries, shorts, and international titles. **Pros:** The dramatic Mt. Timpanogos backdrop. Top-rated dining. Private, understated cottage luxury. Close to slopes, hiking trails. **Cons:** Even a cup of tea is expensive here. ⊠*Sundance Resort, North Fork Provo Canyon, 84604* ☎*801/225–4107 or 800/892–1600* 🖷*801/226–1937* ⊕*www.sundanceresort.com* ⇖*95 units, 11 mountain homes* ⟁*In-room: no a/c, kitchen (some), DVD, VCR. In-hotel: 2 restaurants, bar, spa, concierge, laundry service, parking, no smoking* ▤*AE, D, DC, MC, V* ⊚*BP.*

NIGHTLIFE & THE ARTS

NIGHTLIFE
★

Whether you feel like a quiet midday chess game, or a more lively atmosphere at night, the **Owl Bar** (⊠*Sundance Resort, N. Fork Provo Canyon* ☎*801/225–4107*) provides a good gathering space for guests and local clientele. Here you'll find live music on weekends and a healthy selection of beers and spirits to accompany a limited but satisfying menu. Classic photographs of Paul Newman and Robert Redford as Butch Cassidy and the Sundance Kid hang on the walls, and with the worn plank floors, stone fireplace, and original 1890s rosewood bar (said to have been favored by Cassidy's Hole-in-the-Wall Gang) transported from Thermopolis, Wyoming, you might just feel like cutting loose.

THE ARTS   The **Sundance Art Shack** (⊠ *Sundance Resort, N. Fork Provo Canyon* ☎ *801/223–4535 or 800/892–1600*) offers workshops in photography, jewelry making, wheel-thrown pottery, watercolor painting, and charcoal or pencil drawing. The philosophy that everyone has creative talent is not lost here, and all ages are encouraged to participate. Mirroring the Sundance ethic, these classes blend the natural world with artistic process. If you're interested in a more intensive artistic experience, inquire about three- and four-day Creative Retreats. All workshops and classes are open to resort guests as well as day visitors.

♻   The **Sundance Nature Center** (⊠ *Sundance Resort, N. Fork Provo Canyon* ☎ *801/223–4044 or 800/892–1600*), in operation year-round, offers a variety of programs that introduce you to the area's fauna and flora, as well as seasonal adventures designed to cultivate environmental awareness. Summer Kids Camps (ages 8–12) and workshops for all ages, like stargazing and nature journaling, reinforce the theme of nature and art. Guided naturalist programs are also available.

In January the Sundance Institute, a nonprofit organization supporting independent filmmaking, screenwriters, playwrights, composers, and other film and theater artists, presents the **Sundance Film Festival** (☎ *435/658–3456* ⊕ *www.sundance.org*). A world-renowned showcase for independent film, the 11-day Festival is based in Park City, but has screenings and workshops at Sundance Resort, Salt Lake City, and Ogden.

From mid-July through August, the **Utah Symphony** (☎ *801/355–2787 or 888/451–2787* ⊕ *www.utahsymphonyopera.org*), performs everything from Mozart to opera to Pops, in Sundance's spectacular outdoor amphitheater. Lodging, preconcert dining in the Foundry Grill or Tree Room, and reserved seating packages are available. If you'd rather dine while you listen, Gourmet Baskets are also available. Concerts start at 8 PM and you should arrive 30 minutes in advance. The temperature will drop quickly after sundown, so dress appropriately, in layers.

Throughout the year, the **Sundance Author Series** (⊠ *North Fork Provo Canyon, 84604* ☎ *801/223–4567* ⊕ *www.sundanceresort.com* ✉ *$95*) brings literary and political icons like Sue Monk Kidd and Jimmy Carter to the Tree Room for an intimate brunch and lecture. Call or check the Web site for the event schedule.

2

SHOPPING

The **General Store** (⌧*Sundance Resort, N. Fork Provo Canyon* ☎*801/223–4250*) is the inspiration for the award-winning Sundance catalog, with distinctive home furnishings, clothing, and jewelry reflecting the rustically elegant Sundance style.

Selling foods from American cottage farmers as well as homemade oils, soaps, and bath salts, the **Deli** (⌧*Sundance Resort, N. Fork Provo Canyon* ☎*801/223–4211*) also has a juice bar and is a good place to get tea, coffee, shakes, pastries, deli meats, organic produce, and other tasty snacks. Stop here before your hike to pick up a fresh sandwich.

HEBER VALLEY

20 mi south of Park City via U.S. 40; 22 mi northeast of Sundance via Rte. 92 south and Rte. 189 east.

Bound by the Wasatch Mountains on the west and the rolling foothills of the Uinta Mountains on the east, the Heber Valley, including the towns of Heber, Midway, and Charleston, is well supplied with snow in winter for cross-country skiing, snowmobiling, and other snow sports. Summers are mostly cool and green. Events throughout the year entertain locals as well as visitors.

A 60-car demolition derby is the popular kickoff for the weeklong **Wasatch County Fair** (☎*435/654–3227*) in August; a rodeo caps the action at the week's end.

In September, Midway's **Swiss Days** (☎*435/654–1271*) honor the town's original Swiss settlers with entertainment and contests. More than 300 gallons of sauerkraut are consumed during the two-day event.

☪ Following a line that first ran in 1899, a train ride on the **Heber Valley Historic Railroad** takes you on a nostalgic trip through beautiful Provo Canyon. Each car has been restored, and two of the engines—Number 618 and Number 75—are fully operational, steam-powered locomotives. The railroad offers special events, including comedy murder-mystery rides, the local favorite North Pole Christmas Train, "Raft and Rails" (pairing rafting with a train excursion), and "Tube and Train" (combining a train ride with snow tubing). ⌧*450 S. 600 West St., Heber City* ☎*435/654–5601* ⊕*www.hebervalleyrailroad.org* ⌧*Admission prices vary* ☉*Tues.–Sat. 9–5, Sun. 10–2.*

☪ **Wasatch Mountain State Park** (⌧*1281 Warm Springs Rd., Midway* ☎*435/654–1791, 800/322–3770, 435/654–0532 golf information* ⊕*www.stateparks.utah.gov* ⌧*$5 per car at campground for day use*), a 22,000-acre preserve, is 3 mi from Heber City. Visitors enjoy a number of activities ranging from serene hikes along winding mountain trails to golfing at one of the two 36-hole golf courses. Children have their own fishing pond near the visitor center, which also provides parking places. During winter, hiking turns to snowshoeing, cross-country or backcountry skiing along Dutch Hollow, Snake Creek, or Pine Creek trails winding up through stands of gambel oak, aspen, and maple.

Locals know the best time of year in the park is autumn when the mountainsides light up with deep crimson, ochre, and ruddy salmon-color leaves. On the southern end of the park is **Soldier Hollow** (⊠ *2002 Olympic Dr., Midway* ☎ *435/654–2002* ⊕ *www.soldierhollow.com*), venue for the 2002 Winter Olympic biathlon and cross-country events. Soldier Hollow is open to the public year-round for hiking, horseback riding, cross-country skiing, tubing, snowshoeing, biathlon, and other events. The City Slicker trails cater to beginner and intermediate skiers who may find the Olympic course daunting. A beautiful lodge has food concessions, equipment rentals, and a souvenir shop.

SPORTS & THE OUTDOORS

CROSS-COUNTRY SKIING
You can cross-country ski on the same trails as the 2002 Olympians at **Soldier Hollow** (⊠ *2002 Olympic Dr., Midway* ☎ *435/654–2002* ⊕ *www.soldierhollow.com*), which offers 33 km (21 mi) of groomed trails with cross-country ski lessons, lift-served tubing, and a dedicated trail system just for snowshoers. The **Homestead Resort** (⊠ *700 N. Homestead Dr., Midway* ☎ *435/654–1102 or 800/327–7220* ⊕ *www.homesteadresort.com*) has 12 km (7 mi) of groomed trails as well as cross-country ski and snowshoe rentals.

GOLF
The front nine at the **Homestead Resort** (⊠ *700 N. Homestead Dr., Midway* ☎ *435/654–1102 or 800/327–7220* ⊕ *www.homesteadresort.com*)gives you great views, while the back nine winds through Snake Creek Canyon. With a challenging 18-hole mountain course as well as a gentler 18-hole lake course, **Wasatch Mountain State Park** (⊠ *750 W. Snake Creek Rd., Midway* ☎ *435/654–0532* ⊕ *www.stateparks.utah.gov*) is one of the most popular public courses in the state. Reflecting the Olympic Heritage of **Soldier Hollow Golf Course** (⊠ *1371 W. Soldier Hollow La., Midway* ☎ *435/654–7442*), the names of the 18-hole courses are Gold and Silver. While on these greens, golfers enjoy the beauty of both the Heber Valley to the east and the stunning Mt. Timpanogos to the west. The Gold course is a typical mountain course with significant elevation changes; the Silver course is meadowland style with expanses of native grasslands separating the holes.

HIKING
The path connecting the towns of Heber and Midway is an easy walk with spectacular views of the Wasatch range at a distance and, up close, the Provo River. In **Wasatch Mountain State Park** (⊠ *1281 Warm Springs Rd., Midway* ☎ *435/654–0532* ⊕ *www.stateparks.utah.gov*)hikers will find lots of foliage and wildlife on any number of trails in Dutch Hollow, Pine Canyon, and along Snake Creek. While the trail system at **Soldier Hollow** (⊠ *2002 Olympic Dr., Midway* ☎ *435/654–2002* ⊕ *www.soldierhollow.com*) is more exposed than that in the northern end of Wasatch Mountain State Park, hikers will enjoy the stunning view of the east side of Mt. Timpanogos as well as the vista of the Uinta Mountains to the east across the Heber Valley. For a quiet experience start your hike from the Rock Cliff Nature Center, tucked into tall cottonwoods at the east end of **Jordanelle State Park** (⊠ *Hwy. 32, 10 mi east of Heber* ☎ *435/782–3030* ⊕ *www.stateparks.utah.gov*). Hikers often report excellent wildlife viewing along this section of the upper Provo River. No dogs are allowed.

2

HORSEBACK RIDING
Visitors can enjoy the spectacular setting of Wasatch Mountain State Park and surrounding areas on horseback year-round with **Rocky Mountain Outfitters** (☐ *Box 344, Heber City* ☎*435/654–1655* ⊕*www.rocky mountainoutfitters.com*). Choose from a variety of ride durations and destinations: from one- to four-hour rides, from summiting the Crow's Nest—an original hunting camp of the Ute Indian tribe—to strolling through meadows to a pioneer cabin for lunch.

WATER SPORTS
Consistently good fishing, mild canyon winds, and water warmer than you'd expect are responsible for **Deer Creek State Park's** popularity with windsurfers, sailboaters, swimmers, and those just kicking back in the mountain sunshine. ☒*U.S. 189, 5 mi south of Heber* ☎*435/654–0171* ⊕*www.stateparks.utah.gov* ☜*$9 day-use fee* ⊙*Daily 6 AM–10 PM.*

Jordanelle State Park has two recreation areas on a large mountain reservoir. The Hailstone area, 10 mi north of Heber City via U.S. 40, offers tent and RV camping and day-use areas. There are also boat ramps, a children's playground, a visitor center, and a marina store where water toys (wave runners and the like) can be rented. To the east, across the reservoir on Route 32, the Rock Cliff area and facilities are near the Provo River. This is a quiet part of the park known for excellent wildlife watching, particularly along a series of elevated boardwalks winding through the aspen forest. The 50 campsites here are all walk-ins. The Rock Cliff Nature Center provides interpretation of the area's rich natural history. ☒*Hwy. 32, 10 mi east of Heber* ☎*435/649–9540 Hailstone, 435/782–3030 Rock Cliff* ⊕*www.state parks.utah.gov* ☜*Hailstone $9 per vehicle, Rock Cliff $7 per vehicle* ⊙*May–Sept., daily 6 AM–10 PM; Oct.–Apr., daily 8–5.*

WHERE TO EAT

$$–$$$ ★
✕**Snake Creek Grill.** In a refurbished train depot at the end of the Heber Valley Historic Railroad, Chef Dean Hottle serves comfort food with a twist. Blue cornmeal–crusted red trout, 10-spice salmon with red curry Japanese noodles, and "Belle Isle" baby back ribs with mopping sauce are local favorites. Flowers fresh from the garden add to the elegant country ambience. Whatever you do, leave room for dessert; the black-bottom banana cream pie is to die for. ☒*650 W. 100 South St., Heber Valley* ☎*435/654–2133* ⍂*Reservations essential* ▭*AE, MC, D, V* ⊙*Closed late Apr.–mid-May and mid-Oct.–mid-Nov. Closed Sun.–Tues. No lunch.*

$$–$$$
✕**The Spicy Lady.** Spicy is a state of mind at this eclectic saloon-eatery, and the lounging dame in the giant oil painting above the bar seems to know it. The far-ranging "peasant" cuisine includes Japanese curry, toad in the hole, and goulash—all of which can be washed down with a whiskey or espresso. Live jazz fills the 1880s-era building on weekends. ☒*139 North Main St., Heber City* ☎*435/654–4288* ▭*AE, D, MC, V* ⊙*Closed Mon.*

☾ $–$$$
✕**Fanny's Grill.** Feed the ducks from the patio and enjoy the laid-back company of locals and golfers at one of Midway's original restaurants. Named in honor of Fanabelle Schneitter, whose father-in-law settled the Homestead in the 1800s, this simple eatery is open for three meals a day, serving a fine salmon sandwich, pork tenderloin, and brownie

sundae. ⊠*700 N. Homestead Dr., Box 99, Midway* ☎*435/654–1102* ⊟*AE, D, DC, MC, V.*

$ ✕**Tarahumara.** Note the lack of sombreros. Authentic art from the owner's Chihuahua hometown sets the genuine tone in this lively, self-serve restaurant, where locals lap up the carne asada, seared sea scallops with passion fruit, and other Mexican specialties. Take in a televised soccer game, and try to sample all 15 of the fresh salsas. ⊠*380 E. Main St., Midway* ☎*435/654–3465* ⊟*MC, V* ⊗*Closed Sun.*

☾ ¢   ✕**Dairy Keen.** A welcome respite from chain fast-food, this family-

Fodor'sChoice   owned drive-in serves the best shakes and burgers for miles around.

★   Train artifacts line the walls, and an electric train draws children's attention as it passes over the booths in continuous loops around the inside perimeter of the restaurant. ⊠*199 S. Main St., Heber Valley* ☎*435/654–5336* ⊟*AE, D, MC, V* ⊗*Closed Sun.*

WHERE TO STAY

$$–$$$$ 🏨 **Zermatt Resort & Spa.** Slightly Disney-esque in its re-creation of a Swiss-style estate, this sprawling hotel has everything from a wildlife-theme carousel to a full-service spa. The lederhosen-bedecked staff is friendly without being over-solicitous, the rooms feel both modern and chalet-style old world, and the mountain views are superb. With activities ranging from volleyball to miniature golf, there's something to keep the whole family entertained. **Pros:** Immaculate rooms with stellar views. Plenty to do. **Cons:** Ambiance can feel more theme park than authentically Swiss. ⊠*784 W. Resort Dr., Midway, 84049* ☎*435/657–0180* ⊕*www.zermatt.dolce.com* ➪*427 rooms* ⚐*In-room: safe, kitchen (some), refrigerator (some), Wi-Fi. In-hotel: 2 restaurants, room service, tennis, pool, gym, spa, laundry facilities, laundry service, children's programs* ⊟*AE, D, MC, V.*

$$–$$$ 🏨 **Blue Boar Inn.** Turrets, wrought-iron balconies, an antique alpenhorn, and the boar above the hearth give this château-style inn a warm, romantic feel. Each elegantly furnished room—named for a literary great—has fresh flowers, a fireplace, a jetted tub, and a cuddly "guard boar." Pop into the pub for a pint or play a round at the neighboring golf course. The views of the Wasatch Mountains are as impressive as the in-house chef's cuisine. **Pros:** Freshly made pastries. Hospitable staff. Peaceful, romantic ambiance. **Cons:** It's not the best place to bring the kids. ⊠*1235 Warm Springs Rd., Midway, 84049* ☎*435/654–1400 or 888/650–1400* ⊕*www.theblueboarinn.com* ➪*12 rooms* ⚐*In room: DVD, Wi-Fi. In-hotel: restaurant, bar, parking, no smoking* ⊟*AE, D, MC, V* ⦿*BP.*

★ $–$$$ 🏨 **Johnson Mill Bed & Breakfast.** The waterfall that turned giant grinding stones in the 1800s still flows beside the old mill, which has been renovated as a cozy inn. Implements used at the mill decorate guest rooms and the dining room, where a full breakfast is served. All rooms have fireplaces and jetted tubs. The 26-acre grounds with pathways past ponds and streams offer excellent bird-watching. **Pros:** Expansive grounds. Warm service. Cozy rooms with fireplaces. **Cons:** Location is a bit off the beaten path. ⊠*100 Johnson Mill Rd., Midway, 84049* ☎*435/654–4466 or 888/272–0030* 🖷*435/657–1454* ⊕*www.john sonmill.com* ➪*10 rooms* ⚐*In-room: no phone, refrigerator (some),*

DVD, VCR, Wi-Fi. In-hotel: parking, no kids, no-smoking rooms ⊟AE, D, MC, V ⟨○⟩*BP.*

★ $–$$ 🏨 **Homestead Resort.** Park City silver miners soaked in the hot springs of this resort, which has been in operation since 1886, and you can, too. Garden walkways lead between cottages and main buildings at this sprawling country retreat with a steamy, natural crater at its center. Rooms and common areas are decorated in traditional period furnishings. **Pros:** A Bruce Summerhays-designed golf course. There's both an Aveda spa and the natural hot springs. **Cons:** The only thing missing on-site is a ski hill. ⊠*700 N. Homestead Dr., Box 99, Midway, 84049* ☎*435/654–1102 or 800/327–7220* 🖷*435/654–5087* ⊕*www. homesteadresort.com* ↪*147 rooms* ♿*In-room: safe (some), kitchens (some), refrigerator (some), DVD (some), VCR (some), dial-up, Wi-Fi. In-hotel: 2 restaurants, bar, golf course, tennis courts, pools, gym, spa, laundry facilities, laundry service, public Wi-Fi, no-smoking rooms* ⊟*AE, D, DC, MC, V.*

OFF THE BEATEN PATH **Mirror Lake Highway.** East of Park City, this scenic byway winds through aspens and ponderosa pines, skirts alpine lakes and waterfalls and reaches 11,943-foot Bald Mountain. The ride is good, but getting out of the car is better. A spectacular hike is the five-mile, five-lake, Lofty Lake Loop, which starts at the Pass Lake Trailhead at mile 32. Keep an eye out for moose, wildflowers, and changeable weather. Reward yourself with turkey jerky from Samak Smoke House or a shake at Dick's, both located near the Wasatch-Cache National Forest's Kamas entrance. ⊠*$6 per car for a day pass* ⊕*www.fs.fed.us/r4/wcnf/unit/kamas* ☎*435/783–4338* ☉*road closed in winter, depending on snowfall.*

PARK CITY & THE SOUTHERN WASATCH ESSENTIALS

AIR TRAVEL
All commercial air traffic flies in and out of the Salt Lake International Airport, which is less than an hour from all destinations in the Wasatch and 7 mi northwest of downtown Salt Lake City. The airport is served by American, Continental, Delta, Northwest, Southwest, JetBlue, Frontier, Skywest, US Airways, and United. Provo and Heber have airports open to private planes only.

Information **Salt Lake City International Airport** (☎*801/575–2400*).

BUS TRAVEL
Greyhound Lines serves Provo. The Utah Transit Authority (UTA) has frequent service to all of Salt Lake Valley, Davis and Weber counties, and Utah Valley. UTA buses with ski racks make several runs a day from Salt Lake to ski areas in Little and Big Cottonwood canyons and from Provo to Sundance. UTA bus service from Salt Lake City to the ski resorts of Solitude, Brighton, Snowbird, or Alta, and from Provo to Sundance costs $3.50 each way; most other bus routes cost $1.75 per ride. In addition, several taxi and shuttle companies provide transportation between Salt Lake City and the ski resorts for about $65 round-

trip. A free, efficient Park City shuttle bus will take you between all the area resorts and hotels.

Bus Information All Resort Express (☎ *435/649–3999 or 800/457–9547* ⊕ *www.allresort.com*). **Canyon Transportation** (☎ *801/255–1841 or 800/255–1841* ⊕ *www.canyontransport.com*). **Greyhound Lines** (☎ *801/355–9579 or 800/231–2222* ⊕ *www.greyhound.com*). **Park City Transportation** (☎ *435/649–8567 or 800/637–3803* ⊕ *www.parkcitytransportation.com*). **UTA** (☎ *801/743–3882 or 888/743–3882* ⊕ *www.rideuta.com*).

CAR RENTAL

Most major car rental agencies have branches at the Salt Lake International Airport. Car rentals are also available in Provo and Park City.

Contacts All Resort Car Rental (☎ *435/649–3999 or 800/457–9457* ⊕ *www. allresort.com*). **Avis** (☎ *800/331–1212* ⊕ *www.avis.com*). **Dollar** (☎ *801/575–2580 or 800/800–4000* ⊕ *www.dollar.com*). **Enterprise** (☎ *801/537–7433 or 800/736–8322* ⊕ *www.enterprise.com*). **Hertz** (☎ *801/596–2670 or 800/654–7544* ⊕ *www.hertz.com*).

CAR TRAVEL

Highway travel around the region is quick and easy. The major routes in the area include I–80, which runs from Salt Lake City to Park City; and U.S. 40/189, which connects Park City to Heber City and Provo. Along larger highways, roadside stops with rest rooms, fast-food restaurants, and sundries stores are well spaced. Scenic routes and lookout points are clearly marked, enabling you to slow down and pull over to take in the views. Off the main highways, roads range from well-paved multilane blacktop routes to barely graveled backcountry trails. Watch out for wildlife on the highways. In rural and resort towns, expect gas prices to be considerably higher than in large cities.

Road Conditions Utah Highway Patrol, Mirror Lake area (☎ *435/655–3445*). **Utah Road Condition Information** (☎ *511 Salt Lake City area, 800/492–2400 within Utah*).

EMERGENCIES

Ambulance or Police Emergencies (☎ *911*).

Hospitals Heber Valley Medical Center (✉ *1485 S. Hwy. 40, Heber City* ☎ *435/654–2500*). **Park City Family Health and Urgent Care Center** (✉ *1665 Bonanza Dr., Park City* ☎ *435/649–7640*). **Utah Valley Regional Medical Center** (✉ *1034 N. 500 West St., Provo* ☎ *801/357–7850*).

WHERE TO STAY

CAMPING There are a number of wonderful campgrounds across the Wasatch–Cache National Forest. Between Big and Little Cottonwood canyons there are four higher-elevation sites. In the vicinity of Provo, American Fork, Provo Canyon, and the Hobble Creek drainage there are dozens of possibilities. Additional campgrounds are at the region's state parks and national monuments.

Sites range from rustic (pit toilets and cold running water) to posh (hot showers, swimming pools, paved trailer pads, full hookups). Fees vary, from $6 to $11 a night for tents and up to $35 for RVs, but are usually waived once the water is turned off for the winter. Site reservations are accepted at most campgrounds, but are usually limited to seven days (early birds reserve up to a year in advance). Campers who prefer a more remote setting may camp in the backcountry. You might need a permit, which is available from park visitor centers and ranger stations.

Information U.S. Forest Service (☎ *877/444–6777 reservations* ⊕ *www.recre ation.gov*). **Utah State Parks** (☎ *800/322–3770 reservations* ⊕ *www.stateparks. utah.gov*).

VISITOR INFORMATION

Alta Resort Association (✑ *Box 8031, Alta, 84092* ☎ *888/782–9258* ⊕ *www. altaresortassociation.com*). **Heber Valley County Chamber of Commerce** (✉ *475 N. Main St., Heber Valley, 84032* ☎ *435/654–3666* ⊕ *www.hebervalleycc.org*). **Mountainland Association of Governments** (✉ *586 E. 800 North St., Orem, 84097* ☎ *801/229–3800* ⊕ *www.mountainland.org/travel*). **Park City Chamber of Commerce–Convention and Visitors Bureau** (✑ *Box 1630, Park City, 84060* ☎ *435/649–6100 or 800/453–1360* ⊕ *www.parkcityinfo.com*). **Ski Utah** (✉ *150 W. 500 South St., Salt Lake City, 84101* ☎ *801/534–1779 or 800/754–8824* ⊕ *www.skiutah.com*). **Utah County Convention and Visitors Bureau** (✉ *111 S. University Ave., Provo, 84601* ☎ *801/851–2100 or 800/222–8824* ⊕ *www. utahvalley.org/cvb*).

North of Salt Lake City

WORD OF MOUTH

"When you get in the area of Bear Lake you will see signs for blueberry or raspberry milkshakes. Worth a stop!"

—cmcfong

Updated by
Jenie Skoy
and Jonathan
Stumpf

WHEN MOST PEOPLE THINK OF Utah, they picture the red rock crags and canyons of the south, but the north, with its cattail marshes and pasturelands framed by the gray cliffs of the Wellsville Mountains and the Bear River Range, has its own kind of beauty—without the throngs of tourists you'll encounter in the south.

Here the Shoshones (Sacagawea's tribe) made their summer camps, living on roots, berries, and the plentiful game of the lowlands. In the 1820s and '30s, mountain men came to trap beaver, fox, and muskrat, taking time out for their annual rendezvous on the shores of Bear Lake. Some, like the famous Jim Bridger, took Native

> **TOP REASONS TO GO**
>
> Powder Mountain—America's largest ski resort—is located within 30 minutes of downtown Ogden.
>
> The Hill Aerospace Museum displays over 70 past and present military aircraft.
>
> The annual Brigham City Peach Days: 30,000 attendees can't be wrong.
>
> Warm up or cool down in the natural cold and hot springs at Crystal Hot Springs.
>
> The George C. Eccles Dinosaur Park has broad family appeal.

American wives and settled here; to this day Cache, Rich, and Box Elder counties are collectively known as "Bridgerland." In the 1850s Mormon pioneers were sent by Brigham Young to settle here, and their descendants still populate this rugged land. In 1869 an event occurred here that would change the face of the West, and indeed the nation, forever: the Transcontinental Railroad was celebrated officially at Promontory Summit.

The region is characterized by alternating mountain ranges and valleys, typical of the Basin and Range geologic province that extends westward into Nevada and California. Much of the landscape has remained unspoiled, preserved for 100 years as part of the Wasatch-Cache National Forest. The four counties in this region—Weber, Cache, Rich, and Box Elder—offer a range of outdoor activities for all seasons: hiking, mountain biking, kayaking, skiing, snowmobiling, and birding are popular activities among the locals. The miles of trails here are relatively undiscovered by tourists, who usually head to southern Utah or the Wasatch Mountains east of Salt Lake for such activities.

The largest city north of Salt Lake City is Ogden, with more than 75,000 residents, many of whom live here for the easy-going outdoorsy lifestyle. Ogden offers a diverse selection of cultural and recreational activities and a good balance of urban life mixed with rural flavor. Farther north and roughly half the size of Ogden is the beautiful town of Logan, home to Utah State University and the Utah Festival Opera. Still, in the north of Utah as in the south, it's the landscape that steals the show. If you love a stroll through the backcountry, having breakfast with the locals at a small-town café, or exploring the legacy of the Old West, northern Utah may have a particularly strong appeal for you.

EXPLORING NORTHERN UTAH

Via two mountain ranges, Mother Nature has neatly divided northern Utah into three major sightseeing areas, each with its own attractions. Heading north up I–15 from Ogden (or, if you're in no hurry, up U.S. 89, where you'll find plenty of farm stands), you'll come upon the Golden Spike Empire. Pleasant farmlands in the shadow of the Wellsvilles give way to rolling sagebrush-covered hills and eventually the desolate salt flats of the Great Salt Lake. After a visit to the Bear River Migratory Bird Refuge and the Golden Spike National Historic Site, cut east through the Wellsvilles to Logan and the Cache Valley, soaking up the rural scenery along the way. You'll want to devote a day or two to the thriving college town of Logan, including a visit to the campus of Utah State University with its student-run anthropology museum that will give you a feel for the area's earliest inhabitants, and a stop at the Daughters of Utah Pioneers Museum downtown. About an hour up winding U.S. 89 through spectacular Logan Canyon—a destination in itself—you'll get your first view of startlingly turquoise-color Bear Lake, where the mountain men used to rendezvous. Carefully descend the hairpin curves into the Bear Lake Valley, and plop yourself down for a raspberry shake at one of the local drive-ins as you ponder your next activity—most likely swimming, boating, or fishing the lake's cool waters, or perhaps biking its shoreline. From here, it's just a few hours—about 300 mi—to the Grand Tetons and Yellowstone National Park—but that's another guidebook. If you head back toward Salt Lake City, take at least a couple of hours to recharge yourself at Crystal Hot Springs at Honeyville.

ABOUT THE RESTAURANTS

Both Ogden and Logan have fine restaurants, but in general, the fare in northern Utah is your basic Western-style grub. If your idea of a nice meal out is a big slab of meat that was on the hoof a few days ago and a giant Idaho potato, then you're in luck. If you can't look at another steak, there's at least one decent Mexican or Chinese place in every sizeable town. Do sample the Aggie ice cream made at Utah State University and the Cache Valley Swiss cheese.

ABOUT THE HOTELS

Some reputable chains have made their way here, along with interesting family-owned hostelries and B&Bs in a full range of prices. At Bear Lake, you can rent a condo with kitchen facilities if you feel like putting down roots for a while. Reservations are recommended on summer weekends and holidays; otherwise, you should have no problem exploring your options once you get here.

WHAT IT COSTS					
	¢	$	$$	$$$	$$$$
RESTAURANTS	under $8	$8–$12	$13–$18	$19–$25	over $25
HOTELS	under $70	$70–$110	$111–$150	$151–$200	over $200

Restaurant prices are for a main course at dinner, excluding sales tax of 6%–7%. Hotel prices are for two people in a standard double room in high season, excluding service charges and 6%–7% tax.

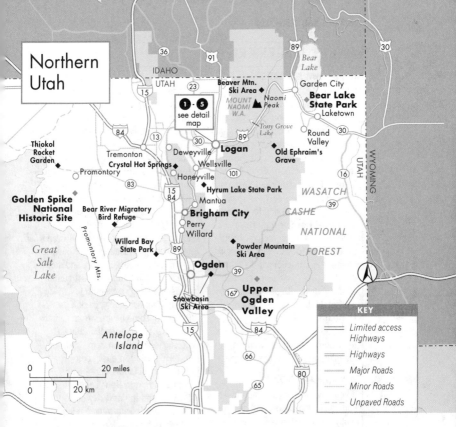

Northern Utah

KEY

═══	Limited access Highways
──	Highways
──	Major Roads
····	Minor Roads
─ ─ ─	Unpaved Roads

TIMING

Unless you're an avid skier, snowshoer, or snowmobiler (in which case you'll find a frozen paradise of ski resorts and trails), you'll probably want to avoid northern Utah in winter, when the mercury can dip below zero for weeks at a time. The other three seasons are beautiful here: spring brings vistas of verdant pastures under the still snow-capped mountains; hot summer afternoons prepare you for a dip in Bear Lake followed by an evening at the Festival Opera; on crisp fall days breathtaking hues of red scrub oak, orange maple, and bright yellow aspen rub shoulders with the blue-green firs. You'll never battle hordes of tourists in this less-discovered part of the state, but you might have to wait in a line of locals for a raspberry shake at Bear Lake on a hot summer weekend.

OGDEN

35 mi from Salt Lake City via I–15 north.

As the Wasatch Front population continues to swell, it's harder to tell where Salt Lake City ends and the next major city, Ogden, begins. In between are a string of towns that serve primarily as bedroom communities. The drive north, through and beyond these communities, bor-

GREAT ITINERARIES

IF YOU HAVE 3 DAYS

Make a quick tour of the attractions in **Ogden** on the morning of Day 1 and then drive north on I–15 to Perry for lunch at the Maddox Ranch House. After lunch head west on Route 83 to **Golden Spike National Historic Site**. When you've had your fill of railroad history, get back on Route 83 heading east and make your way to Honeyville for a cleanse at **Crystal Hot Springs**. Head back north to **Logan**, where you'll settle for the night. Day 2 finds you poking around the attractions in town or on the Utah State University campus, after which you'll pack a lunch for a leisurely drive up Logan Canyon to **Bear Lake State Park**; get a motel or find a campsite and spend the next day boating, swimming, or lounging on Rendezvous Beach.

IF YOU HAVE 5 DAYS

If you have five days in the area, you could skip Ogden and get to the really good stuff. Travel north from Ogden on I–15, exit onto U.S. 89 north and cruise the fruit stands for seasonal delicacies. Enjoy a buffalo steak at Maddox Ranch House on your way to relaxation at **Crystal Hot Springs** before settling in for a laid-back night in **Brigham City**. Spend Day 2 exploring the **Bear River Migratory Game Bird Refuge** and the **Golden Spike National Historic Site**; be sure to pack your lunch because food isn't available here. On Day 3 head northeast to **Logan**, to check out the sites and take in some museums, walk down the tree-lined back streets, and stop at the Bluebird, Utah's oldest continuous operating restaurant, for an ice cream treat. On Day 4, pack a picnic (including some pastries from Crumb Brothers Artisan Bread) and drive up Logan Canyon for some hiking or biking. You can easily enjoy most of the day outdoors here before continuing on to **Bear Lake State Park**. Spend the next day exploring more scenic hiking trails or simply relaxing on the picturesque beaches of Bear Lake.

dered by the shores of the Great Salt Lake on the west and the Wasatch Mountains on the east, takes you through a world of recreational options. With a population of more than 75,000, Ogden combines a small-town feel with the infrastructure of a larger city. The oldest town in Utah, Ogden was founded by mountain man Miles Goodyear, who settled here with his family in the early 1840s. The Mormons arrived in the area in 1847 and in 1869 Ogden became a hub for the Transcontinental Railroad. The city quickly became a major Western crossroads. During World War II there was a considerable military presence here. This continues today, thanks to the proximity of Hill Air Force Base. Ogden is also a college town; Weber State University is within the city limits.

These days, Ogden has become a multisport mecca, where outdoor adventure blends with emerging urban chic. You can head east into the Upper Ogden Valley—only 20 minutes from downtown—for climbing, biking, hiking, and world-class skiing, or paddle the kayak park on the Ogden River. After your adrenaline binge, recharge in the historic 25th Street district, the metropolitan complement to this recreation-

IF YOU LIKE	

SMALL-TOWN LIFE

"Welcome to Utah; set your clocks back 50 years," the local kids say with a smirk, but in fact this is one of the charms of living here. With its friendly folk, low crime rate, and traditions dating back to the pioneers, Utah offers a glimpse of what the rest of the country was like during the Eisenhower years. Nowhere is this more evident than in the north, unjaded as it is by either the tourist throngs of the south or the big-city problems that are starting to plague Ogden and Salt Lake. Although there is plenty to see and do on the tourist beat, you'll enjoy your stay even more if you mingle with the natives at one of the myriad town festivals that dot the calendar throughout the summer and fall, from Mendon's May Day to Paradise's Trout and Berry Days. Check the local newspapers and do a little time-traveling while you're here.

VIEWING WILDLIFE

If you're willing to get out of your car and walk a bit, your chances of encountering wildlife in northern Utah are about 100%. Even from your car you're likely to spot mule deer, moose, elk, coyotes, or bobcats, especially around dawn or dusk (so drive vigilantly, especially in the mountains—many a visitor's trip has been ruined by a collision with an animal). Because of the varied topography—everything from marshes to deserts to mountains—northern Utah has an astounding variety of bird life, and birders come from all over the country to fill out their life lists. To learn about northern Utah wildlife, plan a visit to the Stokes Nature Center in Logan.

heavy stronghold. During the railroad heyday, 25th Street, directly east of the railroad depot, was infamous for its bars and bordellos. The buildings that once contained all the notorious businesses have been preserved and now house restaurants, clubs, crafts and antiques shops, and kitchen stores.

Fodor's Choice ★ Incorporating elements of Ogden's original 1870s train depot, which was destroyed by fire in 1923, the impressive Spanish Revival **Union Station** (built in 1924) houses five museums, two art galleries, a restaurant, gift shop, and visitor center.

The **Browning Firearms Museum** showcases John M. Browning's gun inventions, many of which were built by Winchester, Colt, Remington, and others to become the firearms of choice in the Old West before Browning formed his own company. Original models and working prototypes of many of these weapons are displayed. Gun aficionados will feel like they're in a candy store.

At the **Browning-Kimball Car Museum,** almost 60 unique, restored cars are on display, including a single-cylinder 1901 Oldsmobile and a Cadillac that weighs 3 tons.

Learn about the Great Salt Lake and surrounding areas at the **Natural History Museum,** which displays a collection of Utah trilobites, fossilized wood and plants, and records of paleontological and aquatic life forms.

The **Utah State Railroad Museum** has well-documented exhibits that explain all phases of Utah's railroad history through displays and interpretive signs. You can also watch model trains run through depictions of the Transcontinental Railroad route. The high point of the museum is the Eccles Rail Center, an outdoor exhibit of several dozen restored train cars, engines, and cabooses that date from the late 1800s up to the 2002 Olympic Games cauldron car. ⊠*2501 Wall Ave.* ☎*801/393–9886* ⊕*www.theunionstation.org* ✉*Combined ticket to all 5 museums $5* ⊙*Mon.–Sat. 10–5.*

★ In an impressive Victorian mansion, the **Eccles Community Art Center** has a permanent collection of works by such contemporary artists as LeConte Stewart, Henri Mosher, Pilar Pobil, David Jackson, and Richard Van Wagoner. There is also a sculpture garden; special exhibits change periodically, and there are monthly displays of works by emerging Utah artists. ⊠*2580 Jefferson Ave.* ☎*801/392–6935* ⊕*www.ogden4arts.org* ✉*Free* ⊙*Weekdays 9–5, Sat. 9–3.*

Ở The 5-acre **George S. Eccles Dinosaur Park,** near the mouth of Ogden Canyon, is the stomping grounds for about 100 dinosaur models and the delighted children who come to see them. But be prepared for realism in the form of the bloody teeth of a tyrannosaurus and the remains of its dinner on the ground. A playground with dinosaurs to crawl on is a lure for the younger set. ⊠*1544 E. Park Blvd.* ☎*801/393–3466* ⊕*www.dinosaurpark.org* ✉*$6* ⊙*Memorial Day–Labor Day, Mon.–Sat. 10–8, Sun. noon–6; Labor Day–Memorial Day, Mon.–Sat. 10–6, Sun. noon–6.*

★ Ở If you like airplanes old or new you'll love the **Hill Aerospace Museum,** south of downtown Ogden near the Hill Air Force Base. Among the many planes housed here is a SR-71 Blackbird (a reconnaissance aircraft that made a transatlantic flight in less than two hours), a B-17 Flying Fortress, and a P-51 Mustang. ⊠*Hill Air Force Base, Exit 338 off I–15* ☎*801/777–6868* ⊕*www.hill.af.mil/library/museum* ✉*Free* ⊙*Daily 9–4:30.*

★ Ở As one of very few wildlife sanctuaries set within a city, the 152-acre **Ogden Nature Center** is home to thousands of trees, marshlands, and ponds, with nature trails used for cross-country skiing in winter. You can see Canadian geese, great blue herons, red-tailed hawks, and snowy egrets, as well as red foxes, mule deer, porcupines, and more. The nature center museum has activities for children, and the Nest gift shop sells nature-oriented items. ⊠*966 W. 12th St.* ☎*801/621–7595* ⊕*www.ogdennaturecenter.org* ✉*$3* ⊙*Weekdays 9–5, Sat. 9–4.*

In downtown Ogden the **Ogden River Parkway** runs for 3 mi to the mouth of Ogden Canyon. This urban greenway is perfect for fishing, biking, strolling, running, or playing tennis or baseball. The trail takes you past botanical gardens, pavilion facilities, a swimming pool, a skateboard park, the Eccles Dinosaur Park, and rodeo grounds. ⊠*1544 E. Park Blvd.* ✉*Free.*

3

The massive **Salomon Center at The Junction,** located in a former downtown mall, is a high-adventure recreational playground, complete with a climbing wall, wave pool, wind tunnel, bowling alley, miniature golf, and 13-theater movie complex. ✉*2261 Keisel Ave.* ☎*801/528–5348* ⊕*www.salomoncenter.com* ⬜*Admission varies* ⊘*Call for hours.*

Offering a hands-on learning experience, the **Treehouse Museum** downtown features interactive exhibits for kids ages two–12. Children can visit a replica of the president's Oval Office, "travel" (through a storybook) to countries like Kenya or Russia, and watch—or participate in—plays in the theater. ✉*347 22nd Ave.* ☎*801/394–9663* ⊕*www. treehousemuseum.org* ⬜*$5* ⊘*Mon. 10–4, Tues.–Thurs. and Sat. 10– 6, Fri. 10–8.*

SPORTS & THE OUTDOORS

More than 250 mi of trails for hiking, mountain biking, and horseback riding surround the Ogden area, and the scenic roads are perfect for road biking. The Weber and Ogden rivers provide high-adventure rafting and kayaking and even a free downtown white-water park. Eleven public courses await golfers, and Olympic-caliber skiing is just up the canyon.

GOLF   The 18-hole **Ben Lomond Golf Course** (✉*1800 N. Rte. 89, Harrisville* ☎*801/782–7754*) has a serene setting with Wasatch Mountain views.

While playing 18 holes at the **Mount Ogden Golf Course** (✉*1787 Constitution Way* ☎*801/629–0699*), try not to let the stunning view of Ogden Valley distract you.

Just minutes from downtown Ogden, the 18 holes of the **Schneiter's Riverside Golf Course** (✉*5460 S. Weber Dr.* ☎*801/399–4636*) wind along the scenic Weber River.

For complete information about Ogden area golf courses, contact the **Ogden Convention and Visitors Bureau** (☎*866/867–8824* ⊕*www.ogden. travel*).

HIKING   From an urban stroll along the Ogden River Parkway to a challenging hike on the Beus Canyon Trail to the summit of Mount Ogden, hikes in the Ogden area provide something for everyone. Most of the trail system is connected in some way to the North–South Bonneville Shoreline Trail, a pathway following the high mark of the prehistoric Lake Bonneville along the Wasatch Front. An excellent resource for detailed trails information is **Weber Pathways** (☎*801/393–2304* ⊕*www.weber pathways.org*), a local nonprofit organization dedicated to preserving and maintaining nonmotorized pathways in Weber County.

RAFTING   Located on the Weber River at Exchange Road and 24th Street, **Ogden's Kayak Rodeo Park** (⊕*www.ogden.travel/visitors_outdoor_kayak.asp* ⬜*Free*)offers great rides for kayakers and thrilling action for spectators.For a white-water adventure the whole family can enjoy, try rafting the Weber River on a tour with **Park City Rafting** (✉*1105 N. Taggert La., Morgan* ☎*435/655–3800* ⊕*www.parkcityrafting.com* ⊘*Mid-*

May–mid-Sept.). The relatively gentle two-hour trip ($35 per person) is a great way to experience a rugged canyon, and there are several mild rapids (Class II–III) for excitement. All equipment is provided.

WHERE TO EAT

$$–$$$$ ✕ **Gray Cliff Lodge Restaurant.** Set in scenic Ogden Canyon, this local favorite features Utah trout, prime rib, lamb, and seafood. Lace tablecloths, linen napkins, and a wall of windows offering views of mountains and forests create a quiet, romantic atmosphere. ⊠ *508 Ogden Canyon* ☎ *801/392–6775* ═ *AE, D, MC, V* ⊘ *Closed Mon. No lunch Tues.–Sat.*

$$–$$$$ ✕ **Prairie Schooner.** Desert sand covers the floor, and each table is enclosed in a covered wagon at this Western-style steak house. Although the setting may be a bit much for some, the steak and seafood specialties are top quality. The French dip and other sandwiches give the menu a lighter side. ⊠ *445 Park Blvd.* ☎ *801/621–5511* ⊕ *www.prairieschoonerrestaurant.com* ═ *AE, D, MC, V* ⊘ *No lunch weekends.*

★ $–$$$$ ✕ **Bistro 258.** The decor in this 25th Street hot spot wouldn't be out of place in Manhattan, though the attitude is decidedly laid-back. Brothers Devin and Nick Cash design and prepare upscale fare such as orange chili chicken, pan-seared mahi-mahi, and gorgonzola-balsamic New York steak. For lunch try the curry chicken rice bowl or the creamy pesto tortellini. The outdoor patio and glassed-in back dining area are more casual than the front section accessed from 25th Street. Servers are friendly and offer smart suggestions from the brief but well-appointed wine list. ⊠ *258 25th St.* ☎ *801/394–1595* ═ *AE, D, MC, V* ⊘ *Closed Sun.*

$–$$$ ✕ **Rooster's.** On historic 25th Street, this brewpub is set in a 104-year-
★   old building that was once a Chinese laundry. The pub offers excellent food and libations brewed on-site. Pizzas, steak, and daily seafood specials are popular, as is the herb-crusted rack of lamb. Wash down your meal with a Polygamy Pale Ale or any of the brewmaster's specials, which vary by season. On a sunny day ask for a seat on the patio, which is partly glass-enclosed for year-round seating and makes for a lovely spot to enjoy Sunday brunch. ⊠ *253 25th St.* ☎ *801/627–6171* ⊕ *www.roostersbrewingco.com* ═ *AE, D, DC, MC, V.*

$–$$$ ✕ **Union Grill.** Overlooking the train tracks, this is a great refueling spot when you're museum-hopping at historic Union Station. The menu ranges from mozzarella sandwiches to steak; the service is friendly and casual if occasionally rushed. Save room for the caramel bread pudding. ⊠ *2501 Wall Ave.* ☎ *801/621–2830* ═ *AE, MC, V* ⊘ *Closed Sun.*

⟳ ¢–$$ ✕ **The Greenery.** It's hard to tell if this black- and white-tile riverside restaurant is deliberately kitschy or trying to be one version of authentic Utah, but if a Mormon muffin, ham-it-up sandwich, or homemade caramel apple pie suit your fancy, this is the place. After lunch or dinner browse the thousands of square feet of trinkets, souvenirs, and books at Rainbow Gardens *(⇨ Shopping, below)* next door for just the right piece of Utah to take with you. ⊠ *1875 Valley Dr.* ☎ *801/392–1777* ═ *AE, D, MC, V.*

WHERE TO STAY

$–$$$ 🏨**Ogden Marriott.** Ogden's largest hotel downtown is close to government offices and corporate headquarters for the aerospace industry. It's also within walking distance of historic 25th Street shopping, dining, and nightlife. Relax in one of the spacious rooms, elegantly appointed with mahogany furniture and rich, classic fabrics in complementing florals and stripes. **Pros:** Convenient downtown location. Modern facilities. **Cons:** No in-room Wi-Fi. Prices can be significantly higher on weekdays than on weekends. ✉*247 24th St., 84401* ☎*801/627–1190 or 800/421–7599* 📠*801/394–6312* 🌐*www.marriott.com* 🛏*257 rooms, 35 suites* 🔑*In-room: refrigerator (some), Ethernet. In-hotel: restaurant, bar, pool, gym, laundry facilities, concierge, public Wi-Fi, parking, no-smoking rooms* 🔲*AE, D, DC, MC, V.*

★ $–$$ 🏨**Hampton Inn and Suites.** Gray marble floors, deep-purple chairs, and ornate crown-molded ceilings greet you in the lobby of this art deco beauty. Designed in the Chicago style by architect Leslie S. Hodgson and completed in 1913 as an office center, the building sat vacant for years before it was restored and opened as a hotel in 2002. **Pros:** Huge rooms, updated decor. **Cons:** No fridges in many rooms. ✉*2401 Washington Blvd., 84401* ☎*801/394–9400 or 866/426–7866* 📠*801/394–9500* 🌐*www.ogdensuites.hamptoninn.com* 🛏*124 rooms, 21 suites* 🔑*In-room: refrigerator (some), Ethernet. In-hotel: gym, laundry facilities, laundry service, public Wi-Fi* 🔲*AE, D, DC, MC, V* 🍴*CP.*

$ 🏨**Comfort Suites of Ogden.** Decorated with a Southwestern motif, this is Ogden's only all-suites hotel. Clean well-maintained suites, easy freeway access, and a more-than-adequate list of amenities and services make this a good choice for business or vacation travelers. In warm weather you can unwind playing volleyball or basketball at the outdoor sports court. **Pros:** Nice price, nicer suites. **Cons:** Location is not close to downtown. ✉*2250 S. 1200 West St., 84401* ☎*801/621–2545 or 800/462–9925* 📠*801/627–4782* 🌐*www.ogdencomfortsuites.com* 🛏*144 suites* 🔑*In-room: refrigerator, Ethernet, Wi-Fi. In-hotel: restaurant, bar, pool, gym, laundry facilities, laundry service, public Wi-Fi, some pets allowed* 🔲*AE, D, DC, MC, V* 🍴*BP.*

NIGHTLIFE & THE ARTS

NIGHTLIFE At the height of the railroad era, Ogden's 25th Street housed a bawdy nightlife scene complete with saloons and gambling halls, opium dens, and a thriving red-light district. The area has gentrified since then, but it's still the center of one of Utah's most vibrant nightlife scenes. Beyond 25th Street you'll find good live music and dance clubs spread throughout the city.

★ At **Brewskis** (✉*244 25th St.* ☎*801/394–1713* 🌐*www.brewskisonline. net*), big-screen TVs, pool tables and arcade games, and pub fare such as Italian sandwiches and pizzas often draw a college crowd. Anyone (older than 21) who enjoys good music will love it here on weekends, when national acts ranging from country to punk rock take the stage.

Filled with Beatles memorabilia, the **City Club** (✉*264 25th St.* ☎*801/392–4447*) caters to an upscale thirtysomething crowd. The John Lennon and Yoko Ono bathrooms are worth a visit.

At **Kamikazes** (✉2404 Adams Ave. ☎801/621–9138), in a former church, you can dance to live music on one floor and to DJ tunes on another, or play pool. For two-stepping or line dancing, try the **Outlaw** (✉1254 W. 21st St. ☎801/334–9260 ⊕www.outlawsaloon.com). Stand-up comedians perform Friday and Saturday at **Wiseguys Comedy Café** (✉269 25th St. ☎801/622–5588 ⊕www.wiseguyscomedy.com).

THE ARTS   Local and regional performing artists give free outdoor concerts Tues-
★   days at noon and Wednesday nights, June through August, at the **Ogden Amphitheater** (✉Municipal Gardens, 25th St. and Washington Blvd. ☎801/629–8000 ⊕www.ocae.org). The amphitheater also hosts free outdoor movies on Monday nights, June through August.Built in the 1920s then abandoned for years, the **Peery Egyptian Theater** (✉2415 Washington Blvd. ☎801/395–3200 ⊕www.peerysegyptiantheater. com)is a restored art deco jewel that hosts concerts ranging from world music to national blues, jazz, and country acts, as well as an ongoing film series. The theater also shows screenings and premieres during the Sundance Film Festival in January.The first Friday of each month more than 20 downtown galleries and artists show off their wares at the **Street Stroll** (✉Downtown Ogden ☎801/393–3866), which begins at the Gallery at the Station, Union Station, and ends at the Eccles Community Art Center on the corner of 26th and Jefferson streets.

Enjoy live music, art, and food stalls on Saturday, July through October, at the **25th Street Farmers' & Art Market** (✉25th St. and Municipal Park ☎801/629–8253 ⊕www.ogden.travel/events_farmers.asp). **Weber State University** (✉3750 Harrison Blvd. ☎801/626–6000 ⊕www.weber.edu) regularly offers theater, music, and dance performances by students and visiting artists at the Val A. Browning Center for the Performing Arts, home stage for the Ogden Symphony Ballet Association.

SHOPPING

As with nightlife and dining, you'll find the most interesting concentration of shops on historic 25th Street with a couple of don't-miss shopping stops scattered around the rest of town. Needlepointers from all over the West acclaim the **Needlepoint Joint** (✉241 25th St. ☎801/394–4355)as the best place around to find patterns, yarn, and thread.

The **Bookshelf** (✉2432 Washington Blvd. ☎801/621–4752) is a book lover's dream. Knowledgeable salespeople will point you to the latest titles or to dusty shelves stuffed with used and rare books.

If you're looking for a gift that says Utah, **Rainbow Gardens** (✉1851 Valley Dr. ☎801/621–1606), at the mouth of Ogden Canyon, is the place. More than 20 departments offer souvenirs, cowboy nostalgia, books, baskets, gadgets, and country accessories.

UPPER OGDEN VALLEY

8 mi east of Ogden City.

Locals call it "the valley," as if it were the only valley in the world. It's sleepy and slow and if it had sidewalks they'd roll them up early, but once you see the valley, anchored by Pineview Reservoir, surrounded by the spectacular Wasatch Mountains, and inhabited by the quaint pioneer towns of Eden and Huntsville, you'll see why residents feel this way. With its world-class skiing, accessible water sports, great fishing, golf, climbing, hiking, biking, and camping, the Upper Ogden Valley is a recreation mecca still largely waiting to be discovered.

Thousands of marathon runners kick off the special events season in May with the **Ogden Marathon** (☎ *801/399–1773* ⊕ *www.ogdenmara thon.com*), which starts in the Upper Ogden Valley and follows Ogden Canyon down to the center of Ogden City.

Late August and fall colors bring the **Ogden Valley Balloon Festival** (✉ *3201 N. Wolf Creek Dr., Wolf Creek Resort, Eden* ☎ *801/745– 9591* ⊕ *www.ogdenvalleyballoonfestival.com*), three days of hot-air balloon launches, music, homemade crafts, art, and food vendors.

Just beyond the mouth of Ogden Canyon, the mountains open up to make room for **Pineview Reservoir.** In summer this 2,000-acre lake is festooned with colorful sailboats and the graceful arcs of water-ski-ers. The fishing is good, and beaches, campgrounds, and marinas dot the shore. Anderson Cove, on the lake's southern end, is popular, as is Middle Inlet, on the eastern shore. ✉ *Rte. 39 east to Upper Ogden Valley* ☎ *801/625–5306* ⊕ *www.fs.fed.us/r4/wcnf* 🖱 *$8* ☉ *Daily, dawn–dusk.*

SPORTS & THE OUTDOORS

CROSS-COUNTRY SKIING
Wolf Creek Resort (✉ *3900 N. Wolf Creek Dr., Eden* ☎ *801/745–3737 or 877/492–1061* ⊕ *www.wolfcreekresort.com*) allows cross-country skiers to ski on its golf course in winter.

Weber County Parks and Recreation grooms 8 km (5 mi) of cross-country and snowshoe trails at **North Fork Park** (✉ *North end of Ogden Valley off Rte. 39* ☎ *801/399–8491*).

SKIING
Utah's smallest ski resort, **Wolf Mountain** is a good place to go if you're not quite ready for the high-powered mountains. A great place to learn, this family-oriented resort also offers the most affordable skiing and riding in the state, and the whole mountain is lighted for night skiing. Opening days and hours can be sporadic so it's a good idea to call before you go. ✉ *3657 E. Nordic Valley Way, Eden* ☎ *801/745–3511* ⊕ *www.wolfmountaineden.com* ☉ *Daily Dec.–Apr.* ☞ *1,000-ft verti-cal drop; 100 skiable acres; 30% beginner, 50% intermediate, 20% advanced; 2 double chairs, 1 triple chair* 🖱 *Lift tickets $22–$26.*

Rising north out of Ogden Canyon is **Powder Mountain.** As the name suggests, it receives a generous helping of the white stuff for which Utah is famous. This classic ski resort offers huge terrain (more skiable acres than any other resort in the country) even though it doesn't have as many lifts as some of the destination resorts, and has two terrain parks and a half-pipe. You won't find fancy lodges or haute cuisine here, but crowds are nonexistent and four laid-back slope-side eateries serve everything from scones and hot soup to sandwiches or a flame-broiled Powder Burger at the Powder Keg. ✉ *800 N. 5100 East, Rte.*

158, Eden ☎*801/745–3772* ⊕*www.powdermountain.com* ☞*2,205-ft vertical drop; 5,500 skiable acres; 25% beginner, 40% intermediate, 35% advanced; 2 quad chairs, 1 triple chair, 1 double chair, 3 surface lifts* 🎫*Lift tickets $53.*

A vertical drop of 2,959 feet and a dramatic start at the pinnacle of Mount Ogden made **Snowbasin** the perfect site for the downhill ski races during the 2002 Olympic Winter Games. With nine lifts accessing more than 2,800 acres of skiable terrain, this is one of Utah's largest resorts. Snowbasin shares the same massive log lodges and state-of-the-art lifts and snowmaking as its more established sister resort, Sun Valley in Idaho. There are no overnight accommodations. ✉*Rte. 226, 17 mi from Ogden, Huntsville* ☎*801/399–1135 or 888/437–5488* ⊕*www.snowbasin.com* ☞*2,959-ft vertical drop; 2,820 skiable acres; 7% beginner, 30% intermediate, 67% advanced; 2 high-speed gondolas, 1 tram, 1 high-speed quad chair, 4 triple chairs, 1 double chair, 3 surface lifts* 🎫*Lift tickets $58.*

If you're staying in Ogden and want to head for the mountains for a day of skiing or snowboarding, you can catch the **Ski Bus,** which runs between several downtown Ogden hotels and the ski resorts in the Upper Ogden Valley. The bus schedule is available online at ⊕www. valleylodging.com.

GOLF   On the upper end of the valley, cradled between mountains on both sides, the 18-hole **Wolf Creek Golf Course** (✉*3900 N. Wolf Creek Dr., Eden* ☎*801/745–3365* ⊕*www.wolfcreekresort.com*) is known among Utah golfers as one of the most challenging in the state.

HIKING   Many of the beautiful hikes in the Ogden Valley enable you to discover ski terrain in the off season. Starting at 6,500 feet and ending at 9,600 feet, the moderate 2.5-mi trail (one-way) from the upper parking lot at **Snowbasin** leads to the saddle south of Mount Ogden. Hikers pass through bowls filled with colorful summer wildflowers. Several U.S. Forest Service trails branch off from trails at the resort.For detailed trail maps and information contact the Ogden Ranger District of the Wasatch-Cache National Forest at 801/236–3400, or if you're at Snowbasin you can get maps in the Grizzly Center.

HORSEBACK   The view of these mountains is fine on horseback. **Red Rock Ranch and**
RIDING   **Outfitters** (✉*13555 E. Rte. 39, Huntsville* ☎*801/745–6393* ⊕*www. redrockranch-and-outfitters.com*) will take you on a guided trail ride or a horse-drawn hayride to a Dutch-oven dinner.

SNOWMOBILING   **Red Rock Ranch and Outfitters** (✉*13555 E. Rte. 39, Huntsville* ☎*801/745–6393* ⊕*www.redrockranch-and-outfitters.com*)puts you on a snowmobile and leads you to 200 mi of groomed trails in the Monte Cristo Mountains.

WHERE TO STAY & EAT

$$$–$$$$ ✕**The Grille at Wolf Creek.** Overlooking the golf course with a terrific view of the mountains and Upper Ogden Valley, this resort restaurant serves "contemporary classic" dishes like caramelized king salmon or beef tournedos to those looking for a relaxed meal. Save room for the

cheesecake. ✉ *3900 Wolf Creek Dr.* ☎ *801/745–3737* 🖃 *AE, D, MC, V* ⊘ *No lunch.*

★ ¢–$ ✕ **Shooting Star Saloon.** Welcome to the oldest remaining saloon in Utah, in operation since the 1880s. From the dollar bills pinned to the ceiling to the stuffed head of a 300-pound Saint Bernard on the wall, there's something to look at in every corner of this tavern. The menu doesn't stray far from beer and burgers—many consider those served here to be among the best in the country—and you can't beat the frontier bar atmosphere. ✉ *7350 E. 200 South St., 17 mi from Ogden via Rte. 39, Huntsville* ☎ *801/745–2002* 🖃 *No credit cards* ⊘ *Closed Mon. and Tues.*

$$$–$$$$ ▦ **Moose Hollow Condominiums.** Stone fireplaces, vaulted ceilings, moose antler chandeliers, and massive log beams add rustic touches to this luxury lodging, situated on the second fairway of Wolf Creek Golf Course in the Upper Ogden Valley. **Pros:** Spacious units. Located in a lovely spot. **Cons:** Two-night minimum stay required. ✉ *3605 N. Huntsman Path, Eden, 84310* ☎ *801/745–0333 or 877/945–0333* 🖷 *801/745–0224* ⊕ *www.moosehollowcondos.com* ⇲ *119 units* ⚐ *In-room: kitchen, Wi-Fi. In-hotel: golf course, pool, no elevator, laundry facilities* 🖃 *AE, DC, MC, V.*

$–$$ ▦ **Jackson Fork Inn.** In a restored dairy barn, this comfortable country inn and restaurant are warm and inviting. Antique decor adds to the country charm. Proprietor Vicki Petersen serves the most upscale dinner and Sunday brunch in the valley, with delicious soups and main courses like shrimp with marinated artichokes, boneless pork loin, or prime rib. **Pros:** A great setting in a beautiful valley. **Cons:** No in-room phones. ✉ *Rte. 39, 7345 E. 900 South, Huntsville, 84317* ☎ *801/745–0051 or 800/609–9466* ⊕ *www.jacksonforkinn.com* ⇲ *7 rooms* ⚐ *In-room: no phone. In-hotel: restaurant, no elevator, some pets allowed, no-smoking rooms* 🖃 *AE, D, DC, MC, V* ⦿*CP.*

THE GOLDEN SPIKE EMPIRE

Deserts, marshes, farmlands, mountains: there's enough landscape in the vast reaches of eastern Box Elder County to please any palate. The star attraction here, though, is history, specifically one day in history that changed the world: May 10, 1869. That's the date the Union Pacific and Central Pacific railroad officials met to drive their symbolic golden spike in celebration of the completion of the first transcontinental rail route. It happened at Promontory Summit, an ironically desolate spot about 15 mi north of the Great Salt Lake. The Wild West was about to be tamed.

The **Railroader's Festival** (✉ *32 mi west of Brigham City via Rte. 13/83 at the Golden Spike National Historic Site, Promontory Summit* ☎ *435/471–2209* ⊕ *www.nps.gov/gosp*)takes place annually on the second Saturday in August. Visitors of all ages enjoy reenactments of the celebration of the Transcontinental Railroad completion, talks by railroad historians, and games including a spike-driving contest, and handcar rides. Festival admission is free.

BRIGHAM CITY

21 mi north of Ogden via I–15 or U.S. 89.

Brigham City, first settled in 1851 by Mormon pioneers, reflects the best of both the old and the new. People passing through are charmed by its sycamore-lined Main Street and old-fashioned downtown, but they may not realize they are in one of Utah's most progressive towns. ATK (formerly the Thiokol Corporation), which manufactures rocket motors about 45 minutes west of here, has brought a lot of highly paid, well-educated professionals who have settled here and, over the years, molded Brigham City to their liking. It's one of only three Utah municipalities that fluoridates its drinking water, and the local museum outclasses those in many of the state's larger cities.

★ ☾ In honor of the famous local crop, a **Peach Days Celebration** (☎*435/723–3931*)has been held the weekend after Labor Day since 1904—the longest continually celebrated harvest festival in Utah. There's a Peach Queen pageant, a parade, an auto and motorcycle show, an art show, food and craft booths, and freshly baked peach cobbler.

Documents and artifacts from the city's early settlement and Mormon
★ cooperative periods are the focus of the 3,300-square-foot **Brigham City Museum-Gallery,** which also contains displays on the railroad and agricultural history of the Bear River valley. The large, open gallery is divided in half. The northern part houses pieces such as treasures brought across the plains by the Pioneers and furniture made in Brigham City around 1860. The south end of the gallery holds regional art collections and hosts monthly rotating regional and national touring shows such as Norman Rockwell lithographs and Oklahoma Memorial Art Quilts. ⊠*24 N. 300 West St.* ☎*435/723–6769* ⊕*www.brighamcity.utah.gov* 🔳*Free* ☾*Tues.–Fri. 11–6, Sat. 1–5.*

☾ The **Bear River Migratory Bird Refuge** was established on the brackish
Fodor$Choice marshes where the Bear River empties into the northern tip of the Great
★ Salt Lake. In 1983, however, in the first of a series of flood years, Utah received an unusual amount of rainfall, and the 74,000-acre refuge was inundated by the rising Great Salt Lake. By 1986 the lake had reached its historic high point, destroying all the refuge's facilities, including a just-completed visitor center. After a considerable amount of work, the U.S. Fish and Wildlife Service was able to resurrect a 12-mi driving tour that follows various dikes. The habitat has been reclaimed, and the refuge once again hosts seasonal influxes of ducks, geese, pelicans, swans, and shore birds. The 31,000-square-foot James V. Hansen Wildlife Education Center contains interactive displays, an exhibit hall, a theater, observation decks, and teaching labs. ⊠*2155 W. Forest St., 13 mi west of Brigham City* ☎*435/723–5887* ⊕*www.fws.gov/bearriver* 🔳*Free* ☾*Park daily dawn–dusk, visitor center weekdays 8–5, Sat. 10–4.*

★ ☾ Originally used as a winter camp by the Shoshones, **Crystal Hot Springs** is one of the world's largest natural hot and cold springs. Mixing water from the two springs allows for a variety of pools with temperatures ranging from 80°F to 105°F. The complex, which is in Honeyville, about 8 mi north of Brigham City, has its own campground, a series of three hot tubs, a large soaker pool, a cold freshwater swimming pool, two water slides, and a lap pool. The complex remains open year-round, but hours are variable so it's best to call ahead. ⊠*8215 N. Rte. 38, Honeyville* ☎*435/279–8104 or 801/547–0777* ⊕*www. crystalhotsprings.net* ☜*$6.*

SPORTS & THE OUTDOORS

Box Elder County's long rural roads are great for road biking, but the dirt roads in the Wellsvilles are generally too steep for good mountain biking.

GOLF On the campus of a former Indian school—that's what all the pink-and-green buildings are—**Eagle Mountain Golf Course** (⊠*960 E. 700 South St.* ☎*435/723–3212*), has a PGA pro, complete pro shop, and snack bar. It's a nice mix of challenging holes and straightforward greens, but rent a cart if you're not in shape because the switchbacks up the front nine will leave you puffing. Greens fees are $11.

HIKING The pink-and-gray crags of the Wellsvilles beckon the adventurous, and you can practically hike out your back door in Brigham City because the mountains rise straight up from town. But the range is one of the steepest in the world, so you must pace yourself. Although the peaks are all federal wilderness, gaining access isn't always a straightforward proposition. North of Brigham City, the foothills encompass a string of private ranches. If you knock on a farmhouse door, however, the landowner will usually oblige and tell you the best place to cross his land.

Brigham City's 700 North Street dead-ends in the east at the head of a nice hiking trail. East of Honeyville, the only good public access to the Wellsvilles is from 7200 North Street, 9 mi north of Brigham City on Route 38; the road dead-ends at a gate, which you can open (don't forget to close it behind you) or just climb over. Beyond it are miles of hiking trails to explore.

In spite of all that irrigated farmland you see, you're still in the desert, so bring water on any trip, even if you only plan to be gone an hour.

WHERE TO EAT

★ $–$$$ ✕ **Maddox Ranch House.** Down-home Western food—fried chicken, prime rib, or bison steak—and portions big enough to satisfy a ranch hand make this place, 2 mi south of Brigham City on U.S. 89, quite popular. Every dish is made from scratch, and people drive here from surrounding states just for a piece of the fresh peach pie in season. The restaurant has become such an attraction that it even has its own gift shop. The friendly service is a delight. Reservations are practically a must, even on weeknights. ⊠*1900 S. U.S. 89, Perry* ☎*435/723–8545 or 800/544–5474* ⊕*www.maddoxfinefood.com* ⌂*Reservations essential* ▤*AE, D, DC, MC, V* ⊘*Closed Sun. and Mon.*

¢–$$ ✕ **Idle Isle Café.** Built in 1921, this café maintains its antique atmosphere with original wooden booths and a player piano. The menu features home-style dishes like beef pot roast and halibut steak, along with memorable desserts, which include its trademark "idleberry pie."

FodorsChoice ★

Don't forget to grab a box of chocolates for the road at the Idle Isle's own candy factory across the street. ✉*24 S. Main St.* ☎*435/734–2468* ▭*AE, D, MC, V* ⏲*Closed Sun.*

★ ¢ ✕**Peach City Ice Cream Co.** Travel back in time to the 1950s at this drive-in, complete with carhops. Eat in your car or go inside to pick out a tune on the jukebox and enjoy your homemade ice cream out of a tulip-shaped bowl. ✉*306 N. Main St.* ☎*435/723–3923* ▭*D, MC, V.*

WHERE TO STAY

$ **Crystal Inn.** The spacious rooms of this two-story motel have comfortable sitting areas with desks as well as such conveniences as microwaves, refrigerators, and VCRs; some rooms have whirlpool tubs. There are mountain views from the swimming pool. **Pros:** Quiet location. Wi-Fi in rooms. **Cons:** Old-technology VCRs. ✉*480 Westland Dr., 84302* ☎*435/723–0440 or 800/408–0440* 🖷*435/723–0446* 🌐*www.crystalinns.com* *52 rooms* *In-room: refrigerator, VCR, Wi-Fi. In-hotel: pool, laundry facilities* ▭*AE, D, DC, MC, V* 🍽*CP.*

¢–$ **Howard Johnson Inn.** Ask for an upstairs room with a balcony to enjoy the sunset view from this standard motel not far from the I–15/U.S. 89 split. There are restaurants just through the parking lot and across the street. **Pros:** Excellent views of Willard Bay and beyond. Wi-Fi in rooms. **Cons:** Not handicap-accessible. ✉*1167 S. Main St., 84307* ☎*435/723–8511* 🖷*435/723–0957* 🌐*www.hojobrighamcity.com* *43 rooms, 1 suite* *In-room: Wi-Fi. In-hotel: pool, no elevator, pets allowed, no-smoking rooms* ▭*AE, D, DC, MC, V* 🍽*CP.*

¢ **Galaxie Motel.** You won't believe what a clean, spacious room you can get for the low prices here. And for a few bucks more, six of the rooms add a microwave and refrigerator and four have full kitchenettes. Unless you grew up on a farm, ask for one of the newer rooms toward Main Street—otherwise you risk being awakened at dawn by the neighbor's roosters. **Pros:** Bargain rates, friendly service. **Cons:** No Internet. ✉*740 S. Main St., 84302* ☎*435/723–3439* 🖷*435/734–2049* *28 rooms, 1 suite* *In-room: kitchen (some), refrigerator (some). In hotel: no elevator* ▭*AE, D, DC, MC, V.*

GOLDEN SPIKE NATIONAL HISTORIC SITE

32 mi west of Brigham City via Rte. 83.

The Union Pacific and Central Pacific railroads met here at Promontory Summit on May 10, 1869, to celebrate the completion of the first transcontinental rail route. Under the auspices of the National Park Service, **Golden Spike National Historic Site** has a visitor center and two beautifully maintained locomotives that are replicas of the originals that met here for the "wedding of the rails." Every May 10 (and on Saturday and holidays in summer), a reenactment of the driving of the golden spike is held. In August, boiler stoking, rail walking, and handcar racing test participants' skills at the Railroader's Festival. The Winter Steam Festival around Christmas time gives steam buffs opportunities to photograph the locomotives in the cold, when the steam from the smokestacks forms billowing clouds. ✉*Exit 365 off I–15,*

Hwy. 83, 32 mi west of Brigham City, Promontory ☎*435/471–2209* ⊕*www.nps.gov/gosp* 🎫*$5 per vehicle Columbus Day–Apr., $7 per vehicle May–Columbus Day* ⊙*Daily 9–5.*

CACHE VALLEY

East of Brigham City, U.S. 89/91 tops Sardine Summit in Wellsville Canyon before dropping into the highly scenic Cache Valley. Walled in on the west by the imposing Wellsville Mountains (often touted as having the steepest incline of any range in the country) and on the east by the Bear River Range (a subrange of the Wasatch), Cache Valley is 15 mi wide and 60 mi long.

The valley was originally home to bands of Northwestern Shoshone. During the 1820s it became a favorite haunt for Jim Bridger and other mountain men, who often stashed (or "cached") their furs and held rendezvous here. Mormon pioneers, led by Peter Maughan, arrived in 1856 and created permanent settlements. Today Cache Valley is one of Utah's most important agricultural regions. Topping the list of foods produced here is cheese. One of three cheese factories in the valley, Cache Valley Cheese is one of the nation's largest producers of Swiss cheese.

LOGAN

25 mi northeast of Brigham City via Rte. 89/91.

Mormon pioneers created the permanent settlement of Logan in 1859, but the town didn't become prominent until 1888, when it was chosen as the site for Utah's land-grant agricultural college, now called Utah State University (USU). Logan is now the hub of the Cache Valley. Logan's historic Main Street is best explored on a walking tour; an illustrated brochure, available from the visitor information center, guides you along both sides and up a few cross streets. The more interesting buildings include St. John's Episcopal Church, representing Cache Valley's first non-Mormon denomination; the Ellen Eccles and Lyric theaters; and the Cache County Courthouse.

Numbers in the margin correspond to the Logan map.

★ Each Memorial Day weekend in Blacksmith Fork Canyon is the **Old Ephraim's Mountain Man Rendezvous** (☎*435/245–3778*), a reenactment of an 1820s rendezvous. The celebration features participants dressed in period costumes. Lively games test hatchet, primitive archery, knife, black-powder, and Dutch-oven cooking skills. It's one of the West's largest mountain-man gatherings.

♕ At the Cache County Fairgrounds in August, the **Cache County Fair** (☎*435/716–7150*) is the scene of agricultural and culinary competitions and demonstrations, plus a nightly rodeo.

❶ In the same building as a well-stocked visitor information center, the **Daughters of Utah Pioneers Cache Museum** has mountain-man displays as well as musical instruments, furniture, clothing, and a large collec-

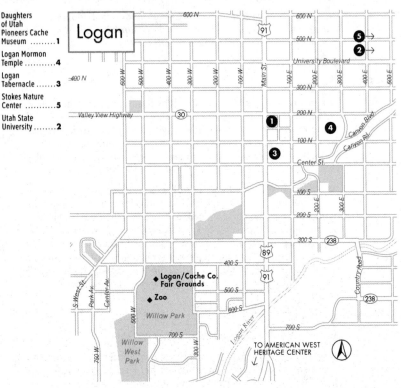

tion of personal journals from the 1850s to the early 1900s. ✉*160 N. Main St.* ☎*435/752–5139 or 435/753–1635* ✆*Free* ⊙*June–Aug., Tues.–Fri. 10–4; Sept.–May by appt only.*

❷ Logan is home to **Utah State University,** a land-grant college established in 1888. Today USU has an enrollment of well over 20,000 and is a leader in such diverse fields as agriculture, natural resources, and space technology. East of downtown Logan, the USU campus is best toured by starting at the historic Old Main administration building—look for the bell tower.

★ Exhibits at the **Museum of Anthropology** (☎*435/797–7545* ⊕*www.usu. edu/anthro/museum* ⊙*Weekdays 9–5, Sat. 10–5* ✆*Free*) in Old Main are entirely designed by students with faculty guidance. A large portion of the museum is devoted to the American West, but cultures from around the world are also represented. Exhibits change frequently, so it's a place you can go back to even if you've seen it before.

★ USU's Chase Fine Arts Center includes the **Nora Eccles Harrison Museum of Art** (✉*650 N. 1100 East St.* ☎*435/797–0163* ⊕*www.artmuseum. usu.edu* ⊙*Tues.–Fri. 10–5, Sat. noon–4*). The free museum has revolving exhibits of works by locally, nationally, and internationally recognized artists.

Housed in a beautifully restored historic mansion, the **Alliance for the Varied Arts** (⌂*35 W. 100 South St.* ☎*435/753–2970* ⊕*www.variedarts. org* ☑*Fees vary* ⏱*Tues.–Fri. 1–6, Sat. 10–2*) offers distinctive traveling exhibits, such as a display of war quilts stitched by women from Afghanistan and Africa. It also showcases artists from around northern Utah; you might see a sculpture created in the same way that a bird makes its nest. This museum is a gathering place for community art events and classes in ceramics, painting, dance, drama, and other media.

3 ➌ It took Mormon settlers 27 years to build the **Logan Tabernacle,** which they completed in 1891. In Logan's early days, the tabernacle hosted church and community meetings; now it's a venue for concerts and lectures. You can search for information about your family history at the genealogical research facility or take a tour of the building in summer. ⌂*50 N. Main St.* ☎*435/755–5598* ☑*Free* ⏱*June–Aug., hrs vary; Closed Sun.*

➍ The twin towers of the **Logan Mormon Temple** (⌂*175 N. 300 East St.*)remind all that this college town is also a conservative community with Mormon roots. Built on a terrace of the ancient Lake Bonneville, this impressive limestone edifice took settlers seven years to complete. The site was chosen by Brigham Young himself in 1877, and the work was directed by architect Truman O. Angell, designer of the Salt Lake temple. As with all Mormon temples, it's open only to followers of the faith.

☪ ➎ A visit to the **Stokes Nature Center,** about a mile up Logan Canyon, is a great way to get acquainted with the natural wonders of this area. The center has animal and bird exhibits and demonstrations. There are special programs for adults and children on some Saturdays; visit the Web site for listings. ⌂*2696 E. U.S. 89* ☎*435/755–3239* ⊕*www. logannature.org* ☑*Free* ⏱*Tues—Fri. 10–4, 2nd Sat. 10–4.*

Come to **Old Ephraim's Grave** to pay your respects to a northern Utah legend. Old Ephraim was the last grizzly bear known to roam and terrorize livestock around Garden City and Logan. His body was buried in 1923 at a site now designated by an 11-foot stone monument, which matches his height while standing on his hind legs; his huge skull is now exhibited in the Special Collections in Utah State University's Merrill Library. You can also look for a wooden sign marking the actual burial place of Old Ephraim originally placed by scouts in 1923. Make sure you have a sturdy four-wheel-drive vehicle with lots of clearance before attempting this trip; do not even attempt it if it's been raining at all. Though it is only roughly 9 mi from the Logan Ranger District Station, the trip takes about 3 hours. Stop in at the ranger station for specific directions and road condition updates. ⌂*1500 E. U.S. 89* ☎*435/755–3620* ⊕*www.fs.fed.us/r4/wcnf.*

OFF THE BEATEN PATH

Hardware Ranch. If you pass through the Logan area in winter, it's worthwhile to take the drive up Blacksmith Fork Canyon to the Hardware Ranch, where the State Division of Wildlife Resources feeds several hundred head of elk through the snowy months. A 20-minute sleigh ride takes you up close to the majestic creatures. Dress warmly in layers. There's also a visitor center and gift shop; bring your own picnic lunch. ✉*Rte. 101, 24 mi southeast of Logan via U.S. 165 and Rte. 101, Hyrum* ☎*435/753–6206 or 435/753–6168* ⊕*www.hardwareranch.com* 🛷*Sleigh rides $5* ⊘*Mid-Dec.–mid-Mar., Thurs.–Fri. and Sun.–Mon. noon–5, Sat. 10–5* ⊟*No credit cards.*

★ ⓒ **American West Heritage Center.** To learn about Cache Valley's history from 1820 to 1920, drive 6 mi south of Logan to visit this living-history complex that spans 160 acres. At the farm, antique implements are on display, draft horses still pull their weight, docents dressed in period clothing demonstrate sheep shearing and quilting, and special events take place throughout the year. The Festival of the American West, held at the center in late July–early August, features additional displays and reenactments, along with food booths, cowboy poetry readings, and concerts. In addition to viewing, visitors can shop for authentic Western jewelry, clothing, and specialty items. ✉*4025 S. U.S. 89/91, Wellsville* ☎*435/245–6050 or 800/225–3378* ⊕*www.americanwestcenter. org* 🖭*$5–$7* ⊘*Memorial Day–Labor Day, Tues.–Sat. 10–5.*

SPORTS & THE OUTDOORS

The outdoors are hard to ignore in beautiful Cache Valley, which is dominated east and west by mountains and by the lazy Bear River snaking through the bottomlands. Fly-fishers enjoy the Logan River and Black Smith Fork, and birders love to canoe the marshes. Hikers, skiers, picnickers, and mountain bikers head for the hills. Trails for all abilities are just minutes away from downtown Logan.

BICYCLING & HIKING
Road cyclists pedal out to the long, flat country roads of scenic Cache Valley or venture up Logan and Blacksmith Fork canyons. Mountain bikers can spend an afternoon on the 9-mi round-trip from Wood Camp, in Logan Canyon, to the 1,500-year-old Jardine juniper tree that grows on a high ridge offering views of Wyoming and Idaho.

Just a few miles up Logan Canyon, hikers and bikers enjoy the wide passageway of the **Red Bridge–River Trail,** which continues 4.2 mi on the south side of the canyon along the Logan River.Mountain bikers and hikers alike can access a prime wilderness area via the 3-mi route from Tony Grove Lake to the summit of **Naomi Peak.** In the Wellsville Mountains, a 2-mi trail climbs steeply from Maple Bench to Stewart Pass, a lofty ridge along the migration route of eagles and hawks; on a clear day the view from here extends for more than 80 mi.You can get maps and brochures for hiking trails in **Wasatch-Cache National Forest** (✉*Logan Ranger District, 1500 E. U.S. 89, 84321* ☎*435/755–3620* ⊕*www.fs.fed.us/r4/wcnf*).

BOATING & FISHING
Fishermen cast dry flies into the Logan River or angle for rare albino trout in the depths of Tony Grove Lake. Although you can paddle a canoe on virtually any body of water in the region, the best places include Tony Grove Lake in Logan Canyon and Bear River, northwest of Logan. Winding in serpentine fashion through Cache Valley, Bear River has several nice stretches, including a particularly satisfying one that runs 11 mi between Amalga and Tremonton. You pass a blue heron rookery along the way, so this is a good float for bird-watchers.

Contact **The Trailhead** (✉*117 N. Main* ☎*435/753–1541* ☉*Weekdays 10–5*) for canoe rentals, which go for about $20 per day, including life vests, paddles, and the car top and straps you need for transport.

Bridgerland Audubon Society (⊕*www.bridgerlandaudubon.org*)often sponsors boat trips on the Bear River.**Hyrum Lake State Park** (✉*405 W. 300 South St., Hyrum* ☎*435/245–6866* ⊕*www.stateparks.utah. gov*) has a 450-acre reservoir that draws boaters in summer and fall. A campground, shady picnic areas, peaceful rural setting, and great views of the Wellsville Mountains and the Bear River Range make this a popular spot for family gatherings. In winter, ice fishing is the activity of choice. Day use is $6 per vehicle.

GOLF The **Logan River Golf Course** (✉*550 W. 1000 South* ☎*435/750–0123* ⊕*www.loganutah*.org) is also a wetlands preserve, as you'll discover when your ball plops irretrievably into one of the many cattail marshes. It's a very challenging course (par 71); the front nine has a tighter width, while the back nine has a tighter length. For $12 you can play 9 holes walking; $22 for 18 holes. Riding, it's $18 and $33, respectively.

Considered by many to be one of the best golf courses in the U.S., **Birch Creek Golf Course** (✉*550 E. 100 North St., Smithfield* ☎*435/563–6825* ⊕*www.birchcreekgolf.com*) is long and exceptionally well maintained. The clubhouse has one of the best views in Cache Valley. There's a full-service pro shop with custom club fitting and a PGA pro. Greens fees for the par-72 course are $22 on weekdays, $23 on weekends.

Roving herds of mule deer are the biggest hazard at the 9-hole **Sherwood Hills Golf Course** (✉*7877 S. U.S. 89/91, 14 mi southwest of Logan, Wellsville* ☎*435/245–6055* ⊕*www.sherwoodhills.com*), but you can't beat the mountain setting. Greens fees for the par-36 course are $12 per person, $10 per cart.

WHERE TO EAT

★ $–$$$ ✗**Le Nonne.** Logan was lucky enough to produce a local lass who caught the eye of Italian chef Pier Antonio Micheli, and after their marriage they opened this sophisticated storefront eatery where you can get an authentic four-course Italian meal with refreshingly brisk service. If your arteries can take it, the four-cheese gnocchi is ecstasy, and you can't go wrong with any of the appetizers. Whatever you do, leave room for a bite of homemade tiramisu. Combine dinner at Le Nonne with an opera at the Eccles Theatre across and down the street, and you might forget you're in the middle of the rural West. ✉*129 N. 100 East* ☎*435/752–9577* ▭*AE, D, MC, V* ☉*Closed Sun. No lunch Sat.*

¢–$$ ✗**Angie's.** One of the last family-owned diners in town, this homey eatery is not much to look at, but the cap-clad retirees and other locals who perch at the counter eating ham and eggs, shooting the breeze with the long-time waitresses, don't seem to mind. You won't either, once you tuck into the malt waffles piled with strawberries and whipped cream. In the evening, you can go decadent with a dessert that includes everything—even the kitchen sink. Angie's "Kitchen Sink" tops mounds of ice cream with hot fudge, blueberries, nuts, or whatever you choose, and serves it all inside a portable kitchen sink! ⊠*690 N. Main St.* ☎*435/752–9252* ☐*AE, D, MC, V.*

★ ¢–$$ ✕**Bluebird.** Utah's oldest continuously operated restaurant serves American classics, including sandwiches, steaks, and ice cream treats, to a loyal clientele. Photographs and murals detail Cache Valley history, and you can sit at the old-fashioned soda counter that dates to the 1920s for a nutty ice-cream sundae or the locally popular Ironport cherry soda. On your way out, stop by the chocolate counter to sample an Aggie Bar (a chocolate- and caramel-covered brazil nut) or a Sea Foam (local honey that's spun and coated in chocolate). ⊠*19 N. Main St.* ☎*435/752–3155* ☐*AE, D, MC, V* ⊗*Closed Sun.*

¢ ✕**Caffé Ibis.** Hang out with Logan's hip and earthy crowd while sipping some of the state's best—and most eco-friendly—coffee. Shiny brass canisters are filled with triple-certified (shade grown, organic, and fair trade) coffee beans ground daily at the Ibis's own local plant. To moderate the caffeine buzz of the double lattes, you can also enjoy homemade soups, savory sandwiches, and hearty breakfasts. Local musicians perform for tips on Friday and Sunday nights. ⊠*52 Federal Ave.* ☎*435/753–4777* ☐*AE, MC, V.*

¢ ✕**Crumb Brothers Artisan Bread.** If you're craving outrageously tasty
Fodor'sChoice pastries or thick-crusted artisan breads, this beloved bakery set in a
★ 1930s Arts and Crafts-style building is your place. Try the apple puff turnovers, cinnamon pull-apart bread, or delicious chocolate-filled croissants. A cup of tea pairs nicely with the traditional English lemon scones, but it's hard to pass up a slice of fruit tart or yummy coffee cake, or the popular ginger cookies spiced up with chunks of crystallized ginger. In summer, take your treats onto the patio overlooking a landscape of native grasses, flowers, and sage. Get there early, though; hours are 7 AM–1 PM Monday through Saturday. ⊠*291 S. 300 West* ☎*435/792–6063* ☐*No credit cards* ⊗*Closed Sun. No dinner.*

WHERE TO STAY

★ $–$$$ ⊞**Providence Inn.** The stone part of the three-story stone and cream-brick inn was once the Old Rock Church, built in 1889. Such architectural embellishments as Palladian windows lend the structure considerable elegance. Rooms are individually decorated—some colonial style, some Georgian, and some Victorian. Breakfast is a hearty affair of omelets or French toast, brought to your room if you choose the higher-end "king rooms" or suites; otherwise, it's served in a lovely parlor decorated to feel like grandma's dining room. **Pros:** Located in a peaceful, rural community. Cozy rooms. **Cons:** When events are held at the adjacent Old Rock Church, you may hear people coming and going. ⊠*10 S. Main St., Providence, 84332* ☎*435/752–3432 or 800/480–4943* ☐*435/752–3482* ⊕*www.providenceinn.com* ⊅*12 rooms, 5 suites* ⊱*In-room: DVD, VCR, dial-up, Wi-Fi. In-hotel: no kids under 16, no-smoking rooms* ☐*AE, D, DC, MC, V* ⊙*BP.*

$–$$ ⊞**Sherwood Hills Resort.** The sense of isolation is part of the charm at
Fodor'sChoice this mountain retreat, set in a swath of wilderness halfway between
★ Logan and Brigham City. You can step out the front door for hiking or cross-country skiing, but don't worry—with a 9-hole golf course, an on-site spa, and postcard views out every window, creature comforts

are never far away. With the best wine list on either side of the Wellsvilles and a menu of feel-good Italian fare, the European-style **Belle Monte** restaurant ($–$$$$) is mighty comforting, too. Settle into a cozy booth by the fireplace and fuel up with a hearty pasta dish, such as the version topped with pancetta, chicken, and roasted sun-dried tomatoes. **Pros:** The bright stars are mesmerizing in this wilderness location. You can often see wildlife just outside your window. **Cons:** If you like to be where things are "happening," you may find the setting a little remote. ✉ *U.S. 89/91, 14 mi southwest of Logan, Wellsville, 84339* ☎ *435/245–5054 or 800/532–5066* ⊕ *www.sherwoodhills.com* ⇨ *60 rooms, 5 suites* ⌂ *In-room: refrigerator, VCR, Wi-Fi. In-hotel: restaurant, golf course, pool, spa, no-smoking rooms* ☰ *AE, D, DC, MC, V* ⊗ *No lunch weekdays. No dinner Sun.* ⍀ *CP.*

¢ ▣ **Zanavoo.** If you're on a tight budget but crave a million-dollar setting, check out this 1948 log cabin lodge 2½ mi up Logan Canyon. The lodge offers ten rooms and a view of some of the area's prettiest scenery: the Logan River below granite cliffs, plus birds, deer, elk, and moose who live on the premises. A low rate of $49 gets you a basic room with satellite TV. **Pros:** Located within walking distance to hiking trails and a trout-stocked river. **Cons:** Limited dining options nearby. ✉ *4880 E. U.S. 89, 84321 1704 South 800 West Logan, 84321* ☎ *435/752–0085* ⇨ *10 rooms* ⌂ *In-hotel: no elevator* ☰ *AE, MC, V* ⍀ *CP.*

NIGHTLIFE & THE ARTS

NIGHTLIFE The underage crowd gathers at **Club NVO** (✉ *339 N. Main St.* ☎ *435/787–8848*), an alcohol-free disco and pool hall, but it's also becoming popular with older couples who like to dance but don't care for the bar scene. Watch for theme nights (salsa, big band, hip-hop, etc.) and come early for dance lessons.

Rub shoulders with both townies and university types at **The White Owl** (✉ *36 W. Center St.* ☎ *435/753–9165*). This convivial downtown watering hole also happens to serve Logan's best burgers. If it's nice out, toast the sunset view of the Wellsvilles from the rooftop beer garden. There's live music on Thursday nights but no dance floor.

THE ARTS Thanks to both the presence of Utah State University and the community's keen interest in the arts, Logan offers many fine theater productions. USU's theater and music departments present a variety of exciting performances. The **Ellen Eccles Theatre** (✉ *43 S. Main St.* ☎ *435/752–0026* ⊕ *www.elleneccestheatre.com*) presents Broadway musicals, Celtic music, and an annual series of performances appropriate for children. The **Caine Lyric Theatre** (✉ *28 W. Center St.* ☎ *435/797–1500*) features plays by the university's repertory company. Each Father's Day weekend in June, **Summerfest, an Art Faire and Music Festival** (✉ *400 South 500 W* ☎ *435/716–9244*)fills the fairgrounds with arts and crafts, music, folk dancing, and other cultural events. The **Utah Festival Opera Company** (☎ *435/750–0300 or 800/262–0074* ⊕ *www.ufoc.org*) performs a five-week season between July and August at the Ellen Eccles Theatre.

SHOPPING

★ **Cox Honeyland and Gifts** (✉*1780 S. U.S. 89/91* ☎*435/752–3234*) sells a wide variety of flavored, creamed honeys, as well as berry juices, candy, and Bear Lake raspberry jam. You can also get home decor items and gifts, and the store will create and ship lovely gift baskets to your family members back home.It's a feast for the nose at **Scentinel Candle Co.** (✉*2788 S. U.S. 89/91* ☎*435/755–6993*), where shoppers find candles of every imaginable color, shape, size, and scent. The shop also stocks some cute decorative items.From mid-May through mid-

★ October, visit the **Cache Valley Gardeners' Market** (✉*100 S. 200 East St.* ⊕*www.gardenersmarket.org*), held every Saturday from 9 AM to 1 PM in Pioneer Park. Buy fresh produce and locally made crafts while listening to local bands.

EN ROUTE From Logan, U.S. 89 continues for 30 mi up Logan Canyon before topping out at the crest of the Bear River Range. Within the canyon are a number of campgrounds and picnic areas administered by the Wasatch–Cache National Forest. For a particularly satisfying excursion, drive the 7-mi side road (marked) to **Tony Grove Lake.** At more than 8,000 feet, this subalpine jewel is surrounded by cliffs and meadows filled in summer with a stunning profusion of wildflowers. A short trail circles the lake, and other backcountry routes enter the Mount Naomi Wilderness Area to the west.

BEAR LAKE COUNTRY

Home of the famed mountain man Jim Bridger, Rich County has only recently been discovered by tourists from outside the region, though residents of Utah and southern Idaho have vacationed here for a century. A few hardy ranchers live here year-round, but raspberries are the only crop besides hay that can stand the short growing season, and you'll see them everywhere in the form of syrup, jam, and the famous Bear Lake raspberry shakes. The deep Bear Lake Valley is generally 5 to 10 degrees cooler than the Cache Valley, so when the mercury hits 90°F in Logan, there's a mass migration over the Bear River Range. The region comes alive in summer when visitors flock to the sandy banks of the turquoise lake to swim, boat, or to catch some sun. The handful of lodgings fill quickly (and in the winter some close shop entirely), so call to check availability.

BEAR LAKE STATE PARK

41 mi from Logan (to Garden City) via U.S. 89 north.

Eight miles wide and 20 mi long, Bear Lake is an unusual shade of blue, thanks to limestone particles suspended in the water. It's home to five species of fish found nowhere else, including the Bonneville cisco, which draws anglers during its spawning season in January. Among the lake's more discreet inhabitants is the Bear Lake Monster, which according to local lore lurks somewhere in the depths like its Loch Ness counterpart.

Along the south shore of Bear Lake, Route 30 traces an old route used by Native Americans, mountain men, and settlers following the Oregon Trail. The lake was a popular gathering place for mountain men, who held two rendezvous here in the 1820s. Harsh winters persuaded most travelers to move on before the first snow flew, but hardy Mormon pioneers settled in the area and founded Garden City. You'll find several hotel and restaurant options in town, which sits at the junction of U.S. 89 and Route 30, on Bear Lake. The abundance of the berry is celebrated each year in early August at **Raspberry Days**. A parade, a craft fair, and entertainment are almost eclipsed by the main event: sampling myriad raspberry concoctions.

> **WORD OF MOUTH**
>
> "I think of Bear Lake as a water skiing lake, not a swimming/kayaking, hiking sort of place. The water is so cold."
>
> –BarbaraS

You can follow the ¼-mi **Garden City Boardwalk** (⊠ *420 S. Bear Lake Blvd., Garden City*)through a small wetlands preserve right to the shore of Bear Lake. **Bear Lake Marina** (⊠ *U.S. 89, Garden City*) has a beach, picnic area, campground, and visitor center with information on all the park's recreation areas. Boats can be rented from several local vendors around Garden City. **Rendezvous Beach** (⊠ *Rte. 30, Laketown*), which is on the south shore of Bear Lake, has more than a mile of sandy beaches, three campgrounds, and picnic areas. Mountain men gathered here for their annual rendezvous in 1827 and 1828. Their meeting place, Rendezvous Beach, now has interpretive signs about the gatherings. Each September a Mountain Man Rendezvous includes period cooking demonstrations, storytelling, cannon and rifle competitions, and a Native American encampment. At **Eastside** (⊠ *10 mi north of Laketown*)the lake bottom drops off quickly, making this a favorite spot among anglers and scuba divers. Facilities include a primitive campground and a boat ramp. ☎ *435/946–3343 or 800/322–3770* ⊕ *www.stateparks.utah.gov* ✉ *$8 per vehicle* ☉ *Daily 8 AM–10 PM.*

SPORTS & THE OUTDOORS

BICYCLING Cyclists of all abilities can enjoy all or any portion of the level 48-mi ride on the road circling Bear Lake. The paved Lakeside Bicycle Path curves from Bear Lake Marina south and east along the shore, with several rest stops. Interpretive signs contain stories about Bear Lake's history and local lore. **Bear Lake KOA** (⊠ *485 N. Bear Lake Blvd., Garden City* ☎ *435/946–3454*), which is right on the trail, rents bikes, including a four-wheel, surrey-top bicycle-built-for-four that can actually carry a family of six.

BOATING

Fodor'sChoice

★

Bear Lake's turquoise waters are a bit chilly for swimming on all but the hottest summer days, but boating is a popular way to enjoy the lake, which is one of the state's top boating destinations. Personal watercraft, sailboats, and motorboats are available at the Bear Lake Marina, at Rendezvous Beach, and in the surrounding towns. Prices vary from about $20 per hour for a catamaran to $60 an hour for a large motorboat capable of towing water-skiers. Be advised that the winds at this mountain lake can change 180 degrees within minutes (or go from 30 knots to completely calm), so inexperienced sailors may want to stick to a motorboat.

At the Bear Lake Marina, **Cisco's Landing** (⊠*Bear Lake Marina, U.S. 89, Garden City* ☎*435/946–2717*) offers everything from personal watercraft to full-size ski boats. Don't neglect to pick owner Bryce Nielson's brain—he's a wildlife biologist and a former Garden City mayor, and he can tell you everything you need to know about the lake and its denizens, both above and below the water.

In addition to sailboats and motorized craft, **Bear Lake Sails** (⊠*Rte. 30, Laketown* ☎*435/946–2900 or 866/867–5912*) rents paddleboats, canoes, and kayaks that are great for poking around the lake's vast shoreline and marshes. You can also rent water skis, wet suits, tubes, and wakeboards here.

GOLF **Bear Lake Golf Course** (⊠*2180 S. Country Club Dr., Garden City* ☎*435/946–8742*) offers 9 holes in a lakeside setting when the weather permits (generally May–October). The 3,400-foot course has a par of 36, and greens fees are $14 on weekdays, $16 on weekends ($20 and $22, respectively, with a cart).

HIKING At 9,980 feet, Naomi Peak is the highest point of the Bear River Range in Cache National Forest. The 3.2-mi **Naomi Peak Trail** starts in the parking lot of the Tony Grove Campground and gains almost 2,000 feet in elevation. You hike through conifer forests and open meadows and along subalpine basins and rocky ledges. A shorter hike to **White Pine Lake**, which begins on the same trail and splits after a quarter of a mile, is also lovely. To reach the trailhead, take U.S. 89 southwest from Garden City approximately 15 mi to the Tony Grove turnoff, then follow the signs. Closer to Garden City is the **Limber Pine Nature Trail**, a popular and easy hike (1 mi round-trip) at the summit between Logan Canyon and Bear Lake and features interpretive information especially designed for children.

SKIING Owned and operated by the same family since 1939, **Beaver Mountain Ski** ★ **Area** offers skiing as it was before it became a rich man's sport. A terrain park invites aerial tricks. There aren't any trendy night spots at the foot of this mountain, just an old-fashioned A-frame lodge with burgers and chili. In summer Beaver Mountain has Logan Canyon's only camping with RV hookups. ⊠*1045½ N. Main St.* ☎*435/753–0921, 435/753–4822, or 435/563–5677* 🖷*435/753–0975* ⊕*www.skithe beav.com* ⬦*1,600-ft vertical drop; 664 skiable acres; 45 runs; 35% beginner, 40% intermediate, 25% advanced; 2 double chairs, 2 triple chairs, 1 surface lift* 🎫*Lift tickets $38.*

WHERE TO STAY & EAT

¢–$ ✕**LaBeau's Drive-in.** Although there's no drive-up window, there's no microwave cuisine either—just old-fashioned fast food. The classic order would be a raspberry shake and a burger topped with ham, cheese, onions, and the homemade sauce. ⊠*69 N. Bear Lake Blvd.,*

Garden City ☎*435/946–8821* ▭*MC, V* ☾*Closed Sun. and mid-Oct.–
late Apr.*

$$$–$$$$ ⊡ **Ideal Beach Resort.** A private beach awaits you at this family-style
resort. You can only rent by the week or "half-week," which is either
three weekend nights or four weekday nights. The condos are all pri-
vately owned and vary in size and amenities, but all have private bed-
rooms and fully equipped kitchens. Restaurants are nearby in Garden
City. **Pros:** A wonderful place for families. Lots of activities. Within
walking distance of the aqua-colored lake. **Cons:** With so many kids
around, it's not a spot for peace and quiet. ⊠*2176 S. Bear Lake Blvd.,
Garden City, 84028* ☎*435/946–3364 or 800/634–1018* ☎*435/946–
8519* ⊕*www.idealbeach.net* ⮌*36 condos* ♿*In-room: no a/c, kitchen.
In-hotel: tennis courts, pools, beachfront, laundry facilities* ▭*AE, DC,
MC, V.*

WHERE TO ⚠ **Bear Lake KOA.** The budget-minded get the best resort in town at
CAMP Bear Lake. This spot, which has cute-as-a-button log cabins (some with
★ ☾ bathrooms and kitchens) as well as campsites, is practically its own city,
with a heated pool, miniature golf course, tennis courts, bicycle rentals,
the biggest convenience store in Garden City, and programmed activi-
ties for kids. There's a pavilion for pancake breakfasts and the like. A
shared outdoor kitchen allows tent campers the luxury of doing their
own cooking. Service is snappier than at the area's luxury resorts. Res-
ervations are essential. ♿*Flush toilets, full hookups, drinking water,
guest laundry, showers, picnic tables, electricity, public telephone, gen-
eral store, service station, swimming (pool)* ⮌*100 full hookups, 130
tent sites, 25 cabins* ⊠*485 N. Bear Lake Blvd., 84028* ☎*435/946–
3454, 800/562–3442 reservations* ⊕*www.koa.com* ▭*AE, D, MC, V*
☾*Mid-Mar.–mid-Nov.*

★ ☾ ⚠ **Rendezvous Beach Campground.** You can camp at all three recreation
areas on Bear Lake, but with 178 sites, the campground at Rendezvous
Beach is by far the largest. It also has hot showers, which are a nice
luxury after a cold plunge in Bear Lake. Plus, you can rent a boat on-
site. ♿*Flush toilets, drinking water, showers, picnic tables, electricity,
swimming (lake)* ⮌*106 full hookups, 72 tent sites* ⊠*Rte. 30, near
Laketown, 84028* ☎*801/538–7220 or 800/322–3770* ⊕*www.state-
parks.utah.gov* ☾*Apr.–mid-Sept.*

NORTHERN UTAH ESSENTIALS

BY AIR

Salt Lake International is 60 mi south of Brigham City on I–15. Ogden-
Hinckley Airport is Utah's busiest general aviation airport. The Logan-
Cache airport is capable of handling small charter jets, and Brigham
City has an airport for propeller planes.

Information Salt Lake International Airport (☎*801/575–2400*). **Brigham City
Airport** (⊠*1780 N. 2000 West St., Brigham City* ☎*435/723–1121*). **Logan-Cache
Airport** (⊠*120 N. 100 West St., Logan* ☎*435/716–7171*). **Ogden-Hinckley
Airport** (⊠*3909 Airport Rd.Ogden* ☎*801/629–8251*).

Cache Valley Limo shuttles between Logan and the Salt Lake International Airport for $52 each way.

Information **Cache Valley Limo Airport Shuttle** (☎ *435/563–6400 or 800/658–8526* ⊕ *www.loganshuttle.com*).

BUS TRAVEL

Greyhound Lines operates on a limited schedule between Tremonton, Logan, and Brigham City. They also run several buses a day between Logan and Salt Lake City. However, a better option for getting to and from the Wasatch Front is the Utah Transit Authority, which runs buses more or less hourly between Brigham City and Ogden with stops in Willard and Perry. From Ogden there are many connections to Salt Lake City. The price is a steal: $1.75 for a two-hour ride (that should get you all the way to Salt Lake); then buy a transfer ticket for an extra $1.75, which will allow you to ride TRAX, Salt Lake City's light rail, once you get there. Within Cache Valley, catch the free blue-and-white Logan Transit District shuttles, which operate within Logan (with an express to Utah State University) or the Cache Valley Transit District between Richmond to the north and Hyrum to the south. The main station is within walking distance of most hotels at 500 North and 100 East streets.

Information **Greyhound Lines** (☎ *801/355–9579 or 800/231–2222* ⊕ *www.greyhound.com*). **Logan Transit District** (☎ *435/752–2877* ⊕ *www.cvtdbus.org*). **Utah Transit Authority** (☎ *801/743–3882 or 888/743–3882* ⊕ *www.rideuta.com*).

CAMPING

There are plenty of campgrounds in northern Utah, and sites vary from the primitive to the luxurious. Ten public campgrounds dot this neck of the Wasatch-Cache National Forest, one near Mantua (4 mi east of Brigham City on U.S. 89/91) and nine in Logan Canyon. National Forest campgrounds cost between $6 and $12 per night. Utah Parks and Recreation also runs campgrounds at the two state parks, Hyrum Reservoir ($16) and Bear Lake ($16–$25). If you want full hookups, showers, and all the amenities, your best bet is a private campground. There are several to choose from in Brigham City, Logan, and Garden City. If you prefer a mountain setting, Beaver Mountain Ski Area in Logan Canyon has RV hookups for rent in summer. Private campgrounds range from $14 to $47 per night. Reservations in the National Forest are handled through a concessionaire, the National Recreation Reservation Service. You can also backpack and camp on most of the public land in Utah; check at the ranger station at the mouth of Logan Canyon for suggestions. During drought years fires are prohibited in summer.

Information **Cache Chamber of Commerce** (✉ *160 N. Main St., Logan, 84321* ☎ *435/752–2161* ⊕ *www.cachechamber.com*). **National Recreation Reservation Service** (☎ *877/444–6777* ⊕ *www.recreation.gov*). **Utah State Parks and Recreation** (☎ *800/322–3770 reservations* ✉ *1594 W. North Temple, Ste. 116, Salt Lake City, 84116* ⊕ *www.stateparks.utah.gov*).

CAR RENTAL

Ogden, Brigham City, and Logan have several car rental agencies. C&R Auto Sales and Rental is in Tremonton, north of Brigham City. Hertz and Enterprise have offices in Logan and Ogden.

Information **C&R Auto Sales and Rental** (✉ 1401 W. Main St., Tremonton ☎ 435/257–0195). **Enterprise** (✉ 2026 N. Main St, Logan ☎ 435/755–6111 or 800/736–8322 ✉ 3565 Riverdale Rd., Ogden ☎ 801/399–5555 ⊕ www.enterprise.com). **Hertz** (✉ 1757 N. 600 West, Logan ☎ 435/752–2961 or 800/654–7544 ⊕ www.hertz.com).

CAR TRAVEL

Northern Utah has two main highways, I–15 running north–south and U.S. 89 running northeast–southwest. The latter is a national scenic byway, and the hour's drive between Logan and Bear Lake will reward you with breathtaking vistas and plenty of places to pull off for a picnic. Off the main highways, roads range from well-paved multilane blacktop routes to barely graveled backcountry trails. If you're going to venture off the beaten track at all, it's a good idea to have a four-wheel-drive vehicle or at least a truck with high clearance. Deer, elk, and even bobcats may try to get to the other side of a road just as you come along, so watch out for wildlife on the highways. In rural and resort towns, expect gas prices to be considerably higher than in large cities.

Information **Utah Highway Patrol Ogden Office** (✉ 461 Stewart St., Box 4-A, Ogden ☎ 801/393–1136). **Utah Highway Patrol Logan Office** (✉ 1225 West Valley View, Ste. 350, Logan ☎ 435/723–1094).

Road Conditions **Utah Road Condition Information** (☎ 511 in Salt Lake City area and 800/492–2400 within Utah).

EMERGENCIES

Ambulance or Police **Emergencies** (☎ 911).

24-Hour Medical Care **Brigham City Community Hospital** (✉ 950 S. Medical Dr., Brigham City ☎ 435/734–9471). **Cache Valley Specialty Hospital** (✉ 2380 N. 400 East St., North Logan ☎ 435/713–9700). **Logan Regional Hospital** (✉ 1400 N. 500 East St., Logan ☎ 43 5/716–1000). **Ogden Regional Medical Center** (✉ 5475 S. 500 East St., Ogden ☎ 801/479–2111).

SPORTS & THE OUTDOORS

FISHING The Logan River and Blacksmith Fork are blue-ribbon trout streams. You can pull indigenous Bear Lake cutthroat, which are found nowhere else in the world, out of Bear Lake, or join the locals in dip-netting Bear Lake cisco when they come to shore to spawn in January. Warm-water species are found in abundance in Mantua Reservoir, 4 mi east of Brigham City on U.S. 89. In the Bear River, it's mostly carp these days. For a novelty fishing experience, boat out to the middle of Tony Grove Lake and use a long line with plenty of sinkers to land one of the rare albino trout that frequent the depths of the lake. You can get a fishing license at most local sporting goods stores but if you want to obtain your license online, go to the **Utah Division of Wildlife Resources Website** (⊕ *www.wildlife.utah.gov*).

Information **Utah Division of Wildlife Resources Fishing Hotline** (☎877/592–5169).

HIKING For great hiking ideas in and around Weber County, contact Weber Pathways for detailed information. Your best source of trail information in the Logan area is the Logan Ranger District office at the mouth of Logan Canyon. It's closed on weekends, though. Most of the hiking trails are also great cross-country ski trails in winter.

Information **Weber Pathways** (☎801/393-2304 ⊕ www.weberpathways.org). **Logan Ranger District** (✉1500 E. U.S. 89, Logan ☎435/755-3620).

VISITOR INFORMATION

Bear Lake–Rendezvous Chamber of Commerce (🖃 Box 55, Garden City, 84028 ☎800/448-2327 ⊕ www.bearlakechamber.com). **Bear River Valley Chamber of Commerce** (🖃 Box 311, Tremonton, 84337 ☎435/257-7585 ⊕ www.bearriverchamber.org). **Brigham City Chamber of Commerce** (✉6 N. Main St., Brigham City, 84302 ☎435/723-3931 ⊕ www.bcareachamber.com).**Cache Valley Visitors Bureau** (✉199 N. Main St., Logan, 84321 ☎435/755-1890 or 800/882-4433 ⊕ www.tourcachevalley.com). **Ogden Convention and Visitors Bureau** (✉2501 Wall Ave., Ogden, 84401 ☎801/627-8288 or 866/867-8824 ⊕ www.ogden.travel). **Ogden Valley Business Association** (✉5460 E. 2200 North, Eden, 84310 ☎801/745-2550 ⊕ www.ovba.org).

NIGHTLIFE & THE ARTS

A lively local favorite since 1977, **Pickleville Playhouse,** which is open from June through Labor Day weekend, features musical-comedy performances and a huge Western cookout on Thursday, Friday, and Saturday nights. ✉2049 S. Bear Lake Blvd., Pickleville ☎435/946–2918 ⊕ www.picklevilleplayhouse.com.

Dinosaurland & Eastern Utah

WORD OF MOUTH

"One of our favorite food stops in Price is Farlai-no's—a classic main street diner. Since Highway 6 is essentially two lanes it's not an issue hopping off whenever you want. Be careful, too, it's one of the most dangerous stretches of road in Utah!"

—katyslc

Updated by
Lucia Stewart

THE RUGGED BEAUTY OF UTAH'S eastern corner, wedged neatly between Wyoming above and Colorado to the east, is the reward for those willing to take the road less traveled. Neither I–80 nor I–70 enter this part of the state, so most visitors who pass through the western United States never even see it. That, of course, is part of its appeal. Small towns, rural attitudes, and a more casual and friendly approach to life are all part of the eastern Utah experience.

TOP REASONS TO GO
Mountain biking outside and around Vernal—no crowds and great trails.
Rafting Split Mountain—adventurous thrills that gives one-of-a-kind perspective of the Dinosaur monument.
Waterslide, bowling, and drive-in in Vernal—frugal fun at its finest!

Eastern Utah is most spectacular when viewed out-of-doors. It's home to great boating and fishing at Flaming Gorge, Red Fleet, Steinaker, and Starvation reservoirs. Hundreds of miles of hiking and mountain-biking trails (often available to cross-country skiers, snowmobilers, or snowshoers in winter) crisscross the region. The Green and Yampa rivers entice white-water rafters as well as less ambitious float-trippers. The pine- and aspen-covered Uinta (pronounced *You-in-tah*) Mountains reveal hidden, pristine lakes and streams to campers and hikers. Even if you don't get out of your car, exploring this region takes you through vast red rock basins, over high mountain passes, and between geologic folds in the earth.

This area of Utah was home to Native American cultures long before the first European fur trappers and explorers arrived. Cliff walls and boulders throughout the region are dotted with thousands of examples of rock art of the Fremont people (AD 300 to 1300), so called because they inhabited the region near the Fremont River. Today the Uintah and Ouray Reservation is the second largest in the United States and covers a significant portion of eastern Utah, though much of the reservation's original land grant was reclaimed by the U.S. government for its mineral and timber resources. The Ute tribe, whose 3,000-some members inhabit the land, hold powwows and other cultural ceremonies, which help visitors understand their way of life.

Museums throughout the region are full of pioneer relics, and you'll find several restored homesteads in and near Vernal. You'll also be able to unearth the dinosaur legacy that's made eastern Utah one of the most important paleontological research areas in the world. You'll discover the rich mining and railroad history of the Price–Helper area. And, of course, you'll hear story after story of outlaws, robberies, mine disasters, and heroic deeds everywhere you go.

EXPLORING EASTERN UTAH

Helper and Price, towns rich in mining and railroad history as well as in dinosaur fossils, are only a couple of hours southeast of Salt Lake City. Price is the largest city on U.S. 6, the major route between the Wasatch

Front and the southeastern portion of the state (and the quickest way to reach I–70 if you're headed east into Colorado). Vernal and Dinosaur National Monument (which spans the Utah–Colorado border) are four hours east of Salt Lake City on Route 40, or three hours northeast of Price via U.S. 191 and U.S. 40. Flaming Gorge is 40 mi north of Vernal via U.S. 191. The Uinta Mountains and the High Uintas Wilderness Area are about 1½ hours east of Salt Lake City, first via I–80 and U.S. 40 to Kamas and then via Route 150.

ABOUT THE RESTAURANTS

Because the towns in eastern Utah are small, dining options are generally more casual and less innovative than in urban areas. Helper has the region's only brewpub (Grogg's Pinnacle Brewing Company); fortunately, it's a good one. Price has a mix of ethnic restaurants that represents its immigrant railroad and mining history. Vernal, a farming and ranching town, has good steak houses. The best dining in this part of the state can be found in upscale lodges—Falcon's Ledge Lodge, between Duchesne and Roosevelt, and Red Canyon Lodge and Flaming Gorge Resort, both near Flaming Gorge—which pride themselves on having gourmet menus. Bear in mind that most locally-owned restaurants are closed on Sunday, so motel restaurants and fast-food places are often the only places you can get food on Sunday.

ABOUT THE HOTELS

Most hotels and motels in eastern Utah are chains, and you can expect clean, comfortable rooms and standard amenities. The area's lodges make for a nice change of pace, surrounding you with natural beauty and more individualized rooms and services.

WHAT IT COSTS					
	¢	$	$$	$$$	$$$$
RESTAURANTS	under $8	$8–$12	$13–$18	$19–$25	over $25
HOTELS	under $70	$70–$110	$111–$150	$151–$200	over $200

Restaurant prices are for a main course at dinner, excluding sales tax of 7%–7.75% (depending on the city). Hotel prices are for two people in a standard double room in high season, excluding service charges and taxes of 9%–10.75% (depending on the city).

TIMING

In eastern Utah, most museums, parks, and other sights extend their hours during the summer season, from Memorial Day to Labor Day. (Some museums and parks are only open in summer.) Summer also brings art festivals, rodeos, pioneer reenactments, and other celebrations. Of course, it's also the hottest period of the year, when temperatures can reach 100°F, so it's an ideal time for rafting trips down the Green River or boating on the region's reservoirs. Spring and autumn are cooler and less crowded, therefore nicer for hiking or biking, but you'll miss out on some of the festivities. Some campgrounds are open year-round, but the drinking water is usually turned off after Labor Day, so bring your own. In winter you can cross-country ski or snowshoe on many of the hiking trails; maps are available at local visitor centers.

EAST–CENTRAL UTAH (CASTLE COUNTRY)

Spanish explorers and traders crossed East-Central Utah as early as 1598 on a trail now followed by Route 10. In the 19th century fur trappers passed through the mountains in their search for beaver and other animals, and in the 1870s some of them decided to return to do some ranching. However, the area didn't thrive until a new kind of wealth was discovered in the mountains—coal. Railroad tracks were laid in the valley in 1883 to bring miners from around the world to dig the black mineral and to carry the coal out to markets across the country. Coal continues to provide the economic base for many towns in Castle Country, so nicknamed for the impressive castlelike rock formations that grace many parts of the landscape.

PRICE

7 mi south of Helper via U.S. 6.

Thousands of visitors annually come to Price to look at Utah's prehistoric past in the College of Eastern Utah Prehistoric Museum. Like many Utah towns, Price began as a Mormon farming settlement in the late 1800s. In 1883 the railroad arrived, bringing immigrants from around the world to mine coal reserves that had barely been acknowledged up until that point. Mining became the town's primary industry, which it remains to this day.

☾ Miners working in the coal fields around Price in the late 1800s often saw and excavated rare treasures that most scientists could only dream of finding—dinosaur bones, eggs, skeletons, and fossilized tracks. These are all on view at the **College of Eastern Utah Prehistoric Museum.** A second hall is devoted to early humans, with displays of beadwork, clay figurines, and other area artifacts, as well as a gigantic wooly mammoth and a saber-toothed cat. In 2008, the museum began construction of a gigantic glass pyramid, which will house the world's only Mesozoic garden with hundreds of plants similar to those that lived 65 million years ago. The museum is also home to the **Castle County Regional Information Center,** where you can pick up area information, maps, and directions. ⊠*155 E. Main St.* ☎*435/613–5060 or 800/817–9949* ⊕*www.museum.ceu.edu* ⊠*$5* ☾*Apr.–Sept., daily 9–6; Oct.–Mar., Mon.–Sat. 9–5.*

The 200-foot-long **Price Mural** inside the Price Municipal Building is a visual narration of the history of the town as well as Carbon County, beginning with the first trappers and white settlers. The painting took artist Lynn Fausett almost four years to complete back in the 1930s. ⊠*185 E. Main St.* ☎*435/637–5010* ⊠*Free* ☾*Weekdays 8–5.*

Fodor'sChoice   The hundreds of petroglyphs etched into the boulders and cliffs of **Nine**
★   **Mile Canyon** may be one of the world's largest outdoor art galleries.

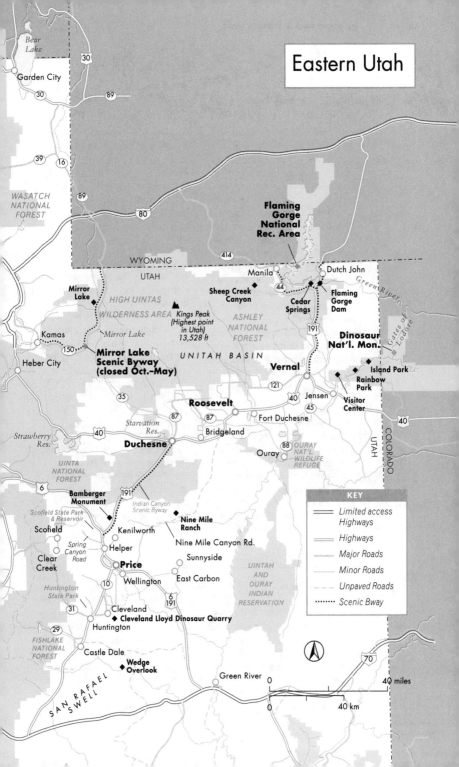

Eastern Utah

Bear Lake

Garden City

30

30

89

39

16

89

WASATCH NATIONAL FOREST

89

80

WYOMING

UTAH

414

Mirror Lake

HIGH UINTAS WILDERNESS AREA

Kings Peak (Highest point in Utah) 13,528 ft

ASHLEY NATIONAL FOREST

Manila

44

Sheep Creek Canyon

Cedar Springs

Flaming Gorge National Rec. Area

Dutch John

Flaming Gorge Dam

Green River

Kamas

Mirror Lake

150

Mirror Lake Scenic Byway (closed Oct.–May)

UNITAH BASIN

191

Dinosaur Nat'l. Mon.

Gates of Lodore

Heber City

Vernal

121

Island Park

Rainbow Park

Jensen

40

45

Visitor Center

40

35

Roosevelt

87

87

Fort Duchesne

88

OURAY NAT'L. WILDLIFE REFUGE

UTAH

COLORADO

Strawberry Res.

40

Starvation Res.

Bridgeland

Duchesne

Ouray

UINTA NATIONAL FOREST

6

Bamberger Monument

191

Indian Canyon Scenic Byway

Nine Mile Ranch

Scofield State Park & Reservoir

Scofield

Kenilworth

Nine Mile Canyon Rd.

UINTAH AND OURAY INDIAN RESERVATION

Clear Creek

Spring Canyon Road

Helper

Price

Sunnyside

East Carbon

Huntington State Park

10

Wellington

31

Cleveland

6

191

Cleveland Lloyd Dinosaur Quarry

Huntington

FISHLAKE NATIONAL FOREST

29

Castle Dale

Wedge Overlook

70

SAN RAFAEL SWELL

Green River

KEY

———	Limited access Highways
———	Highways
———	Major Roads
———	Minor Roads
- - -	Unpaved Roads
·········	Scenic Bway

0   40 miles

0   40 km

IF YOU LIKE

THE OUTDOORS

Towns in eastern Utah are small, and the population is sparse. The lure of this area is not indoors, air-conditioned, and antiseptic. It's all about being outside. This country is magnificent, whether you're perfecting that barely perceptible whisk of your hand-tied fly inches from the surface of a sun-dazzled creek in the High Uintas, listening to thousands of birds rising into the cool evening air over the Ouray National Wildlife Refuge, laughing out loud at the taste of cold river water drenching you as an experienced guide rafts you through the narrow walls of Dinosaur National Monument's sunset-color canyons, or savoring the smells of sage and wind-scoured sandstone as you pause during your hike along a high-ridge plateau over Price. Get outside. Take sunblock and water. And leave your walls at home.

HISTORY

America's Wild West grabs the imagination like few other time periods. There's something about pioneers, cowboys, Native Americans, mountain men, outlaws, miners, and intrepid explorers that keeps us fascinated. In eastern Utah, the Wild West wasn't really so long ago. Homesteaders were still staking out their claims in the 1900s, and ranchers still ride horses and use sheep dogs to round up their livestock. A good portion of eastern Utah is actually the sovereign land of the Uintah and Ouray Indian Reservation. Experience the real West by searching for rock art, seeing a rodeo, watching the Northern Ute Pow Wow, touring the local history museums, visiting restored homesteads, or hiking or biking through landscapes that once sheltered outlaws and humbled pioneers.

PREHISTORY

Throughout millions of years, eastern Utah was lush and verdant with giant ferns, flooded by seas, or frozen in ice. Now, all those layers of time have begun to reveal their secrets. Dinosaurs once trod footprints into mud or lay down to die beside fast-moving rivers in the regions we now know as Vernal and Price. When you come to eastern Utah, you are entering one of the world's most important areas of dinosaur and fossil research. Let yourself be swept up in dino-mania, and visit the College of Eastern Utah Prehistoric Museum in Price, the Utah Field House of Natural History State Park in Vernal, and, of course, the astounding scenic wonders of Dinosaur National Monument just outside Vernal. And keep your eyes peeled for fossils wherever you hike.

They're the handiwork of the Fremont Indians, who lived in much of what is now Utah from AD 300 to 1250. The canyon also shelters the remnants of many early homesteads, stage stops, and ranches. However, the petroglyphs and pictographs are the main draws. It's important not to touch the fragile rock art because oils from your fingers can damage them. Most of this 80-mi round-trip is on a gravel road, so plan a day to complete it. Bring water and a picnic, because there are no services. A brochure detailing significant sites is available at the visitor center in the College of Eastern Utah Prehistoric Museum in Price. Without it, many panels will go unnoticed. At the gas station where you turn off U.S. 6 in Wellington to head to the canyon, you can also buy a self-published book that contains a complete list of sites, photos, and directions. To reach the canyon, go 7½ mi east of Price on U.S. 6 and then turn north on Nine Mile Canyon Road. ⊠*Nine Mile Canyon Rd., 7½ mi east of Price* ☎*435/637–3009 or 800/842–0789.*

★ ☾ Paleontologists and geologists have excavated more than 15,000 dinosaur bones from the **Cleveland-Lloyd Dinosaur Quarry,** making this "predator trap" the densest concentration of Jurassic fossils ever found. Since the quarry's discovery by herders in the 1920s, scores of dinosaur remains have been discovered here, including the oldest fossilized egg. Although many of the bones found in the quarry now reside in museums around the world, a trip to the remote landscape surrounding the quarry pit is worth the journey. The Visitor Center, which generates its own electricity from rooftop solar panels, has a reconstructed dinosaur skeleton and exhibits about the quarry, and the area has some short hiking trails. The center is 15 mi on a gravel road from the nearest services, so bring food and water and dress for desert conditions. To get here, take Rte. 10 south from Price to the Cleveland/Elmo turnoff and follow the signs. ⊠*20 mi south of Price off Rte. 10* ☎*406/636–3600* ⊕*www.blm.gov/ut* ⊡*$5* ☾*Memorial Day–Labor Day, Mon.–Sat. 10–5, Sun. noon–5; Apr.–Memorial Day and Labor Day–Oct., Fri.–Sat. 10–5, Sun. noon–5.*

☾ The **Western Mining & Railroad Museum,** which is in the Old Helper Hotel
Fodor'sChoice in Helper's National Historic District, is a treasure and doubles as a
★ visitor center. Elaborate model trains make their rounds through a simulated coal tunnel, and exhibits show the history of mining. Rooms depict everyday activities of Helper's past and include a medical room, a children's toy room, a school room, a railroad office, and a beauty salon. One room is dedicated to the more illicit side of Helper, with a jail cell, stills, and early beer bottles. Incredible photographs and paintings put a face on Helper's history, and there's an outdoor exhibit of trains and mining equipment. ⊠*296 S. Main St.,Helper* ☎*435/472–3009* ⊕*www.wmrrm.org* ⊡*$2 donation* ☾*May–Sept., Mon.–Sat. 10–5; Oct.–Apr., Tues.–Sat. 11–4.*

SPORTS & THE OUTDOORS
Carbon County covers a wide range of geography, from mountains to gorges to plateaus. Hundreds of miles of hiking and biking trails crisscross the region.

GOLF The 18-hole championship course at the **Carbon Country Club** (⊠*3055 N. U.S. 6* ☎*435/637–2388*) is open to the public. Keep in mind that it may be hard to concentrate on your game when you're surrounded by sandstone cliffs, a waterfall, hidden Native American petroglyphs, and a pioneer burial ground.

MOUNTAIN The canyons and expanses around Price boast trails that rival the slick-
BIKING rock of Moab, but without the crowds. The visitor center at the **College of Eastern Utah Prehistoric Museum** (⊠*155 E. Main St.* ☎*435/613–5060 or 800/817–9949*) has a mountain-biking guide that shows several trails you can tackle, including Nine Mile Canyon. Adventurous hik-

CLOSE UP

San Rafael Is Swell

Deep in the emptiest region of Utah, the San Rafael Swell is a place of quiet and a place of adventure. If you're seeking unrivaled opportunities for solitude—or for outdoor activities without the national park crowds, consider exploring this vast stretch of remote and ruggedly beautiful terrain.

Tremendous geological upheavals pushed through the earth's surface eons ago, forming a giant oval-shaped dome of rock 50 mi long and 30 mi wide, giving rise to the name "swell." Over the years, the harsh climate beat down the dome, eroding it into a wild array of multi-colored sandstone and creating buttes, pinnacles, mesas, and canyons that spread across more than 600,000 acres—an area slightly smaller than the state of Rhode Island.

Managed by the Bureau of Land Management, the Swell offers visitors spectacular sights similar to those in the Utah's national parks but without the crowds. In the northern Swell, the Wedge Overlook peers into the Little Grand Canyon and the San Rafael River below, for one of the most scenic vistas in the state. The strata at the edges of the southern Swell are angled near vertical, creating the San Rafael Reef. Both are known for fantastic hiking, canyoneering, and mountain biking.

I-70 bisects the northern and southern sections of the San Rafael Swell and is the only paved road in the region. While there are many off-road opportunities, the main gravel road and many of the graded dirt roads through the Swell are accessible to two-wheel-drive vehicles. The Swell is about 25 mi south of Price, and the closest towns—Green River, Castle Dale, and Cleveland—are not that close, so bring whatever supplies you might need, including plenty of water, food, and a spare tire.

Proposals have been made to designate the Swell a national monument. Until then, the San Rafael Swell remains one of the little-known natural wonders of the American West. ⊠ *BLM San Rafael Resource Area, 900 North and 700 East, Price* ☎ *435/637-4584* ⊕ *www.blm.gov/ut.*

ers can use many of these trails as well. At **Fuzzy's Bicycleworks** (⊠ *640 E. Main St.* ☎ *435/637-2433* ⊕ *www.fuzzysbicycleworks.com*), owner Fuzzy "the Bike Guy" Nance is Price's go-to guy for trail details, fix-its, or area information.

WHERE TO EAT

¢–$$ ✕ **Farlaino's Cafe.** In a historic building on Main Street, this casual restaurant attracts the locals with its large menu of American fare for breakfast and lunch. It's known for its curly fries, milkshakes, and homemade Italian sausage sandwiches prepared from an old family recipe. ⊠ *87 W. Main St.* ☎ *435/637-9217* ⊟ *AE, MC, V* ⊘ *Closed Sun. No dinner.*

¢–$ ✕ **Greek Streak.** On the site of a Greek coffeehouse from the early
FodorśChoice 1900s, this café is a reminder of Price's strong Greek heritage. The
★ menu includes traditional recipes from Crete: gyros, dolmades, lemon-rice soup, and such. The baklava and other desserts made here are among the best Greek pastries in the state. ⊠ *84 S. Carbon Ave.*

☎ *435/637–1930* ▤ *AE, MC, V* ⊘ *Closed Sun.*

¢–$ ✗ **El Salto Mexican Café.** Traditional Mexican specialties, such as corn tamales smothered in green sauce, spicy or mellow chiles rellenos, and crispy taquitos to share around the table, make this one of the area's most popular restaurants. Sit down to an endless basket of chips with homemade salsa, or order your meal to go. ✉ *19 S. Carbon Ave.* ☎ *435/637–6545* ▤ *MC, V* ⊘ *Closed Sun. No lunch Sat.*

¢ ✗ **Sherald's Burger Bar.** If you hanker for the nostalgia of an old-fashioned hamburger stand, where you order at the window and sit in your car, or sit outside at a picnic table where a carhop takes your order, you're in luck. Stop at Sherald's and see why locals stand in line here for their burgers, scones, malts, and shakes, ignoring the McDonald's across the street. ✉ *434 E. Main St.* ☎ *435/637–1447* ▤ *No credit cards* ⊘ *Closed Sun.*

> ### GOOD BREW
>
> **Grogg's Pinnacle Brewing Company.** A surprising discovery on the road toward Price, this small microbrewery has a comfortable, modern feel. A stone fireplace welcomes you as warmly as the staff, and outdoor patio seating with umbrellas beckons in the warmer months. Try any of Grogg's own microbrewed beers with your pizza, steak, or sandwich. ✉ *1653 N. Carbonville Rd. Helper* ☎ *435/637-2924* ▤ *AE, D, MC, V.*

WHERE TO STAY

$–$$ ⌂ **Holiday Inn Hotel and Suites.** This tastefully decorated hotel has a large atrium containing the pool, and the hotel's nightclub and restaurant have partial glass ceilings and walls for a sunroom effect. Suites have jetted tubs and kitchenettes. The restaurant is one of the few in Price open on Sunday; guests receive a complimentary membership to the nightclub, which serves alcohol. **Pro:** Comfortable atmosphere. **Con:** Continental breakfast served only occasionally. ✉ *838 Westwood Blvd., 84501* ☎ *435/637–8880 or 800/465–4329* 🖷 *435/637–7707* ⊕ *www. ichotelsgroup.com* ➥ *151 rooms, 14 suites* ♿ *In-room: kitchen (some), refrigerator (some), Wi-Fi. In-hotel: restaurant, bar, pool, gym, laundry facilities, no elevator, no-smoking rooms* ▤ *AE, D, DC, MC, V.*

¢–$ ⌂ **Greenwell Inn & Convention Center.** With more amenities than most local hotels, but still reasonably priced, the Greenwell is a good choice. Every room has a refrigerator and coffeemaker; a 15% discount to the restaurant and membership to the hotel's private club are included with the room. The suites have whirlpool tubs, big-screen TVs, and remote-control fireplaces. **Pros:** Convenient downtown location. Nice pool. **Con:** Can feel hectic when conventions are in town. ✉ *655 E. Main St., 84501* ☎ *435/637–3520 or 800/666–3520* 🖷 *435/637–4858* ⊕ *www. greenwellinn.com* ➥ *125 rooms, 3 suites* ♿ *In-room: kitchen (some), refrigerator, Wi-Fi. In-hotel: restaurant, bar, pool, gym, laundry facilities, no elevator, no-smoking rooms* ▤ *AE, D, DC, MC, V.*

¢–$ ⌂ **Best Western Carriage House Inn.** Behind a white, colonial-style facade, the motel-basic rooms all have coffeemakers, and you get a complimentary daily newspaper. Restaurants and shops are within reasonable walking distance, as this hotel is located near the College of Eastern

Utah. The roof over the pool retracts in summer to let the sun in. **Pros:** Close to the university. Friendly staff. **Cons:** Basic rooms with few amenities. Small TVs. ✉ *590 E. Main St., 84501* ☎ *435/637–5660 or 800/780–7234* 🖷 *435/637–5157* ⊕ *www.bestwestern.com* ⌨ *40 rooms, 3 suites* ♿ *In-room: refrigerator (some), Wi-Fi. In-hotel: pool, no elevator, no-smoking rooms* ▤ *AE, D, MC, V* ⦿ *CP.*

WHERE TO CAMP ⚠ **Nine Mile Ranch.** Ben Mead grew up in beautiful Nine Mile Canyon and now runs a "bunk and breakfast" and campground here. If you camp or rent a sparsely furnished log cabin or teepee, arrange ahead of time for a cowboy breakfast or Dutch-oven dinner. If you rent a room in the Meads's house, breakfast is included. Play your cards right, and Ben may recite some of his cowboy poetry—he's the real deal, and there's nothing "dime store" about him. There's no electricity in the cabins and no hookups for the campsites, but there is electricity in the restrooms. To reach the ranch, go 7½ mi east of Price on U.S. 6, then 25 mi north on Nine Mile Canyon Road. ♿ *Flush toilets, dump station, drinking water, fire pits, picnic tables* ⌨ *18 sites, 2 cabins, 1 teepee, 2 rooms* ✉ *Nine Mile Canyon Rd., Box 212, Wellington* ☎ *435/637–2572* ⊕ *www.ninemilecanyon.com.*

NIGHTLIFE & THE ARTS

THE ARTS A sizable number of Greeks came to the Price area to work in the mines. At the **Greek Festival** (✉ *Assumption Greek Orthodox Church, 61 S. 200 East St.* ☎ *435/637–3009 or 800/842–0789*) in mid-July, traditional Greek food, dance, and music celebrate this heritage.

At the end of July, **International Days** (✉ *Washington Park, 150 E. 450 North St.* ☎ *435/637–3009 or 800/842–0789*) uses music, dance, and food to celebrate the many nationalities that make up the Price community.

NIGHTLIFE Inside the Holiday Inn, **Rockie's Lounge** (✉ *838 Westwood Blvd.* ☎ *435/637–8880 or 800/465–4329*) is a private club for hotel guests, but nonguests can buy inexpensive memberships. A pool table and big-screen TV keep patrons amused when there isn't a comedy act performing.

Tucked away downstairs at the Greenwell Inn, **Wooly's Private Club** (✉ *655 E. Main St.* ☎ *435/637–2020*) offers inexpensive memberships (free for hotel guests). You can watch the game on the big-screen TV or throw some darts.

EN ROUTE The **Indian Canyon Scenic Byway** is the section of U.S. 191 that climbs up out of the Helper vicinity, cresting at Indian Creek Pass at an elevation of 9,100 feet. Then it begins a long descent into the Uinta Basin area, ending at Duchesne. The 43-mi route takes you through canyons, over plateaus, and into the heart of the geology and natural beauty that make up this part of Utah.

THE UINTA BASIN (DINOSAURLAND)

The Uinta Basin, originally home to the ancient Fremont people, is a vast area of gently rolling land bordered by the Uinta Mountains to the north, the Wasatch Mountains to the west, and a series of high plateaus and cliffs to the south. In the late 1800s, the Mormons thought about settling here but decided the land was not fit for agriculture. At their suggestion, President Abraham Lincoln set aside several million acres of the basin as an Indian reservation and moved members of Ute and other tribes here from their traditional lands in the Salt Lake and Utah Lake valleys. In the 1900s, the U.S. government took back much of the Uinta Basin land that had been set aside as a reservation and opened it to settlers from the East. Following the Indian Reorganization Act of 1934, the Northern Ute Tribe repurchased the majority of this land, which now constitutes the second largest reservation in the U.S.

In the early 1900s, an unbelievably rich trove of dinosaur fossils was discovered in the sandstone layers near the eastern Utah border. Since then, archaeologists have unearthed hundreds of tons of fossils, and the region encompassing Daggett, Duchesne, and Uintah counties has become known as Dinosaurland. An area particularly rich in fossils, straddling the Utah and Colorado borders, has been preserved as Dinosaur National Monument.

ROOSEVELT

80 mi northeast of Price via U.S. 191.

Roosevelt, a small town named for President Theodore Roosevelt, lies between blocks of the sovereign land of the Uintah and Ouray Indian Reservation.

The 1.3 million acres of the **Uintah and Ouray Indian Reservation** spreads out in patchwork fashion across the Uinta Basin and northeastern Utah to the eastern edge of the state. Fort Duchesne is the tribal headquarters for the Ute Indians. Because it's sometimes difficult to tell whether you're on reservation land, public land, or private land, you are asked to stay on main roads unless you have permission to be on the reservation lands.

Each July Fourth weekend, the **Northern Ute Pow Wow** (⊠ *8 mi east of Roosevelt on U.S. 40, at Fort Duchesne turnoff, Fort Duchesne* ☎ *435/722–5141* ⊕ *www.utetribe.com*) has drumming, dancing, and singing competitions, a rodeo, golf and softball tournaments, and an arts-and-crafts fair. One of the biggest powwows in the West, it's free to the public, who are welcome to attend and camp on the powwow grounds. Another, smaller powwow is held over Thanksgiving weekend at the tribal gymnasium in Fort Duchesne.

Established in 1960, the **Ouray National Wildlife Refuge** consists of 11,987 acres of land along the Green River, where you can see more than 200 species of migratory birds in spring and fall, mule deer and golden eagles year-round, and bald eagles in early winter. An information kiosk at the refuge has a 12-mi auto-tour guide and a bird check-list. Best times to visit are in the early morning and early evening. To reach the refuge, go 15 mi east of Roosevelt on U.S. 40, then 13 mi south on Route 88. ⊠*Rte. 88, Ouray* ☎*435/545–2522* ⊕*www.fws. gov/ouray* 🗇*Free* ⊙*Daily.*

SPORTS & THE OUTDOORS

Information about camping, sporting, and photo safaris on the Uintah and Ouray Indian Reservation is available from the **Ute Tribe Fish & Wildlife Department** (☎*435/722–5511* ⊕*www.uitfwd.com*).

PACK TRIPS **J/L Ranch Outfitters and Guides** (✎*Box 129, Whiterocks, 84085* ☎*435/ 353–4049* ⊕*www.jlranch.com*) leads fishing trips into the Uinta Mountains and the Ashley National Forest. Fishing the lakes, rivers, and mountain streams of the Ashley National Forest and High Uintas will give you an up-close perspective of their natural beauty.

WHERE TO STAY

$$$ **Falcon's Ledge Lodge.** With an emphasis on escaping the workaday
Fodor'sChoice world, guest rooms at this lodge are luxurious; all have vaulted ceil-
★ ings and two have jetted tubs. The lodge also offers luxury sporting packages, including fly-fishing and wing-shooting. There are no TVs in the rooms, but you can wheel in a portable TV with video games or visit the central big-screen TV room if you must. The five- to seven-course meals ($$$$) are the best in the area, but bring your own wine or alcohol. Specialties include whiskey-grilled, glazed filet mignon, bacon-wrapped ahi tuna, and fresh home-baked bread. Guests and nonguests must make advance reservations for the restaurant. **Pros:** Stunning lodge on 600-acre private ranch. Exquisite food. **Cons:** Location is quite remote. ⊠*Rte. 87, Box 67, 15 mi north of Duchesne or 25 mi west of Roosevelt, Altamont, 84001* ☎*435/454–3737 or 877/879–3737* ⊕*www.falconsledge.com* 🛏*9 rooms* ⌂*In-room: no phone, no TV, Wi-Fi. In-hotel: restaurant, no kids under 12, no elevator, no-smoking rooms* ☰*AE, D, MC, V* ⏼*BP.*

$$–$$$ **J/L Ranch.** The J/L Ranch is a place for the family to come explore, where you can sleep in cowboy-theme comfort, and hike, birdwatch, and fish in the numerous lakes, rivers, and mountain streams. The Chepeta cabin sleeps four; the "bunkhouse suite" on the second floor of the log horse barn (yes, there really are horses down there) sleeps six. Both are surprisingly nice, furnished with handmade log furniture, full baths, and fully-equipped kitchens so you can prepare your own meals. There is no air-conditioning, but there are fans in each room. The price you pay varies depending on the number of people in your party. **Pro:** Perfect for a fly-fishing getaway. **Con:** If you're not into outdoor activities, you may not be happy in this remote setting. ✎*Box 129, Whiterocks, 84085* ☎*435/353–4049* ⊕*www.jlranch.com* 🛏*2 cabins* ⌂*In-room: no a/c, kitchen, VCR. In-hotel: laundry facilities, no-smoking rooms* ☰*No credit cards*

$–$$ **Best Western Inn.** In small towns like this, lodging choices are limited, so chains are often comforting in their sheer familiarity. The pool and restaurant make this a popular place to stay in Roosevelt. Rooms have fridges and coffeemakers. **Pro:** Large, clean rooms. **Con:** Staff isn't always accommodating. ⊠*2203 E. U.S. 40, 84066* ☎*435/722–4644 or 800/780–7234* 🖷*435/722–0179* ⊕*www.bestwestern.com* 🛏*40 rooms* ⚬*In-room: refrigerator, Ethernet. In-hotel: restaurant, pool, no-smoking rooms* ⊟*AE, D, MC, V.*

¢–$ 🍴**Frontier Grill & Motel.** Accommodations at this downtown motel are simple but adequate and inexpensive, and the location puts you close to shops. A golf course is ½ mi away. The restaurant ($–$$) is the most popular in town and serves American fare like steak, fried chicken, burgers, and strawberry pie. **Pro:** Good value for the price. **Cons:** Aging facilities and decor. ⊠*75 S. 200 East St., 84066* ☎*435/722–2201* 🖷*435/722–2212* 🛏*54 rooms* ⚬*In-room: kitchen (some), refrigerator (some), Ethernet. In-hotel: restaurant, pool, no elevator, public Wi-Fi, no-smoking rooms, some pets allowed* ⊟*AE, D, DC, MC, V.*

VERNAL

22 mi east of Fort Duchesne via U.S. 40.

Vernal is the hub of "Dinosaurland," mixing the region's ancient heritage with a certain kitschy charm—think giant dino statues, a dino-themed bowling alley, and an old-time drive-in movie theater. Dinosaurs aren't the only things they're proud of in Vernal, however. The town claims the ancient Fremont Indians, a rowdy ranching past, and more than a passing acquaintance with outlaws like Butch Cassidy, who frequented the area whenever he felt it was safe to be seen around town. Legend has it that the saloonkeepers of Vernal gave Butch's gang the name "Wild Bunch," muttering, "there goes that wild bunch" whenever the outlaws rolled in. Now the largest town (population 8,000) in the northeast corner of the state, the cattle-ranching community of Vernal is one of the few Utah towns founded by non-Mormons. However, it was the town's remote location—at the eastern edge of Utah, far from government authorities—not a lack of religion, that led to its early reputation as a wild and lawless place. Each July, Vernal celebrates the town's western heritage when it hosts what has been voted one of the top five professional rodeos in the world—the **PRCA Dinosaur Roundup Rodeo** (⊠*Western Park Convention Center, 302 E. 200 South St.* ☎*435/789–1352 or 800/421–9635*). Four days of rodeo events, dances, and parades on Main Street celebrate the real-life cowboys who wear cowboy boots because they're practical, not because they're fashionable.

Each June, Vernal celebrates its feisty past during the **Outlaw Trail Ride** (☎*866/658–7433* ⊕*www.outlawtrailride.com*). Guided horseback rides along outlaw trails, camping, cookouts, and Western-theme entertainment are among the main events.

★ ☺ One hundred and fifty million years ago this land was the stomping ground of dinosaurs. At **Utah Field House of Natural History State Park** you can see rock samples, fossils, Fremont and Ute Indian artifacts, and a large mural depicting the last 2.7 billion years of the Uinta Basin's geologic history. The biggest attraction for kids is undoubtedly the outdoor Dinosaur Garden with its 18 life-size dinosaur models. The

Field House also doubles as a visitor center for all of Dinosaurland, so stop here for maps and guides for the entire area. ⊠*496 E. Main St.* ☏*435/789–3799* ⊕*http://stateparks.utah.gov/parks/field-house/* 💲*$6* ⊙*Memorial Day–Labor Day, daily 8–7; Labor Day–Memorial Day, daily 9–5.*

Inside the big, open **Western Heritage Museum** are collections of Fremont and Ute Indian artifacts, including baskets, water jugs, and beadwork pieces, as well as pioneer items like carriages, guns, saddles, and old-fashioned children's toys. Outside, you can see various horse-drawn farm implements, and every month the museum hosts a different show of local and national artists. ⊠*328 E. 200 South St.* ☏*435/789–7399* ⊕*www.co.uintah.ut.us/museum/whmuseum.php* 💲*Free* ⊙*Memorial Day–Labor Day, weekdays 9–6, Sat. 10–4; Labor Day–Memorial Day, weekdays 9–5, Sat. 10–2.*

The Daughters of Utah Pioneers Museum provides a window into the daily lives of pioneers. The large collection of artifacts (most donated by descendents of the area's early settlers) range from a working loom to guns to a mortician's tools. Most everything is displayed in period rooms, including a shop, a house, and even a local doctor's office. ⊠*158 S. 500 West St.* 💲*Free* ⊙*June–Aug., Tues.–Sat. 10–4.*

☾ An impressive array of easily accessible Native American petroglyphs adorn the 200-foot-high cliffs in **Dry Fork Canyon**, making the 22-mi round-trip drive from Vernal well worth your time. Next to the parking lot where you'll park to explore the petroglyphs is the Jean McConkie McKenzie house on the **Sadie McConkie Ranch.** You can see pioneer displays here, including a replica of a saloon. ⊠*11 mi north of Vernal on 3500 West St. (Dry Fork Canyon Rd.)* ☏*435/789–6733* 💲*Free, donations requested* ⊙*Daily.*

OFF THE BEATEN PATH

Browns Park. If you hanker for a glimpse of the Wild West, head to Browns Park. Lying along a quieter stretch of the Green River and extending into Colorado, this area features plenty of high-desert scenery, a national waterfowl refuge, and a history complete with notorious outlaws of the late 1800s. Inside the park, you can explore several buildings on the **John Jarvie Ranch.** Buildings date from 1880 to the early 1900s, and there's also a cemetery containing the graves of a few men who met violent ends nearby. In addition to his ranch, Jarvie ran a post office, store, and river ferry, and his spread was a major hideout on the so-called "Outlaw Trail." Each June (usually Father's Day weekend), the Jarvie Festival celebrates with mountain men, wagon rides, pioneer demonstrations, and live music. Reach the park and ranch by driving 65 mi north of Vernal on U.S. 191, then 22 mi east on a gravel road, following signs to the ranch. ⊠*Browns Park* ☏*435/885–3307 John Jarvie Ranch* ⊕*www.blm.gov/utah/vernal* 💲*Free* ⊙*May–Oct., daily 10–5; Nov.–Apr., Tues.–Sun. 10–5.*

SPORTS & THE OUTDOORS

BICYCLING Because Dinosaurland is less known than other parts of the state, bikers can often escape the crowds and enjoy some scenic solitude. The area has some 200 mi of trails. Bring plenty of water and sunblock.

To talk to knowledgeable cyclists about local trails off the beaten path, stop in at **Altitude Cycle** (✉*580 E. Main St.* ☎*435/781–2595* ⊕*www. altitudecycle.com*), where they can set you up with trail guides, repairs, and accessories. You'll find family-friendly biking trails with great vistas and opportunities for seeing some of Utah's diverse wildlife in Browns Park, with trailheads near the **John Jarvie Ranch** (✉*Browns Park* ☎*435/885–3307*).

BOATING **Red Fleet State Park** (✉*10 mi north of Vernal off U.S. 191* ☎*435/789–4432* ⊕*www.stateparks.utah.gov*), like the other reservoirs in the region, is great for boating and fishing. What really attracts visitors are the colorful sandstone formations surrounding the lake. In addition, a section of 200-million-year-old dinosaur tracks can be reached by a short hike or by boat, and camping is available. Day use is $5. Boating and waterskiing enthusiasts love **Steinaker Lake State Park** (✉*U.S. 191, 7 mi north of Vernal* ☎*435/789–4432* ⊕*www.stateparks.utah.gov*). More than 2 mi long, Steinaker Reservoir relinquishes a fair number of largemouth bass and rainbow trout. There's a sandy swimming beach, hiking trails begin at the park, and wildlife viewing areas are nearby. A campground and covered group pavilions make this a popular park. You'll pay $5 for day use.

HIKING One of the most beautiful hikes in the area begins at the Jones Hole National Fish Hatchery, 40 mi northeast of Vernal on the Utah-Colorado border, and follows **Jones Hole Creek** through riparian woods and canyons, past petroglyphs and wildlife. The full trail is an 8-mi round trip to the Green River and back, but you can stop halfway at Ely Creek and return for an easier, but still lovely, 4-mi hike. There are numerous trails in this area that are unmarked and not maintained, but easy to follow if you use reasonable caution. Or check with the rangers at the **Dinosaur Quarry Visitor Center** (☎*435/781–7700* ⊕*www.nps.gov/dino*) for more information about the numerous hiking trails in the area.

RAFTING For a unique perspective of Dinosaur National Monument, and the best way to experience its geologic depths, take a white-water rafting trip on the Green or Yampa rivers. Joining forces near Echo Park in Colorado, the two waterways have each carved spectacular canyons through several eons' worth of rock, and contain thrilling white-water rapids such as Whirlpool Canyon, SOB, Disaster Falls, and Hell's Half Mile. A one-day trip down Split Mountain is a good choice if you don't have four days to spare. River-running season is May–September.

Adrift Adventures (⌂*4500 East 6000 S., Jensen, 84035* ☎*435/789–3600 or 800/824–0150* ⊕*www.adrift.com*) offers one-day or multiday rafting trips, as well as a package that includes rafting in the morning and a horseback ride in the afternoon. **Dinosaur Expeditions** (✉*550 Main St.* ☎*435/781–0717 or 800/345–7238* ⊕*www.dinosaurexpeditions.com*) offers trips on the Green, Yampa, and White rivers, all concluding at their local boater-friendly restaurant in Vernal for tall tales and cold beers.

Hatch River Expeditions (⌂*221 North 400 E., Vernal, 84078* ☎*435/789–4316 or 800/342–8243* ⊕*www.hatchriver.com*) is the original river-running company; they've been at it since 1929. Their one-day and multiday rafting trips take you through both calm and white waters, and if fishing is your passion, they'll equip you for that, too.

SCENIC FLIGHTS
For a bird's-eye view of Dinoland's deep canyons, wide-open deserts, and blue reservoirs, take to the air with **Dinaland Aviation** (⊠ *800 E. 500 South St.* ☎ *435/789–4612 or 800/789–4614*). They offer flightseeing tours from 30 minutes to more than an hour; prices start at $39 per person.

WHERE TO EAT

★ $–$$$$
✕**Curry Manor.** Vernal's most elegant restaurant resides within the century-old home that once belonged to a state representative and is now on the National Register of Historic Places. In Victorian-era decorated rooms, indulge in steak, seafood, and pasta entrées, fresh-daily bread, and homemade desserts. And don't worry about a dress code—they'll welcome you right off the trail or river. Beer and wine are available. ⊠ *189 S. Vernal Ave.* ☎ *435/789–0789* ⊟ *AE, D, MC, V* ⊗ *Closed Sun.–Mon. No lunch Sat.*

¢–$$
✕**7–11 Ranch Restaurant.** No, this restaurant is not associated in any way with the convenience-store chain. Specialties are prime rib, steaks, and homemade soups and pies. It's open for breakfast, lunch, and dinner, and the down-home food is so good that locals have been crowding the place since it opened in 1965. A gift shop sells souvenirs from the area. ⊠ *77 E. Main St.* ☎ *435/789–1170* ⊟ *AE, D, MC, V* ⊗ *Closed Sun.*

¢–$$
✕**Cobble Rock Restaurant.** Craving mesquite-smoked ribs and a beer? Satisfy that craving at this family-style restaurant, where they smoke their own ribs and chicken, and serve steak, fajitas, burgers, and creative pasta dishes, too. The outdoor seating area borders a city park. ⊠ *25 S. Vernal Ave.* ☎ *435/789–8578* ⊟ *AE, D, MC, V.*

¢–$$
✕**Dinosaur Brew Haus.** After a long day on the trails or the river, unwind at this casual sports-oriented restaurant over cold microbrews, dino-sized sandwiches, salads, and ribs. Videos of wild outdoor adventures play on the dining room's TVs, courtesy of rafting outfitter Dinosaur Expeditions, which also runs the restaurant. ⊠ *550 E. Main St. 84078* ☎ *435/781–0717* ⊟ *AE, MC, V.*

¢–$
✕**Betty's Cafe.** Locals come here for breakfast, or for the tasty Italian sausage sandwiches. You can get burgers, catfish, and other sandwiches, too. Everything is homemade, including the jams, salsa, and pies. ⊠ *416 W. Main St.* ☎ *435/781–2728* ⊟ *MC, V* ⊗ *No dinner Sun.–Wed.*

WHERE TO STAY

★ ¢–$$$
🏠**Landmark Inn Bed & Breakfast.** Despite its history as a Baptist church building, this lovely inn has a homey feel. Rooms are decorated with quilts and Western Americana. Suites have gas fireplaces and jetted tubs. A breakfast of cereals, breads, yogurts, fruits, and juices is served in the dining room, and you're welcome to congregate around the living room fireplace in the evening. **Pros:** Quaint, historic building. Friendly owners. **Cons:** Not the best spot for privacy. ⊠ *288 E. 100 South St.,*

84078 ☎435/781–1800 or 888/738–1800 ⊕www.landmark-inn.com ⚲7 rooms, 3 suites ♿In-room: VCR, Wi-Fi. In-hotel: no elevator, no-smoking rooms ☰AE, D, DC, MC, V ⦿CP.

$$ 🏨**Best Western Dinosaur Inn.** This basic one-story motel is a few blocks from downtown museums and restaurants. Most rooms have two queen beds, but "family rooms" accommodate more sleepers. You might even find a tiny plastic toy dinosaur or two in your room. The motel also has a gift shop with dinosaur toys, fossils, and Native American jewelry. **Pro:** Family friendly. **Con:** Feels busy rather than quiet. ⊠*251 E. Main St., 84078 ☎435/789–2660 or 800/780–7234 ☄435/789–2467 ⊕www.bestwestern.com ⚲60 rooms, 3 suites ♿In-room: refrigerator (some), Wi-Fi. In-hotel: restaurant, pool, no elevator, public Internet, no-smoking rooms ☰AE, D, DC, MC, V ⦿CP.*

$–$$ 🏨**Weston Lamplighter Inn.** The simply furnished rooms here are larger than average, and a half-dozen family suites can accommodate up to eight people (on two queen and two double beds). The motel is within a few blocks of area shops, theaters, restaurants, and attractions. **Pros:** Moderate prices. Breakfast available at on-site restaurant. **Cons:** Can be noisy. Older mattresses won't win any comfort prizes. ⊠*120 E. Main St., 84078 ☎435/789–0312 ☄435/781–1480 ⚲88 rooms, 6 suites ♿In-room: refrigerator, dial-up (some). In-hotel: restaurant, pool, no-smoking rooms ☰AE, DC, MC, V.*

THE ARTS
In June and July, enjoy musicals, melodramas, or comedies under the ★ stars at the **Outlaw Trail Theater** (⊠ *Western Park Outdoor Amphitheater, 302 E. 200 South St. ☎888/240–2080 ⊕www.myartscouncil. org/outlawtr.html*). Shows typically run Tuesday through Saturday.

SHOPPING
Dinosaur memorabilia, rocks, fossils, and Native American jewelry and baskets are available at the **Ashley Trading Post** (⊠*236 E. Main St. ☎435/789–8447*).If you prefer your rocks in stunning 14-karat gold settings, stop in at the **R. Fullbright Studio and Rock Shop** (⊠*216 E. Main St. ☎435/789–2451*)to see what local artist Randy Fullbright has created. He often works bits of dinosaur fossils into his upscale jewelry or produces bronze or paper castings of petroglyphs. He does photographs of the surrounding area, too.

EN ROUTE   Past Red Fleet Reservoir north of Vernal, U.S. 191 begins to ascend the eastern flank of the Uinta uplift as you head toward Flaming Gorge. The section of U.S. 191 and Route 44 between Vernal and Manila, Utah, is known as the **Flaming Gorge-Uintas National Scenic Byway.** Within a distance of 30 mi, the road passes through 18 uptilted geologic formations, including the billion-year-old exposed core of the Uinta Mountains, with signs identifying and describing them. The route also provides plenty of opportunity for wildlife watching and fossil hunting. Before setting out, pick up a guide to the road at the Utah Field House of Natural History.

DINOSAUR NATIONAL MONUMENT

20 mi east of Vernal via Rte. 149.

Dinomania rules at this 330-square-mi park that straddles the Utah–Colorado border.

The monument's collection of fossils resulted when floods deposited an astounding number of dinosaur carcasses on a sandbar; subsequent geologic deposits covered the bodies where they lay until the cache of paleontological treasures was discovered by Earl Douglass in 1909, when he stumbled upon eight enormous dinosaur tailbones exposed on a sandstone ridge. Although most of the park's acreage is in Colorado, its prime attraction is on the Utah side: the **Dinosaur Quarry and Visitor Center.** Unfortunately, the main visitor center has been closed indefinitely, due to structural problems plaguing the building, but a temporary visitor center has a small display of dinosaur fossils, and more are on view a short hike away. ⊠ *Rte. 149, 20 mi east of Vernal* ☎ *435/781–7700* ⊕ *www.nps.gov/dino* ⬜ *$10 per vehicle* ☉ *Memorial Day–Labor Day, daily 8:30–5:30; Labor Day–Memorial Day, daily 8:30–4:30.*

Although most people visit Dinosaur National Monument to see dinosaur bones, the backcountry scenery itself is alluring. An especially scenic 22-mi round-trip drive, the **Tour of the Tilted Rocks,** runs from the Dinosaur Quarry east to the **Josie Morris Cabin.** Josie was the sister of Ann Bassett, the "Etta Place" of Butch Cassidy legends. Ms. Morris lived alone for 50 years on her isolated homestead, keeping company with the likes of Butch Cassidy. Along the drive, watch for ancient rock art, geological formations, views of Split Mountain and rafters on the Green River, and hiking trails.

A scenic drive on the unpaved **Island Park Road,** along the northern edge of the park, not only passes some impressive Fremont petroglyph panels but also reaches a put-in point for rafters, who toss about on the white water of the Green and Yampa rivers.

The Journey Through Time self-guided 64-mi auto tour begins at the national monument Headquarters Visitor Center in Colorado and winds along the Utah–Colorado border, providing overlooks of the spectacularly colored canyons and landscape that make up the park.

SPORTS & THE OUTDOORS

HIKING   Four miles past the Dinosaur Quarry, the moderate 2-mi **Desert Voices Nature Trail** has interpretive signs (including some designed by children for children) that describe the arid environment you're hiking through. The more challenging 3-mi **Sound of Silence Trail,** which begins 2 mi past the Dinosaur Quarry, tests (or boosts) your hiking knowledge by asking you to find your way using landmarks. To hike both trails without returning to your car, use the easy ¼-mi **Connector Trail,** which links the two.

RAFTING   The best way to experience the geologic depths of Dinosaur National
Fodor's Choice   Monument is to take a white-water rafting trip on the Green or Yampa
★   rivers. Joining forces near Echo Park in Colorado, the two waterways

Environmental Echoes at Echo Park

CLOSE UP

Few public land controversies tell the tale of the modern environmental movement like the debate over the Echo Park Dam in Dinosaur National Monument.

To achieve economic expansion after World War II and encourage settlement in the arid American West, the federal Bureau of Reclamation created the Colorado River Compact, a proposal to build a series of hydroelectric dams on the West's greatest river. One of these proposed dams was at Echo Park, in the heart of the remote Dinosaur National Monument where two Colorado River tributaries, the Green and the Yampa, meet.

Although relatively unknown Dinosaur National Monument wasn't the public icon that parks such as Yosemite, Yellowstone, or the Grand Canyon were, the dam proposal galvanized a number of environmental organizations. The National Parks Association, Sierra Club, Izaak Walton League, and Wilderness Society began an unprecedented national campaign to raise awareness of the potentially drowned national monument. Together, they raised the question: if national parks

and monuments—areas that are supposedly under government protection—could not escape development, how could we safeguard these stunning places?

Through photographs, these organizations showcased the area's astounding geologic history, wild whitewater rivers, spectacular canyons, and its role as a wildlife haven. Historians view the Echo Park Dam controversy as the start of an era—the first time conservation organizations used their voices to oppose government actions on public lands. When Secretary of the Interior Douglas McKay announced in 1955 that the Echo Park Dam project would not go forward, it was the first of several major conservationist victories that led to future legislation to protect the nation's resources, including the Wilderness Act (1964) and the Wild and Scenic Rivers Act (1968).

As a result of the Echo Park controversy, the U.S. public began to understand the value of national parks and monuments, even those located in extremely remote locations. The word "environmental" had entered the American vocabulary.

have each carved spectacular canyons through several eons' worth of rock, and contain thrilling white-water rapids such as Whirlpool Canyon, SOB, Disaster Falls, and Hell's Half Mile. River-running season is May through September.

Adrift Adventures (📍*9500 East 6000 S., Jensen, 84035* ☎*435/789–3600 or 800/824–0150* ⊕*www.adrift.com*) offers one-day or multiday rafting trips, as well as a package that includes rafting in the morning and a horseback ride in the afternoon. **Dinosaur Expeditions** (✉*550 Main St., Vernal* ☎*435/781–0717 or 800/345–7238* ⊕*www.dinosau rexpeditions.com*) offers trips on the Green, Yampa, and White rivers, all concluding at their local boater-friendly restaurant in Vernal for tall tales and cold beers. **Hatch River Expeditions** (📍*221 N. 400 East St., Vernal, 84078* ☎*435/789–4316 or 800/342–8243* ⊕*www. hatchriver.com*)is the original river-running company; they've been at it since 1929. Their one-day and multiday rafting trips take you through both calm and white waters, and if fishing is your passion, they'll equip you for that, too.

WHERE TO CAMP

⚠ **Dinosaur National Monument Campgrounds.** You can camp alongside the Green River at two spots inside the monument. Both campgrounds have a bit of shade and are surrounded by canyon scenery. Green River campground is only open when the water is turned on, from approximately April to October, and it has a boat ramp for rafters. Split Mountain campground is open year-round, but only larger groups can camp there from approximately April to October. After the water is turned off in the fall, it's open to all, and vault toilets are available. Reservations are not accepted at either campground, except for groups at Split Mountain in the summer. ♿ *Flush toilets, pit toilets, drinking water, fire grates, picnic tables* 🏕*92 sites, no hookups* ✉*Rte. 149, 4 mi east of Dinosaur Quarry* ☎*435/781–7700 information 435/781–7759 reservations* ⊕*www.nps.gov/dino* ⊗*Green River campground approx. Apr.–Oct., Split Mountain yr-round.*

FLAMING GORGE NATIONAL RECREATION AREA

40 mi north of Vernal (to Flaming Gorge Dam) via U.S. 191.

In May 1869, during his mapping expedition on the Green and Colorado rivers, explorer John Wesley Powell named this canyon Flaming Gorge for its "flaming, brilliant red" color. Flaming Gorge remained one of Utah's most remote and least-developed inhabited areas well into the 1950s. In 1964, Flaming Gorge Canyon and the Green River running through it were plugged with a 500-foot-high wall of concrete. The result is a 91-mi-long reservoir that twists and turns among canyon walls. Much of Flaming Gorge Reservoir, a major area destination for fishing and boating, stretches north into Wyoming; however, most facilities lie south of the state line in Utah.

★ The main information center for the Utah side is the **Flaming Gorge Dam Visitor Center** (✉*U.S. 191, 2 mi north of Greendale Junction* ☎*435/885– 3135* ⊕*www.recreation.gov*). Displays and a movie explain aspects of this engineering marvel, and depending on national terrorism alert levels and weather conditions, the dam may be open for free guided tours leaving every hour. The visitor center is open from mid-March to mid-October, daily 8–5, and from mid-October to mid-March, daily 10–4. The **Swett Ranch** (✉*Off U.S. 191* ☎*435/784–3445*) was an isolated homestead that belonged to Oscar and Emma Swett and their nine children through most of the 1900s. The U.S. Forest Service has turned the ranch into a working historic site, complete with restored and decorated houses and buildings. At the Greendale Junction of U.S. 191 and Route 44, stay on U.S. 191; about ½ mi north of the junction there's a sign for the 1½-mi dirt road to the ranch, which is open from Memorial Day to Labor Day, Thursday–Monday 10–5. The **Red Canyon Visitor Center** (✉*Rte. 44* ☎*435/889–3713*) explains the geology, flora and fauna, and human history of the Flaming Gorge area, but the most magnificent thing about the center is its location atop a cliff that towers 1,300 feet above the lake. The views here are outstanding, and you can enjoy them while having a picnic on the grounds. To reach the visitor center, turn left at the Greendale Junction of U.S. 191 and Route 44, and follow the signs. The visitor center is open from Memorial Day to Labor Day, daily 8–6.A scenic 13-mi drive (on paved and gravel roads) crosses the **Sheep Creek Canyon Geological Area** (✉ *Sheep Creek Canyon Loop Rd., 28 mi west of Greendale Junction off U.S. 191 and Rte. 44* ☎ *435/784–3445*), which is full of upturned layers of rock, craggy pinnacles, and hoodoos pointing toward the sky. Watch for wild horses, bighorn sheep, and a bat cave alongside the road. In the fall salmon return to Sheep Creek to spawn; a viewing kiosk and several bridges provide unobtrusive locations from which to watch the spawning runs. The area is open from May to October.The **Spirit Lake Scenic Backway,** a 17-mi round-trip add-on to the Sheep Creek Canyon Loop road, leads past the **Ute Lookout Fire Tower,** which was in use from the 1930s through the 1960s.

SPORTS & THE OUTDOORS

BICYCLING Because it mixes high-desert vegetation—blooming sage, rabbit brush, cactus, and wildflowers—and red rock terrain with a cool climate, Flaming Gorge National Recreation Area is an ideal destination for road and trail biking. The 3-mi round-trip **Bear Canyon–Bootleg** ride begins south of the dam off U.S. 191 at the Firefighters' Memorial Campground and runs west to an overview of the reservoir. For the intermediate rider, **Dowd Mountain Hideout** offers a 10-mile ride with spectacular views of Flaming Gorge through forested single-track trail, leaving from Dowd Springs Picnic Area off Route 44. A free brochure, *Flaming Gorge Trails,* describes these and other cycling routes. The brochure is distributed at area visitor centers or online at ⊕ *www.dinoland.com/hikebike.html.* Several local lodges rent bikes.

FISHING & Flaming Gorge Reservoir provides ample opportunities for boating and
BOATING water sports of all kinds, whether you prefer lounging on the deck of
Fodor'sChoice a rented houseboat or skiing behind a high-performance speedboat.
★ Old-timers maintain that Flaming Gorge provides the best lake fishing in the state, yielding rainbow and lake trout, smallmouth bass, and Kokanee salmon. Only artificial lures and fly-fishing are permitted; bait fishing isn't allowed. For the best river fishing, try the Green River below Flaming Gorge Dam, where rainbow and brown trout are plentiful and big. Fed by cold water from the bottom of the lake, this stretch has been identified as one of the best trout fisheries in the world. The Green River below Flaming Gorge Dam is a calm, scenic stretch of water, ideal for risk-averse folk or for families who want to take smaller children on rafting trips, but who don't want to worry about them falling into white water. Most boating facilities close from October through mid-March.

If you have your own boat, you can launch it, gas it up, or rent a slip from **Cedar Springs Marina** (✉ *U.S. 191, approximately 2 mi southwest of Flaming Gorge Dam* ☎ *435/889–3795* ⊕ *www.cedarspringsmarina. com*), where you can also rent a boat or hire a fishing guide.**Flaming Gorge Recreation Services** (✉ *U.S. 191 at Dutch John Blvd.* ☎ *435/885–*

3191 ⊕www.fgrecservices.com) provides boat rentals, guided fishing trips, and daily float trips on the Green River. The **Lucerne Valley Marina** (⊠*1 Lucerne Valley Blvd., 7 mi east of Manila ☏435/784–3483 or 888/820–9225 ⊕www.flaminggorge.com*) has a boat launch, slips, mooring buoys, boat rentals, fishing licenses, mechanical services, gas, full-service RV camping, and houseboat and floating-cabin rentals.

HIKING Plenty of hiking opportunities exist in the Flaming Gorge area. Ask at any of the local visitor centers or lodges for recommended hikes. From the Red Canyon Visitor Center, you can take three different hikes along the **Canyon Rim Trail** through the pine forest: an easy ½-mi trek will take you to the Red Canyon Rim Overlook (above 1,300-foot cliffs), a moderate 3½-mi hike finds you at the Swett Ranch Overlook, and a 7-mile hike winds through brilliant layered colors to the Green River at the canyon's bottom below the dam.

In the Sheep Creek Canyon Geological Area, the 4-mi **Ute Mountain Trail** leads from the Ute Lookout Fire Tower down through pine forests to Brownie Lake, then back the same way. The **Spirit Lake Trail** begins at Spirit Lake (on Route 44, go past the Ute Lookout Fire Tower turnoff and take F.S. Road 221 to Spirit Lake) and takes you to Tamarack Lake and back for a moderate 4-mi trek.

WHERE TO STAY

$–$$ **Flaming Gorge Resort.** The lodge has motel rooms and condos, a good American-style restaurant ($–$$$), a store, and affiliation with Flaming Gorge Recreation Services, who rent rafts and boats and provide fishing-guide service. Each one-bedroom condo has air-conditioning, a queen bed, twin bed, queen sofa bed, living room, dining room, and full kitchen. There is no air-conditioning in the motel rooms. **Pros:** Plenty of amenities and recreational options. **Cons:** Can be extremely busy in summer, and too quiet in winter. ⊠*1100 E. Flaming Gorge Resort, off U.S. 191, Dutch John, 84023 ☏435/889–3773 ☐435/889–3788 ⊕www.flaminggorgeresort.com ⤶21 rooms, 24 condos ⚷In-room: no a/c (some), kitchen (some), DVD, Wi-Fi. In-hotel: restaurant, no elevator, no-smoking rooms ☰AE, D, MC, V.*

★ $–$$ **Red Canyon Lodge.** A pleasant surprise in the woods, this lodge is surrounded by well-built, handcrafted log cabins that face a private trout-stocked lake; the cabins have kitchenettes, and a few have wood-burning stoves. The great restaurant ($–$$$) is open for breakfast, lunch, and dinner from April to October and for weekend dinners only from November to March; dinner might include buffalo, elk medallions, or wild trout with pasta. The lodge provides recreation services like boat and bike rentals, horseback riding, and snowshoeing. It's a pleasant spot for birdwatching, too. **Pros:** Beautiful setting. Cabins are comfortable for families or groups. **Cons:** Don't expect to make last-minute reservations. ⊠*2450 W. Red Canyon Lodge, Dutch John, 84023 ☏435/889–3759 ☐435/889–5106 ⊕www.redcanyonlodge. com ⤶18 cabins ⚷In-room: no a/c, no phone, kitchen (some), no TV. In-hotel: restaurant, bicycles, some pets allowed ☰AE, D, MC, V.*

WHERE TO
CAMP
⛺ **Canyon Rim Campground.** This small campground sits along the Canyon Rim hiking trail atop 1,300-foot cliffs overlooking Flaming Gorge Reservoir. The location provides ample scenery, cool air, scattered shade, and close proximity to both the Red Canyon visitor center and the Red Canyon Lodge. The campground is 4 mi west of the Greendale Junction of U.S. 191 and Route 44, then 2½ mi down Red Canyon Road (look for the turnoff). ♿ *Pit toilets, drinking water, fire pits, picnic tables* 🏕 *18 sites* ✉ *Red Canyon Rd.* ☎ *435/784–3445 information, 877/444–6777 reservations* ⊕ *www.recreation.gov* ⊙ *Mid-May–mid-Sept.*

MIRROR LAKE SCENIC BYWAY

4

Kamas is 49 mi from Salt Lake City via I–80 and Rte. 32 south.

Although the Wasatch may be Utah's best-known mountain range, the Uinta Mountains, the only major east–west mountain range in the United States, are its tallest, topped by 13,528-foot Kings Peak. The Uinta Mountains area, particularly in the High Uintas Wilderness where no vehicles are allowed, is prime country for pack trips, horseback day rides, hiking, and overnight backpacking between late June and September. The Uintas are ribboned with streams, and they have hundreds of small lakes set in rolling meadows. Access to the Uinta Mountains is either from Kamas (40 mi east of Salt Lake City on I–80) or from Route 150, 30 mi south of Evanston, Wyoming.

Fodor'sChoice
★
Winding its way up to the High Uinta country is the **Mirror Lake Scenic Byway,** which begins in Kamas. The 65-mi drive follows Route 150 through heavily wooded canyons past mountain lakes and peaks, cresting at 10,687-foot Bald Mountain Pass. A good place to stop en route is at **Upper Provo Falls,** near mile marker 24, where you can stroll the boardwalk to the terraced falls cascading with clear mountain water. Because of heavy winter snows, much of the road is closed from October to May. You can buy a guide to the byway from the Wasatch–Cache National Forest's Kamas Ranger District office in Kamas. ✉ *Wasatch–Cache National Forest, Kamas Ranger District, 50 E. Center St., Box 68, Kamas* ☎ *435/783–4338* ⊕ *www.fs.fed.us/r4/wcnf/unit/kamas.*

Nearby **Mirror Lake** (1 mi north of the crest of Bald Mountain Pass on Route 150) is arguably the best-known lake in the High Uintas Wilderness. At an altitude of 9,000 feet, it offers a cool respite from summer heat, it's easy to reach by car, and families enjoy fishing, hiking, and camping along its rocky shores. Its campgrounds provide a base for hikes into the surrounding mountains, and Highline Trail accesses the 460,000-acre High Uintas Wilderness Area to the east. There's a $6 day-use fee for Mirror Lake.

SPORTS & THE OUTDOORS
Bear River Lodge (✉ *Mile marker 49 on Mirror Lake Route 150* ☎ *801/936–0780 or 800/559–1121*) is 49 mi northeast of Kamas, or 30 mi south of Evanston, Wyoming, an ideal location for beginning your exploration of the Uinta Mountains. Employees at the lodge are

intimately familiar with the area and can tell you about any number of the hundreds of hiking trails you can try. The lodge also rents fishing gear, ATVs, snowmobiles, and cross-country skis.

WHERE TO STAY

$$–$$$$ ▢ **Bear River Lodge.** Thirteen log cabins in the forest let you reconnect with nature without giving up creature comforts. Simply appointed with log and wood furniture, the cabins are near the lodge, where you can outfit yourself for a variety of outdoor adventures. The lodge's Burly Bear Grill (¢–$$) serves up breakfast as well as burgers and sandwiches for lunch or dinner. Autumn rates (October to December) are often deeply discounted. From October to May, the route from Kamas on Route 150 is closed, so access is from Evanston, Wyoming. **Pros:** Comfortable cabins. Plenty of outdoor activities nearby. **Cons:** Prices seem high for level of amenities. ⊠*Mile marker 49 on Mirror Lake Highway (Route 150), 49 mi northeast of Kamas, or 30 mi south of Evanston, WY* ☎*801/451–0275 or 800/559–1121* ▤*801/451–0174* ⊕*www.bearriverlodge.com* ➷*13 cabins* ⅃*In-room: no a/c, no phone, kitchen (some), refrigerator, DVD (some), VCR (some). In-hotel: restaurant, no elevator, no-smoking rooms* ▤*AE, D, MC, V.*

WHERE TO   ⛺ **Christmas Meadows Campground.** Escape the summer heat and sur-
CAMP   round yourself in a beautiful setting that just begs to be hiked or mountain biked. To reach the campground, go 45 mi northeast of Kamas on Route 150, then east 4 mi on Christmas Meadows Road. ⅃*Pit toilets, drinking water, fire pits, picnic tables* ➷*11 sites* ⊠*Christmas Meadows Rd., 49 mi northeast of Kamas* ☎*307/789–3194 information, 877/444–6777 reservations* ⊕*www.recreation.gov* ☉*June–Aug.*

⛺ **Mirror Lake Campground.** A popular destination in the summertime, this lovely campground borders Mirror Lake, in the thick Uinta forest. ⅃*Pit toilets, drinking water, fire pits, picnic tables* ➷*79 sites* ⊠*Rte. 150, 32 mi northeast of Kamas* ☎*435/783–4338 information, 877/444–6777 reservations* ⊕*www.recreation.gov* ☉*July–early Sept.*

EASTERN UTAH ESSENTIALS

AIRPORTS

The closest major airport is Salt Lake International Airport—two hours from Price and four hours from Vernal; it's served by most major airlines.

CAMPING

Campgrounds are scattered liberally throughout eastern Utah. Many are state-run campgrounds with no hookups, but you'll usually find flush toilets, drinking water, fire pits, barbecue grills, and picnic tables. The Ashley National Forest offers forested sites; areas around Price, Vernal, and the reservoirs tend to be more open. Summer temperatures are cooler in the high-alpine camping areas in the Uinta Mountains and the Wasatch-Cache National Forest. Many campsites can be reserved through Recreation.gov or through the Utah State Parks.

Information **Recreation.gov** (☎877/444–6777 ⊕ *www.recreation.gov*). **Utah State Parks** (☎800/322–3770 ⊕ *www.stateparks.utah.gov/reservations*).

CAR TRAVEL

Both U.S. 40 and U.S. 191 are well maintained; however, there are some curvy, mountainous stretches. If you're headed away from major towns, be prepared for dirt roads. Keep your vehicle fueled up because gas stations can be far apart, and not all of them are open on Sunday. Watch for wildlife on the road, especially at night.

Information **Road Conditions** (☎800/492–2400).

EMERGENCIES

For emergencies, call the local Utah Highway Patrol phone number or 911.

Ambulance or Police **Emergencies** (☎911). **Utah Highway Patrol dispatch** (☎435/789–7222 *Vernal area*, 435/637–0890 *Price area*, 435/336–3600 *Mirror Lake area* ⊕ *www.highwaypatrol.utah.gov*).

24-Hour Medical Care **Ashley Valley Medical Center** (✉151 W. 200 North St., Vernal ☎435/789–3342). **Castleview Hospital** (✉300 N. Hospital Dr., Price ☎435/637–4800). **Uintah Basin Medical Center** (✉250 W. 300 North St., Roosevelt ☎435/722–4691).

TOURS

In Vernal, Dinaland Aviation offers flights over Dinosaur National Monument, Flaming Gorge, and the canyons of the Green River.

Tour Operators **Dinaland Aviation** (✉830 E. 500 South St., Vernal ☎435/789–4612).

TRAIN TRAVEL

Amtrak's daily *California Zephyr* stops in Helper en route between Chicago and San Francisco.

Train Information **Amtrak** (☎800/872–7245 ⊕ *www.amtrak.com*).

VISITOR INFORMATION

Information **Bureau of Land Management** (✉125 S. 600 West St., Price, 84501 ☎435/636–3600 ✉170 S. 500 East St., Vernal, 84078 ☎435/781–4400 ⊕ *www.blm.gov*). **Carbon County Chamber of Commerce** (✉81 N. 200 East St., #3, Price, 84501 ☎435/637–2788 ⊕ *www.carboncountychamber.com*). **Castle Country Travel Region–Carbon County Visitors Bureau** (✉81 N. 200 East St., Price, 84501 ☎435/637–3009 or 800/842–0789 ⊕ *www.castlecountry.com*). **Dinosaurland Travel Board** (✉25 E. Main St., Vernal, 84078 ☎435/789–6932 or 800/477–5558 ⊕ *www.dinoland.com*). **Duchesne County Chamber of Commerce** (✉50 E. 200 South St., Duchesne, 84066 ☎435/722–4598). **Flaming Gorge Chamber of Commerce** (✉ General Delivery, Manila, 84046 ☎435/784–3154 or 435/789–3445). **Northeastern Utah Visitor Center** (✉Utah Field House of Natural History, 496 E. Main St., Vernal, 84078 ☎435/789–7894). **Vernal Chamber of Commerce** (✉134 W. Main St., Vernal, 84078 ☎435/789–1352 or 800/421–9635 ⊕ *www.vernalchamber.com*).

Capitol Reef National Park

WORD OF MOUTH

"We loved Cohab Canyon hike—didn't go all the way since it started raining and got stormy. But we took a million pics of all those incredible dripping rocks and weird formations. Love that stuff!"

—sharondi

WELCOME TO CAPITOL REEF

Gifford Farmhouse in Fruita

TOP REASONS TO GO

★ **The Waterpocket Fold:** See an excellent example of a monocline—a fold in the earth's crust with one very steep side in an area that is otherwise horizontal. This one's almost 100-mi long.

★ **No crowds:** Experience the best of Southern Utah weather, rock formations, and wide-open spaces without the crowds of nearby parks such as Zion and Bryce Canyon.

★ **Fresh fruit:** Pick apples, pears, apricots, and peaches in season at the pioneer-planted orchards at historic Fruita. These trees still produce plenty of fruit.

★ **Rock art:** View ancient pictographs and petroglyphs left by the Fremont people, who lived in this area from 700 to 1300 AD.

★ **Pioneer artifacts:** Buy faithfully reproduced tools and utensils like those used by Mormon pioneers, at the Gifford Homestead.

Chimney Rock

1 Fruita. This historic pioneer village is at the heart of what most people see of Capitol Reef. The one and only park visitor center nearby is the place to get maps, and travel and weather information. The scenic drive through Capitol Gorge provides a view of the Golden Throne.

2 Cathedral Valley. The views are stunning and the silence deafening in the park's remote northern section. High-clearance vehicles are required, as is a crossing of the Fremont River. Driving in this valley is next to impossible when the Cathedral Valley Road is wet, so ask at the visitor center about current weather and road conditions.

3 Muley Twist Canyon. At the southern reaches of the park, this canyon is accessed via Notom-Bullfrog Road from the north, and Burr Trail Road from the west and southeast. High-clearance vehicles are required for much of it.

GETTING ORIENTED

At the heart of this 378-square-mi park is the massive natural feature known as the Waterpocket Fold, which runs roughly northwest to southeast along the park's spine. Capitol Reef itself is named for a formation along the fold near the Fremont River. A historic pioneer settlement, the green oasis of Fruita is easily accessed by car, and a 9-mi scenic drive provides a good overview of the canyons and rock formations that populate the park. Colors here range from deep, rich reds to sage greens to crumbling gray sediments. The absence of large towns nearby ensures that night skies are brilliant starscapes.

Springtime blossoms

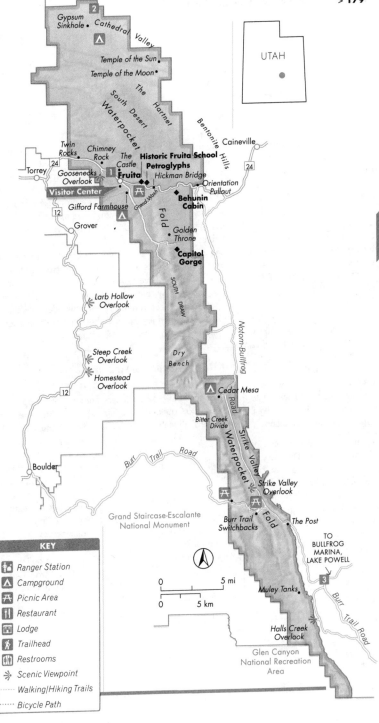

UTAH

2

Gypsum
Sinkhole
Cathedral Valley

Temple of the Sun

Temple of the Moon

The Hartnet

South Desert

Waterpocket

Bentonite Hills

Caineville

24

Twin
Rocks
Chimney
Rock
The
Castle
Historic Fruita School
Petroglyphs
Fruita
Hickman Bridge
*Orientation
Pullout*

Torrey

Goosenecks
Overlook
Visitor Center

Gifford Farmhouse

1

Grand Wash

Fold

**Behunin
Cabin**

12

Grover

*Golden
Throne*

**Capitol
Gorge**

Larb Hollow
Overlook

SOUTH DRAW

Steep Creek
Overlook

Dry
Bench

Homestead
Overlook

12

Cedar Mesa

Notom–Bullfrog

Bitter Creek
Divide

Waterpocket

Strike Valley

Burr   Trail   Road

Boulder

Strike Valley
Overlook

Grand Staircase-Escalante
National Monument

Burr Trail
Switchbacks

Fold

The Post

TO
BULLFROG
MARINA,
LAKE POWELL

3

Burr Trail Road

Muley Tanks

Halls Creek
Overlook

Glen Canyon
National Recreation
Area

0   5 mi

0   5 km

5

KEY

👥	*Ranger Station*
⛺	*Campground*
🏕	*Picnic Area*
🍴	*Restaurant*
🏠	*Lodge*
🚶	*Trailhead*
🚻	*Restrooms*
☀	*Scenic Viewpoint*
	Walking/Hiking Trails
	Bicycle Path

CAPITOL REEF PLANNER

When to Go

Spring and early summer bring the most visitors to the park. Folks clear out in the height of summer as temperatures reach the mid-90s°F, and then early fall brings people back to the park for the apple harvest and crisp autumn temperatures. Still, the park could seldom be called crowded—though the campground does fill daily throughout spring, summer, and fall. Trails remain fairly unpopulated year-round, perhaps because of the difficult nature of many of them. You're not bound to get wet, since annual rainfall is only about 7 inches. When it does rain, devastating flash floods can wipe out park roads and leave you stranded. Snowfall is usually light, especially at lower elevations.

Spring is undoubtedly one of the most beautiful times to visit this region, but weather can be unpredictable, and sudden, short-lived snowstorms are not uncommon. Although summer days can be uncomfortably hot and winter storms potentially fierce, central Utah has a generally moderate climate with four distinct seasons.

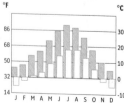

Flora & Fauna

The golden rock and rainbow cliffs are at their finest at sunset, when it seems as if they are lighted from within. That's also when mule deer wander through the orchards near the campground. The deer are quite tame, but do not feed them; their digestive systems are harmed by people food. Many of the park's animals move about only at night to escape the heat of the day, but pinyon jays and black-billed magpies flit around the park all day. The best place to see wildlife is near the Fremont River, where animals are drawn to drink. Ducks and small mammals such as the yellow-bellied marmot live nearby. Desert bighorn sheep also live in Capitol Reef, but they are elusive. Your best chance of spotting the sheep is during a long hike deep within the park. If you should encounter a sheep, do not approach it, as they've been known to charge human beings.

Getting There & Around

Though far from big cities, there are a variety of approaches to Capitol Reef country. The main high-speed arteries through the region are Interstates 70 and 15, but any route will require travel of some secondary roads such as U.S. 50, U.S. 89, Highway 24, or Route 72. All are well-maintained, safe roads that bisect rich agricultural communities steeped in Mormon history (such as the nearby towns of Bicknell and Loa). Interstate 15 is the fastest way through central Utah, but U.S. 89 and the local roads that feed onto it will give you a more direct path into Utah's past and present-day character. Highway 24 runs across the middle of Capitol Reef National Park, so even those traveling between points west and east of the park with no intention of touring the park get a scenic treat on their way. Once inside the park, there is no shuttle service like at nearby Zion and Bryce Canyon national parks.

Updated
by Janet
Buckingham

YOUR SENSES WILL BE DELIGHTED by a visit to Capitol Reef National Park. Here, the land is saturated in colors that are more dramatic than anywhere else in the West. The dominant Moenkopi rock formation is a rich, red-chocolate hue. Deep blue-green juniper and pinyon stand out against it. Other sandstone layers are gold, ivory, and lavender. Sunset brings out the colors in an explosion of copper, platinum, and orange, then dusk turns the cliffs purple and blue. The texture of rock deposited in ancient inland seas and worn by subsequent erosion is pure art.

The park preserves the Waterpocket Fold, a giant wrinkle in the earth that extends a hundred miles between Thousand Lake Mountain and Lake Powell. When you climb high onto the rocks or into the mountains, you can see this remarkable geologic wonder and the jumble of colorful cliffs, massive domes, soaring spires, and twisting canyons that surround it. It's no wonder Native Americans called this part of the country the "land of sleeping rainbow."

But your eyes will not be alone in their joy. The fragrance of pine and sage rises from the earth, and canyon wrens sing to you as you sit by the water. Flowing across the heart of Capitol Reef is the Fremont River, a narrow little creek that can turn into a swollen, raging torrent during desert flash floods. The river sustains cottonwoods, wildlife, and verdant valleys rich with fruit. During the harvest, your sensory experience is complete when you bite into a perfect ripe peach or apple from the park's orchards. Your soul, too, will be gratified here. You can walk the trails in relative solitude and enjoy the beauty without confronting crowds on the roads or paths. All around you are signs of those who came before: ancient Native Americans of the Fremont culture, Mormon pioneers who settled the land, and other courageous explorers who traveled the canyons. It is a rare thrill to feel the past overtake the present.

SCENIC DRIVE

Capitol Reef Scenic Drive. This paved road starts at the visitor center and winds its way through the Fruita Historic District and colorful sandstone cliffs into Capitol Gorge; a side street, Grand Wash Road, provides access into the canyon. At Capitol Gorge, the route becomes unpaved, and road conditions may vary because of weather and amount of use. Check with the visitor center before entering Capitol Gorge. Capitol Reef Scenic Drive, called simply Scenic Drive by locals, is 9 mi long, with about the last quarter of it unpaved.

See Four-Wheeling in the Sports & the Outdoors section for the **Cathedral Valley Scenic Backway** *drive.*

CAPITOL REEF IN ONE DAY

Pack a picnic lunch, snacks, and cold drinks to take with you, because there are no restaurants in the park. As you enter the park, look to your left for Chimney Rock; in a landscape of spires, cliffs, and knobs, this deep-red landmark is unmistakable. Start your journey at the **visitor center,** where you can study a three-dimensional map of the area, watch the short slide show, and browse the many books and maps related to the park. Then head for the park's scenic drive, stopping at the **Fruita Historic District** to see some of the sites associated with the park's Mormon history. Stop at the **Historic Gifford Farmhouse** for a tour and a visit to the gift shop. As you continue on with your tour, check out the **Fremont Indian Petroglyphs,** and if you feel like some exertion, take a hike on the Hickman Bridge Trail. Next you'll have to backtrack a few miles on Highway 24 to find the **Goosenecks Trail.** At the same parking lot you'll find the trailhead for **Sunset Point Trail;** take this short hike in time to watch the setting sun hit the colorful cliffs.

WHAT TO SEE

HISTORIC SITES

Fruita Historic District. In 1880 Nels Johnson became the first homesteader in the Fremont River Valley, building his home near the confluence of Sulphur Creek and the Fremont River. Other Mormon settlers followed and established small farms and orchards, creating the village of Junction. The orchards thrived, and in 1902 the settlement's name was changed to Fruita. Capitol Reef's **fruit orchards** (⊠ *Scenic Dr., less than 1 mi from visitor center*)are still lovingly maintained by the National Park Service. You can often see mule deer wandering here at dusk, making for great photographs. During harvest season, you can pick cherries, apricots, peaches, pears, and apples.

FodorsChoice
★

Originally built by Mormon settler Calvin Pendleton in 1908, the **historic Gifford Farmhouse** (⊠ *Scenic Dr., less than 1 mi from visitor center* ☎ *435/425–3791* ⊗ *Memorial Day–Labor Day, daily 9–4: 30*)is one of the few remaining buildings in the area. The Gifford family—the last residents of Fruita—lived in the house from 1928 to until they sold their home to the National Park Service in 1969. Several rooms in the restored house are furnished with period furniture and housewares. The former kitchen has been converted to a gift shop. It's open daily from 11 to 5. The grounds are an idyllic spot for a picnic, too.

Pioneer Register. Travelers passing through Capitol Gorge in the 19th and early 20th centuries etched the canyon wall with their names and the date they passed. Directly across the canyon from the Pioneer Register and about 50 feet up are signatures etched into the canyon wall by an early United States Geologic Survey crew. It's illegal to write or scratch on the canyon walls today. You can reach the register via an easy 1-mi hike from the end of the road. ⊠ *Off Scenic Dr., 9 mi south of visitor center.*

SCENIC STOPS

Capitol Gorge. At the entrance to this gorge Scenic Drive becomes unpaved. The narrow, twisting road on the floor of the gorge was a route for pioneer wagons traversing this part of Utah starting in the 1860s. After every flash flood, pioneers would laboriously clear the route so wagons could continue to go through. The gorge became the main automobile route in the area until 1962, when Highway 24 was built. The short drive to the end of the road leads to some interesting hiking trails. ⊠ *Scenic Dr., 9 mi south of visitor center.*

Chimney Rock. Even in a landscape of spires, cliffs, and knobs, this deep-red landform is unmistakable. ⊠ *Hwy. 24, about 3 mi west of the visitor center.*

♺ **Fremont Indian Petroglyphs.** Nearly 1,000 years ago the Capitol Reef area was occupied by the Fremont Indians, whose culture was tied closely to the ancestral Puebloan culture. Fremont rock art can be identified by the large trapezoidal figures often depicted wearing headdresses and ear baubles. ⊠ *Hwy. 24, 1 2/10 mi east of visitor center.*

The Waterpocket Fold. A giant wrinkle in the earth that extends almost 100 mi between Thousand Lake Mountain and Lake Powell, the Waterpocket Fold is not to be missed. You can glimpse the fold by driving south on Scenic Drive—after it branches off Highway 24—past the Fruita Historic District, but for complete immersion enter the park via the 66-mi Burr Trail from the town of Boulder. Travel through the southernmost reaches of the park requires a substantial amount of driving on unpaved roads. It's accessible to most vehicles during dry weather; check at the visitor center for road conditions and recommendations.

VISITOR CENTER

Watch a film, talk with rangers, or peruse the many books, maps, and materials offered for sale in the bookstore. Towering over the center is the Castle, one of the park's most prominent rock formations. ⊠ *Hwy. 24, 11 mi east of Torrey* ☎ *435/425–3791* ⊙ *May–Sept., daily 8–6; Oct. and mid-Apr.–May, daily 8–5; Nov.–mid-Apr., daily 8–4:30.*

SPORTS & THE OUTDOORS

The main outdoor activity at Capitol Reef is hiking. There are trails for all levels. Remember: whenever you venture into the desert—that is, wherever you go in Capitol Reef—take, and drink, plenty of water.

BICYCLING

Bicycles are allowed only on established roads in the park. Since Highway 24 is a state highway and receives a substantial amount of through traffic, it's not the best place to pedal. Scenic Drive is better, but the road is narrow, and you have to contend with drivers dazed by the beautiful surroundings. Four-wheel-drive roads are certainly less traveled, but they are often sandy, rocky, and steep. You cannot ride your bicycle in washes or on hiking trails. ⇨ *Multisport Outfitters & Expeditions box.*

MULTISPORT OUTFITTERS & EXPEDITIONS

Hondoo Rivers & Trails. Fast gaining a reputation for high-quality, educational trips into the backcountry of Capitol Reef National Park, these folks pride themselves on delivering a unique, private experience. From May to October, the company offers adventures on horseback, on foot, or via four-wheel-drive vehicle in Capitol Reef and the mountains and deserts surrounding it. Trips are designed to explore the geologic landforms in the area, seek out wildflowers in season, and to encounter free-roaming mustangs, bison, and bighorn sheep when possible. Single- or multiday trips can be arranged. ⊠ *90 E. Main St., Torrey* ☎ *435/425–3519 or 800/332–2696* ⊕ *www.hondoo.com.*

Wild Hare Expeditions. For a real taste of Capitol Reef National Park backcountry, take a hiking, biking, or 4x4 expedition with this enthusiastic outfitter. Guides will teach you more in one fun day about geology, wildlife, and land ethics than you thought possible. ⊠ *116 W. Main St., Torrey* ☎ *435/425–3999 or 888/304–4273* ⊕ *www.color-country. net/~thehare.*

Cathedral Valley Scenic Backway. In the remote northern end of the park you can enjoy solitude and a true backcountry ride on this trail. You'll be riding on surfaces that include dirt, sand, bentonite clay, and rock, and you will also ford the Fremont River; you should be prepared to encounter steep hills and switchbacks, wash crossings, and stretches of deep sand. Summer is not a good time to try this ride, as water is very difficult to find and temperatures may exceed 100°F. The entire route is about 60 mi long; during a multiday trip you can camp at the primitive campground with five sites, about midway through the loop. ⊠ *Off Hwy. 24 at Caineville, or at River Ford Rd., 5 mi west of Caineville on Hwy. 24.*

South Draw Road. This is a very strenuous ride that traverses dirt, sand, and rocky surfaces, and crosses several creeks that may be muddy. It's not recommended in winter or spring because of deep snow at higher elevations. If you like fast downhill rides, though, this trip is for you—it will make you feel like you have wings. The route starts at an elevation of 8,500 feet on Boulder Mountain and ends 15 mi later at 5,500 feet in the Pleasant Creek parking area at the end of Scenic Drive. ⊠ *At the junction of Bowns Reservoir Rd. and Hwy. 12, 13 mi south of Torrey.*

FOUR-WHEELING

You can explore Capitol Reef in a 4x4 on a number of exciting backcountry routes. Road conditions can vary greatly depending on recent weather patterns. Spring and summer rains can leave the roads muddy, washed out, and impassable even to four-wheel-drive vehicles. Always check at the park visitor center for current conditions before you set out, and take water, supplies, and a cell phone with you. ⇨ *Multisport Outfitters & Expeditions box for guided four-wheeling trips.*

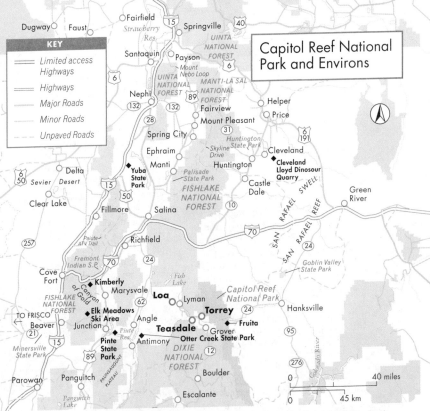

Capitol Reef National
Park and Environs

Cathedral Valley Scenic Backway. The north end of Capitol Reef, along this backcountry road, is filled with towering monoliths, panoramic vistas, and a stark desert landscape. The area is remote and the road through it unpaved, so do not enter without a high-clearance vehicle, some planning, and a cell phone. The drive through the valley is a 58-mi loop that you can begin at River Ford Road off Highway 24. From there, the loop travels northwest, giving you access to Glass Mountain, South Desert, and Gypsum Sinkhole. Turning southeast at the sinkhole, the loop takes you past the side road that accesses the Temples of the Moon and Sun, then becomes Caineville Wash Road before ending at Highway 24, 7 mi east of your starting point. Caineville Wash Road has two water crossings. Including stops, allow a half day for this drive. ■TIP➔ If your time is limited, you may want to tour only the Caineville Wash Road, which takes about two hours. At the visitor center you can check for road conditions and pick up a self-guided auto tour brochure for $1. ⊠ River Ford Rd., 11 7/10 mi east of visitor center on Hwy. 24.

HIKING

Many park trails in Capitol Reef include steep climbs, but there are a few easy-to-moderate hikes. A short drive from the visitor center takes you to a dozen trails, and a park ranger can advise you on combining trails or locating additional routes. ⇨*Multisport Outfitters & Expeditions box for hiking trips.*

EASY   **Goosenecks Trail.** This nice little walk gives you a good introduction to the land surrounding Capitol Reef, as well as dizzying views from the overlook. It's only 3/10 mi round-trip. ⊠*Hwy. 24, about 3 mi west of the visitor center.*

Grand Wash Trail. At the end of unpaved Grand Wash Road you can continue on foot through the canyon to its end at the Fremont River. This flat hike takes you through a wide wash between canyon walls. It's an excellent place to study the geology up close. The round-trip hike is 4½ mi; allow two to three hours for your walk. Check at the ranger station for flash-flood warnings before entering the wash. ⊠*Hwy. 24, east of Hickman Bridge parking lot, or at end of Grand Wash Rd., off Scenic Dr. about 5 mi from visitor center.*

> ## GEOLOGY BEHIND THE PARK'S NAME
>
> When water wears away layers of sandstone, basins can appear in the rock. These are called waterpockets. The 100-mi-long Waterpocket Fold—a massive rift in the Earth's crust, where geothermal pressure pushed one side 7,000 feet higher than the other—is full of these waterpockets. Early explorers with seafaring backgrounds called the fold a reef, since it was a barrier to travel. Some of the rocks, due to erosion, also have domelike formations resembling capitol rotundas.

Sunset Point Trail. The trail starts from the same parking lot as the Goosenecks Trail. Benches along this easy, 7/10-mi round-trip invite you to sit and meditate surrounded by the colorful desert. At the trail's end, you will be rewarded with broad vistas into the park; it's even better at sunset. ⊠*Hwy. 24, about 3 mi west of visitor center.*

MODERATE   **Capitol Gorge Trail and the Tanks.** Starting at the Pioneer Register, about
Fodor'sChoice   a mile from the Capitol Gorge parking lot, is a trail that climbs to
★   the Tanks. After a scramble up about 2/10 mi of steep trail with cliff drop-offs, you can look down into the Tanks and can also see a natural bridge below the lower tank. Including the walk to the Pioneer Register, allow an hour or two for this interesting hike. ⊠*At end of Scenic Dr., 9 mi south of visitor center.*

♺   **Cohab Canyon Trail.** Children particularly love this trail for the geological features and native creatures, such as rock wrens and Western pipistrelles (canyon bats), that you see along the way. One end of the trail is directly across from the Fruita Campground on Scenic Drive, and the other is across from the Hickman Bridge parking lot. The first ¼ mi from Fruita is pretty strenuous, but then the walk becomes easy except for turnoffs to the overlooks, which are strenuous but short. Along the way you'll find miniature arches, skinny side canyons, and honeycombed patterns on canyon walls where the wrens make nests. The trail is 3 2/10 mi round-trip to the Hickman Bridge parking lot. The Overlook Trail adds 2 mi to the journey. Allow one to two hours to overlooks and back; allow two to three hours to Hickman Bridge parking lot and back. ⊠*About 1 mi south of visitor center on Scenic Dr., or about 2 mi east of visitor center on Hwy. 24.*

Fremont River Trail. What starts as a quiet little stroll beside the river turns into an adventure. The first ½ mi of the trail is wheelchair accessible as you wander past the orchards next to the Fremont River. After you pass through a narrow gate, the trail changes personality and you're in for a steep climb on an exposed ledge with drop-offs. The views at the top of the 770-foot ascent are worth it as you look down into the Fruita Historic District. The trail is 2½ mi round-trip; allow two hours. ⊠*Near amphitheater off Loop C of Fruita Campground, about 1 mi from visitor center.*

Golden Throne Trail. As you hike to the base of the Golden Throne, you may be fortunate enough to see one of the park's elusive desert bighorn sheep. You're more likely, however, to spot their small, split-hoof tracks in the sand. The trail itself is 2 mi of gradual elevation gain with some steps and drop-offs. The Golden Throne is hidden until you near the end of the trail, then suddenly you find yourself looking at a huge sandstone monolith. If you hike near sundown the throne burns gold, salmon, and platinum. The round-trip hike is 4 mi and you should allow two to three hours. ⊠*At end of Capitol Gorge Rd., at Capitol Gorge trailhead, 9 mi south of visitor center.*

Fodor'sChoice
★ **Hickman Bridge Trail.** This trail is a perfect introduction to the park. It leads to a natural bridge of Kayenta sandstone, which has a 135-foot opening carved by intermittent flash floods. Early on, the route climbs a set of steps along the Fremont River, and as the trail tops out onto a bench, you'll find a slight depression in the earth. This is what remains of an ancient Fremont pit house, a kind of home that was dug into the ground and covered with brush. The trail splits, leading along the right-hand branch to a strenuous uphill climb to the Rim Overlook and Navajo Knobs. Stay to your left to see the bridge, and you'll encounter a moderate up-and-down trail. As you continue up the wash on your way to the bridge, you'll notice a Fremont granary on the right side of the small canyon. Allow about 1½ hours to walk the 2-mi round-trip. The walk to the bridge is one of the most popular trails in the park, so expect lots of company along the way. ⊠*Hwy. 24, 2 mi east of visitor center.*

DIFFICULT **Chimney Rock Trail.** You're almost sure to see ravens drifting on thermal winds around the deep red Mummy Cliff that rings the base of this trail. This loop trail begins with a steep climb to a rim above Chimney Rock. The trail is 3½ mi round-trip, with a 600-foot elevation change. Allow three to four hours. ⊠*Hwy. 24, about 3 mi west of visitor center.*

HORSEBACK RIDING

Many areas in the park are closed to horses and pack animals, so it's a good idea to check with the visitor center before you set out with your animals. Day use does not require a permit, but you need to get one for overnight camping with horses and pack animals. Hondoo Rivers & Trails and Wild Hare Expeditions run horseback tours into the national park *(⇨ Multisport Outfitters & Expeditions box).* Unless you ride with a park-licensed outfitter, you have to bring your own horse, as no rentals are available.

EDUCATIONAL OFFERINGS

RANGER PROGRAMS

From May to September, ranger programs, including guided walks and talks as well as evening programs in the Fruita Campground amphitheater, are offered at no charge. You can obtain current information about ranger talks and other park events at the visitor center or campground bulletin boards.

Evening Program. Learn about Capitol Reef's geology, Native American cultures, wildlife, and more at a free lecture, slide show, or other ranger-led activities. Programs are offered from May to September nightly, ½ hour after sunset. A schedule of topics and times is posted at the visitor center. ✉ *Amphitheater, Loop C, Fruita Campground, about 1 mi from visitor center on Scenic Dr.* ☎ *435/425–3791.*

Junior Ranger Program. Each child who participates in this self-guided program completes a combination of activities in the Junior Ranger booklet, attends a ranger program, interviews a park ranger, and/or picks up litter. ✉ *At the visitor center* ☎ *435/425–3791* 💳 *$1.50.*

Ranger Talks. Each day at the visitor center rangers give brief talks on park geology. Times of these talks vary, so check at the center for a current schedule. ✉ *At the visitor center* ☎ *435/425–3791* 💳 *Free* ⊙ *May–Sept., daily.*

NEARBY TOWNS & ATTRACTIONS

Probably the best home base for exploring the park, the pretty town of **Torrey,** just outside the park, has lots of personality. Giant old cottonwood trees make it a shady, cool place to stay, and the townspeople are friendly and accommodating. A little farther west on Highway 24, tiny **Teasdale** is a charming settlement cradled in a cove of the Aquarius Plateau. The homes, many of which are well-preserved older structures, look out onto brilliantly colored cliffs and green fields. **Bicknell** lies another few miles west of Capitol Reef. Not much happens here, making it a wonderfully quiet place to rest your head. The Wayne County seat of **Loa,** 10 mi west of Torrey, was settled by pioneers in the 1870s. If you head south from Torrey instead of west, you can take a spectacular 32-mi drive along Highway 12 to **Boulder,** a town so remote that its mail was carried on horseback until 1940. Nearby is Anasazi State Park. In the opposite direction, 51 mi east, is **Hanksville,** more a crossroads than anything else.

Anasazi State Park. Anasazi is a Navajo word interpreted to mean "ancient enemies." What the Anasazi called themselves we will never know, but their descendants, the Hopi people, prefer the term Ancestral Puebloan. This state park is dedicated to the study of that mysterious culture, with a largely unexcavated dwelling site, an interactive museum, and a reproduction of a pueblo. ⌧*460 N. Hwy. 12, Boulder* ☎*435/335–7308* ⊕*www.stateparks.utah.gov* 🗃*$4 per person* ⊗*Memorial Day–Labor Day, daily 8–6; Labor Day–Memorial Day, daily 9–5.*

🄫 **Goblin Valley State Park.** All of the landscape in this part of the country is strange and surreal, but Goblin Valley takes the cake as the weirdest of all. It's full of hundreds of gnome-like rock formations colored in a dramatic orange hue. Short, easy trails wind through the goblins, which delight children. ⌧*Hwy. 24, 12 mi north of Hanksville* ☎*435/564–3633* ⊕*www.stateparks.utah.gov* 🗃*$7 per vehicle* ⊗*Daily 8 AM–sunset.*

San Rafael Swell. About 80 mi long and 30 mi wide, this massive fold and uplift in the Earth's crust rises 2,100 feet above the desert. The Swell, as it is known locally, is northeast of Capitol Reef, between Interstate 70 and Highway 24. You can take photos from several viewpoints (⇨ also box in Chapter 4). ⌧*BLM San Rafael Resource Area, 900 North and 700 East, Price* ☎*435/637–4584* ⊕*www.blm.gov/ut.*

> **FAMILY PICKS**
>
> **Anasazi State Park.** Learn how the Ancestral Puebloans lived.
>
> **Bicknell International Film Festival.** Time your visit so you can attend the opening parade.
>
> **Goblin Valley State Park.** Play hide-and-seek among the strange orange rock formations.

AREA ACTIVITIES

SPORTS & THE OUTDOORS

FISHING Sitting at an elevation of 8,800 feet is Fish Lake, which lies in the heart of its namesake, 1.4-million-acre **Fishlake National Forest.** The area has several campgrounds and wonderful lodges. The lake is stocked annually with lake and rainbow trout, mackinaw, and splake. A large population of brown trout is native to the lake. The Fremont River Ranger District office can provide all the information you need on camping, fishing, and hiking in the forest. *Fremont River Ranger District office* ⌧*138 S. Main St., Loa* ☎*435/836–2811* ⊕*www.fs.fed.us/r4/fishlake.*

Boulder Mountain Adventures & Alpine Angler's Flyshop. This outfitter has a stellar reputation for personalized attention during fly-fishing trips into the high backcountry around Capitol Reef, as well as 4x4 and horseback tours. ⌧*310 W. Main St., Torrey* ☎*435/425–3660 or 888/484–3331* ⊕*www.alpineadventuresutah.com.*

ARTS & ENTERTAINMENT

The **Robbers' Roost** (⌧*185 W. Main St. (Hwy. 24), Torrey* ☎*435/425–3265* ⊗*Mar.–Oct.*)is part coffee bar, part bookstore, and part performance space, all contained in the late Utah writer Ward Roylance's practically pyramid-shape house. The Roost, whose name comes from

Butch Cassidy's hideout region, is an excellent place to stop to browse, talk about trails, or find out what's going on around town.

SHOPPING

The pleasing **Gallery 24** (⊠*135 E. Main St., Torrey* ☎*435/425–2124*) sells contemporary fine art from Utah-based artists that includes sculpture, handcrafted furniture, folk art, photography, and ceramics.

Unique and unexpected, the nifty **Flute Shop** (⊠*2650 S. Hwy. 12, 4 mi south of junction of Hwy. 12 and Hwy. 24* ☎*435/425–3144*) is open year-round and sells Native American-style flutes and gifts.

SCENIC DRIVES

★ **Burr Trail Scenic Backway.** Branching east off Highway 12 in Boulder, Burr Trail travels through the Circle Cliffs area of Grand Staircase–Escalante National Monument into Capitol Reef. The views are of backcountry canyons and gulches. The road is paved between Boulder and the eastern boundary of Capitol Reef. It leads into a hair-raising set of switchbacks—not suitable for RVs or trailers—that ascends 800 feet in a half mile. Before attempting to drive this route, check with the Capitol Reef Visitor Center for road conditions. From Boulder to its intersection with Notom-Bullfrog Road the route is 36 mi long.

Fodor's Choice
★
Utah Scenic Byway 12. Named as one of only 20 All-American Roads in the United States by the National Scenic Byways Program, Highway 12 is not to be missed. The 32-mi stretch between Torrey and Boulder winds through alpine forests and passes vistas of some of America's most remote and wild landscape. It is not for the faint of heart or those afraid of narrow, winding mountain roads.

Utah Scenic Byway 24. For 62 mi between Loa and Hanksville, you'll cut right through Capitol Reef National Park. Colorful rock formations in all their hues of red, cream, pink, gold, and deep purple extend from one end of the route to the other. The closer you get to the park the more colorful the landscape becomes. The vibrant rock finally gives way to lush green hills and the mountains west of Loa.

WHERE TO EAT

There is not even a snack bar within Capitol Reef, but dining options exist close by in Torrey, where you can find everything from one of Utah's best restaurants serving high-end Southwestern cuisine to basic hamburger joints offering up consistently good food.

WHAT IT COSTS				
	¢	$	$$	$$$	$$$$
RESTAURANTS	under $8	$8–$12	$13–$20	$21–$30	over $30
HOTELS	under $50	$50–$100	$101–$150	$151–$200	over $200

Restaurant prices are per person for a main course at dinner. Hotel prices are for two people in a standard double room in high season.

$$$-$$$$
Fodor'sChoice
★
✕**Cafe Diablo.** This popular Torrey restaurant keeps getting better, and indeed is one of the state's best. Saltillo-tile floors and matte-plaster walls lined with Southwestern art set the stage for innovative Southwestern cuisine that includes fire-roasted pork tenderloin, artichoke and sun-dried tomato tamales, and local trout crusted with pumpkin seeds and served with a cilantro-lime sauce. The rattlesnake cakes, made with free-range desert rattler and served with ancho-rosemary aioli, are delicious. ⊠*599 W. Main St. (Hwy. 24), Torrey* ☏*435/425–3070* ⊕*www.cafediablo.net* ⊟*AE, D, MC, V* ⊗*Closed mid-Oct.–mid-Apr. No lunch.*

$$-$$$$
Fodor'sChoice
★
✕**Hell's Backbone Grill.** One of the best restaurants in Southern Utah, this remote spot is worth the drive from any distance. The menu is inspired by Native American, Western Range, Southwestern, and Mormon pioneer recipes. Chef-owners Jen Castle and Blake Spalding use only fresh, organic foods that have a historical connection to the area. Because they insist on fresh foods, the menu changes weekly. Their cookbook is a gem worth owning, too. ⊠*20 N. Hwy. 12, Boulder* ☏*435/335–7464* ⊕*www.hellsbackbonegrill.com* ⊟*AE, D, MC, V* ⊗*Closed Nov.–Mar. No lunch.*

$-$$$
✕**Capitol Reef Café.** For standard fare that will please everyone in the family, visit this unpretentious restaurant. Favorites include the 10-vegetable salad and the flaky fillet of locally caught rainbow trout, and the breakfasts are both delicious and hearty. Numerous vegetarian offerings make for a refreshing break from beef and beans. ⊠*360 W. Main St. (Hwy. 24), Torrey* ☏*435/425–3271* ⊕*www.capitolreefinn. com* ⊟*AE, D, MC, V* ⊗*Closed Nov.–Mar.*

¢
✕**Stan's Burger Shack.** This is the traditional pit stop between Lake Powell and Capitol Reef, featuring great burgers, fries, and shakes—and the only homemade onion rings you'll find for miles. ⊠*140 S. Hwy. 95, Hanksville* ☏*435/542–3330* ⊟*AE, D, MC, V.*

WHERE TO STAY

There are no lodging options within Capitol Reef, but you'll have no problem finding clean and comfortable accommodations no matter what your budget in nearby Torrey, and not far beyond in Bicknell and Loa. Drive farther into the region's towns, and you are more likely to find locally owned low- to moderate-price motels and a few nice bed-and-breakfasts. Reservations are recommended in summer.

Campgrounds in Capitol Reef fill up fast between Memorial Day and Labor Day, though that goes mainly for the super-convenient Fruita Campground and not the more remote backcountry sites. Most of the area's state parks have camping facilities, and the region's two national forests offer many wonderful sites.

IN THE PARK
△**Cathedral Valley Campground.** You'll find this primitive campground, about 30 mi from Highway 24, in the park's remote northern district. The only way here is via a high-clearance road that should not be attempted when wet. ⊠*Hartnet Junction, on Caineville Wash*

5

Rd. ☎435/425–3791 ➥6 tent sites ♿*Pit toilets, grills, picnic tables* 🛇*Reservations not accepted.*

🏕 **Cedar Mesa Campground.** Wonderful views of the Waterpocket Fold and Henry Mountains surround this primitive campground in the park's southern district. The road to the campground does not require a high-clearance vehicle, but it's not paved and you should not attempt to drive it if the road is wet. ✉*Notom-Bullfrog Rd., 22 mi south of Hwy. 24* ☎435/425–3791 ➥5 tent sites ♿*Pit toilets, grills, picnic tables* 🛇*Reservations not accepted.*

🏕 **Fruita Campground.** Near the orchards and the Fremont River, this shady campground is a great place to call home for a few days. The sites nearest the river or the orchards are the best. Loop C is most appropriate for RVs, although the campground has no hookups. In summer, the campground fills up early in the day. ✉*Scenic Dr., about 1 mi south of the visitor center* ☎435/425–3791 ➥71 sites ♿*Flush toilets, drinking water, grills, picnic tables* 🛇*Reservations not accepted* ▤*No credit cards.*

OUTSIDE THE PARK

★ $$–$$$$ 🏨 **Lodge at Red River Ranch.** You'll swear you've walked into one of the great lodges of Western legend when you walk through the doors at Red River Ranch. The great room is decorated with wagon-wheel chandeliers, Native American rugs, leather furniture, and original Frederick Remington sculptures. Guest rooms are meticulously and individually decorated with fine antiques and art; each has a fireplace and most have a patio or balcony overlooking the grounds. **Pros:** Furnishings and artifacts so distinctive they could grace the pages of a design magazine. **Cons:** Rooms are on the small side, and in summer you may wish for air-conditioning. ✉*2900 W. Hwy. 24, Box 22, Teasdale, 84773* ☎435/425–3322 or 800/205–6343 🖷435/425–3329 ⊕*www.redriverranch.com* ➥*15 rooms* ♿*In-room: no a/c, no TV. In-hotel: restaurant, no elevator, public Wi-Fi, no-smoking rooms* ▤*AE, DC, MC, V.*

$–$$$$ 🏨 **Fish Lake Lodge and Lakeside Resort.** This large, lakeside lodge built in 1932 exudes rustic charm and character and has great views. It houses the resort's restaurant, gift shop, game room, and even a dance hall. Guests stay in cabins that sleep 2 to 22 people. The larger houses are excellent for family reunions. Some of the lodgings are quite rustic. The larger cabins are the newest, but all focus on function rather than cute amenities. The lodge, general store, and restaurant are closed from early September to late May; cabins are available year-round. An RV park also has 24 sites for $20 a night, May–October. **Pros:** Great place for families and groups to congregate. **Cons:** Some cabins are a little close together, so not the best for solitude. ✉*HC80, Rte. 25, Loa, 84701* ☎435/638–1000 🖷435/638–1001 ⊕*www.fishlake.com* ➥*55 cabins* ♿*In-room: no a/c, kitchen, no TV (some). In-hotel: restaurant, no elevator* ▤*D, MC, V.*

$$–$$$ 🏨 **SkyRidge Bed and Breakfast.** Each of the inn's windows offers an exceptional year-round view of the desert and mountains surrounding Capitol Reef National Park. The walls are hung with the works of local artists, and unusual furniture—each piece chosen for its look

and feel—makes the guest rooms and common areas both stimulating and comfortable. Breakfasts here, which might have you feasting on apple-stuffed croissants or homemade cinnamon rolls, are excellent, and you are served evening hors d'oeuvres as well. ⊠ *950 E. Hwy. 24, Box 750220, Torrey, 84775* ☎ *435/425–3222 or 800/448–6990* 🖷 *435/425–3222* ⊕ *www.skyridgeinn.com* 🛏 *6 rooms* △ *In-room: VCR, Wi-Fi. In-hotel: restaurant, no elevator* ☐ *AE, MC, V.*

$–$$$ 🏨 **Boulder Mountain Lodge.** If you're traveling between Capitol Reef and
Fodor'sChoice Bryce Canyon national parks, don't miss this wonderful lodge along sce-
★ nic Highway 12. A 5-acre pond on the pastoral grounds is a sanctuary for ducks, coots, and other waterfowl, and horses graze in a meadow opposite. Large, modern rooms with balconies or patios offer gorgeous views of the wetlands. The main lodge contains a great room with fire-place, and there's a fine art gallery and remarkably good restaurant on the premises. The service and care given to guests here is impeccable. **Pros:** A perfect spot for peace and solitude. **Cons:** Some might find the middle-of-nowhere location too remote. ⊠ *Hwy. 12 at Burr Trail, Boulder, 84716* ☎ *435/335–7460 or 800/556–3446* 🖷 *435/335–7461* ⊕ *www.boulder-utah.com* 🛏 *20 rooms* △ *In-room: Wi-Fi. In-hotel: no elevator, some pets allowed, no-smoking rooms* ☐ *D, MC, V.*

★ **$–$$** 🏨 **Muley Twist Inn.** This gorgeous B&B sits on 30 acres of land, with expansive views of the colorful landscape that surrounds it. A wrap-around porch, contemporary furnishings, and classical music drifting through the air add to a stay here. **Pros:** Dramatic setting against a beautiful rock cliff, a place you can slow down and unwind. **Cons:** Living quarters feel a little tight. ⊠ *125 S. 250 West, Teasdale, 84773* ☎ *435/425–3640 or 800/530–1038* 🖷 *435/425–3640* ⊕ *www.rof.net/ yp/muley/index.html* 🛏 *5 rooms* △ *In-room: no a/c, no TV. In-hotel: no elevator, no-smoking rooms* ☐ *AE, MC, V* ⊗ *Closed Nov.–Mar.*

¢–$ 🏨 **The Snuggle Inn.** On the second floor of a row of shops on Main Street, this hostelry has the feel of an old-time hotel. The rooms are spacious, with modern decorations and touches like Internet access. Each room has a pillow-top queen bed. For families, there's a sofa bed in one room. The suite has two separate bedrooms, a living room, and a full kitchen. **Pros:** Character, character, character! **Cons:** Located in a small farming community with few restaurants. ⊠ *55 S. Main St., Loa, 84747* ☎ *435/836–2898* 🖷 *435/836–2700* ⊕ *www.thesnuggleinn.com* 🛏 *11 rooms, 1 suite* △ *In-room: no a/c, kitchen (some), refrigerator (some), Wi-Fi. In hotel: no elevator, public Wi-Fi* ☐ *AE, D, MC, V.*

¢–$ 🏨 **Rim Rock Inn.** Situated on a bluff with outstanding views of the desert, this motel was the first one built to accommodate visitors to Capitol Reef. Under energetic management, its rooms are clean and ample—and a good bargain, to boot. The on-site restaurant is a local favorite. **Pros:** Stunning views in every direction. **Cons:** Predictable motel-style rooms, no shade on property. ⊠ *2523 E. Hwy. 24, Tor-rey, 84775* ☎ *435/425–3398 or 888/447–4676* ⊕ *www.therimrock.net* 🛏 *19 rooms* △ *In-hotel: restaurant, no elevator, public Wi-Fi* ☐ *AE, MC, V* ⊗ *Closed Nov.–Mar.*

5

¢ 🛏**Sunglow Motel & Restaurant.** This well-maintained and inexpensive motel is right in the heart of Bicknell. Try the buttermilk and oatmeal pie at the restaurant next door—and don't knock the sounds of Pickle Pie and Pinto Bean Pie, for they are legendary, and rightfully so. **Pros:** Friendly owner who makes amazing pies! **Cons:** Few amenities, either at this motel or in this small town. ✉*91 E. Main St., Bicknell, 84715* ☎*435/425–3821* 🖨*435/425–3821* ⊕*www.sunglowpies.com* ⤴*15 rooms* ⚙*In room: Wi-Fi. In-hotel: restaurant, no elevator* ☰*AE, D, MC, V.*

CAMPGROUNDS 🏕**Fish Lake Campgrounds.** There are four Forest Service campgrounds in the Fish Lake area, about 7–15 mi northwest on Route 25 or Route 72. All are comfortable and well maintained. The two best are **Doctor Creek** and **Mackinaw.** Doctor Creek is a short drive from Fish Lake in a grove of aspen and pine. Mackinaw sits on a hill overlooking Fish Lake, giving campers a good view of the surrounding basin. The showers here are a rarity in Forest Service campgrounds. ✉*Fremont River Ranger District Office, 138 S. Main St., Loa, 84747* ☎*435/836–2811, 877/444–6777 reservations* ⊕*www.reserveamerica.com* ⤴*60 tent sites at Mackinaw, 30 tent sites at Doctor Creek* ⚙*Pit toilets, dump station (Doctor Creek only), drinking water, showers (Mackinaw only)* ☰*AE, D, MC, V (for online or phone reservations only)* 🕐*May–Oct.*

🏕**Sunglow Campground.** Managed by the U.S. Forest Service, this secluded little campground is next to red cliffs in a pinyon forest. All of the sites are suitable for moderately sized RVs or tents, but RVers should know that the campground's roads are narrow and winding with some tight turns. ✉*Hwy. 24, 1 mi east of Bicknell, Bicknell, 84747* ☎*435/836–2811* ⤴*7 sites* ⚙*Pit toilets, drinking water* 🗝*Reservations not accepted* ☰*No credit cards* 🕐*May–Oct.*

🏕**Thousand Lakes RV Park and Campground.** This is one of the area's most popular RV parks. There's lots of grass and shade, and the level 22-acre site provides good views of the surrounding red cliffs. The cabins come either bare-bones or with bath, microwave, refrigerator, and TV. There's free wireless Internet access. ✉*1050 W. Rte 24, Torrey, 84775* ☎*435/425–3500 or 800/355–8995* 🖨*435/425–3510* ⊕*www.thousandlakesrvpark.com* ⤴*36 full hookups, 16 partial hookups, 9 tent sites, 8 cabins* ⚙*Flush toilets, full hookups, partial hookups (water and electricity), dump station, drinking water, guest laundry, showers, fire pits, grills, picnic tables, electricity, public telephone, general store, play area, swimming (pool), Wi-Fi* ☰*D, MC, V* 🕐*Apr.–Oct.*

CAPITOL REEF ESSENTIALS

ACCESSIBILITY

Like many of the undeveloped Western national parks, Capitol Reef doesn't have many trails that are accessible to people in wheelchairs. The visitor center, museum, slide show, and restrooms are all accessible, as is the campground amphitheater where evening programs are held. The Fruita Campground Loop C restroom is accessible, as is the boardwalk to the petroglyph panel on Highway 24, 1 2/10 mi east of the visitor center.

ADMISSION FEES
There is no fee to enter the park, but it's $5 per vehicle to drive on Scenic Drive beyond Fruita Campground; this fee is good for one week.

ADMISSION HOURS
The park is open year-round. It is in the Mountain time zone.

ATMS/BANKS
The nearest ATM is at the travel plaza at the junction of Highways 24 and 12 in Torrey.

AUTOMOBILE SERVICE STATIONS
Contacts **Blackburn Sinclair and Towing** (⊠178 E. Main St., Bicknell ☎435/425–3432). **Brian Auto Parts and Service** (⊠233 S. Main, Loa ☎435/836–2343).

Hidden Falls Hotel Travel Center (⊠2424 E. Hwy. 24, Torrey ☎435/425–3956). **M & D Auto Parts & Repair** (⊠390 W. 100 N, Bicknell ☎435/425–3280). **Stan's Chevron** (⊠350 S. Hwy. 95, Hanksville ☎435/542–2017).

Wonderland Texaco (⊠Hwys. 12 and 24, Torrey ☎435/425–3345).

EMERGENCIES
Dial 911, contact a park ranger, or report to the visitor center. For park police, dial 435/425–3791. The nearest 24-hour medical center is the Beaver Valley Hospital in Beaver.

LOST AND FOUND
It's at the visitor center.

PERMITS
Backcountry camping permits are free; pick up at the visitor center.

POST OFFICES
Contacts **Torrey Contract Post Office** (⊠75 W. Main, Torrey ☎435/425–3716).

PUBLIC TELEPHONES
They're at the visitor center and at Fruita Campground. Cell-phone reception is best near the visitor center and campground areas.

RELIGIOUS SERVICES
There are no religious services in Capitol Reef.

RESTROOMS
Restrooms are available at the visitor center, Fruita Campground, and Chimney Rock and Hickman Bridge trailheads.

SHOPS & GROCERS
Contacts **Austin's Chuckwagon General Store** (⊠12 W. Main St., Torrey ☎435/425–3288).

Capitol Reef National Park

NEARBY TOWN INFORMATION

Contacts **Capitol Reef Country Travel Council (Bicknell, Hanksville, Loa, Teasdale, Torrey)** ✆ *Box 7, Teasdale, 84773* ☎ *435/425–3365 or 800/858–7951* ⊕ *www.capitolreef.org* . **Garfield County Tourism Office (Boulder)** ✉ *55 S. Main St., Panguitch, 84759* ☎ *435/676–1160 or 800/444–6689* ⊕ *www.brycecanyon-country.com* .

VISITOR INFORMATION

Contacts **Capitol Reef National Park** ✉ *HC 70 Box 15, Torrey, 84775* ☎ *435/425–3791* ⊕ *www.nps.gov/care* .

Zion
National Park

WORD OF MOUTH

"In Zion, I'd recommend the Riverside walk (which ends at the narrows), and the Emerald Pools hikes as easy hikes with great views. Have lunch at the lodge in the dining room. You can stay in Springdale since it is totally accessible to the park. There is little advantage to staying in the park lodge in this park. The highway that passes through the park is very scenic to drive. You will travel through a historic tunnel and maybe see bighorn sheep if you are lucky."

—Ellya

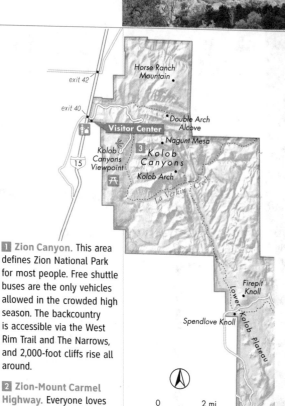

WELCOME TO ZION

TOP REASONS TO GO

★ **To Hike Where Angels Land:** Though not for the timid or the weak, the Angels Landing Trail culminates in one of the park's most astounding viewpoints.

★ **To Leave Traffic Behind:** During the busy summer season, cars are no longer allowed in Zion Canyon, allowing for a relaxing and scenic shuttle bus ride.

★ **To Veg Out:** Zion Canyon is home to approximately 900 species of plants, more than anywhere else in Utah.

★ **To Take the Subway:** Only the hardiest of hikers venture through the pools and tunnels of the Subway in the Zion Canyon backcountry.

★ **To Experience Highs & Lows:** Zion Canyon area geography ranges from mountains to desert, offering a diverse selection of places to explore.

1 Zion Canyon. This area defines Zion National Park for most people. Free shuttle buses are the only vehicles allowed in the crowded high season. The backcountry is accessible via the West Rim Trail and The Narrows, and 2,000-foot cliffs rise all around.

2 Zion-Mount Carmel Highway. Everyone loves driving through the tunnel hewn from stone, even RVers who have to pay a fee and get a ranger escort. Canyon Overlook Trail provides a quick overlook of the West Temple and other majestic formations.

The Virgin River

3 **Kolob Canyons.** The quiet northwest corner of Zion, this area lets you see some of the park's attractions, such as the West Temple, from an angle many visitors never witness. Kolob Arch is easily reached via a relatively short trail.

Hiking through the river in Zion Narrows

4 **Lava Point.** Infrequently visited, this area has a primitive campground and nearby are two reservoirs that provide the only significant fishing opportunities in Zion National Park. Lava Point Overlook provides a view of Zion Canyon from the north.

UTAH

GETTING ORIENTED

The heart of Zion Canyon National Park is Zion Canyon itself, which follows the North Fork of the Virgin River for 6½ mi beneath cliffs that approach 2,000 feet in elevation. The Kolob area is considered by some to be superior in beauty, and you aren't likely to run into any crowds here. Both sections hint at the extensive backcountry beyond, open for those with the stamina, time, and the experience to go off the beaten paths of the park.

6

KEY	
🏠	Ranger Station
🅰	Campground
🌲	Picnic Area
🍴	Restaurant
🏨	Lodge
🥾	Trailhead
🚻	Restrooms
✳	Scenic Viewpoint
-----	Walking/Hiking Trails
·····	Bicycle Path

ZION PLANNER

When to Go

Getting There & Around

Zion is the most heavily visited national park in Utah, receiving nearly 2.5 million visitors each year. **Most visitors come between April and October,** when upper Zion Canyon is accessed only by free shuttle bus to reduce traffic congestion.

Summer in the park is hot and dry except for sudden cloudbursts, which can create flash flooding and spectacular waterfalls. Expect afternoon thunderstorms between July and September. In the summer sun, wear sunscreen and drink lots of water, regardless of your activity level.

Winters are mild at lower desert elevations, so consider planning your visit for some time other than peak season. You can expect to encounter winter driving conditions November through March, and although most park programs are suspended, winter is a wonderful and solitary time to see the canyons. During these months the shuttle does not operate.

⚠ **Extreme highs in Zion can often exceed 100°F in July and August.**

In southwestern Utah, not far from the Nevada border, Zion National Park is closer to Las Vegas (158 mi) than to Salt Lake City (310 mi). The nearest commercial airport is 46 mi away in St. George, Utah. Off Route 9, the park is 21 mi east of Interstate 15 and 24 mi west of U.S. 89.

November through March, private vehicles are allowed on Zion's main park road, Zion Canyon Scenic Drive. From April through October, however, it is closed to private vehicles. During this time, the park's easy-to-use shuttle system ferries people into the canyon from the Zion Canyon Visitor Center, where the parking lot is typically full, 10 to 3 daily, May through September. To avoid parking hassles, leave your car in the nearby town of Springdale and ride the town shuttle to the park entrance where you can connect with the park shuttle. Town shuttle stops are at Majestic View, Driftwood Motel, Quality Inn, Bit & Spur Restaurant, Zion Park Inn, Bumbleberry Inn, Pizza and Noodle Company, Zion Canyon Clothing, Flanigan's Inn, and Zion Giant Screen Theater. The shuttles are free, but you must pay the park entrance fee.

If you enter or exit Zion via the east entrance you will have the privilege of driving a gorgeous, twisting 24-mi stretch of the Zion–Mount Carmel Highway (Route 9). Two tunnels, including the highway's famous 1 1/10-mi tunnel, lie between the east park entrance and Zion Canyon. The tunnels are so narrow that vehicles more than 7 feet, 10 inches wide or 11 feet, 4 inches high require traffic control while passing through. Rangers, who are stationed at the tunnels 8 AM to 8 PM daily, April through October, stop oncoming traffic so you can drive down the middle of the tunnels. Large vehicles must pay an escort fee of $15 at either park entrance. West of the tunnels the highway meets Zion Canyon Scenic Drive at Canyon Junction, about 1 mi north of the Zion Canyon Visitor Center.

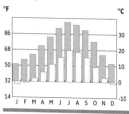

By John
Blodgett

THE WALLS OF ZION CANYON soar more than 2,000 feet above the valley below, but it's the character, not the size, of the sandstone forms that defines the park's splendor. The domes, fins, and blocky massifs bear the names and likenesses of cathedrals and temples, prophets and angels. But for all Zion's grandeur, trails that lead deep into side canyons and up narrow ledges on the sheer canyon walls reveal a subtler beauty. Tucked among the monoliths are delicate hanging gardens, serene spring-fed pools, and shaded spots of solitude. So diverse is this place that 85% of Utah's flora and fauna species are found here. Some, like the tiny Zion snail, appear nowhere else in the world.

At the genesis of Zion is the Virgin River, a tributary of the Colorado River. It's hard to believe that this muddy little stream is responsible for carving the great canyon you see, until you witness it transformed into a rumbling red torrent during spring runoff and summer thunderstorms. Cascades pour from the cliff tops, clouds float through the canyon, and then the sun comes out and you know you are walking in one of the West's most loved and sacred places. If you're lucky, you may catch such a spectacle, but when the noisy waters run thick with debris, make sure that you keep a safe distance—these "flash floods" can, and do, kill.

The park comprises two distinct sections—Zion Canyon, and the Kolob Plateau and Canyons. Most people restrict their visit to the better-known Zion Canyon, especially if they have only one day to explore, but the Kolob area has much to offer and should not be missed if time allows. There's little evidence of Kolob's beauty from the entrance point off Interstate 15, but once you negotiate the first switchback on the park road, you are hit with a vision of red rock cliffs shooting out of the earth. As you climb in elevation you are treated first to a journey through these canyons, then with a view into the chasm. Due to geography—no roads connect Zion Canyon with Kolob Canyon—and to access points that are far apart, it is not feasible to explore both sections in one day.

SCENIC DRIVES

Zion Canyon's grandeur is best experienced on foot whenever possible, but there is something to be said for covering a lot of ground in the car—and indeed, there is a lot to see if you've only a short amount of time in the area. Driving is the only way to easily access Kolob Canyon, for example, and from November through March, driving your own vehicle is the only way to access the Zion Canyon scenic drive.

★ **Kolob Canyons Road.** From Interstate 15 you get no hint of the beauty that awaits you on this 5-mi road. Most visitors gasp audibly when they get their first glimpse of the red canyon walls that rise suddenly and spectacularly out of the earth. The scenic drive winds amid these towers as it rises in elevation, until you reach a viewpoint that overlooks the whole Kolob region of Zion National Park. The shortest hike in this section of the park is the Middle Fork of Taylor Creek Trail, which is 2$\frac{7}{10}$ mi one way to Double Arch Alcove, and gets fairly rugged toward the end (⇨ *Hiking in the Sports & the Outdoors section*). During heavy snowfall Kolob Canyons Road may be closed. ⊠ *Kolob Canyons Rd. east of I–15, Exit 40.*

★ **Zion–Mount Carmel Highway & Tunnels.** Two narrow tunnels lie between the east park entrance and Zion Canyon on this breathtaking 24-mi stretch of Route 9. As you travel through solid rock from one end of the longest (1 1/10 mi) tunnel to the other, portals along one side provide a few glimpses of cliffs and canyons, and when you emerge on the other side you find that the landscape has changed dramatically. The tunnels are so narrow that large vehicles more than 7 feet, 10 inches wide or 11 feet, 4 inches high require traffic control while passing through, available 8 AM–8 PM daily, April–October, and must pay a $15 escort fee. ⊠ *Zion–Mount Carmel Rte. 9, about 5 mi east of Canyon Junction.*

HISTORIC SITES

★ **Zion Human History Museum.** Enrich your visit with a stop here, where you'll get a complete overview of the park with special attention to human history. Exhibits explain how settlers interacted with the geology, wildlife, plants, and unpredictable weather in the canyon from prehistory to the present. A 22-minute film plays throughout the day. ⊠ *Zion Canyon Scenic Dr., 1 mi north of south entrance* 🖀 *435/772–3256, ext. 168* ⊕ *www.nps.gov/zion/HHMuseum.htm* 🎞 *Free* ☉ *Late May–early Sept., daily 9–7; early May and early-Sept.–mid-Oct., daily 10–6; Mar.–Apr. and late Oct., daily 10–5.*

Zion Lodge. The Union Pacific Railroad constructed the first Zion National Park Lodge in 1925, with buildings designed by architect Stanley Gilbert Underwood. A fire destroyed the original building, but it was rebuilt to recapture some of the look and feel of the first building. The original Western-style cabins are still in use today. Among giant cottonwoods across the road from the Emerald Pools trailhead, the lodge houses a restaurant, snack bar, and gift shop. ⊠ *Zion Canyon Scenic Dr., about 3 mi north of Canyon Junction* 🖀 *435/772–7700* ⊕ *www.zionlodge.com.*

SCENIC STOPS

Checkerboard Mesa. The distinctive pattern on this huge, white mound of sandstone was created by a combination of vertical fractures and the exposure of horizontal bedding planes by erosion. ⊠ *Zion–Mount Carmel Hwy., 1 mi west of the east entrance.*

★ **Court of the Patriarchs.** This trio of peaks bears the names of, from left to right, Abraham, Isaac, and Jacob. Mount Moroni is the reddish peak on the far right, which partially blocks your view of Jacob. You can see the Patriarchs better by hiking a half mile up Sand Bench Trail. ⊠ *Zion Canyon Scenic Dr., 1½ mi north of Canyon Junction.*

ZION IN ONE DAY

Begin your visit at the **Zion Canyon Visitor Center,** where outdoor exhibits inform you about the park's geology, wildlife, history, and trails. Catch the shuttle or drive—depending on the season—into Zion Canyon. On your way in, make a quick stop at the **Zion Human History Museum** to watch a 22-minute park orientation program and to see exhibits chronicling the human history of the area. Board the shuttle and travel to the **Court of the Patriarchs** viewpoint to take photos and walk the short path. Then pick up the next bus headed into the canyon. Stop at Zion Lodge and cross the road to the **Emerald Pools** trailhead, and take the short hike up to the pools themselves.

Before reboarding the shuttle, grab lunch in the snack shop or dining room at **Zion Lodge.** Take the shuttle as far as **Weeping Rock** trailhead for a brief, cool walk up to the dripping, spring-fed cascade.

Ride the next shuttle to the end of the road, where you can walk to the gateway of the canyon's narrows on the paved, accessible **Riverside Walk.**

Reboard the shuttle to return to the Zion Canyon Visitor Center to pick up your car. Head out onto the beautiful **Zion–Mount Carmel Highway,** with its long, curving tunnels, making sure your camera is loaded and ready for stops at viewpoints along the road. Once you reach the park's east entrance, turn around, and on your return trip stop to take the short hike up to **Canyon Overlook.** Now you're ready to rest your feet at a screening of *Zion Canyon—Treasure of the Gods* at the **Zion Canyon Theater.** In the evening, you might want to attend a **ranger program** at one of the campground amphitheaters or at Zion Lodge. Or you can follow a relaxing dinner in nearby **Springdale** with a stroll downtown.

Great White Throne. Towering over the Grotto picnic area near Zion Lodge is this massive 6,744-foot rock peak. ⊠*Zion Canyon Scenic Dr., about 3 mi north of Canyon Junction.*

★ **Weeping Rock.** A short, paved walk leads up to this flowing rock face, where wildflowers and delicate ferns thrive near a spring-fed waterfall that seeps out of a cliff. In fall, this area bursts with color. The ⅕-mi trail to the west alcove takes about 25 minutes round-trip. It is paved, but too steep for wheelchairs. ⊠*Zion Canyon Scenic Dr., about 4 mi north of Canyon Junction.*

VISITOR CENTERS

Zion Canyon National park has two visitor centers, one for each section of the park, and they are open year-round. The main center is at the south entrance of the park, and is larger than the one at Kolob Canyon. There is a bookstore at each location, plus rangers to answer your questions or point you to a good hike or picnic area. Both feature exhibits and photographs that cover the park's natural and cultural history. Plan to get snacks, lunch, or coffee elsewhere.

Kolob Canyons Visitor Center. At the origin of Kolob Canyons Road, this park office has a small bookstore plus exhibits on park geology and helpful rangers to answer questions. ⊠*Exit 40 off I–15* ☎*435/586–9548* ⊙*Oct.–Apr., daily 8–4:30; May–Sept., daily 8–5.*

Zion Canyon Visitor Center. Unlike most national park visitor centers, which are filled with indoor displays, Zion's presents most of its information in an appealing outdoor exhibit. Beneath shade trees beside a gurgling brook, displays help you plan your stay and introduce you to the area's geology, flora, and fauna. Inside, a large bookstore operated by the Zion Natural History Association sells field guides and other publications. **Ranger-guided shuttle tours** of Zion Canyon depart from the parking lot and travel to the Temple of Sinawava, with several photo-op stops along the way. The tour schedule and free tour tickets are available inside. You can also pick up backcountry permits here. ⊠*At south entrance, Springdale* ☎*435/772–3256, ext. 616* ⊕*www.nps.gov/zion* ⊙*Apr.–May and Sept.–mid-Oct., daily 8–6; June–Aug., daily 8–7; mid-Oct.–Mar., daily 8–5.*

SPORTS & THE OUTDOORS

Zion Canyon has plenty of opportunities to get out of the car for recreation, with activities suited to all ages and abilities. Hiking is by far the most popular activity, and cyclists rejoiced when Zion Canyon was deemed off-limits to cars during the busy summer season. Some sections of the Virgin River are ideal for swimming or floating on an inner tube. In the winter, hiking boots can be exchanged for snowshoes and cross-country skis, but check with a ranger to determine backcountry snow conditions.

AIR TOURS

Bryce Canyon Airlines & Helicopters. For a once-in-a-lifetime view of Zion National Park, join professional pilots and guides for an airplane ride over the park (and Bryce Canyon National Park during the same flight). Flights depart from Ruby's Inn Heliport near Bryce Canyon National Park. There is a two-person minimum. ☎*435/834–8060* ⊕*www.rubysinn.com/bryce-canyon-airlines.html* 🖃*$175 per person.*

BICYCLING

The introduction of the park shuttle has improved bicycling conditions in Zion National Park, for during the busy months, April through October, cyclists no longer share Zion Canyon Scenic Drive with thousands of cars—though two-wheelers do need to be cautious of the large buses plying the park road throughout the day. Within the park proper, bicycles are only allowed on established park roads and on the 3½-mi Pa'rus Trail, which winds along the Virgin River in Zion Canyon. You cannot ride your bicycle through the Zion–Mount Carmel tunnels; the only way to get your bike past this stretch of the highway is to transport it by motor vehicle. (*For information on bike outfitters, see the Southwestern Utah chapter.*)

BIRD-WATCHING

Approximately 290 bird species call Zion Canyon home or else pass through its environs on occasion. Some species, such as the white-throated swift and the powerful peregrine falcon, take full advantage of the towering cliffs. Closer to the ground are the common pinyon jay and, if you look closely enough, perhaps a Gambel's quail. Wild turkeys are not only common, but some aren't very wild, venturing up to visitors looking for a handout. If you're quick, you might spot one of nine species of hummingbirds that have been spotted feeding at various Zion Canyon blossoms.

HIKING

The best way to experience Zion Canyon is to walk beneath, between and, if you can bear it (and have good balance!), along its towering cliffs. There is something for everyone, from paved and flat river strolls to precarious cliff-side scrambles. You can buy a detailed guide to the trails of Zion at the Zion Canyon Visitor Center bookstore. Whether you're heading out for a day of rock-hopping or an hour of strolling, you should carry—and drink—plenty of water to counteract the effects of southern Utah's arid climate. Wear a hat, sunscreen, and sturdy shoes or boots; make sure to bring a map, and be honest with yourself about your capabilities. Getting in over your head can have serious health consequences.

EASY **Emerald Pools Trail.** Two small waterfalls cascade (or drip, in dry weather) into pools at the top of this relatively easy trail. The way is paved up to the lower pool and is suitable for baby strollers and wheelchairs with assistance. Beyond the lower pool, the trail becomes rocky and steep as you progress toward the middle and upper pools. A less crowded and exceptionally enjoyable return route follows the Kayenta Trail connecting on to the Grotto Trail. Allow 50 minutes round-trip to the lower pool and 2½ hours round-trip to the middle and upper pools. ⊠*Zion Canyon Scenic Dr., about 3 mi north of Canyon Junction.*

🕲 **Grotto Trail.** This flat and very easy trail takes you from Zion Lodge to the Grotto picnic area, traveling for the most part along the park road. Allow 20 minutes or less for the walk. If you are up for a longer hike, and have two to three hours, connect with the Kayenta Trail after you cross the footbridge, and head for the Emerald Pools. You will begin gaining elevation, and it's a steady, steep climb to the pools. ⊠*Zion Canyon Scenic Dr., about 3 mi north of Canyon Junction.*

Pa'rus Trail. This 2-mi walking and biking path parallels and occasionally crosses the Virgin River, starting at South Campground and proceeding north along the river to the beginning of Zion Canyon Scenic Drive. It's paved and gives you great views of the Watchman, the Sentinel, the East and West Temples, and Towers of the Virgin. Dogs are allowed on this trail as long as they are leashed. Cyclists must follow traffic rules on this heavily used trail. ⊠*Canyon Junction, ½ mi north of south entrance.*

🕲 **Riverside Walk.** Beginning at the Temple of Sinawava shuttle stop at the end of Zion Canyon Scenic Drive, this easily enjoyed 1-mi round-trip stroll shadows the Virgin River. The river gurgles by on one side of the trail; on the other, wildflowers bloom out of the canyon wall in fascinating hanging gardens. This is the park's most trekked trail; it is paved and suitable for baby strollers and for wheelchairs with assistance. A round-trip walk takes between one and two hours. The end of the trail marks the beginning of the Narrows Trail. ⊠ *Zion Canyon Scenic Dr., 5 mi north of Canyon Junction.*

MODERATE **Canyon Overlook Trail.** It's a little tough to locate this trailhead, but you'll find it if you watch for the parking area just east of Zion–Mount Carmel tunnel. The trail is moderately steep but only 1 mi round-trip; allow an hour to hike it. The overlook at trail's end gives you views of the West and East Temples, Towers of the Virgin, the Streaked Wall, and other Zion Canyon cliffs and peaks. ⊠ *Rte. 9, east of Zion–Mount Carmel Tunnel.*

Taylor Creek Trail. In the Kolob Canyons area of the park, this trail immediately descends parallel to Taylor Creek, sometimes crossing it, sometimes shortcutting benches beside it. The historic Larsen Cabin precedes the entrance to the canyon of the Middle Fork, where the trail becomes rougher. After the old Fife Cabin, the canyon bends to the right and delivers you into Double Arch Alcove, a large, colorful grotto with a high arch towering above. The distance one way to Double Arch is 2¾ mi. Allow about four hours round-trip for this hike. ⊠ *Kolob Canyons Rd., about 1½ mi east of Kolob Canyons Visitor Center.*

Watchman Trail. For a view of the town of Springdale and a look at lower Zion Creek Canyon and the Towers of the Virgin, take the moderately strenuous hike that begins on a service road east of Watchman Campground. Some springs seep out of the sandstone to nourish hanging gardens and attract wildlife here. There are a few sheer cliff edges on this route, so children should be supervised carefully. Allow two hours for this 3-mi hike. ⊠ *East of Rte. 9 (main park road), on access road inside south entrance.*

DIFFICULT **Angels Landing Trail.** Truly one of the most spectacular hikes in the park, this trail is an adventure for those not afraid of heights. On your ascent you must negotiate Walter's Wiggles, a series of 21 switchbacks built out of sandstone blocks, and traverse sheer cliffs with chains bolted into the rock face to serve as handrails. In spite of its hair-raising nature, this trail attracts many people. Small children should skip it, however, and older children should be carefully supervised. Allow 2½ hours round-trip if you stop at Scout's Lookout, and four hours if you keep going to where the angels (and birds of prey) play. ⊠ *Zion Canyon Scenic Drive, about 4½ mi north of Canyon Junction.*

Fodor'sChoice ★

★ **Narrows Trail.** On a hot, clear day there are few things more enjoyable than a walk in the river. This route does not follow a trail or path; rather, you are walking on the riverbed, no matter how much water is in it. The gateway of the Narrows admits adventurous souls deeper into Zion Canyon than most visitors go. As beautiful as it is, this hike is not for everyone. To see the Narrows you must wade upstream through chilly water and over uneven, slippery rocks. Just to cross the river, you must walk deliberately and slowly using a walking stick. Be prepared to swim, as chest-deep holes may occur even when water levels are low. Like any narrow desert canyon, this one is famous for sudden flash flooding even when skies are clear. *Before attempting to hike into the Narrows, check with park rangers about the likelihood of flash floods.* A day trip up the lower section of the Narrows is 6 mi one way to the turnaround point. Allow at least five hours round-trip. ⊠*At the end of Riverside Walk.*

HORSEBACK RIDING

Grab your hat and boots and see Zion Canyon the way the pioneers did—on the back of a horse or mule. This is a sure way to make your trip to Zion National Park memorable. Only one outfitter is licensed to guide tours within park boundaries. Easy going, one-hour and half-day trips are available, with a minimum age of 7 and 10 years respectively. Maximum weight on either trip is 220 pounds.

OUTFITTERS & EXPEDITIONS

Canyon Trail Rides. These friendly folks have been around for years, and they are the only outfitter for trail rides inside the park. Anyone over age seven can participate in guided rides along the Virgin River. The horses work from late March through October; you may want to make reservations ahead of time. ⊠*Across the road from Zion Lodge* ☎*435/679–8665* ⊕*www.canyonrides.com* ⊠*$30–$65.*

SWIMMING

Swimming is allowed in the Virgin River within and outside park boundaries, but be careful of cold water, slippery rock bottoms, and the occasional flash floods whenever it rains. Swimming is not allowed in the Emerald Pools, and the use of inner tubes is prohibited within park boundaries.

WINTER SPORTS

Cross-country skiing and snowshoeing are best experienced in the park's higher elevations during the winter, where snow stays on the ground longer. Inquire at the Zion Canyon Visitor Center for backcountry conditions. Snowmobiling is only allowed for residential access.

EDUCATIONAL OFFERINGS

CLASSES & SEMINARS

Zion Canyon Field Institute. Turn Zion Canyon into a classroom by participating in a seminar on edible plants, geology, photography, adobe-brick making, or any number of other educational programs provided year-round by the Zion Canyon Field Institute, in the nature center. Classes, held outdoors throughout the park, are limited to small groups; reserve ahead to assure placement. ☎*800/635–3959* ⊕*www.zionpark.org* ⊠*$12–$250.*

RANGER PROGRAMS

Evening Programs. Held each evening in campground amphitheaters and in Zion Lodge from April through September, these entertaining 30–45-minute ranger-led programs inform you on subjects such as geology and history. You may learn about the bats that swoop through the canyons at night, the surreptitious ways of the mountain lion, or how plants and animals adapt to life in the desert. Programs may include a slide show or audience participation. ☎*435/772–3256* ☑*Free.*

Junior Ranger Program. Kids 6–12 can have fun learning about plants, animals, geology, and archaeology through hands-on activities, games, and hikes. They can earn a certificate, pin, and patch by attending one session of the Junior Ranger Program at the Zion Nature Center and one other ranger-led activity in the park. Children 5 or younger can earn a Junior Ranger decal by completing an activity sheet available at the Zion Canyon Visitor Center. Kids can earn a Junior Ranger badge by working through an activity booklet (available at the Zion Canyon and Kolob Canyons visitor centers) during their visit to Zion. Kids need to sign up for Junior Ranger programs at the Zion Nature Center half an hour before they begin. ⊠*Zion Nature Center, near South Campground entrance, ½ mi north of south entrance* ☎*435/772–3256* ☑*Free* ⊙*Daily.*

Morning and Afternoon Hikes. These 1- to 2-mi ranger-led walks can greatly enhance your understanding of the geology, wildlife, and history of Zion National Park. Each park ranger selects a favorite destination, which may change daily. Inquire at the Zion Canyon Visitor Center or check park bulletin boards for locations and times. Wear sturdy footgear and bring a hat, sunglasses, sunscreen, and water.

Shuttle Tours. To learn about the geology, ecology, and history of Zion Canyon, join a park ranger for a 90-minute narrated tour by shuttle bus. Tours depart from the Zion Canyon Visitor Center. You'll make several stops along the way to take photographs and hear park interpretation from the ranger. Tour times are posted at the Zion Canyon Visitor Center, which is also where you can pick up your free but mandatory tour tickets up to 24 hours in advance. ⊠*Zion Canyon Center* ☎*435/772–3256* ☑*Free* ⊙*May–Sept., daily.*

NEARBY TOWNS

Springdale, on the southern boundary of Zion National Park, has plenty of hotels, restaurants, and shops, yet the community still manages to maintain its small-town charm. On Route 9 between St. George and Zion stands the small town of **Hurricane,** home to one of Utah's most scenic 18-hole golf courses; it's also a less expensive and less crowded base for exploring Zion National Park. On Route 9, 13 mi east of the park is **Mount Carmel Junction,** an intersection offering some funky small-town lodging and the don't-miss studio of Maynard Dixon, the artist many consider the finest painter of the American West.

For more information on these nearby towns see Chapter 8.

WHERE TO EAT

ABOUT THE RESTAURANTS

There is only one full-service restaurant in Zion National Park, so for more dining options, head for the nearby town of Springdale (⇨ *Chapter 8*), which has the area's best restaurants.

WHAT IT COSTS				
¢	$	$$	$$$	$$$$
RESTAURANTS under $8	$8–$12	$13–$20	$21–$30	over $30

Restaurant prices are per person for a main course at dinner.

$$-$$$ ✕**Red Rock Grill at Zion Lodge.** This is the only full-service restaurant inside the park. A rustic reproduction of the original lodge dining room, the restaurant is hung with historic photos. You can dine on the patio overlooking the front lawn of the lodge. A good selection of steak, fish, and poultry is offered for dinner, and lunch includes sandwiches and salads. Breakfast is also served. ⊠*Zion Canyon Scenic Dr., 3¼ mi north of Canyon Junction* ☎*435/772-7760* ⊕*www.zionlodge.com* ⏵*Reservations essential (for dinner)* ▤*AE, D, DC, MC, V.*

¢ ✕**Castle Dome Café.** Right next to the Zion Lodge shuttle stop and adjoining the gift shop, this small fast-food restaurant defines convenience. Hikers on the go can grab a banana or a sandwich here, or you can while away an hour with ice cream on the sunny patio. ⊠*Zion Canyon Scenic Dr., 3¼ mi north of Canyon Junction* ☎*435/772-7700* ⊕*www.zionlodge.com* ▤*AE, D, DC, MC, V.*

PICNIC AREAS Whether in the cool of Zion Canyon or on a point overlooking the drama of Kolob Canyons, a Zion picnic can be a relaxing break in a busy day of exploring.

The Grotto. A shady lunch retreat with lots of amenities—drinking water, fire grates, picnic tables, and restrooms—the Grotto is ideal for families. A short walk takes you to Zion Lodge, where you can pick up fast food. ⊠*Zion Canyon Scenic Dr., 3½ mi north of Canyon Junction.*

Kolob Canyons Viewpoint. Enjoy the views while you have your lunch at the picnic table. Restrooms and drinking water are available at the Kolob Canyons Visitor Center. ⊠*Kolob Canyons Rd., 5 mi from Kolob Canyons Visitor Center.*

Zion Nature Center. On your way to or from the Junior Ranger Program feed your kids at the Nature Center picnic area. When the nature center is closed, you can use the restrooms in South Campground. ⊠*Near the entrance to South Campground ½ mi north of the south entrance* ☎*435/772-3256.*

WHERE TO STAY

ABOUT THE HOTELS

Lodging within Zion is very limited and rustic. Still, in the summer high season, you'll want to make reservations if you want to stay in or close to the park. Nearby Springdale has many lodging options, from quaint smaller motels and bed-and-breakfasts, to upscale hotels with modern amenities and riverside rooms. If you are willing to find a room upward of an hour or two away, perhaps with fewer amenities, you may be surprised not only by same-day reservations in some cases, but also much lower room rates. Panguitch and Hurricane have some particularly good options for budget and last-minute travelers.

For lodging recommendations outside the park, *see Where to Stay in Springdale, Panguitch, Hurricane, and Mt. Carmel Junction in Chapter 8.*

ABOUT THE CAMPGROUNDS

Campgrounds within Zion National Park are family friendly, convenient, and quite pleasant, but in the high season they do fill up fast. Your best bet is to reserve ahead of time whenever possible. How quickly camping choices outside of the park fill up varies according to how far away they are, but most all cater to tent campers and RVers alike, with features such as playgrounds, showers, and picnic areas. Backcountry camping in the park is an option for overnight backpackers, but make sure to get a permit at the Zion Canyon Visitor Center. The primitive Lava Point Campground has no water and is closed during the winter. Its six sites are first-come, first-served.

> ### WORD OF MOUTH
>
> "We recently stayed in Springdale at the west entrance to Zion NP at the Best Western Zion Park Inn. We were pleased with our room. There is a nice pool but no breakfast."
>
> –happytrailstoyou

	WHAT IT COSTS				
	¢	$	$$	$$$	$$$$
HOTELS	under $50	$50–$100	$101–$150	$151–$200	over $200

Hotel prices are for two people in a standard double room in high season.

$$$ 🏨 **Zion Lodge.** Although the original lodge burned down in 1966, the rebuilt structure convincingly re-creates the classic look of the old inn. Knotty pine woodwork and log and wicker furnishings accent the lobby. Lodge rooms are modern but not fancy, and the historic Western-style cabins have gas-log fireplaces. This is a place of quiet retreat, so there are no TVs—kids can amuse themselves outdoors on the abundant grassy lawns. The lodge is within easy walking distance of trailheads, horseback riding, and, of course, the shuttle stop, all of which are less than ½ mi away. **Pro:** Prime location in the heart of Zion Canyon. **Con:** Reservations tend to fill far in advance. Make yours at least six months ahead. ⊠ *Zion Canyon Scenic Dr., 3¼ mi north of Canyon Junction* 🕾 *435/772–7700, 888/297–2757 reservations* 🖷 *435/772–7790* ⊕ *www.zionlodge.com* 🛏 *122 rooms, 6 suites* 🖧 *In-room: refrigerator (some), no TV, dial-up. In-hotel: 2 restaurants, bar, public Internet, no-smoking rooms* 🚍 *AE, D, MC, V* 🍴 *EP.*

🏕 **South Campground.** All the sites here are under big cottonwood trees, granting campers some relief from the summer sun. The campground operates on a first-come, first-served basis, and sites are usually filled before noon each day during high season. Many of the sites are suitable for either tents or RVs, although there are no hookups. Reservations not accepted. ☒ *Rte. 9, ½ mi north of south entrance* ⟳ *127 sites* ♿ *Flush toilets, dump station, drinking water, fire grates, picnic tables* ☎ *435/772–3256* ☱ *No credit cards* ⊙ *Mar.–Oct.*

★ 🏕 **Watchman Campground.** This large campground on the Virgin River operates on a reservation system from April to October, but you do not get to choose your own site. Sometimes you can get same-day reservations, but don't count on it. ☒ *Access road off Zion Canyon Visitor Center parking lot* ☎ *435/772–3256, 877/444–6777 reservations* ⊕ *www.recreation.gov* ⟳ *152 sites, 63 with hook-ups* ♿ *Flush toilets, partial hookups (electric), dump station, drinking water, fire grates, picnic tables* ☱ *D, MC, V.*

🏕 **Zion Canyon Campground & RV Park.** In Springdale about a half mile from the south entrance to the park, this campground is surrounded on three sides by the canyon's rock formations. Many of the sites are on the river. ☒ *479 Zion Park Blvd., Springdale* ☎ *435/772–3237* 🖷 *435/772–3844* ⊕ *www.zion-camp.com/rv_park.html* ⟳ *110 RV sites, 110 tent sites* ♿ *Flush toilets, full hookups, dump station, drinking water, guest laundry, showers, fire grates, picnic tables, food service, electricity, public telephone, general store, play area, swimming (river), Wi-Fi* ☱ *D, MC, V.*

🏕 **Zion River Resort RV Park & Campground.** This resort in Virgin, 8 mi east of Hurricane, has everything an RV camper could want, with the possible exception of shade. Most of the trees haven't grown up yet, but there are some premium sites along the river where the cottonwoods are mature. You can also rent a cabin, tent site, or tepee. The RV hookups include phone or modem connections. Ask about the shuttle to Zion National Park. ☒ *730 E. Rte. 9, Box 790219, Virgin, 84779* ☎ *435/635–8594* 🖷 *435/635–3934* ⊕ *www.zionriverresort.com* ⟳ *114 sites, 114 with hookups* ♿ *Flush toilets, full hookups, drinking water, guest laundry, showers, grills, picnic tables, electricity, public telephone, general store, play area, swimming (pool)* ☱ *D, MC, V.*

ZION NATIONAL PARK ESSENTIALS

ACCESSIBILITY
Both visitor centers, all shuttle buses, and Zion Lodge are fully accessible to wheelchairs. Several campsites (sites A24 and A25 at Watchman

Campground and sites 103, 114, and 115 at South Campground) are reserved for people with disabilities, and two trails—Riverside Walk and Pa'rus Trail—are accessible with some assistance.

ADMISSION FEES
Entrance to Zion National Park is $25 per vehicle for a seven-day pass. People entering on foot or by bicycle or motorcycle pay $12 per person (not to exceed $25 per family) for a seven-day pass. Entrance to the Kolob Canyons section of the park costs $25, and includes access to Zion Canyon.

ADMISSION HOURS
The park is open daily year-round, 24 hours a day. The park is in the Mountain time zone.

ATMS/BANKS
The park has no ATM.

Contacts Zions Bank (⊠ *921 Zion Park Blvd., Springdale* ☎ *435/772–3274*).

AUTOMOBILE SERVICE STATIONS
In nearby Kanab and Springdale, you can fuel up, get your tires and oil changed, and have auto-repair work done.

Contacts Kanab Tire Center (⊠ *265 E. 300 S, Kanab* ☎ *435/644–2557*). **Springdale Chevron** (⊠ *1593 Zion Park Blvd., Springdale* ☎ *435/772–3922*).

EMERGENCIES
In the event of an emergency, dial 911, report to a visitor center, or contact a park ranger at 435/772–3322. The nearest hospitals are in St. George, Cedar City, and Kanab.

Contacts Zion Canyon Medical Clinic (⊠ *120 Zion Blvd., Springdale* ☎ *435/772–3226* ☽ *Mid-May–mid-Oct., Tues.–Sat. 9–5*)accepts walk-in patients.

LOST AND FOUND
The park's lost-and-found is at the Zion Canyon Visitor Center.

PERMITS
Permits are required for backcountry camping and overnight climbs. The maximum size of a group hiking into the backcountry is 12 people. The cost for a permit for 1–2 people is $10; 3–7 people, $15; and 8–12 people, $20. Permits and hiking information are available at the Zion Canyon Visitor Center.

POST OFFICE
Within the park, you can mail letters and buy stamps at Zion Lodge.

Contacts Springdale Branch (⊠ *625 Zion Park Blvd., Springdale, 84767* ☎ *800/275-8777*).

PUBLIC TELEPHONES
Public telephones may be found at South Campground, Watchman Campground, Zion Canyon Visitor Center, Zion Lodge, and Zion

Museum. Cell-phone reception is decent in Springdale but spotty in Zion Canyon itself.

RELIGIOUS SERVICES

Interdenominational services are held during the summer at Zion Lodge and South Campground. Check bulletin boards at the Zion Canyon Visitor Center for times.

RESTROOMS

Public restrooms are located at the Grotto, Kolob Canyons Visitor Center, Temple of Sinawava, Weeping Rock Trailhead, Zion Canyon Visitor Center, Zion Human History Museum, and Zion Lodge.

SHOPS & GROCERS

Contacts **Sol Foods Market** (✉ *95 Zion Park Blvd., Springdale* ☎ *435/772–3402*).

Springdale Fruit Company (✉ *2491 Zion Park Blvd.Springdale* ☎ *435/772–3822*).

Zion Park Market (✉ *865 Zion Park Blvd., Springdale* ☎ *435/772-3251*).

VISITOR INFORMATION

Contacts **Zion National Park** (✉ *Springdale, UT 84767-1099* ☎ *435/772-3256* ⊕ *www.nps.gov/zion*).

6

Bryce Canyon National Park

WORD OF MOUTH

"The sunrise at Bryce Point should not be missed. Navajo Loop–Queen's Garden hike is beautiful and easy. It will take you down into the Hoodoos. You will not get an appreciation for the place without going down."

—Myer

WELCOME TO BRYCE CANYON

TOP REASONS TO GO

★ **Hoodoos Galore:** Bryce Canyon attracts visitors for its hundreds, if not thousands, of brightly colored, limestone spires, more commonly known as hoodoos.

★ **Famous Fresh Air:** To say the air around Bryce Canyon is rarified is not an exaggeration. With some of the clearest skies anywhere, the park offers views that, on a clear day, extend 200 mi and into three states.

★ **Spectacular Sunrises & Sunsets:** The deep orange and crimson hues of the park's hoodoos are intensified by the light of the sun at either end of the day.

★ **Getting into the Zone(s):** Bryce Canyon's elevation range—2,000 feet—is such that it spans three climatic zones: spruce/fir forest, ponderosa pine forest, and pinyon pine/juniper forest. The result is a park rich in biodiversity.

★ **Gaspworthy Geology:** A series of horseshoe-shaped amphitheaters comprise much of the park, and are the focus of most scenic turnouts.

Spire in Bryce Canyon

1 Bryce Amphitheater. Here is the park's densest collection of attractions, including the historic Bryce Canyon National Park Lodge and the points Sunrise, Sunset, and Inspiration. Paria View looks far south into Grand Staircase–Escalante National Monument.

2 Under-the-Rim Trail. Though it more or less parallels most of the scenic drive and accesses many popular sites, from Bryce Point to the vicinity of Swamp Canyon, this trail is the best way to reach the Bryce Canyon backcountry. A handful of primitive campgrounds line the route.

Hoodoo Towers

Inspiration Point at Bryce Canyon

3 Rainbow and Yovimpa Points. The end of the scenic road, but not of the scenery, here you can hike a trail to see some ancient bristlecone pines and look south into Grand Staircase–Escalante National Monument.

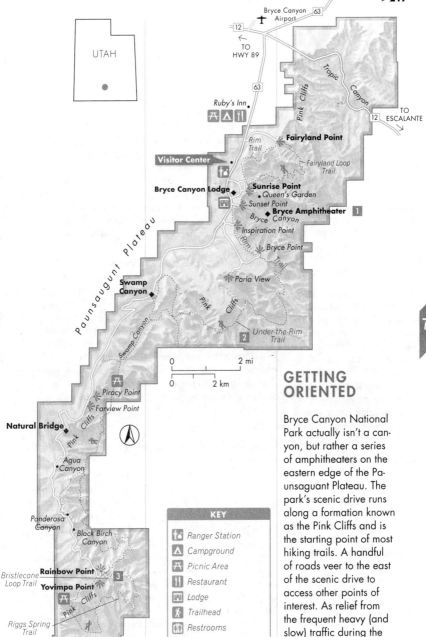

GETTING ORIENTED

Bryce Canyon National Park actually isn't a canyon, but rather a series of amphitheaters on the eastern edge of the Paunsaguant Plateau. The park's scenic drive runs along a formation known as the Pink Cliffs and is the starting point of most hiking trails. A handful of roads veer to the east of the scenic drive to access other points of interest. As relief from the frequent heavy (and slow) traffic during the high season of summer, consider riding in one of the park's shuttle buses.

UTAH

Bryce Canyon Airport

TO HWY 89

Ruby's Inn

Visitor Center

Bryce Canyon Lodge

Fairyland Point

Fairyland Loop Trail

Rim Trail

Sunrise Point
Queen's Garden
Sunset Point
Bryce Amphitheater
Bryce Canyon
Inspiration Point
Bryce Point
Rim Trail

Paria View

Pink Cliffs

Under-the-Rim Trail

Swamp Canyon

Paunsaugunt Plateau

Piracy Point
Farview Point
Natural Bridge
Pink Cliffs
Agua Canyon
Ponderosa Canyon
Black Birch Canyon
Bristlecone Loop Trail
Rainbow Point
Yovimpa Point
Pink Cliffs
Riggs Spring Trail

TO ESCALANTE

KEY

Ranger Station
Campground
Picnic Area
Restaurant
Lodge
Trailhead
Restrooms
Scenic Viewpoint
Walking/Hiking Trails
Bicycle Path

0   2 mi
0   2 km

BRYCE CANYON PLANNER

When to Go

Around Bryce Canyon National Park, elevations approach and surpass 9,000 feet, making for temperamental weather, intermittent and seasonal road closures due to snow, and downright cold nights well into June. At this altitude, the warm summer sun is perfectly balanced by the coolness of the alpine forests during the day.

If you choose to see Bryce Canyon in July, August, or September, you'll be visiting with the rest of the world. During these months, traffic on the main road can be crowded with cars following slow-moving RVs, so consider taking one of the park buses from the visitor center. Also in summer, lodging may be difficult to find.

If it's solitude you're looking for, come to Bryce any time between October and March. The snow may be flying, but imagine the multihued rocks under an icing of white. Strap on snowshoes or cross-country skis, and you might just have a trail all to yourself.

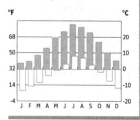

Flora & Fauna

Due to elevations approaching 9,000 feet, many of Bryce Canyon's 400 plant species are unlike those you'll see at less lofty places. Look at exposed slopes and you might catch a glimpse of the gnarled, 2,000-year-old bristlecone pine. More common, and far younger, are the Douglas fir, ponderosa pine, and the quaking aspen, most striking in its bright golden fall color. No fewer than three kinds of sagebrush—big, black, and fringed—grow here, as well as the blue columbine.

Their reputation as a pest among Southern Utah ranchers notwithstanding, the Utah prairie dog is designated a threatened species. Be cautious around them. Though cute and seemingly approachable, they might bite if you get too close, and the bacteria that causes bubonic plague has been found on their fleas. Other animals include elk, black-tailed jackrabbits, and the desert cottontail. Below 7,000 feet, black bear have been seen in the trees, but infrequently. It's far more likely you'll see the soaring forms of golden and bald eagles, or perhaps a peregrine falcon diving into the amphitheaters at speeds approaching 200 mph.

Getting There & Around

The closest major cities to Bryce Canyon are Salt Lake City and Las Vegas, each about 270 mi away. The nearest commercial airport is 80 mi west in Cedar City, Utah. The park is reached via Route 63, just 3 mi south of the junction with Highway 12.

You can see the park's highlights by driving along the well-maintained road running the length of the main scenic area. Bryce has no restrictions on automobiles, but in the summer you may encounter heavy traffic and full parking lots. A shuttle bus system operates from mid-May through September. It is free, though you still must pay the park entrance fee. The shuttle departs from the staging area off Highway 12 about 3 mi north of the park entrance every 10 to 15 minutes. Stops include Best Western Ruby's Inn, the North Campground, the visitor center, and all major overlooks in the northern portion of the park.

By John
Blodgett

A LAND THAT CAPTURES THE imagination and the heart, Bryce is a visitor favorite among Utah's national parks. The park was named for Ebenezer Bryce, a pioneer cattleman and the first permanent settler in the area. His description of the landscape not being hospitable to cows has oft been repeated. Even more than his famous quote, however, Bryce Canyon is known for its fanciful "hoodoos," best viewed at sunrise or sunset, when the light plays off the red rock.

In geological terms, Bryce is actually an amphitheater, not a canyon. The hoodoos in the amphitheater took on their unusual shapes because the top layer of rock—"cap rock"—is harder than the layers below it. If erosion undercuts the soft rock beneath the cap too much, the hoodoo will tumble. But Bryce will never be without hoodoos, because as the amphitheater's rim recedes, new hoodoos are formed.

SCENIC DRIVE

Fodor'sChoice
★

Main Park Road. One of the delights of Bryce Canyon National Park is that much of the park's grandeur can be experienced from scenic overlooks along its main thoroughfare, which meanders 18 mi from the park entrance south to Rainbow Point. Allow two to three hours to travel the entire 36 mi round-trip. The road is open year-round, but may be closed temporarily after heavy snowfalls to allow for clearing. Major overlooks are rarely more than a few minutes' walk from the parking areas, and many let you see more than 100 mi on clear days. All overlooks lie east of the road—to keep things simple (and left turns to a minimum), you can proceed to the southern end of the park and stop at the overlooks on your northbound return. Trailers are not allowed beyond Sunset Campground. Day users may park trailers at the visitor center or other designated sites; check with park staff for parking options. RVs can drive throughout the park, but vehicles longer than 25 feet are not allowed at Paria View.

WHAT TO SEE

HISTORIC SITE

Bryce Canyon National Park Lodge. Gilbert Stanley Underwood designed this lodge, built in 1924, for the Union Pacific Railroad. The National Historic Landmark has been faithfully restored, right down to the lobby's huge limestone fireplace and log and wrought-iron chandelier, plus bark-covered hickory furniture made by the same company that created the originals. Inside the historic building are a restaurant and a gift shop, as well as plenty of information on park activities. Guests of the lodge stay in the numerous log cabins on the wooded grounds. ⊠ *2 mi south of park entrance* ☎ *435/834–5361.*

SCENIC STOPS

Agua Canyon. When you stop at this overlook in the southern section of the park, pick out among the hoodoos the formation known as the Hunter, which actually has a few small hardy trees growing on its cap.

BRYCE CANYON IN ONE DAY

Begin your day at the **visitor center** to get an overview of the park and to purchase books and maps. Watch the video and peruse exhibits about the natural and cultural history of Bryce Canyon. Thus informed, drive to the historic **Bryce Canyon National Park Lodge.** From here, stroll along the relaxing **Rim Trail.** Afterward, drive the 18-mi **Main Park Road,** stopping at the overlooks along the way. Allowing for traffic, and if you stop at all 13 overlooks, this drive will take you between two and three hours.

If you have the time and energy for a hike, the easiest route into the amphitheater is the **Queen's Garden Trail** at Sunrise Point. A short,

rolling hike along the **Bristlecone Loop Trail** at Rainbow Point rewards you with spectacular views and a cool walk through a forest of bristlecone pines. If you don't have time to drive the 18 mi to the end of the park, skip Bryce Canyon National Park Lodge and drive 2 mi from the visitor center to **Inspiration Point** and the next 2 mi to **Bryce Point.**

End your day with sunset at Inspiration Point and dinner at Bryce Canyon National Park Lodge (you'll want to have made your reservations that morning). As you leave the park, stop at **Ruby's Inn** for Native American jewelry, souvenirs for the kids, and snacks for the road.

The plays of light and colorful contrasts are especially noticeable here. ✉ *12 mi south of park entrance.*

Bryce Point. After absorbing views of the Black Mountains and Navajo Mountain, you can follow the trailhead for the Under-the-Rim-Trail and go exploring down in the amphitheater to the cluster of top-heavy hoodoos known collectively as the Hat Shop. Along the Peekaboo Loop Trail, which also descends from this point, is the **Wall of Windows.** Openings carved into a wall of rock illustrate the drama of erosion that formed Bryce Canyon. ✉ *5½ mi south of park entrance on Inspiration Point Rd.*

★ **Fairyland Point.** At the scenic overlook closest to the park entrance (look for the sign marking the route off the main park road), there are splendid views of Fairyland Amphitheater and its delicate, fanciful forms. The Sinking Ship and other formations stand before the grand backdrop of the Aquarius Plateau and distant Navajo Mountain. ✉ *1 mi off main park road, 1 mi north of visitor center.*

Inspiration Point. Not far at all (³⁄₁₀ mi) east along the Rim Trail from Bryce Point is Inspiration Point, site of a wonderful panorama and one of the best places in the park to see the sunset. ✉ *5½ mi south of park entrance on Inspiration Point Rd.*

★ **Natural Bridge.** Despite its name, this formation is actually an arch carved in the rock by rain and frost erosion; true natural bridges must be bored out by streams and rivers. Pine forests are visible through the span of the arch. ✉ *11 mi south of park entrance.*

Rainbow and Yovimpa Points. While Rainbow Point's orientation allows a view north along the southern rim of the amphitheater and east into Grand Staircase–Escalante National Monument, the panorama from Yovimpa Point spreads out to the south and on a clear day you can see as far as 100 mi to Arizona. Yovimpa Point also has a shady and quiet picnic area with tables and restrooms. The Bristlecone Loop Trail connects the two viewpoints and leads through a grove of bristlecone pine trees. There are informative displays on flora, fauna, and geological history at Rainbow Point. ⊠ *18 mi south of park entrance.*

★ **Sunrise Point.** Named for its stunning views at dawn, this overlook is a popular stop for the summer crowds that come to Bryce Canyon and is the starting point for the Queen's Garden Trail and the Fairyland Loop Trail. You have to descend the Queen's Garden Trail to get a regal glimpse of **Queen Victoria,** a hoodoo that appears to sport a crown and glorious full skirt. The trail is popular and marked clearly, but moderately strenuous. ⊠ *2 mi south of park entrance near Bryce Canyon National Park Lodge.*

Sunset Point. Bring your camera to watch the late-day sun paint its magic on the hoodoos here. You can only see **Thor's Hammer,** a delicate formation similar to a balanced rock when you hike 521 feet down into the amphitheater on the Navajo Loop Trail. ⊠ *2 mi south of park entrance near Bryce Canyon National Park Lodge.*

VISITOR CENTER
Bryce Canyon Visitor Center. You can visit with park rangers, watch a video about Bryce Canyon, study exhibits, or shop for informative books, maps, and other materials at this spacious visitor center. First aid, emergency, and lost-and-found services are offered here, and rangers dole out backcountry permits. If you want coffee, head to nearby Ruby's Inn. ⊠ *1 mi south of park entrance* ☎ *435/834–5322* ⊕ *www.nps.gov/brca* ⊗ *May–Sept., daily 8–8; Apr. and Oct., daily 8–6; Nov.–Mar., daily 8–4:30.*

SPORTS & THE OUTDOORS

Most visitors explore Bryce Canyon by car, and though many stick only to the easiest of trails, there are plenty of other ways in which to enjoy Bryce Canyon. At these elevations, it gets warm in the summer but rarely uncomfortably hot, so hiking farther into the depths of the park is not difficult so long as you don't pick a hike that is beyond your abilities.

AIR TOURS
Bryce Canyon Airlines & Helicopters. For a once-in-a-lifetime view of Bryce Canyon National Park, join professional pilots and guides for a helicopter ride over the park. Flights depart from Ruby's Inn Heliport. You can swoop over the amphitheater for as long as 15 minutes to more than an hour. Small airplane tours and charter services are also available. ☎ *435/834–8060* ⊕ *www.rubysinn.com/bryce-canyon-airlines.html* ⊠ *$59–$349.*

BIRD-WATCHING

More than 170 bird species have been identified in Bryce. Violet-green swallows and white-throated swifts are common, as are Steller's jays, American coots, Rufous hummingbirds, and mountain bluebirds. Lucky bird-watchers will see golden eagles floating across the skies above the pink rocks of the amphitheater. The best time in the park for avian variety is from May through July, during the migration.

HIKING

To get up close and personal with the park's hoodoos, set aside a half day to hike into the amphitheater. Just about any hike that descends below the rim is moderately strenuous (and no below-rim trails are paved). The uneven terrain calls for sturdy hiking boots. In summer, consider hiking in the morning to avoid the day's warmest temperatures and strongest sun. Keep in mind that if you're not used to exercising at elevation, you can fall victim to altitude sickness. For trail maps, information, and ranger recommendations, stop at the visitor center. Bathrooms are located at most trailheads but not down in the amphitheater.

EASY **Bristlecone Loop Trail.** Hike through dense spruce and fir forest to exposed cliffs where ancient bristlecone pines somehow manage to survive the elements; some of the trees here are more than 1,700 years old. You might see yellow-bellied marmots and blue grouse, critters not found at lower elevations in the park. The popular 1-mi trail takes about an hour to hike. ⊠ *Rainbow Point, 18 mi south of park entrance.*

Queen's Garden Trail. This hike is the easiest into the amphitheater and therefore the most crowded. Allow two to three hours to hike the 2 mi down and back. ⊠ *Sunrise Point, 2 mi south of park entrance.*

MODERATE **Navajo Loop Trail.** A steep descent via a series of switchbacks leads to Wall Street, a narrow canyon with high rock walls and towering fir trees. The northern end of the trail brings Thor's Hammer into view. Allow one to two hours on this 1½-mi trail. ⊠ *Sunset Point, 2 mi south of park entrance.*

★ **Navajo/Queen's Garden Combination Loop.** By walking this extended 3-mi loop, you can see some of the best of Bryce; it takes two to three hours. The route passes fantastic formations and an open forest of pine and juniper on the amphitheater floor. Descend into the amphitheater from Sunset Point on the Navajo Trail and ascend via the less demanding Queen's Garden Trail; return to your starting point via the Rim Trail. ⊠ *Sunset and Sunrise points, 2 mi south of park entrance.*

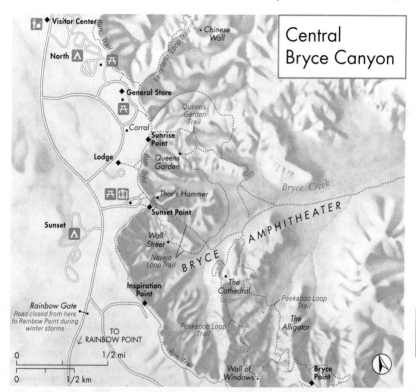

DIFFICULT **Fairyland Loop Trail.** Hike into whimsical Fairyland Canyon on this strenuous but uncrowded 8-mi trail. It winds around hoodoos, across trickles of water, and finally to a natural window in the rock at Tower Bridge, 1½ mi from Sunrise Point and 4 mi from Fairyland Point. The pink-and-white badlands and hoodoos surround you the whole way. Allow four to five hours round trip. You can pick up the loop at Fairyland Point or Sunrise Point. ⊠ *Fairyland Point, 1 mi off main park road, 1 mi south of park entrance; Sunrise Point, 2 mi south of park entrance.*

Peekaboo Loop. For a good workout, hike this steep trail past the Wall of Windows and the Three Wise Men. Horses use this trail in spring, summer, and fall and have the right-of-way. Start at Bryce, Sunrise, or Sunset points and allow three to four hours to hike either the 5-mi or 7-mi loop. ⊠ *Bryce Point, 2 mi off main park road, 5½ mi south of park entrance; Sunrise and Sunset points, 2 mi south of park entrance.*

Riggs Spring Loop Trail. One of the park's more rigorous day hikes, or a relaxed overnighter, this 9-mi trail between Yovimpa and Rainbow points takes about four to five hours to hike. ⊠ *Yovimpa and Rainbow points, 18 mi south of park entrance.*

Trail to the Hat Shop. Once you reach the end you understand how the trail got its name. Hard gray caps balance precariously atop narrow pedestals of softer, rust-colored rock. Allow three to four hours to travel this strenuous 4-mi round-trip trail. ⊠ *Bryce Point, 2 mi off main park road, 5½ mi south of park entrance.*

Under-the-Rim Trail. This is how serious backpackers immerse themselves in the landscape of Bryce. Starting at Bryce Point, the trail travels 22½ mi to Rainbow Point, passing through the Pink Cliffs, traversing Agua Canyon and Ponderosa Canyon, and taking you by several springs. Most of the hike is on the amphitheater floor, characterized by up-and-down terrain among stands of ponderosa pine; the elevation change totals about 1,500 feet. Four trailheads along the main park road allow you to connect to the Under-the-Rim Trail and cover its length as a series of day hikes. Allow at least two days to hike the route in its entirety. Obtain a backcountry permit at the visitor center if you intend to stay in the amphitheater overnight. Also inquire about the current availability of water along the trail. ⊠ *Access from Bryce Point, Swamp Canyon, Ponderosa Canyon, and Rainbow Point.*

HORSEBACK RIDING

Few activities conjure up the Old West like riding a horse, and Bryce Canyon offers plenty of opportunities to see the sights from the saddle. Many of the park's hiking trails were first formed beneath the hooves of cattle wranglers, and their modern-day counterparts now guide tourists over these and other trails. Area outfitters prefer reservations, and will sometimes cancel rides if not enough people sign up. Minimum rider age and maximum rider weight vary according to the chosen ride (anywhere from half an hour to a full day or more in length), but typically those under the age of seven and over the weight of 230 pounds are prohibited.

OUTFITTERS &
EXPEDITIONS
Canyon Trail Rides. Via horse or mule descend to the floor of the Bryce Canyon amphitheater. Most who take this expedition have no riding experience, so don't hesitate to join in. A two-hour ride ambles along the amphitheater floor to the Fairy Castle before returning to Sunrise Point. The half-day expedition follows Peekaboo Trail, winds past the Fairy Castle and the Alligator, and passes the Wall of Windows before returning to Sunrise Point. To reserve a trail ride, call or stop by their desk in the lodge. ⊠ *Bryce Canyon National Park Lodge* ☎ 435/679–8665.

Mecham Outfitters. This outfitter offers a full-day ride in Bryce Canyon, as well as a half-day ride in Grand Staircase-Escalante National Monument. They can also arrange multi-day excursions. ✉ *Box 71, Tropic, 84776* ☎ 435/679–8823 ⊕ *www.mechamoutfitters.com.*

Ruby's Red Canyon Horseback Rides. Retrace trails taken by outlaw Butch Cassidy in Red Canyon. Rides last from one and half hours to all day. For the full-day tour, a strenuous ride to Thunder Mountain, riders must be at least 10 years old and weigh no more than 220 pounds. ☎ 866/782–0002 ⊕ *www.horserides.net.*

WINTER SPORTS

Unlike Utah's other national parks, Bryce Canyon usually receives plenty of snow, making it a popular cross-country ski area. The park's 2½-mi Fairyland Ski Loop is marked but ungroomed, as is the 5-mi Paria Loop, which runs through ponderosa forests into long, open meadows.

The National Park Service lends out snowshoes free of charge at the visitor center; just leave your driver's license or a major credit card with a ranger. You can snowshoe on the rim trails, but the Park Service discourages their use below the rim.

OUTFITTERS & EXPEDITIONS **Best Western Ruby's Inn.** The property grooms a 31-mi private trail that connects to an ungroomed trail in the park. Rental equipment is available. ⊠ *Rte. 63, 1 mi north of park entrance* ☎ *435/834–5341.*

EDUCATIONAL OFFERINGS

PROGRAMS AND TOURS

Bryce Canyon Scenic Tours. Enjoy a scenic two-hour tour of Bryce Canyon with knowledgeable guides who describe the area's history, geology, and flora and fauna. Choose from a sunrise tour, sunset tour, or general tour of the park. Specialized or private tours can also be arranged. ☎ *435/834–5351 or 866/834–0043* ⊕ *www.brycetours.com* ☎ *$26 and up.*

Campfire and Auditorium Programs. Bryce Canyon's natural diversity comes alive in the park's two campgrounds or at Bryce Canyon National Park Lodge. Lectures, slide programs, and audience participation introduce you to geology, astronomy, wildlife, history, and many other topics related to Bryce Canyon and the West. ☎ *435/834–5322.*

RANGER PROGRAMS

The base of operations for all ranger activities is the visitor center, located 4½ mi south of the intersection of highways 12 and 63. Admission is free, but meeting times and locations vary. Stop by the visitor center or call 435/834–5322 for more information.

Canyon Hike. Take an early morning walk among the hoodoos of Queen's Garden or Navajo Loop Trail. A ranger points out the formations and explains some of the amphitheater's features as you go. The hike is 2- to 3-mi long and takes two to three hours to complete.

Geology Talk. Rangers relate the geologic story of Bryce Canyon in 30-minute sessions held at various times and locations around the park.

Junior Ranger Program. The program runs from Memorial Day to Labor Day; children ages 6 to 12 can sign up at the park visitor center. Activities vary depending on the park ranger, but a session might involve learning about geology and wildlife using arts and crafts and games. Schedules of events and topics are posted at the visitor center, Bryce Canyon National Park Lodge, and on North and Sunset campground bulletin boards.

7

Full Moon Hike. Four times a month, at or near full moon, rangers lead this two-hour hike. You must make reservations in person at the visitor center on the morning of the hike. Reservations are free but often fill up by 9 AM. Learn more about these hikes, and about the full array of the park's astronomy programs, at ⊕ www.nps.gov/brca/planyourvisit/astronomyprograms.htm.

Sunset Walk. Stroll along the gorgeous rim of Bryce Canyon at Sunset Point with a park ranger on a 1-mi, 1½-hour outing.

SHOPPING

Ruby's General Store. Shopping at Ruby's souvenir heaven is an integral part of the Bryce Canyon experience. This large, lively store is open year-round, and is packed with everything imaginable emblazoned with the park's name, from thimbles to sweatshirts. Native American arts and crafts, Western wear, camping gear, groceries, and sundries are plentiful. There is a large selection of children's toys and trinkets. ⊠ *Rte. 63, north of the park* ☎ *435/834–5341.*

NEARBY TOWNS

Many people check out Bryce Canyon without exploring its environs, but nearby small towns offer good choices for lodging, especially during the busy summer season. Decent amenities, inexpensive lodging, and an excellent location 24 mi northwest of Bryce Canyon National Park on U.S. 89 make **Panguitch** (⇨ *Chapter 8*) a comfortable launching pad for recreation in the area. The town is noted for the distinctive brick architecture of its early homes and outbuildings, and for the original facades of some of its late-19th-century Main Street commercial structures. Northeast of Bryce 47 mi, **Escalante** (⇨ *Chapter 8*) has modern amenities and is a western gateway to the Grand Staircase–Escalante National Monument. If you're traveling through southwestern Utah on Interstate 15, **Cedar City** (⇨ *Chapter 8*) will be your exit to Bryce. The largest city you'll encounter in this part of Utah, it's 78 mi from Bryce Canyon. The city's claims to fame are its popular Utah Shakespearean Festival and a major state university, and it's also steeped in Mormon pioneer heritage.

WHERE TO EAT

ABOUT THE RESTAURANTS
Dining options in the park proper are limited to Bryce Canyon National Park Lodge; the nearby Ruby's Inn complex (⇨ *Where to Stay*) is your best eating bet close by. For other dining options outside the park, which tend to be of the meat-and-potatoes variety, ⇨ *Where to Eat in Panguitch and Escalante in Chapter 8.*

$$–$$$ ✕**Bryce Canyon National Park Lodge.** Set among towering pines, this rustic old lodge is the only place to dine within the park. The simple breakfast menu features eggs, flapjacks, and lighter fare such as oatmeal

and granola. For dinner, try the red canyon grilled trout almandine or the cherry-glazed pork chops. Reservations are essential for dinner. ⊠*About 2 mi south of the park entrance* ☎*435/834–8760* ⊕*www. brycecanyonlodge.com* ⚑*Reservations essential (for dinner)* ▭*AE, D, DC, MC, V* ⊙*Closed Nov.–Mar.*

PICNIC AREAS **North Campground.** This area, a shady, alpine setting among ponderosa pine, has picnic tables and grills. ⊠*About ¼ mi south of the visitor center.*

Yovimpa Point. At the southern end of the park, this shady, quiet spot looks out onto the 100-mi vistas from the rim. There are tables and restrooms. ⊠*18 mi south of the park entrance.*

WHERE TO STAY

ABOUT THE HOTELS

Lodging options in Bryce Canyon include both rustic and modern amenities, but all fill up fast in summer. The big advantage of staying here is proximity, though Bryce Canyon National Park Lodge also has views. Outside the park, Panguitch (⇨ *Chapter 8*) has some good options for budget and last-minute travelers, and there are comfortable options within 10 mi of the park entrance.

ABOUT THE CAMPGROUNDS

Campgrounds in Bryce Canyon fill up fast, especially during the summer, and are family friendly. All are drive-in, except for the handful of backcountry sites that only backpackers and gung-ho day hikers ever see. Most are first-come, first-served during the high season, but call to inquire about those available for reservation. Most of the area's state parks have camping facilities, and Dixie National Forest contains many wonderful sites. Campgrounds may close seasonally because of lack of services (one loop of North Campground remains open year-round), and roads may occasionally close in winter while heavy snow is cleared.

WHAT IT COSTS				
$$$$	**$$$**	**$$**	**$**	**¢**
HOTELS	over $200	$151–$200	$101–$150	$50–$100	under $50

Hotel prices are per night for two people in a standard double room in high season.

$$$ 🏨 **Bryce Canyon National Park Lodge.** A few feet from the amphitheater's
Fodor's Choice rim and trailheads is this rugged stone-and-wood lodge. You have your
★ choice of suites on the lodge's second level, motel-style rooms in separate buildings (with balconies or porches), and cozy lodgepole-pine cabins, some with cathedral ceilings and gas fireplaces. Reservations are hard to come by, so call several months ahead. Horseback rides into the park's interior can be arranged in the lobby. Reservations are essential for dinner at the lodge restaurant. **Pro:** Fine Western-style lodging with bright orange hoodoos only a short walk away. **Con:** Closed in the winter. ⊠*2 mi south of park entrance, 84764* ☎*435/834–5361*

or 888/297–2757 🖷435/834–5464 ⊕www.brycecanyonlodge.com
🖢114 rooms, 3 suites ♿In-room: no a/c, no TV. In-hotel: restaurant, no elevator, no-smoking rooms ☰AE, D, MC, V ⊙Closed Nov.–Mar.

★ $$–$$$ 🖭**Best Western Ruby's Inn.** North of the park entrance and housing a large restaurant and gift shop, this is "Grand Central Station" for visitors to Bryce. Rooms vary in age, with sprawling wings added as the park gained popularity. All of the guest rooms are consistently comfortable and attractive, however. Centered between the gift shop and restaurant, the lobby of rough-hewn log beams and poles sets a Southwestern mood. There's a liquor store on-site. **Pro:** Has it all—general store, post office, campground, restaurants, gas and more. **Con:** Expansion has caused it to lose some of its charm. ⊠1000 South Rte. 63, Box 640001, Bryce 84764 🕾435/834–5341 or 866/866–6616 🖷435/834–5265 ⊕www.rubysinn.com 🖢368 rooms, 6 suites ♿In-room: refrigerator, Ethernet, dial-up, Wi-Fi. In-hotel: 2 restaurants, pools, bicycles, laundry facilities, concierge, public Internet, public Wi-Fi, airport shuttle, some pets allowed, no-smoking rooms ☰AE, D, DC, MC, V.

$–$$ 🖭**Bryce Valley Inn.** Rest your head in this down-to-earth motel in the tiny town of Tropic, about 8 mi from the Park entrance. The accommodations are clean, and a small gift shop sells Native American crafts. ⊠199 N. Main St. (Rte. 12), Tropic, 84776 🕾435/679–8811 or 800/442–1890 🖷435/679–8846 ⊕www.brycevalleyinn.com 🖢65 rooms, 13 suites ♿In-room: refrigerator (some), Wi-Fi. In-hotel: restaurant, laundry facilities, public Internet, some pets allowed, no-smoking rooms ☰AE, D, MC, V ⎮◎⎮CP.

$ 🖭**Bryce Canyon Pines.** This quiet, no-surprises motel complex is tucked into the woods 6 mi from the park entrance. Most of the rooms have excellent mountain views. There's a campground on the premises. ⊠6 mi northwest of park entrance on Rte. 12, Bryce, 84764 🕾800/892–7923 🖷435/834–5330 ⊕www.brycecanyonmotel.com 🖢51 rooms ♿In-hotel: restaurant, pool ☰AE, D, DC, MC, V.

$ 🖭**Bryce Canyon Resort.** This rustic lodge stands across from the local airport and 3 mi from the park entrance. Cabins and cottages are also available if you're seeking a tad more privacy. ⊠13500 E. Rte. 12, Bryce, 84764 🕾866/834–0043 ⊕www.brycecanyonresort.com 🖷435/834–5256 🖢71 rooms, 2 suites, 2 cabins ♿In-room: dial-up. In-hotel: restaurant, pool, laundry facilities, some pets allowed ☰MC, V.

$ 🖭**Bryce View Lodge.** Next to the park entrance and across from the Best Western Ruby's Inn complex, this motel has reasonable rates. The rooms are updated and comfortable, and the lodge is operated by Ruby's Inn, so you can use the pool and other amenities across the way. ⊠Rte. 63, 1 mi south of Rte. 12, Bryce, 84764 🕾435/834–5180 or 888/279–2304 🖷435/834–5181 ⊕www.bryceviewlodge.com 🖢160 rooms ♿In-hotel: some pets allowed ☰AE, D, DC, MC, V.

CAMPING ⛺ **Best Western Ruby's Inn Campground and RV Park.** North of the entrance
Fodor's Choice to Bryce Canyon National Park, this campground sits amid pine and fir
★ trees. ⊠Rte. 63, 1 mi off Hwy. 12, Bryce 🕾866/866–6616 ⊕www.

brycecanyoncampgrounds.com 🔄114 RV sites (full hookups), 13 RV sites (partial hookups), 73 tent sites, 5 cabins, 8 tepees 🚻Flush toilets, full hookups, partial hookups, dump station, drinking water, guest laundry, showers, grills, picnic tables, electricity, public telephone, general store, swimming (pool) 🗐AE, D, DC, MC, V ⊘Apr.–Oct.

🗻 **Bryce Canyon Pines Campground.** This campground, 6 mi from the park entrance, is shady and quiet. It's on the grounds of Bryce Canyon Pines Motel. ⊠Rte. 12, 6 mi northwest of the park entrance, Bryce ☎435/834–5441 or 800/892–7923 🖷435/834–5330 ⊕www.brycecanyonmotel.com/campground 🔄40 sites, 24 with hookups 🚻Flush toilets, full hookups, drinking water, showers, fire grates, electricity, public telephone, play area, swimming (pool) 🗐D, DC, MC, V ⊘Apr.–Nov.

🗻 **North Campground.** A cool, shady retreat in a forest of ponderosa pines, this is a great home base for your exploration of Bryce Canyon. You're near the general store, Bryce Canyon National Park Lodge, trailheads, and the visitor center. Reservations are accepted at 32 sites from May through September; the remaining 75 are available on a first-come, first-served basis. The campground usually fills by early afternoon in July, August, and September. ⊠Main park road, ½ mi south of visitor center ☎435/834–5322, 877/444–6777 reservations ⊕www.recreation.gov 🔄107 sites, 47 for RVs 🚻Flush toilets, dump station (closed during winter), drinking water, fire grates, picnic tables, public telephone, general store 🗐No credit cards ⊘Daily.

🗻 **Sunset Campground.** This serene alpine campground is within walking distance of Bryce Canyon National Park Lodge and many trailheads. All sites are filled on a first-come, first-served basis. The campground fills by early afternoon in July, August, and September, so get your campsite before you sightsee. Reservations not accepted. ⊠Main park road, 2 mi south of visitor center ☎435/834–5322 🔄101 sites, 49 for RVs 🚻Flush toilets, dump station, drinking water, fire grates, picnic tables, public telephone, general store 🗐No credit cards ⊘May–Oct.

BRYCE CANYON ESSENTIALS

ACCESSIBILITY

Most park facilities were constructed between 1930 and 1960. Some have been upgraded for handicap accessibility, while others can be used with some assistance. Because of the park's natural terrain, only a ½-mi section of the Rim Trail between Sunset and Sunrise points is wheelchair accessible. The 1-mi Bristlecone Loop Trail at Rainbow Point has a hard surface and could be used with assistance, but several grades do not meet standards. Handicapped parking is marked at all overlooks and public facilities. Accessible campsites are available at Sunset Campground.

ADMISSION FEES

The entrance fee is $25 per vehicle for a seven-day pass and $12 for pedestrians, bicyclists, or motorcyclists. An annual Bryce Canyon park pass, good for one year from the date of purchase, costs $30. This pass can also be used on the park shuttle. If you leave your private vehicle outside the park, the one-time entrance fee, including transportation on the shuttle, is $12.

ADMISSION HOURS
The park is open 24/7, year-round. It's in the Mountain time zone.

ATMS / BANKS
Ruby's Inn has an ATM. The nearest bank is in Panguitch.

Contacts **Ruby's Inn** (✉ *Rte. 63, 1 mi north of the park entrance, Bryce* ☎ *435/834–5341*) . **Zions Bank** (✉ *90 E. Center St., Panguitch* ☎ *435/676–8855*).

AUTOMOBILE SERVICE STATIONS
Just outside the park you can fuel up, get your oil and tires changed, and have car repairs done.

Contacts **Bryce Canyon Towing** (✉ *1 mi north of the park on Rte. 63, Bryce* ☎ *435/834–5232*). **Chevron at Ruby's Inn** (✉ *Rte. 63, 1 mi north of the park entrance, Bryce* ☎ *435/834–5484*).

EMERGENCIES
In an emergency, dial 911. To contact park police or if you need first aid, go to the visitor center or speak to a park ranger. (In the summer months only, there is also first aid at Bryce Canyon National Park Lodge.) The nearest hospital is in Panguitch.

Hospital **Garfield Memorial Hospital** (✉ *200 N. 400 East St., Panguitch* ☎ *435/676–8811*).

PERMITS
A $5 backcountry permit, available from the visitor center, is required for camping in the park's interior, allowed only on Under-the-Rim Trail and Rigg's Spring Loop, both south of Bryce Point. Campfires are not permitted.

RESTROOMS
Bryce Canyon National Park Lodge, Bryce Canyon Pines General Store, the south end of North Campground, Ruby's General Store, Ruby's Inn, Sunset Campground, Sunset Point, the visitor center, and Yovimpa Point all have public restrooms.

NEARBY TOWN INFORMATION
Contacts **Garfield County Travel Council (Bryce, Escalante, Panguitch).** ✉ *55 S. Main St., Panguitch, 84759* ☎ *435/676–1160 or 800/444–6689* ⊕ *www.brycecanyoncountry.com.* **Iron County Visitor Center (Cedar City)** ✉ *581 N. Main, Box 1007, Cedar City, 84720* ☎ *800/354–4849* ⊕ *www.scenicsouthernutah.com.*

VISITOR INFORMATION
Contacts **Bryce Canyon National Park** ✉ *Box 640201, Bryce Canyon, UT 84764* ☎ *435/834–5322* ⊕ *www.nps.gov/brca.*

Southwestern Utah

WORD OF MOUTH

"Cedar City is about the same distance and travel time to Springdale as St. George. It is a bit closer to the Kolob Canyon section of Zion, and probably about 30 minutes or so closer to Bryce than St. George. The drive between Cedar City and Bryce would be much better (scenery-wise) in fall than from Zion to Bryce. Cedar Breaks National Monument is not far from Cedar City and should be nice in fall, provided there isn't an early snowfall."

—BibE1

By John
Blodgett

SOUTHWESTERN UTAH IS A LAND of opposites. The state's lowest point, Beaver Dam Wash, is here, south and west of St. George, while the Pine Valley Mountains north of that growing city are among the tallest in Utah. The region is often perceived as a hot, dry place, yet from the desert depths you can see snowy peaks and evergreens and shiver.

Such contrasts have always attracted the curious. Famed explorer John Wesley Powell charted the uncharted; the young idealist and dreamer Everett Reuss left his well-to-do family and lost himself without a trace in the canyons; the author and curmudgeon Ed Abbey found himself, and has since been though of, depending on whom you ask, as either a voice crying in the wilderness or a pariah in Pareah. But that's the beauty of this place, the joy of choice in a land that confronts and challenges. We come, ostensibly, to escape; yet we really come to discover.

Southwestern Utah is a land of adventure and contemplation, of adrenaline and retreat. It's not an either-or proposition; you rejuvenate whether soaking at a luxury spa or careening on a mountain bike down an alpine single-track headed straight for an aspen tree. The land settlers tamed for planting cotton and fruit is now a playground for golfers, bikers, and hikers. Arts festivals and concerts under canyon walls have smoothed the rough edges hewn by miners and the boomtowns that evaporated as quickly as they materialized. Ruins, petroglyphs, pioneer graffiti, and ghost towns—monuments to what once was—beckon new explorers. The region's secrets reveal themselves to seekers, yet some mysteries remain elusive—the paradox of the bustling world that lies hidden under the impression of spare, silent, and open space.

EXPLORING SOUTHWESTERN UTAH

Southwestern Utah is remarkable in the range of activities and terrain it has to offer. On one summer day you can explore an arid desert canyon at Snow Canyon State Park, the next you can camp in a high-alpine aspen grove in Dixie National Forest and bundle up for warmth. In winter you can sample mountain biking (at Gooseberry Mesa near Hurricane) and skiing (at Brian Head Resort) on the same trip.

Getting around is usually straightforward. The region's biggest cities, Cedar City and St. George, spring up alongside I–15, the major north–south travel corridor to the west. Farther east, U.S. 89 is a more scenic north–south route with access to Bryce Canyon National Park, the east side of Zion National Park, and the Kanab area. Routes 14 and 9 are the major east–west connectors between the two main highways, with Route 9 being the primary access to Springdale and Zion National Park. ■TIP➡ **However, be warned: if you need to travel between I–15 and U.S. 89 via Route 9 during the day, you must pay the $25 admission fee to Zion National Park even if you do not plan to stop and visit.** Access to the massive and remote Grand Staircase–Escalante National Monument is via Route 12 to the north and U.S. 89 to the south.

TOP REASONS TO GO

To Go With the (Lava) Flow: As you hike along the lower trails of Snow Canyon State Park, look up to see ridges capped in lava from eruptions possibly as recent as 20,000 years ago.

To Sit in a Stagecoach: Check out the one restored stagecoach that visitors can hop aboard at Iron Mission State Park Museum.

To Camp Beneath the Aspens: The 26 campgrounds in Dixie National Forest might seem like a lot, but it's still easy to lose yourself amidst the forest's two million acres.

To Pay Your Respects to the Bard: Watch the likes of *Othello* on a stage that replicates the Old Globe Theatre during the Utah Shakespearean Festival.

To Watch Where a Dinosaur Stepped: The St. George Dinosaur Discovery Site at Johnson Farm would be developed real estate if a backhoe hadn't unearthed ancient footprints in 2000.

In winter the primary access roads to Brian Head and Cedar Breaks National Monument are either closed occasionally for snow removal (Route 143 from the north and east) or closed for the season (Route 148 from the south). Call the Cedar City office of the Utah Department of Transportation at ☎435/865–5500 for current road conditions.

ABOUT THE RESTAURANTS

In the southwestern corner of the state, reflecting the pioneer heritage of the region, traditional and contemporary American cuisines are most common, followed closely by those with Mexican and Southwestern influences. St. George and Springdale have the greatest number and diversity of dining options. Around St. George, there are a number of restaurants that serve seafood; keep in mind that at nicer restaurants, the fish is flown in daily from the West Coast; at the less expensive locales, the fish is usually frozen. Because this is conservative Utah, don't presume a restaurant serves beer, much less wine or cocktails, especially in the smaller towns. Most restaurants are family friendly, and dress tends to be casual.

ABOUT THE HOTELS

Southwestern Utah is steeped in pioneer heritage, and you'll find many older homes that have been refurbished as bed-and-breakfasts. Green Gate Village in St. George, a collection of pioneer homes gathered from around the state, is an excellent example. The area also has its share of older independent motels in some of the smaller towns. Most of the major hotel and motel chains have opened up at least one facility in the region. With the exception of Brian Head, the high season is summer, and logic dictates that the closer you want to be to a major attraction, the further in advance you have to make reservations. If you are willing to find a room upward of an hour from your destination, perhaps with fewer amenities, you may be surprised not only by same-day reservations in some cases, but also much lower room rates. Panguitch has some particularly good options for budget and last-minute travelers.

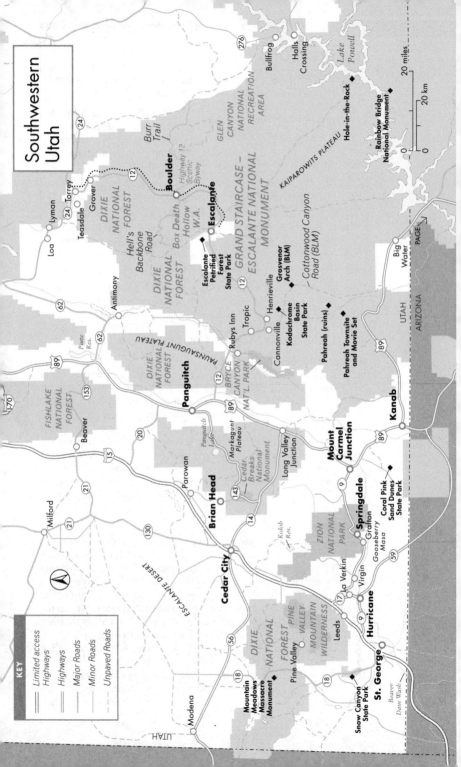

Southwestern Utah

KEY
- Limited access Highways
- Highways
- Major Roads
- Minor Roads
- Unpaved Roads

20 miles
20 km

UTAH

Modena

Milford

Beaver

Parowan

Cedar City

Brian Head

FISHLAKE NATIONAL FOREST

Panguitch

Panguitch Lake

Markagunt Plateau

Cedar Breaks National Monument

Kolob Res.

DIXIE NATIONAL FOREST

Mountain Meadows Massacre Monument

Pine Valley

Snow Canyon State Park

PINE VALLEY MOUNTAIN WILDERNESS

St. George

Beaver Dam Wash.

Hurricane

Leeds

La Verkin

Virgin

ZION NATIONAL PARK

Grafton

Springdale

Gooseberry Mesa

ESCALANTE DESERT

PAUNSAUGUNT PLATEAU

DIXIE NATIONAL FOREST

Rubys Inn

BRYCE CANYON NAT'L. PARK

Tropic

Cannonville

Henrieville

Kodachrome Basin State Park

Long Valley Junction

Mount Carmel Junction

Coral Pink Sand Dunes State Park

Kanab

Big Water

PAGE

UTAH
ARIZONA

Pahreah (ruins)

Pahreah Townsite and Movie Set

GRAND STAIRCASE – ESCALANTE NATIONAL MONUMENT

Grosvenor Arch (BLM)

Cottonwood Canyon Road (BLM)

KAIPAROWITS PLATEAU

Escalante

Escalante Petrified Forest State Park

Box Death Hollow W.A.

DIXIE NATIONAL FOREST

Hell's Backbone Road

Boulder

Highway 12 Scenic Byway

Burr Trail

Grover

Torrey

Teasdale

Lyman

Loa

Antimony

GLEN CANYON NATIONAL RECREATION AREA

Bullfrog

Halls Crossing

Lake Powell

Hole-in-the-Rock

Rainbow Bridge National Monument

IF YOU LIKE

HIKING & BACKPACKING

The horizon is the limit when it comes to exploring southwestern Utah by foot. There are hiking trails to fit all levels of experience and fitness. If you're short on time, make it a point to spend at least half a day out of the car and on the trail. For what seems like a small, parched, and desolate corner of the state, southwestern Utah offers an impressive diversity of hiking climates, from cool evergreen forests at alpine elevations near 10,000 feet to hot desert washes sprinkled with sandstone and sage.

If you have the motivation and ability, consider a multiday backpacking trip into the region's wild backcountry. Time your trip right and you can experience true wilderness at comfortable temperatures and, most importantly, without the crowds of the Wasatch. The peaks of the Pine Valley Wilderness warm to comfortable levels in spring, summer, and fall and are generally forsaken for the parks on the other side of I-15 during these seasons. Grand Staircase–Escalante National Monument contains nearly 2 million acres of desert plains, canyons, and badlands, though you will probably want to wait until the cooler fall and winter months to set out on your backcountry adventure here. Safety precautions are critical on any trip: travel in groups, prepare for all weather conditions in any season, and don't embark without notifying several people of your itinerary. If you don't feel comfortable leading your own trip, consider contacting a local outfitter about the availability of guided trips.

WHAT IT COSTS					
	¢	$	$$	$$$	$$$$
RESTAURANTS	under $8	$8–$12	$13–$18	$19–$25	over $25
HOTELS	under $70	$70–$110	$111–$150	$151–$200	over $200

Restaurant prices are for a main course at dinner, excluding sales tax of 7½%–8½%. Hotel prices are for two people in a standard double room in high season, excluding service charges and 11%–12¼% tax.

TIMING

Year-round, far southwestern Utah is the warmest region in the state; St. George is usually the first city to break 100°F every year, and even the winters remain mild at lower desert elevations. Despite the heat, most people visit from June to September, making the off-season a pleasantly uncrowded experience for those willing and able to travel from fall to spring. Incidentally, Utahns from the north tend to stay away from the southern parts of the state during peak months for the very reasons—intense, dry heat and unyielding sun—that attract so many travelers from out of state. If you decide to brave the heat, wear sunscreen and drink lots of water, regardless of your activity level.

Farther east, around the Brian Head–Cedar Breaks National Monument area, elevations approach and surpass 9,000 feet, making for more temperamental weather, intermittent and seasonal road closures due to snow, and downright cold nights well into June. At this altitude, the warm summer sun is perfectly balanced by the coolness of the alpine forests during the day. While the peak season at most locations is summer, it's a different story at Brian Head, where snow sports dominate; still, the resort has been pushing its summer recreation lineup of mountain biking and hiking, and the trails here are some of the finest in all of Utah.

UTAH'S DIXIE

Mormon pioneers from the American South settled this part of Utah to grow cotton and brought the name Dixie with them. Some thought the move was a gamble, but the success of the settlement may be measured in the region's modern-day definition of risk: hopping the border to nearby Mesquite, Nevada, to roll the dice. St. George is often the hottest place in the state, but the Pine Valley Mountains and Brian Head offer alpine relief and summer recreation.

CEDAR CITY

250 mi southwest of Salt Lake City via I–15 south.

Rich iron-ore deposits here grabbed Mormon leader Brigham Young's attention, and he ordered a Church of Jesus Christ of Latter-day Saints (LDS) mission established. The first ironworks and foundry opened in 1851 and operated for only eight years; problems with the furnace, flooding, and hostility between settlers and Native Americans eventually put out the flame. Residents then turned to ranching and agriculture for their livelihood, and Cedar City thrived thereafter.

Cedar City calls itself "The Festival City." The Southern Utah University campus hosts the city's major event, the Utah Shakespearean Festival, which has been stretching its season longer and longer as its reputation has grown. Though better known for festivals than recreation, the city is well placed for exploring the Brian Head area.

Inside the Iron County Visitor Center, the **Daughters of the Utah Pioneers Museum** displays pioneer artifacts such as an old trundle sewing machine, an antique four-poster bed, and photographs of old Cedar City and its inhabitants. ⊠*582 N. Main St.* ☎*435/586-4484* ☞*Free* ⊗ *Weekdays 1–4.*

The **Iron Mission State Park Museum** is a memorial to the county's iron-industry heritage. Explore the bullet-scarred stagecoach that ran in the days of Butch Cassidy, plus tools and other mining artifacts. A log cabin built in 1851—the oldest standing home in southern Utah—and a collection of wagon wheels and farm equipment are displayed outside. Local artisans demonstrate pioneer crafts. ⊠*635 N. Main St.* ☎*435/586-9290* ⊕*www.stateparks.utah.gov* ☞*$3* ⊗*Mid-May–mid-Sept., daily 9–6; mid-Sept.–Oct. and Mar.–mid-May, daily 9–5; Nov.–Feb., Mon.–Sat. 9–5.*

SPORTS & THE OUTDOORS

The **Dixie National Forest** (✉ *1789 N. Wedgewood La.* ☎ *435/865–3700* ⊕ *www.fs.fed.us/dxnf*) administers an area encompassing almost 2 million acres, stretching 170 mi across southwestern Utah, and containing 26 designated campgrounds. The forest is popular for such activities as horseback riding, fishing, and hiking.

HIKING Join **Southern Utah Scenic Tours** (☎ *435/867–8690 or 888/404–8687* ⊕ *www.utahscenictours.com*) for an all-day tour from Cedar City to either Zion National Park or Bryce National Park, including a short, easy-to-moderate hike. The price includes pick-up and drop-off at your hotel; snacks and lunch; and all applicable park fees.

WHERE TO STAY & EAT

★ $$–$$$$ ✕ **Milt's Stage Stop.** This dinner spot in beautiful Cedar Canyon is known for its 12-ounce rib-eye steak, prime rib, fresh crab, lobster, and shrimp dishes. In winter, deer feed in front of the restaurant as a fireplace blazes away inside. A number of hunting trophies decorate the rustic building's interior, and splendid views of the surrounding mountains delight patrons year-round. ✉ *Cedar Canyon, 5 mi east of town on Rte. 14* ☎ *435/586–9344* ⊟ *AE, D, DC, MC, V* ⊗ *No lunch.*

¢–$ ✕ **The Pastry Pub.** Don't be fooled by the name—coffee and tea are the only brews on tap here, and sandwiches and salads join pastries on the chalkboard menu. Build a sandwich of meat, egg, cheese, and more on a bagel, croissant, sliced bread, or one of five flavors of wraps. Festival-goers, take note: this is the best bet for a late-night bite after the show. ✉ *86 W. Center St.* ☎ *435/867–1400* ⊟ *AE, D, MC, V* ⊗ *Closed Sun.*

$–$$ ▦ **Best Western Town & Country Inn.** Actually two buildings directly across the street from each other, this two-story motel has good amenities and a friendly staff. You can easily walk the few blocks to the Shakespearean Festival and the downtown shopping district. **Pro:** Conveniently located near downtown. **Con:** Can get crowded during festival season. ✉ *189 N. Main St., 84720* ☎ *435/586–9900 or 800/493–4089* 🖶 *435/586–1664* ⊕ *www.bwtowncountry.com* ⇄ *157 rooms* ⌂ *In-room: refrigerator, Ethernet (some), Wi-Fi. In-hotel: 2 restaurants, pools, no elevator, laundry facilities, airport shuttle, no-smoking rooms* ⊟ *AE, D, DC, MC, V* ⍟*CP.*

$ ▦ **Bard's Inn Bed and Breakfast.** Rooms in this restored turn-of-the-20th-century house are named after heroines and heroes in Shakespeare's plays. There are antiques throughout and handcrafted quilts grace the beds. Hosts Jack and Audrey prepare a full breakfast that includes fresh home-baked breads such as Amish friendship bread and croissants, plus fruit, juices, and shirred eggs. Bone up on your Shakespeare before attending a play by reading from a supply of on-site Cliff Notes. **Pros:** Close to the festival grounds, dining options nearby. **Con:** Rooms fill up in advance during festival season. ✉ *150 S. 100 West St., 84720* ☎ *435/586–6612* ⊕ *www.bardsbandb.com* ⇄ *7 rooms* ⌂ *In-room: no phone, refrigerator (some), Wi-Fi. In-hotel: no elevator, public Internet, public Wi-Fi, airport shuttle, no-smoking rooms* ⊟ *AE, MC, V.*

8

Fodor'sChoice
★

THE ARTS

From June to October, the **Utah Shakespearean Festival** (☎*435/586–7880 or 800/752–9849 ⊕www.bard.org*) puts on plays by the Bard and others, drawing tens of thousands over the course of the season. The outdoor theater at Southern Utah University is a replica of the Old Globe Theatre from Shakespeare's time, showcasing Shakespearean costumes and sets during the season. Call ahead for a schedule of performances.

BRIAN HEAD

29 mi northeast of Cedar City via Rte. 14 east and Rte. 143 and Rte. 148 north.

Brian Head made a name for itself as a ski town (Brian Head Resort is Utah's southernmost and highest ski area at well over 9,000 feet), but the area's summer recreation, especially mountain biking, has been developed and promoted energetically. There are now more than 200 mi of trails for mountain bikers, many of which are served by chairlift or shuttle services. The bright red-orange rock formations of Cedar Breaks Monument are several miles south of town.

The snow season is still the high season in Brian Head, so book winter lodging in advance and don't be surprised by the high room rates. Food prices are high year-round. The fall "mud season" (October to November) and spring "slush season" (April to May) shut down many area businesses.

SPORTS & THE OUTDOORS

At **Brian Head Ski Resort,** eight lifts service 50 trails covering almost 500 acres of terrain starting at a base elevation of 9,600 feet. The Peak Express snowcat takes expert skiers to the 11,300-foot summit of Brian Head Peak for access to ungroomed runs. A half-pipe, rails, and terrain park attract hordes of snowboarders. From the top you can see the red rock cliffs of Cedar Breaks National Monument to the southwest. ⊠*329 S. Rte. 143* ☎*435/677-2035* ⊕*www.brianhead.com* ☼*Late Nov.–late Apr., daily 9:30–4:30* 🎫*Lift tickets $45.*

The largest outfitter in town, **Brianhead Sports** (⊠*269 S. Rte. 143* ☎*435/677-2014*)caters to cyclists, skiers, and snowboarders with equipment and accessories for rent or purchase. The store runs a mountain-bike shuttle that's handy for riding area trails that end far from where they start.Down the road from Brian Head Resort, **Georg's Ski Shop and Bikes** (⊠*612 S. Rte. 143* ☎*435/677-2013*) has new and rental skis, snowboards, and bikes.

BICYCLING   Brian Head is a good place to base mountain-biking excursions. The area's most popular ride is the 12-mi **Bunker Creek Trail,** which winds its way through forests and meadows to Panguitch Lake. Brian Head Resort runs one of its ski lifts in summer, providing access to several mountain-bike trails, and Brianhead Sports, among others, shuttles riders to other trails on the resort property. Five miles south of Brian Head, road cyclists can explore Cedar Breaks National Monument and vicinity.

Cedar Breaks National Monument

CLOSE UP

Cedar Breaks National Monument, a natural amphitheater similar to Bryce Canyon, spans almost 3 mi and plunges 2,000 feet into the Markagunt Plateau. Short alpine hiking trails along the rim and thin crowds make this a wonderful summer stop. Although its roads may be closed in winter due to heavy snow, the monument stays open for cross-country skiing and snowmobiling.

It's never crowded here, and most people who visit are content to photograph the monument from one of

the handful of overlooks alongside the road—which means the intrepid hiker, skier, or snowshoer can easily find solitude along the trails. In fact, winter is one of the best times to visit, when snow drapes the red-orange formations; though call ahead for road conditions and keep in mind that all visitor facilities are closed from October through late May.

⊠ *Rte. 148, 9 mi south of Brian Head* ☎ *435/586–9451* ⊕ *www.nps. gov/cebr* ☒ *$4 per person* ⊙ *Visitor center June–early-Oct., daily 8–6.*

WHERE TO STAY & EAT

★ $-$$$$ ✕**Double Black Diamond Steak House.** Elk medallions and ribeye steaks are favorites at this elegant yet relaxed steak and seafood restaurant in Cedar Breaks Lodge. Low lights, a crackling fire, and the clink of wine glasses set an upscale mood, but there's no need to dress up for the occasion. The restaurant is open Friday and Saturday evenings only. ⊠*223 Hunter Ridge Rd. (Rte. 143)* ☎*435/677–4242* ⊟*AE, D, MC, V* ⊙*Closed Sun.–Thurs. No lunch.*

$ ✕**The Bump and Grind.** Eat here or grab takeout—the service is quick if you can't wait to hit the trails. Classic American deli sandwiches and burgers offer no surprises, just good quality for hearty appetites. ⊠*259 S. Rte. 143* ☎*435/677–3111* ⊟*AE, MC, V.*

$$-$$$$ ▦ **Brian Head Reservation Center.** The studio and condominium units rented out by central reservations are privately owned and individually decorated, so facilities and layout vary; ask about fireplaces and whirlpool baths. All kitchens are equipped, and linens provided. Reservations well in advance are recommended in winter. ⊠*356 S. Brian Head Blvd., 84719* ☎*435/677–2042 or 800/845–9781* ▤*435/677–2827* ⊕*www.brianheadtown.com/bhrc* ⇄*40 units* ⌂*In-room: no a/c. In-hotel: laundry facilities, no-smoking rooms* ⊟*AE, D, MC, V.*

★ $$-$$$$ ▦ **Cedar Breaks Lodge & Spa.** On the north end of town, this casual but upscale resort sits among aspen and pine trees. Large studio rooms have kitchenettes and suites have sleeper sofas in the sitting areas. **Pro:** The warmth of a mountain lodge with home-away-from-home rooms. **Con:** The cozy interior makes it tempting to stay inside rather than enjoy the outdoors. ⊠*223 Hunter Ridge Rd. Box 190248, 84719* ☎*435/677–3000 or 888/282–3327* ▤*435/677–2211* ⊕*www.cedarbreakslodge. com* ⇄*28 rooms, 90 suites* ⌂*In-room: no a/c, safe (some), kitchen (some), refrigerator (some), DVD (some), VCR (some), dial-up. In-hotel: 3 restaurants, bar, pool, gym, spa, laundry facilities, concierge, public Internet, public Wi-Fi, no-smoking rooms* ⊟*AE, MC, V.*

ST. GEORGE

50 mi southwest of Cedar City via I–15.

Believing the mild year-round climate ideal for growing cotton, Brigham Young dispatched 309 LDS families in 1861 to found St. George. They were to raise cotton and silkworms and to establish a textile industry, to make up for textile shortages resulting from the Civil War. The area was subsequently dubbed "Utah's Dixie," a name that stuck even after the war ended and the "other" South could once again provide cotton to Utah. The settlers—many of them originally from southern states—found the desert climate preferable to northern Utah's snow, and they remained as farmers and ranchers. Crops included fruit, molasses, and grapes for wine that the pioneers sold to nearby mining communities. St. Georgians now number more than 60,000, many of whom are retirees attracted by the hot, dry climate and the numerous golf courses. But historic Ancestor Square, the city's many well-preserved, original pioneer and Mormon structures, and a growing shopping district make St. George a popular destination for families, as well.

Numbers in the margin correspond to the St. George map.

① Mormon leader Brigham Young spent the last five winters of his life in the warm, sunny climate of St. George. Built of adobe on a sandstone-and-basalt foundation, **Brigham Young Winter Home** has been restored to its original condition. A portrait of Young hangs over one fireplace, and furnishings authentic to the late-19th-century time period have been donated by supporters. Guided tours are available. ⊠ *67 W. 200 North St.* ☎ *435/673–5181* ⊡ *Free* ☉ *Daily 9–6.*

② The red-sandstone **St. George Temple,** plastered over with white stucco, was completed in 1877 and served as a meeting place for both Mormons and other congregations. It's still in use today, and though only Mormons can enter the temple, a visitor center next door offers guided tours for everyone. ⊠ *250 E. 400 South St.* ☎ *435/673–5181* ⊡ *Free* ☉ *Visitor center daily 9–9.*

③ Mormon settlers began work on the **St. George Tabernacle** in June 1863, a few months after the city of St. George was established. Upon completion of the sandstone building's 140-foot clock tower 13 years later, Brigham Young formally dedicated the site. This is one of the best-preserved pioneer buildings in the entire state, and is still used for public meetings and programs for the entire community. ⊠ *18 S. Main St.* ☎ *435/673–5181* ☉ *Daily 9–6.*

★ ④ Chances are the **Rosenbruch Wildlife Museum** in St. George is unlike any museum you've ever seen. This modern 25,000-square-foot facility displays more than 300 species of wildlife (stuffed) from around the globe, displayed in an uncanny representation of their native habitat—the plains of Africa, the forests of North America, and the mountains of Asia. A wheelchair-accessible pathway of almost ¼ mi winds through the different environments. Two waterfalls cascade from a two-story mountain, and more than 50 hidden speakers provide ambient wildlife and nature sounds. Before your tour, check out the video presentation

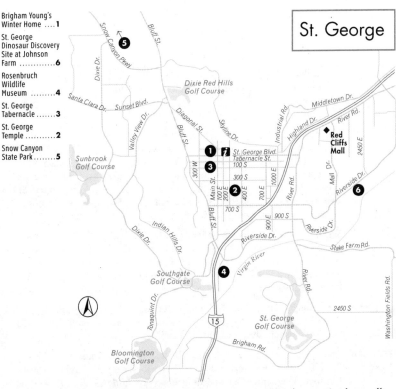

in the 200-seat theater, and be sure not to miss the massive bug collection. ⊠*1835 Convention Center Dr.* ☎*435/656–0033* ⊕*www.rosen bruch.org* ⊠*$8* ⊙*Mon. noon–9, Tues.–Sat. 10–6.*

★ ❺ Red Navajo sandstone mesas and formations are crowned with black lava rock, creating high-contrast vistas from either end of **Snow Canyon State Park.** From the campground you can scramble up huge sandstone mounds and overlook the entire valley. ⊠*1002 Snow Canyon Dr., Ivins, 8 mi northwest of St. George* ☎*435/628–2255* ⊕*www.state parks.utah.gov* ⊠*$5* ⊙*Daily 6 AM to 10 PM.*

☾ ❻ Follow footsteps cast in stone millions of years ago at **St. George Dinosaur Discovery Site at Johnson Farm,** where property development came to a halt when the ancient prints from the Jurassic period were unearthed in 2000. To reach the tracks, take 700 South Street east to Foremaster Drive and continue past the sod farm. ⊠*2180 E. Riverside Dr.* ☎*435/574–3466* ⊕*www.dinotrax.com* ⊠*$3* ⊙*Mon.–Sat. 10–6.*

Beaver Dam Wash. Utah's lowest point happens to mark the convergence of the Colorado Plateau, the Great Basin, and the Mojave Desert. In this overlapping of ecosystems, you'll find a large diversity of plants and animals, especially of birds. In the southern part of the wash stands the greatest concentration of Joshua trees in the area. To get here, take

Route 18 north of St. George and turn west onto Route 8, the paved road that runs 12 mi through Santa Clara. ⊠ *12 mi southwest of Shivwits on Old Hwy. 91* ☎*801/539–4001* 🎟*Free.*

SPORTS & THE OUTDOORS

BICYCLING   The folks at **Bicycles Unlimited** (⊠*90 S. 100 East St.* ☎*888/673–4492* ⊕*www.bicyclesunlimited.com*) are a font of information on mountain biking in southern Utah. They rent bikes and sell parts, accessories, and guidebooks.

GOLF   **Bloomington** (⊠*3174 E. Bloomington Dr.* ☎*435/673–2029*)offers a striking combination of manicured fairways and greens beneath sandstone cliffs. **Dixie Red Hills** (⊠*645 W. 1250 North St.* ☎*435/634–5852*)has 9 holes.The 18-hole **Entrada** (⊠*2537 W. Entrada Trail* ☎*435/986–2200*) is Utah's first Johnny Miller Signature Course.**St. George Golf Club** (⊠*2190 S. 1400 East St.* ☎*435/634–5854*) is a popular 18-hole course with challenging par-3 holes.

Water provides challenges at **Southgate Golf Club** (⊠*1975 S. Tonaquint Dr.* ☎*435/628–0000*), with several holes bordering ponds or crossing the Santa Clara River. Designed by Ted Robinson, fairway features at **Sunbrook** (⊠*2366 Sunbrook Dr.* ☎*435/634–5866*) include rock walls, lakes, and waterfalls.

HIKING   **Snow Canyon State Park** (⊠*8 mi northwest of St. George on Rte. 18* ★   ☎*435/628–2255* ⊕*www.stateparks.utah.gov*)has several short trails and lots of small desert canyons to explore.

HORSE RACING   The St. George Lions Club hosts the **Dixie Downs Horse Races** (☎*435/632–* & RODEO   *8502*)on two April weekends to prepare horses for the larger tracks in summer. The September **Dixie Roundup** (☎*435/656–8998*) rodeo has been a tradition for decades. The novelty of this professional rodeo event is that it's held on the green grass of Sun Bowl stadium.

WHERE TO EAT

$$$–$$$$ ✕**Painted Pony.** Patio dining and local art hanging on the walls provide suave accompaniment to the creative meals served in this downtown restaurant. Be sure to try the Dixie pork chop or the bacon-wrapped duck. ⊠*2 W. St. George Blvd., Ancestor Sq.* ☎*435/634–1700* ⊕*www. painted-pony.com* ▭*AE, D, MC, V* ⊗*No lunch Sun.*

$$$–$$$$ ✕**Sullivan's Rococo Steakhouse & Inn.** Specializing in beef and seafood, this St. George restaurant is known for its prime rib, but its vistas are worthy noting, too. It sits atop a hill overlooking town, so you can enjoy spectacular views right from your table. ⊠*511 Airport Rd.* ☎*435/628– 3671* ⊕*www.rococo.net/steakhouse.html* ▭*AE, D, MC, V.*

★ ¢–$ ✕**Bear Paw Coffee Company.** The menu is full of flavor, with elements of Southwestern, Tex-Mex, American, and Italian cuisines all represented, but breakfast is the star of the show here (served all day, every day). The coffee is hot, the teas loose, the juice fresh, and the servers smiling. Home brewers (of coffee and tea, that is) can get their fresh beans and leaves here, too. ⊠*75 N. Main St.* ☎*435/634–0126* ▭*AE, D, MC, V* ⊗*No dinner.*

WHERE TO STAY

$$$$ ☷**Green Valley Spa & Tennis Resort.** Minutes from downtown but in a world of its own, this serene, luxurious resort and inn consistently ranks among the best in the world. Here you can arrange your days around morning hikes, golf or tennis lessons, exercise classes, massage therapy, facials, and delicious low-calorie meals. All meals, and some spa services, are included in the weekly rate. Dozens of fitness classes are offered, as well as guided treks into the red rock canyon country surrounding the resort. A three-day minimum stay is required. **Pros:** Fourteen tennis courts, seven swimming pools, and a 4,000-sq-ft gym pamper athletes. **Cons:** Setting is adult-oriented (which may not be a negative for some); children under 10 not allowed in dining room. ⌧*1871 W. Canyon View Dr., 84770* ☎*435/628–8060 or 800/237–1068* 🖷*435/673–4084* ⊕*www.greenvalleyspa.com* 🛏*45 suites* &*In-room: safe, refrigerator, dial-up, Wi-Fi. In-hotel: restaurant, golf course, tennis courts, pools, gym, spa, laundry service, concierge, airport shuttle, parking (no fee), some pets allowed, no-smoking rooms* ⊟*AE, D, MC, V* ⦿|*FAP.*

$$$$
Fodor'sChoice
★

☷**Red Mountain Spa.** Located near the mouth of Snow Canyon, this active resort is a retreat designed for fitness and rejuvenation. Breakfast and lunch buffets list the nutritional contents of each item, while dinner is a more traditional sit-down experience. But it's not just about the food; there are fitness classes, hikes, yoga, and plenty of other activities that leave you with a healthy glow. The well-appointed rooms aren't especially large, but with so many things to do, you won't want to lounge around your room anyway. **Pros:** Down-to-earth spa experience, healthy food. **Cons:** You might feel guilty if you don't wake up at dawn to hit the gym or the trails. ⌧*1275 E. Red Mountain Cir., Ivins, 7 mi northwest of St. George, 84738* ☎*435/673–4905 or 800/407–3002* ⊕*www.redmountainspa.com* 🛏*82 rooms, 24 suites* &*In-room: safe, Ethernet. In-hotel: 2 restaurants, tennis court, pools, gym, spa, water sports, bicycles, no elevator, laundry facilities, concierge, public Internet, airport shuttle, some pets allowed, no kids under 12, no-smoking rooms* ⊟*AE, D, MC, V* ⦿|*FAP.*

★ **$–$$$$** ☷**Green Gate Village Historic Inn.** Step back in time in these restored pioneer homes dating to the 1860s. The inn takes its name from the green gates and fences that surrounded the homes of St. George's LDS leaders in the late 1800s. The last remaining original gate is displayed in the inn's garden and served as a model for those now surrounding Green Gate Village. Behind the gates is a village of nine fully restored pioneer homes filled with antique furnishings and modern amenities. Guests with children need to get prior approval from the management. **Pros:** Each building is the real historic deal. Location is close to tabernacle and downtown walking tour. **Cons:** Village-like setting might not appeal to those seeking privacy. ⌧*76 W. Tabernacle St., 84770* ☎*435/628–6999 or 800/350–6999* 🖷*435/628–6989* ⊕*www.green gatevillageinn.com* 🛏*4 rooms, 10 suites* &*In-room: kitchen (some), refrigerator, DVD (some), VCR, Wi-Fi (some). In-hotel: 2 restaurants, room service, pool, gym, spa, no elevator, public Internet, parking (no fee), no-smoking rooms* ⊟*AE, D, MC, V* ⦿|*BP.*

8

$$ 🏨**Best Western Coral Hills.** The town's walking tour of historic pioneer buildings begins a block from this motel, which is next to the old courthouse and close to many restaurants. You can spend a hot afternoon relaxing in the shade of palm trees next to the outdoor pool. **Pro:** Walking distance to downtown attractions. **Con:** High-traffic location. ✉*125 E. St. George Blvd., 84770* ☎*435/673–4844 or 800/542–7733* 🖷*435/673–5352* ⊕*www.coralhills.com* 🛏*95 rooms, 3 suites* ♿*In-room: refrigerator, DVD (some), VCR (some), Ethernet (some), Wi-Fi. In-hotel: pools, gym, no elevator, laundry facilities, laundry service, public Wi-Fi, airport shuttle, no-smoking rooms* ☰*AE, D, DC, MC, V* ⊚*CP.*

$–$$ 🏨**Comfort Suites.** Two blocks from the Dixie Convention Center, this hotel's "minisuites" have comfortable sitting areas and large TVs. The shaded outdoor common areas offer additional space in good weather. **Pro:** Great location for conventioneers. **Con:** Too far from downtown to walk. ✉*1239 S. Main St., 84770* ☎*435/673–7000* 🖷*435/628–4340* ⊕*www.stgeorgecomfortsuites.com* 🛏*122 suites* ♿*In-room: refrigerator, Wi-Fi. In-hotel: pool, gym, laundry facilities, laundry service, public Internet, airport shuttle, no-smoking rooms.* ☰*AE, D, DC, MC, V* ⊚*CP.*

$–$$ 🏨**Seven Wives Inn Bed & Breakfast.** It's said that Brigham Young slept here, and that one of the buildings may have been a hiding place for polygamists after the practice was outlawed in the 1880s. In fact, the inn is named for an ancestor of the owner who indeed had seven wives. Not surprisingly the rooms are named after those wives. Antiques are liberally placed throughout the rooms, which are elaborately decorated with flowers and pastels. One room has a jetted tub installed in a Model T Ford. In-room spa treatments are available (an unexpected treat!). ✉*217 N. 100 West St., 84770* ☎*800/600–3737* 🖷*435/628–5646* ⊕*www.sevenwivesinn.com* 🛏*9 rooms, 4 suites* ♿*In-room: refrigerator (some), DVD (some), VCR (some), Wi-Fi. In-hotel: pool, public Wi-Fi, some pets allowed, no-smoking rooms.* ☰*AE, D, MC, V* ⊚*BP.*

NIGHTLIFE & THE ARTS

NIGHTLIFE   Ask locals where to go for nightlife in this conservative city and they'll say, with a straight face, Mesquite, Nevada (almost 40 mi away). Then they'll remember the aptly named **The One & Only Watering Hole** (✉*800 E. St. George Blvd.* ☎*435/673–9191*), a beer-only joint in a strip mall with billiards, televised sports, and live music on many weekends.

THE ARTS   Artisan booths, food, children's activities, and entertainment, including cowboy poets, are all part of the **St. George Arts Festival** (☎*435/634–5942*), held the Friday and Saturday of Easter weekend.

Spend a few quiet hours out of the Dixie sun at the **St. George Art Museum** (✉*47 E. 200 North St.* ☎*435/627–4525*). The permanent collection celebrates local potters, photographers, painters, and more. Special exhibits highlight local history.

A rotating series of musicals such as *Joseph and the Amazing Technicolor Dream Coat* and *Les Misérables* entertain at **Tuacahn** (✉*1100 Tuacahn*

Dr., Ivins ☎435/652–3200 or 800/746–9882 🌐www.tuacahn.org), an outdoor amphitheater nestled in a natural sandstone cove.

SHOPPING

★ Historic **Ancestor Square** (*✉St. George Blvd. and Main St. ☎435/628–1658*)is the shopping and dining centerpiece of downtown St. George. Occupants of the tiny old Jailhouse Coffee now serve java instead of time, providing a pick-me-up from browsing the many galleries, shops, and restaurants.Pick up recreational items that made the packing list but not the pack at the **Outdoor Outlet** (*✉1062 E. Tabernacle St. ☎435/628–3611 or 800/726–8106 🌐www.outdooroutlet.com*). Shop for bargains at their frequent clearance sales.

Zion Factory Stores (*✉250 N. Red Cliffs Dr., I–15 Exit 8 ☎435/674–9800 🌐www.zionfactorystores.com*)is southern Utah's only factory-outlet center.

HURRICANE

17 mi northeast of St. George via I–15 north and Rte. 9 east.

An increasing number of lodging establishments makes Hurricane a fine alternate base for exploring Dixie. Nearby Gooseberry Mesa is one of the best places to mountain bike in Utah.

SPORTS & THE OUTDOORS

BICYCLING ★ The mountain biking trails on **Gooseberry Mesa,** off Route 59 south of Hurricane, rival those of world-famous Moab on the other side of southern Utah, yet don't have the hordes of fat-tire fanatics. Come here for solitary and technical single-track challenges.

GOLF Hurricane has **Sky Mountain** (*✉1030 N. 2600 West St. ☎888/345–5551*), one of the state's most scenic 18-hole golf courses. Many fairways are framed by red-rock outcroppings; the course has a front-tee view of the nearby 10,000-foot Pine Valley Mountains.

WHERE TO STAY & EAT

★ ¢ ✕**Main Street Café.** One of the best cups of coffee in Dixie is poured right here in Hurricane. A full espresso bar will satisfy "caffiends," while vegetarians and others can choose from salads, sandwiches, breakfast burritos, homemade breads, and desserts. Sit inside to admire the works of local artists, or share the patio with the hummingbirds. *✉138 S. Main St. ☎435/635–9080 ▭MC, V ⊙Closed Sun. No dinner.*

$ **Travelodge.** This basic motel will provide you with a comfortable night's rest if you want few other amenities, though there is a pool. It's a comfortable distance—a 35-mi drive—from Zion National Park. **Pro:** In the heart of downtown. **Con:** There's not much to do in downtown Hurricane. *✉280 W. State St., 84737 ☎435/635–4647 or 800/578–7878 🖷435/635–0848 🌐www.travelodgezion.com ⇆62 rooms ♿In-room: refrigerator, Wi-Fi. In-hotel: pool, spa, no elevator, laundry facilities, public Internet, public Wi-Fi, no-smoking rooms ▭AE, D, MC, V 🍽CP.*

8

¢ ⬚**Comfort Inn Zion.** Golfers will appreciate the package deals available with nearby courses, and everyone benefits from being fairly close to Zion National Park, which is a 35-mi drive away. If the hot southern Utah sun has sapped your energy, a dip in the pool will wake you for your next adventure. Pro: Minutes from two 18-hole golf courses. Con: Location in a newly developed area lacks charm. ✉ *43 N. 2600 West, 84737* ☎ *435/635–3500 or 800/635–3577* 🖷 *435/635–7224* ⊕ *www. comfortinnzion.com* ➯ *53 rooms* ⚒ *In-room: Wi-Fi. In-hotel: pool, no elevator, laundry facilities, public Internet, public Wi-Fi, no-smoking rooms* ▤ *AE, D, MC, V* ⦿| *CP.*

SPRINGDALE

21 mi east of Hurricane via Rte. 9.

Springdale's growth has followed that of next-door neighbor Zion National Park, the most popular park destination in Utah and one of the most popular in the United States. Hotels, restaurants, and shops keep popping up, yet the town still manages to maintain its small-town charm. And oh, that view! Many businesses along Zion Park Boulevard, the main drag, double as shuttle stops for the bus system that carts tourists into the jaw-dropping sandstone confines of Zion Canyon, the town's main attraction.

WHERE TO EAT

$$–$$$$ ✕**Bit & Spur Restaurant and Saloon.** This restaurant has been a legend Fodor'sChoice in Utah for more than 25 years. The house favorites' menu lists tra-
★ ditional Southwestern dishes like *flautas verde* (deep-fried burritos with tomatillo salsa), but the kitchen also gets creative. Try the *bistec asado* (chile-rubbed steak) or pasta with rosemary cream sauce. When the weather is nice, arrive early so you can eat outside and enjoy the lovely grounds and views. ✉ *1212 Zion Park Blvd.* ☎ *435/772–3498* ⊕ *www.bitandspur.com* ▤ *AE, D, MC, V* ⊗ *No lunch.*

$$–$$$$ ✕**Spotted Dog Cafe at Flanigan's Inn.** Named in honor of the family dog of Springdale's original settlers, this contemporary American restaurant offers dinner entrées such as regional red mountain trout and tenderloin of pork. Breakfast is also served, and the sidewalk patio fills quickly. ✉ *428 Zion Park Blvd.* ☎ *435/772–0700* ▤ *AE, MC, V, D* ⊗ *No lunch.*

★ $$–$$$$ ✕**The Switchback Grille.** Crowded with locals and tourists alike, this restaurant is known for its wood-fired pizzas, ribs, and vegetarian dishes. Favorites include corn-crusted Utah mountain trout and crown rack of barbecue ribs. The vaulted ceilings make the dining room feel open and comfortable. They're open for breakfast; both lunch and more casual dinner items are served next door at Switchback Jack's Sports Grill. ✉ *1149 Zion Park Blvd.* ☎ *435/772–3700* ⊕ *www.switchbacktrading. com* ▤ *AE, D, MC, V.*

$–$$ ✕**Zion Pizza and Noodle Co.** The "Cholesterol Hiker" and veggie-friendly "Good for You" pizzas and the selection of microbrews put some pizzazz into the menu at this casual restaurant in a former church building. Whether you dine indoors or in the beer garden, you can also order pasta dishes like linguine with pesto, mushrooms, and fresh tomatoes. ✉ *868 Zion Park Blvd.* ☎ *435/772-3815* ⊕ *www.zionpizzanoodle.com* 🚫 *No credit cards* 🕐 *Closed Dec.–Feb.*

¢–$ ✗ **Sol Foods.** For a quick, healthful meal any time of day, stop here for organic, ethnic, and gourmet food items. Daily specials include spanakopita, quiche, lasagna, and salads. They can also prepare picnic baskets or box lunches for your day

in the park. Nearby is Sol's ice cream parlor, with hand-dipped ice cream cones, banana splits, and espresso. The patio seating is near the Virgin River, with views into the park. There is public Wi-Fi available, and beer is served. ✉ *95 Zion Park Blvd.* ☎ *435/772-0277* ⊕ *www.solfoods.com* 🚫 *MC, V.*

WHERE TO STAY

$$–$$$$

Fodor'sChoice
★

🏠 **Desert Pearl Inn.** You may never want to leave this comfortable inn, where every room has vaulted ceilings, thick carpets, cushy throw pillows, Roman shades, oversize windows, and sleeper sofas, as well as a large balcony or patio overlooking either the Virgin River or the pool. The pool area is exceptionally well landscaped and fully equipped, with a double-size hot tub and a shower–and–rest room block. **Pro:** Spacious, condo-like rooms. **Con:** Fills up early during high season. ✉ *707 Zion Park Blvd., Box 405, 84767* ☎ *435/772-8888 or 888/828-0898* 🖨 *435/772-8889* ⊕ *www.desertpearl.com* 🛏 *69 rooms, 4 suites* 🚹 *In-room: safe, kitchen, refrigerator, DVD, VCR, Ethernet, dial-up, Wi-Fi. In-hotel: pool, laundry facilities, public Internet, no-smoking rooms* 🚫 *AE, D, MC, V.*

★ $$–$$$ 🏠 **Cliffrose Lodge and Gardens.** Flowers adorn the 5-acre grounds of this friendly, charming lodge. Comfortable rooms will keep you happy after a long hike, and from your balcony you can continue to enjoy views of the towering, colorful cliffs. The Virgin River runs right along the property, so you can have a picnic or barbecue out back to the sound of rushing water. The Cliffrose is within walking distance of the Zion Canyon visitor center and shuttle stop. **Pro:** It's the closest lodging to Zion's South Entrance. **Con:** You'll need to book early in high season. ✉ *281 Zion Park Blvd., Box 510, 84767* ☎ *435/772-3234 or 800/243-8824* 🖨 *435/772-3900* ⊕ *www.cliffroselodge.com* 🛏 *29 rooms, 10 suites* 🚹 *In-room: refrigerator, Wi-Fi. In-hotel: pool, laundry facilities, no-smoking rooms* 🚫 *AE, D, MC, V.*

$$–$$$ 🏠 **Flanigan's Inn, Spa, and Café.** Close to the park with canyon views, this rustic country inn has contemporary furnishings. The pool area is small but scenic. You can walk to the Zion visitor center from here (it's a few blocks), though the shuttle to the canyon stops on the property. **Pro:** Close to Zion Canyon Theatre. **Con:** Not centrally located to downtown. ✉ *428 Zion Park Blvd., 84767* ☎ *435/772-3244 or 800/765-7787* 🖨 *435/772-3396* ⊕ *www.flanigans.com* 🛏 *28 rooms,*

8

4 suites, 2 villas ♿In-room: refrigerator, DVD, VCR (some), dial-up, Wi-Fi. In-hotel: restaurant, bar, pool, spa, no elevator, parking (no fee), no-smoking rooms. ⊟AE, D, MC, V.

$–$$ ⊡ **Best Western Zion Park Inn.** This spacious and modern facility has large rooms. The Switchback Grille will get you going in the morning with a hearty breakfast, and since the inn is a stop on the park shuttle route, take one step out the door and you're on your way to Zion Canyon. **Pros:** Restaurants serve some of Springdale's tastiest fare. On-site liquor store is only place in town that sells wine by the bottle. **Con:** Not for the quaint-at-heart. ⊠*1215 Zion Park Blvd., Box 800, 84767* ☎*435/772–3200 or 800/934–7275* 🖷*435/772–2449* ⊕*www.zionparkinn.com* 🛏*120 rooms, 6 suites* ♿*In-room: refrigerator, Ethernet, Wi-Fi. In-hotel: 2 restaurants, pool, laundry facilities, public Internet, public Wi-Fi, some pets allowed, no-smoking rooms* ⊟*AE, D, DC, MC, V.*

WHERE TO CAMP ⚠ **Zion Canyon Campground & RV Park.** About a half mile from the south entrance to the park, this campground is surrounded on three sides by the canyon's rock formations. Many of the sites are on the river. ♿*Flush toilets, full hookups, dump station, drinking water, guest laundry, showers, fire grates, picnic tables, food service, electricity, public telephone, general store, play area, swimming (river), Wi-Fi* 🛏*110 RV sites, 110 tent sites* ⊠*479 Zion Park Blvd.* ☎*435/772–3237* 🖷*435/772–3844* ⊕*www.zioncamp.com* ⊟*D, MC, V.*

THE ARTS

The **O. C. Tanner Amphitheater** (⊠*Lion Blvd., Springdale* ☎*435/652–7994* ⊕*www.dixie.edu/tanner*) is set amid huge sandstone boulders at the base of the enormous red cliffs spilling south from Zion National Park. In summer, live concerts are held each weekend, when everything from local country-music bands to the Utah Symphony Orchestra takes to the stage.

☮ If it's too hot for you outside, escape to the cool confines of the **Zion Canyon Theatre** (⊠*145 Zion Park Blvd.* ☎*435/772–2400 or 888/256–3456* ⊕*www.zioncanyontheatre.com*), where the six-story-high screen earns its superlative name. The 40-minute *Zion Canyon: Treasure of the Gods* takes you on an adventure through Zion and other points in canyon country. Two other films, including a Hollywood feature, are regularly shown here.

ART GALLERIES **Worthington Gallery.** Opened in 1980 by a single potter in a pioneer-era home near the mouth of Zion Canyon, Worthington Gallery now features more than 20 artists who create in clay, metal, glass, paint, and more. ⊠*789 Zion Park Blvd.* ☎*800/626–9973.*

ALONG U.S. 89—UTAH'S HERITAGE HIGHWAY

Winding north from the Arizona border all the way to Spanish Fork Canyon an hour south of Salt Lake City, U.S. 89 is known as the Heritage Highway for its role in shaping Utah history. At its southern end, Kanab is known as "Little Hollywood," having provided the backdrop for many famous Western movies and television commercials. The town has since grown considerably to accommodate tourists who flock here to see where Ronald Reagan once slept and Clint Eastwood drew his guns. Other towns north along this famous road may not have the same notoriety in these parts, but they do provide a quiet, uncrowded, and inexpensive place to stay near Zion and Bryce Canyon National Parks. East of Kanab, U.S. 89 runs along the southern edge of the Grand Staircase–Escalante National Monument, providing access to one of the most remote areas of Utah via the area near the old townsite of Paria.

MT. CARMEL JUNCTION

13 mi east of Zion National Park via Rte. 9 east.

Little more than where Route 9 meets U.S. 89, Mt. Carmel Junction does offer some funky small-town lodging for those willing to stay about 15 minutes east of Zion National Park's east entrance. But don't miss the studio of Maynard Dixon, the artist many consider the finest painter of the American West.

The **Maynard Dixon Home and Studio** was the final residence of the best-known painter of the American West, who died here in 1946. The property and log cabin structure are now maintained by the nonprofit Thunderbird Foundation for the Arts, which gives tours and schedules artist workshops and retreats. ⊠ *2 mi north of Mt. Carmel Junction on U.S. 89, mile marker 84, Mt. Carmel* ☎ *435/648–2653 or 801/533–5330* ⊕ *www.thunderbirdfoundation.com* ✉ *$20* ⊙ *Tours by appointment only May–Oct., Mon.–Sat.*

WHERE TO STAY

☼ **$$–$$$$** 🏨 **Zion Ponderosa Ranch Resort.** This multi-pursuit resort on an 8,000-acre ranch just east of Zion National Park offers activities from horseback riding to spa treatments, and just about everything in between. Lodging options include suites that sleep six and luxurious mountain homes for up to 13. Hearty meals are included. ⊠ *5 mi. north of route marker 46 on North Fork Country Rd., Mount Carmel* ☎ *800/293–5444* ⊕ *www.zionponderosa.com* ➷ *16 suites, 8 cabins, 17 houses* ⌂ *In-room: kitchen (some), DVD (some), Wi-Fi (some). In-hotel: restaurant, tennis courts, pool, spa, bicycles, children's programs (ages 4–11)* ☱ *AE, D, MC, V* ✸ *EP, AP* ⊙ *Closed Dec.–Feb.*

$ 🏨 **Best Western East Zion Thunderbird Lodge.** A quick 13 mi east of Zion National Park, this red-adobe motel is a good option if lodging in Springdale has filled, or if you want to be within an hour's drive of Bryce Canyon National Park as well. Surrounded by the Zion Mountains and bordered by a scenic golf course, the rooms are spacious and bright. **Pro:** A convenient base for visiting Zion and Bryce (and even the North Rim of the Grand Canyon). **Con:** No attractions within walking distance. ⊠ *Junction of U.S. 89 and Rte. 9, Box 5531, 84755* ☎ *435/648–2203 or 888/848–6358* 🖷 *435/648–2239* ⊕ *www.bestwestern.com* ➷ *62 rooms* ⌂ *In-room: kitchen (some), Ethernet (some), Wi-Fi. In-hotel: restaurant, golf course, pool, spa, no* *elevator, laundry facilities, public Internet, no-smoking rooms* ▤*AE, D, DC, MC, V.*

¢–$ 🏨**Golden Hills Motel.** This clean and simple establishment right at Mt. Carmel Junction is an inexpensive and no-frills lodging option. Its funky pink-and-blue roadside diner serves good, basic country-style fare like country-fried steak, liver and onions, and homemade breads and pies. Some rooms in this ground-level facility are on the riverside. **Pro:** One of the most affordable lodgings in the vicinity of Zion National Park. **Con:** Because prices are so reasonable, you'll need to reserve early. ✉*Junction of U.S. 89 and Rte. 9, 84755* ☎*435/648–2268 or 800/648–2268* 🖷*435/648–2558* ⊕*www.goldenhillsmotel. com* ⇨*30 rooms* ⌂*In-room: refrigerator, DVD (some), Wi-Fi. In-hotel: restaurant, pool, gym, bicycles, no elevator, laundry facilities, public Internet, public Wi-Fi, some pets allowed, no-smoking rooms* ▤*MC, V.*

KANAB

17 mi southeast of Mt. Carmel Junction via U.S. 89 south.

Kanab is Hollywood's vision of the American West. Soaring vermilion sandstone cliffs and sagebrush flats with endless vistas have lured filmmakers to this area for more than 75 years. The welcoming sign at city limits reads "Greatest Earth on Show"—Kanab has been used as a setting in more than 100 movies and television shows. Abandoned film sets have become tourist attractions, and old movie posters or still photographs are a decorating staple at local businesses. In addition to a movie-star past, Kanab is ideally positioned as a base for exploration. With major roads radiating in four directions, it offers easy access to three national parks, three national monuments (including Grand Staircase–Escalante), two state parks, and several historic sites.

The nostalgic **Western Legends Roundup** (☎*800/733–5263*) is for anyone who loves cowboys, pioneer life, or Native American culture. For four days every August, Kanab fills with cowboy poets and storytellers, musicians, Western arts-and-crafts vendors, and Native American dancers and weavers.

Eroding sandstone formed the sweeping expanse of pink sand at **Coral Pink Sand Dunes State Park.** Funneled through a notch in the rock, the wind picks up speed and carries grains of sand into the area. Once the wind slows down, the sand is deposited, creating this giant playground for dune buggies, ATVs, and dirt bikes. A small area is fenced off for walking, but the sound of wheeled toys is always with you. Children love to play in the sand, but before you let them loose, check the surface temperature; it can become very hot. ✉*Yellowjacket and Hancock Rds., 12 mi off U.S. 89, near Kanab* ☎*435/648–2800* ⊕*www.stateparks.utah.gov* 🎟*$6* ⊙*Daily, dawn–dusk.*

WHERE TO STAY & EAT

★ **$$–$$$$** ✕**Rocking V Cafe.** Fresh fish, including mahimahi when available, arrives several times a week at this respected café that prides itself on "slow food." Buffalo tenderloin is a favorite, but vegetarians and vegans have plenty of choices, as well. Save room for dessert—the crème brûlée is perfectly prepared. Lunch offers a more casual selection of wraps, sandwiches, burgers, and salads. A full liquor license supports a decent wine and beer list, but cocktails are limited to standards such as margaritas. The Web site is a must-read—trust us. ⊠*97 W. Center St.* ☎*435/644–8001* ⊕*www.rockingvcafe.com* ▭*MC, V* ⊗*Closed Jan.–late Mar.*

¢–$ ✕**Fernando's Hideaway.** Fernando's mixes the best margarita for miles—it's mighty fine with a quesadilla as a warm-up for dinner. The house salsa is chunky and fresh-tasting, and menu items are available as dinner platters or à la carte. Steaks and seafood will please those with a hankering for American food. Accommodations are made for vegetarians. Colorful Mexican folk art adorns the bright dining room, and the patio may encourage you to linger with another margarita. ⊠*332 N. 300 West St.* ☎*435/644–3222* ▭*AE, MC, V* ⊗*Closed Oct.–mid-Feb.*

$–$$ ▦**Best Western Red Hills.** One of Kanab's larger motels has a hearty dose of cowboy flavor accenting its city-style amenities. The downtown shopping and dining district is only a few blocks away. **Pros:** Located within 30 min of Zion National Park. Children under 17 stay free. **Cons:** No on-site restaurant. ⊠*125 W. Center St., 84741* ☎*435/644–2675 or 800/830–2675* ᕧ*435/644–5919* ⊕*www.bestwesternredhills.com* ↻*75 rooms* ♿*In-room: refrigerator, VCR, Wi-Fi. In-hotel: pool, no elevator, laundry facilities, public Internet, public Wi-Fi, some pets allowed, no-smoking rooms* ▭*AE, D, MC, V* ��*CP.*

★ $ ▦**Parry Lodge.** The lobby of this colonial-style building, constructed in 1929, is lined with photos of movie stars, including Ronald Reagan and Barbara Stanwyk, who stayed here while filming in the area. Some of the spacious rooms have plaques over the doors to tell you who stayed here before you. The lodge barn, which housed Victor Mature's camels during the making of *Timbuktu*, is now a playhouse, where old-time Western melodramas are performed in summer. **Pro:** Film buffs will enjoy sleeping among the ghosts of Hollywood past. **Con:** The dining room serves breakfast only from April through October. ⊠*89 E. Center St., 84741* ☎*435/644–2601 or 888/289–1722* ᕧ*435/644–2605* ⊕*www.parrylodge.com* ↻*89 rooms* ♿*In-hotel: restaurant, pool, laundry facilities, no-smoking rooms* ▭*AE, D, MC, V* ⊗*Reservations required Nov.–Mar.*

PARIA

43 mi east of Kanab on U.S. 89.

The town once known as Paria—or, historically, Pahreah—is long gone, but the name remains to describe the area around the intermittently flowing Paria River. Pahreah, incidentally, was Ute for "muddy water."

CLOSE UP

Edward Abbey: A Pariah in Pahreah

Most people who are aware of Edward Abbey (1927–89) in passing are probably familiar with his landmark book *Desert Solitaire*, written while he was a park ranger at Arches National Park in southeastern Utah. Though he was born in Pennsylvania's Appalachian region, he went west at the age of 17 and never really left again—at least in his heart. Those familiar with his work and his radical environmentalist ideas also know that he spent many days and nights wandering and writing about the entire western United States, and this included southwestern Utah. One of his more memorable essays devoted to this part of the state is "Days and Nights in Old

Pariah," which documents a hiking trip down Buckskin Gulch in what is now the Paria Canyon–Vermilion Cliffs Wilderness Area, not far from The Wave. Abbey's self-mocking sense of humor is evident in his essay's title. The Ute Indians named the area Pahreah, or "muddy water," after the river running through the region. Later settlers simplified it to Paria, but as Abbey put it in the first paragraph: "I like Pariah." (No doubt his detractors found that term suitable, too.) Among the adventures he documents in the essay are the rescue of a cow that had become stuck in quicksand and a swim in a 150-foot-wide pothole filled by recent rains.

Fodor's Choice
★

Hike the world-famous rock expanse known as "The Wave" in the remote and rugged **Paria Canyon–Vermilion Cliffs Wilderness,** beyond the southern boundary of the Grand Staircase–Escalante National Monument and along the Arizona border. Permits to hike the Wave—envision ocean waves frozen in striated red, orange, and yellow sandstone— and some of the other trails here are available online and usually are reserved many months in advance. However, if you arrive before 9 AM, you may be one of the 10 lucky walk-ins who can score a permit to hike the *following* day. It's not first-come, first-served; if more than 10 people show up, names are placed in a hat and drawn at random. By limiting the number of people who access the backcountry, the Bureau of Land Management hopes to preserve this area for years to come. From November 16 to March 14, apply for walk-in permits at 318 N. 100 East Street in Kanab; the rest of the year visit the Paria Information Station at the turnoff for the monument. ⊠ *43 mi east of Kanab on U.S. 89, mile marker 21* ☎*435/644-4600* ⊕*www.blm.gov* ⊠*$5 fee, reservations and permits required for some hikes* ⊗*Information station open mid-Mar.–mid-Nov. daily 8–5.*

Visit two ghost towns at once at the **Pahreah Townsite and Movie Set,** one settled by hardy pioneers and one built by Hollywood (and then rebuilt by locals when the famous movie set was damaged by floods in 1999). In fact, floods also caused the demise of the original settlements along the Pahreah River. The last movie filmed here was Clint Eastwood's *The Outlaw Josey Wales* in 1976. The set is 35 mi east of Kanab. First stop by the **Kanab field office** (⊠*318 N. 100 East St.* ☎*435/644-4600*)for Grand Staircase–Escalante National Monument to get maps and an update on road conditions. ⊠*35 mi east of Kanab via U.S. 89; turn north at monument onto Paria River Valley Rd.*

PANGUITCH

67 mi north of Kanab via U.S. 89.

An elevation of 6,650 feet helps this town of 1,600 residents keep its cool. Main Street is lined with late-19th-century buildings, and its early homes and outbuildings are noted for their distinctive brick architecture. Decent amenities, inexpensive lodging (mainly strip motels), and an excellent location 24 mi northwest of Bryce Canyon National Park make Panguitch a comfortable launching pad for recreation in the area.

During the bitter winter of 1864, Panguitch residents were on the verge of starvation. A group of men from the settlement set out over the mountains to fetch provisions from the town of Parowan, 40 mi away. When they hit waist-deep snow drifts they were forced to abandon their oxen. Legend says the men, frustrated and ready to turn back, laid a quilt on the snow and knelt to pray. Soon they realized the quilt had kept them from sinking into the snow. Spreading quilts before them as they walked, leapfrog style, the men traveled to Parowan and back, returning with life-saving provisions. Every June, the four-day **Quilt Walk Festival** (☎435/676–2418 ⊕*www.quiltwalk.com*) commemorates the event with quilting classes, a tour of Panguitch's pioneer homes, crafts shows, and a dinner-theater production in which the story is acted out.

WHERE TO STAY & EAT

★ $–$$ ✕**Cowboy's Smokehouse Café.** Stuffed animal trophies and hundreds of business cards and photographs from customers line the walls at this barbecue joint. Specialties include mesquite-smoked beef, pork, turkey, and chicken, and a sauce with no fewer than 15 secret ingredients. Try homemade peach, apricot, or cherry cobbler if you have room for dessert. Breakfast is served, too. ⊠*95 N. Main St.* ☎*435/676–8030* ▤*MC, V* ⊗*Closed Sun.*

☾ ¢–$ ▧**Marianna Inn Motel.** Rooms at this clean, family-friendly, one-story motel have up to four beds; those with whirlpool baths are $25 extra. You can barbecue your own supper on one of the grills and eat your meal on the covered patio. Relax afterward on a hammock or in the summer-only outdoor spa. **Pro:** Distance from Bryce means reservations typically are easier to come by. **Con:** Some may find Panguitch too sleepy. ⊠*699 N. Main St., 84759* ☎*435/676–8844* ▤*435/676–8340* ⊕*www.mariannainn.com* ⇆*32 rooms* ☖*In-room: refrigerator (some). In-hotel: no elevator, some pets allowed, no-smoking rooms* ▤*AE, D, DC, MC, V.*

¢ ▧**Panguitch Inn.** This quiet inn occupies a 100-year-old, two-story building a few blocks from downtown restaurants and shops. Rooms are simple and no-frills, but clean. **Pro:** Covered indoor parking. **Con:** Rooms don't match building's quaintness. ⊠*50 N. Main St., 84759* ☎*435/676–8871* ⊕*www.panguitchinn.com* ▤*435/676–8340* ⇆*25 rooms* ☖*In-room: Wi-Fi. In-hotel: no-smoking rooms* ⊗*Closed Nov.–Mar.* ▤*AE, D, DC, MC, V.*

8

GRAND STAIRCASE–ESCALANTE NATIONAL MONUMENT

In September 1996, President Bill Clinton designated 1.7 million acres in south-central Utah as the Grand Staircase–Escalante National Monument. Its three distinct sections—the Grand Staircase, the Kaiparowits Plateau, and the Canyons of the Escalante—offer remote backcountry experiences hard to find elsewhere in the Lower 48. Waterfalls, Native American ruins and petroglyphs, shoulder-width slot canyons, and improbable colors all characterize this wilderness. Straddling the northern border of the monument, the small towns of Escalante and Boulder offer access, information, outfitters, lodging, and dining to adventurers. The highway that connects them, Route 12, is one of the most scenic stretches of road in the Southwest.

ESCALANTE

47 mi east of Bryce Canyon National Park entrance via Rte. 12 east.

Though the Dominguez and Escalante expedition of 1776 came nowhere near this area, the town's name does honor the Spanish explorer. It was bestowed nearly a century later by a member of a survey party led by John Wesley Powell, charged with mapping this remote area. These days Escalante has modern amenities and is a western gateway to the Grand Staircase–Escalante National Monument.

Created to protect a huge repository of fossilized wood and dinosaur bones, **Escalante Petrified Forest State Park** has two short interpretive trails to educate visitors. There's an attractive swimming beach at the park's Wide Hollow Reservoir, which is also good for boating, fishing, and birding. ⊠*710 N. Reservoir Rd.* ☎*435/826–4466* ⊕*www.stateparks. utah.gov* ⊠*$5* ⊙*Daily 8* AM*–10* PM.

NEED A BREAK?
A fine place to stop along the way for the view (and a brew) is **Kiva Koffeehouse** (⊠*Near mile marker 74 on Rte. 12, 13 mi east of Escalante* ☎*435/826–4550*), constructed by a local artist and inventor when in his 80s. He quarried the sandstone for the walls and floors on this very site and spent two years finding and transporting the 13 Douglas-fir logs surrounding the structure. It's open from April to October, and there are two rooms for rent in a cabin below.

Fodor's Choice ★ Keep your camera handy and steering wheel steady along **Highway 12 Scenic Byway** between Escalante and Loa, near Capitol Reef National Park. Though the highway starts at the intersection of U.S. 89, west of Bryce Canyon National Park, the stretch that begins in Escalante is one of the most spectacular. The road passes through Grand Staircase–Escalante National Monument and on to Capitol Reef along one of the most scenic stretches of highway in the United States. Be sure to stop at the scenic overlooks; almost every one will give you an eye-popping view. Don't get distracted, though; the paved road is twisting and steep, and at times climbs over a hogback with sheer drop-offs on both sides.

SPORTS & THE OUTDOORS

Larger than most national parks at 1.7 million acres, the Grand Staircase–Escalante National Monument is popular with backpackers and hard-core mountain bike enthusiasts. You can explore the rocky landscape, which represents some of America's last wilderness, via dirt roads with a four-wheel-drive vehicle; most roads depart from Route 12. Roadside views into the monument are most impressive from Route 12 between Escalante and Boulder. It costs nothing to enter the park, but fees apply for camping and backcountry permits. Contact the **Escalante Interagency Visitor Center** (⊠*755 W. Main St.* ☎*435/826–5499* ⊕*www.ut.blm.gov/monument* ⊗*Mid.-Mar.–mid-Nov., daily 7:30–5:30; mid-Nov.–mid-Mar., weekdays 8–4:30*)for permits and detailed information.

Canyoneering and hiking are the focus of **Excursions of Escalante,** where tours are custom-fit to your schedule and needs. All necessary gear is provided, and tours last from one to eight days. ⊠*125 E. Main St.* ☎*800/839–7567* ⊕*www.excursions-escalante.com* ⊗*Wed.–Mon. 8–5 or by appointment.*

BICYCLING A good long-distance mountain-bike ride in the isolated Escalante region follows the 44-mi **Hell's Backbone Road** from Escalante to Boulder. The grade is steep and, if you're driving, a four-wheel-drive vehicle is recommended, but the views of Box Death Hollow make it all worthwhile. The road leaves from the center of town. Inquire about road conditions before departing.

HIKING Some of the best backcountry hiking in the area lies 15 mi east of Escalante on Route 12, where the **Lower Escalante River** carves through striking sandstone canyons and gulches. You can camp at numerous sites along the river for extended trips, or you can spend a little time in the small park where the highway crosses the river.With a guided tour from **Utah Canyons** (⊠*325 W. Main St.* ☎*435/826–4967* ⊕*www.utah canyons.com*), you can slip into the slot canyons with confidence or end a day of adventure by watching a sunset from the rim of a canyon.

WHERE TO STAY & EAT

¢–$ ✕**Esca-Latte Coffee Shop & Cafe.** Fuel up for your hike with the best coffee in town. When you're hot and spent after your day of exploration, there's no better place to sit back and relax with friends. Try a turkey sub or homemade pizza with a cold draft microbrew, or opt for a salad. Watch hummingbirds fight the wind at the feeders while dining on the patio. ⊠*310 W. Main St.* ☎*435/826–4266* ▭*AE, D, MC, V.*

★ $$ ⊞**Escalante's Grand Staircase Bed & Breakfast Inn.** Rooms have skylights, tile floors, log furniture, and murals reproducing area petroglyphs. You can relax on the outdoor porches or in the library, or make use of the rental bikes to explore the adjacent national monument. **Pro:** Southwestern rusticity with modern flair. **Con:** Escalante's wonderful remoteness may not be for everyone. ⊠*280 W. Main St., Box 657, Escalante, 84726* ☎*435/826–4890 or 866/826–4890* ⊕*www.escalantebnb.com*

➔8 *rooms* ♨*In-room: no a/c, no phone, no TV, Wi-Fi. In-hotel: no elevator, public Wi-Fi, no kids under 12, no-smoking rooms* ▭*AE, D, MC, V* ⦿I*BP.*

BOULDER

29 mi northeast of Escalante via Rte. 12 north.

That mail was delivered to Boulder by horse and mule until 1940 should give you an idea of how remote it is. The town was founded by cattle ranchers, and ranching continues to occupy many residents. The town of Escalante is larger with more services, but Boulder has one of the finest lodges and restaurants in the state.

Believed to be one of the largest Ancestral Puebloan sites west of the Colorado River, the village at **Anasazi State Park Museum** is largely unexcavated. A paved outdoor trail leads to the protected ruins of a surface pueblo pit house that predates AD 1200. Within a reproduction of an ancient dwelling is a museum featuring interactive exhibits and views into the climate-controlled environment where artifacts are stored. ✉*460 N. Rte. 12* ☎*435/335–7308* ⊕*www.stateparks.utah.gov* 🖂*$4* ⊙*Daily 9–5.*

SPORTS & THE OUTDOORS

BICYCLING Mountain bikers may want to pedal a portion of the **Burr Trail**, a 66-mi backcountry route (also passable by most vehicles when dry) that crosses east through the monument into the southern portion of Capitol Reef National Park.

HIKING **Calf Creek Falls** (✉*8 mi south of Boulder on Rte. 12*)is an easy 6-mi
★ round-trip hike from the trailhead at Calf Creek Recreation Area. At the end of the trail, a large waterfall explodes over a cliff hundreds of feet above.

If you want to take a few days to hike and backpack in Grand Staircase–Escalante National Monument, let the professionals at **Escalante Canyon Outfitters** (✉*842 W. Rte. 12* ☎*888/326–4453* ⊕*www.ecohike. com*)guide you. Founded in 1991 by a husband-and-wife team with extensive knowledge of the area, the service provides some gear and all of your meals.Explore the slot canyons in the Boulder vicinity during the spring and fall on three to six individual day trips with **Earth Tours** (☎*435/691–1241* ⊕*www.earth-tours.com*).

WHERE TO STAY & EAT

$$–$$$$ ✕ **Hell's Backbone Grill.** One of the best restaurants in Southern Utah,
Fodor's Choice this remote spot is worth the drive from any distance. The menu is
★ inspired by Native American, Western Range, Southwestern, and Mormon pioneer recipes. Chef-owners Jen Castle and Blake Spalding use only fresh, organic foods that have a historical connection to the area, so you might find buffalo burgers or cornmeal-molasses-pecan trout on the menu, and salads might contain strawberries, jicama, pine nuts, and dried corn. Their cookbook is a gem worth owning, too. ✉*20 N. Rte. 12, in Boulder Mountain Lodge* ☎*435/335–7464* ⊕*www.hellsback bonegrill.com* ▭*AE, D, MC, V* ⊙*Closed Nov.–Mar. No lunch.*

$$\text{-}$$$
Fodor'sChoice
★

☷ **Boulder Mountain Lodge.** A 15-acre pond serves as sanctuary to ducks, coots, and other waterfowl at this pastoral lodge. Large, modern rooms with either balconies or patios have gorgeous views of the wetlands. The main lodge contains a great room with fireplace, and there's a fine art gallery and remarkably good restaurant on the premises. **Pro:** A perfect spot for peace and solitude. **Con:** Some might find the middle-of-nowhere location too remote. ✉*20 N. Rte. 12, Box 1397, 84716* ☎*435/335–7460 or 800/556–3446* 📠*435/335–7461* ⊕*www.boulder-utah.com* ➥*20 rooms, 2 suites* ⚐*In-room: kitchen (some), refrigerator (some), DVD, Wi-Fi. In-hotel: restaurant, no elevator, laundry service, public Wi-Fi, some pets allowed, no-smoking rooms* ▤*AE, D, MC, V* ❑*BP.*

SOUTHWESTERN UTAH ESSENTIALS

AIR TRAVEL

SkyWest flies to St. George municipal airport, and operates as a carrier for both United Express and Delta Connection flights. Las Vegas's McCarran International Airport is 116 mi from St. George; the St. George Shuttle makes nine trips a day between it and St. George.

Airport Information McCarran International Airport (✉*5757 Wayne Newton Blvd., Las Vegas, NV* ☎*702/261–5211* ⊕*www.mccarran.com*). **St. George Municipal Airport** (✉*317 S. Donlee Dr., St. George* ☎*435/634–5822* ⊕*www.sgcity.org/airport/*).

Carriers Delta Connection (☎*800/221–1212* ⊕*www.delta.com*). **SkyWest Airlines** (☎*435/634–3400* ⊕*www.skywest.com*). **United Express** (☎*800/864–8331* ⊕*www.united.com*).

Shuttle Van St. George Shuttle (✉*915 Bluff St.* ☎*435/628–8320 or 800/933–8320* ⊕*www.stgshuttle.com*).

BUS TRAVEL

Greyhound Bus Lines serves the I–15 corridor, making stops in Parowan and St. George.

Information Greyhound Bus Lines (☎*800/229–9424* ⊕*www.greyhound.com*).

CAR RENTAL

St. George has major car rental agencies at the airport and within town.

Information Avis (✉*620 S. Airport Rd., St. George Airport, St. George* ☎*435/627–2002* ⊕*www.avis.com*). **Budget** (✉*620 S. Airport Rd., St. George Airport, St. George* ☎*435/673–6825* ⊕*www.budget.com*) . **Enterprise** (✉*289 E. St. George Blvd., St. George* ☎*435/634–1556* ✉*166 W. 1700 South, St. George* ☎*435/673–5647* ⊕*www.enterprise.com*).

CAR TRAVEL

I–15 is the main route into southwestern Utah, from Las Vegas to the southwest and Salt Lake City to the northeast. U.S. 89, which leads to Kanab, is a good, well-traveled road with interesting sights, as well as

8

gas stations and convenience stores. Routes 143 and 14 are the main east–west connecting routes. Some mountain curves can be expected on these roads, and winter months may see hazardous conditions and occasional closures in the higher elevations around Brian Head and Cedar Breaks. Keep the gas tank topped off, especially if you start to venture along any of the region's old Jeep roads. Contact the Utah Department of Transportation for construction delays and road conditions.

Information **AAA** (☎ *800/222-4357* ⊕ *www.csaa.com*). **Utah Department of Transportation** (☎ *801/965-4000* ⊕ *www.dot.state.ut.us*).

EMERGENCIES

In most towns, call ☎911 for police, fire, and ambulance service. In rural areas, the Utah Highway Patrol has jurisdiction, as do county sheriff departments.

Ambulance or Police Emergencies (☎ *911*). **Utah Highway Patrol** (☎ *435/634-2890*).

Hospitals Dixie Regional Medical Center (✉ *544 S. 400 East St., St. George* ☎ *435/251-1000*).**Kane County Hospital** (✉ *355 N. Main St., Kanab* ☎ *435/644-5811*). **Valley View Medical Center** (✉ *1303 N. Main St., Cedar City* ☎ *435/586-6587*).

LODGING

The official travel site of the State of Utah is your single best bet for information on lodging and amenities in the southwestern part of the state.

Information Utah Office of Tourism (✉ *300 N. State St., Salt Lake City, 84114* ☎ *800/200-1160* ⊕ *www.utah.com*).

CAMPING In this region of Utah, campers can choose from low-desert to high-mountain facilities and more than 100 commercial campgrounds. Most of the area's state parks have camping facilities, and Dixie National Forest contains many wonderful sites. The Utah Bureau of Land Management also runs campgrounds in the area.

Information Dixie National Forest (✉ *1789 N. Wedgewood Ln., Cedar City, 84720* ☎ *435/865-3700* ⊕ *www.fs.fed.us/dxnf/*). **Utah Bureau of Land Management** (✉ *345 East Riverside Dr., St. George, 84720* ☎ *435/688-3200* ⊕ *www.blm.gov/ut*). **Utah State Parks** (✉ *1594 W. North Temple, Salt Lake City, 84114* ☎ *801/538-7220* ⊕ *www.stateparks.utah.gov*).

SPORTS & THE OUTDOORS

You should not visit southwestern Utah without exploring some of its wide-open and remote spaces using a mode of transportation other than a car or bus. In many instances, four wheels will not take you to the best sights. Consider a half- or full-day tour by bike, foot, or horseback—or spend a few nights out on the range. The following outfitters offer tours that cover a wide geographical area with many different types of terrain; check the Sports & the Outdoors section of each town in this chapter for listings of outfitters which target a specific area.

BICYCLING   The "other" southern corner of the state tends to grab the cycling spotlight, but southwestern Utah is making a name for itself as a destination for the discriminating road or mountain biker. The higher elevations of Brian Head are popular in summer, when temperatures are relatively cool; the winter climate at lower desert elevations is mild enough for off-season riding. The outfitters listed here are a great source of information on trails and conditions, but consider signing on for a professionally guided tour.

Contacts **Escape Adventures** (✉ *8221 W. Charleston, Suite 101, Las Vegas, 89117* ☎ *800/596-2953* ⊕ *www.escapeadventures.com*). **Rim Tours** (✉ *1233 S. U.S. 191, Moab, 84532* ☎ *800/626-7335* ⊕ *www.rimtours.com*).

TOURS

Hondoo Rivers & Trails arranges full-day four-wheel-drive vehicle tours into portions of the Grand Staircase–Escalante National Monument.

Contacts **Hondoo Rivers & Trails** (✉ *95 E. Main St., Box 98, Torrey, 84775* ☎ *435/425-3519 or 800/332-2696* ⊕ *www.hondoo.com*).

VISITOR INFORMATION

Information **Garfield County Travel Council** (✉ *55 S. Main St., Panguitch, 84759* ☎ *800/444-6689* ⊕ *www.brycecanyoncountry.com*). **Iron County Visitors Center** (⌂ *581 N. Main St., Cedar City, 84720* ☎ *800/354-4849* ⊕ *www. scenicsouthernutah.com*). **Kane County Office of Tourism** (⌂ *78 S. 100 East St., Kanab, 84741* ☎ *800/733-5263* ⊕ *www.visitsouthernutah.com*). **St. George Area Convention & Visitors Bureau** (✉ *1835 Convention Center Dr., St. George, 84790* ☎ *800/869-6635* ⊕ *www.utahstgeorge.com*). **Utah Office of Tourism** (✉ *300 N. State St., Salt Lake City, 84114* ☎ *800/200-1160* ⊕ *www.utah.com*).

8

Arches
National Park

WORD OF MOUTH

"Delicate Arch is the most beautiful spot in Utah! You can do Del Arch late in the day or very early morning for great photos and to avoid the heat. Other hikes in Arches are easy and in shade. Try to do Fiery Furnace with a ranger, but reserve ahead. Without a ranger, tourists can get lost! Visitor center is very helpful; ask about best time for each hike for your time of year."

—stweaver00

Delicate Arch

WELCOME TO ARCHES

TOP REASONS TO GO

★ **Unique terrain:** There's nowhere else on Earth that looks like this.

★ **Memorable snapshots:** You have to have a picture of Delicate Arch at sunset.

★ **Treasures hanging in the balance:** Landscape Arch is the longest open span in the world. Come quick! Due to its delicate nature, it could fall before you see it.

★ **Fiery Furnace:** A hike through this maze of rock walls and fins is sure to make you fall in love with the desert and appreciate nature at its most spectacular.

★ **Window to nature:** The park has the largest collection of natural arches in the world—more than 2,000. They make great frames through which to view moonrises, mountains, and more.

Balanced Rock

1 Devil's Garden. About 18 mi from the visitor center, this is the end of the road in Arches. Trails lead to Landscape Arch and numerous other natural rock windows. This area also has picnic tables, the park's only campground, and an amphitheater where campfire programs are held.

2 Fiery Furnace. This forbiddingly named area is so labeled because its orange spires of rock look much like tongues of flame, especially in the late-afternoon sun. About 14 mi inside from the visitor center, it's the site for ranger-guided walks.

3 The Windows. Reached on a spur 9⅓ mi from the visitor center, this area of the park is where visitors with little time stop. Here you can see many of the park's natural arches from your car or on an easy rolling trail.

4 Petrified Dunes. Just a tiny pull-out about 5 mi from the visitor center, this scenic stop is where you can take pictures of acres and acres of petrified sand dunes.

5 Courthouse Towers. The Three Gossips, Sheep Rock, and Tower of Babel are the rock formations to see here. Enter this section of the park 3 mi past the visitor center. The Park Avenue Trail winds through the area, which was named for its steep walls and towers that look like buildings.

Bighorn Sheep

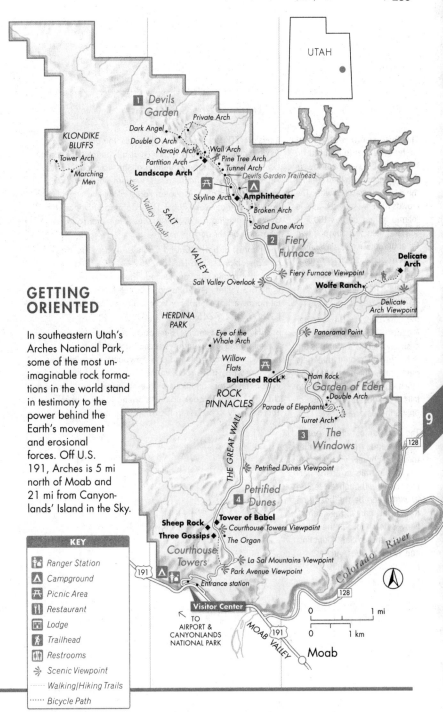

UTAH

1 Devils Garden

KLONDIKE BLUFFS

Tower Arch

Marching Men

Private Arch

Dark Angel

Double O Arch

Navajo Arch

Partition Arch

Landscape Arch

Wall Arch

Pine Tree Arch

Tunnel Arch

Devils Garden Trailhead

Skyline Arch

Amphitheater

Broken Arch

Sand Dune Arch

SALT VALLEY WASH

SALT VALLEY

2 Fiery Furnace

Fiery Furnace Viewpoint

Salt Valley Overlook

Delicate Arch

Wolfe Ranch

Delicate Arch Viewpoint

HERDINA PARK

Eye of the Whale Arch

Panorama Point

Willow Flats

Balanced Rock

Ham Rock

Garden of Eden

Double Arch

ROCK PINNACLES

Parade of Elephants

Turret Arch

3 The Windows

128

9

THE GREAT WALL

Petrified Dunes Viewpoint

4 Petrified Dunes

Tower of Babel

Courthouse Towers Viewpoint

Sheep Rock

Three Gossips

The Organ

Courthouse Towers

La Sal Mountains Viewpoint

Park Avenue Viewpoint

Entrance station

Colorado River

128

191

Visitor Center

← TO AIRPORT & CANYONLANDS NATIONAL PARK

MOAB VALLEY

191

Moab

GETTING ORIENTED

In southeastern Utah's Arches National Park, some of the most un-imaginable rock formations in the world stand in testimony to the power behind the Earth's movement and erosional forces. Off U.S. 191, Arches is 5 mi north of Moab and 21 mi from Canyonlands' Island in the Sky.

KEY	
👪	Ranger Station
🅰	Campground
🌲	Picnic Area
🍴	Restaurant
🏨	Lodge
🚶	Trailhead
🚻	Restrooms
🔆	Scenic Viewpoint
⋯	Walking/Hiking Trails
⋯	Bicycle Path

0 _____ 1 mi

0 _____ 1 km

ARCHES PLANNER

When to Go	Getting There & Around

The busiest times of year at Arches are spring and fall. In the spring, blooming wildflowers and temperatures in the 70s bring the year's largest crowds. The crowds thin in summer as the thermostat approaches 100°F in July and then soars beyond that for about four weeks. In August, sudden cloudbursts create rainfalls over red rock walls and dramatic skies for a part of the day.

Fall brings everybody back to the park because the weather is perfect—clear, warm days, and crisp, cool nights. October is the only autumn month that gets much rain, but even that isn't much, considering how little rain falls in the desert: an average of only 8 inches a year.

The park almost clears out in winter, and from December through February you can hike any of the trails in nearly perfect solitude. Though few realize it, winter can be the best time to visit this part of the country. Snow seldom falls in the valley beneath the La Sal Mountains, and when it does, Arches is a photographer's paradise.

Interstate 70 is the speedway that gets you across Utah. To dip southeast toward Moab, veer off the interstate onto U.S. 191, a main artery running all the way south to the Arizona border, skirting Arches' western border, Moab, and the Monti-La Sal National Forest along the way. Alternatively, you can take Route 128, Colorado River Scenic Byway, traveling just east of Arches. On either road services can be far apart.

The nearest airport is Grand County Airport, also know as Canyonlands Field (☎435/259-7419), 18 mi north of Moab. Flights are very limited. The nearest train "station" is a solitary Amtrak stop in Green River, about 60 mi northwest of Moab. For train inquiries, call Amtrak (☎800/872-7245).

Branching off the main, 18-mi park road are two spurs, a 2½-mi one to The Windows section and a 1⅗-mi one to the Delicate Arch trailhead and viewpoint. There are several four-wheel-drive roads in the park; always check at the visitor center for conditions before attempting to drive them. U.S. 191 tends to back up mid-morning to early afternoon. There's likely to be less traffic at 8 AM or sunset.

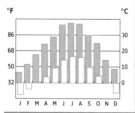

By Janet
Buckingham

THE RED ROCK LANDSCAPE OF Arches National Park awakens the spirit and challenges the imagination: balanced rocks teeter unthinkably on pedestals; sandstone arches—of which there are more than 2,000—frame the sky with peekaboo windows; and formations like the Three Penguins greet you at points throughout the 73,379-acre park. Far from a stereotypical beige-tone palette with the occasional cactus, the desert here is adorned with a rich tapestry of colors: red, orange, purple, pink, creamy ivory, deep chocolate, and even shades of turquoise. The Fiery Furnace burns like a wildfire at sunset, and acres of petrified sand dunes rise across the horizon.

The sky is big here, so it's easy to spot many of the arches from your car. But despite the endless horizon, you should really step outside and walk beneath the spans and giant walls of orange rock. This gives you a much better idea of their proportion. No doubt you will feel as writer Edward Abbey did when he awoke on his first day as a park ranger in Arches: that you're walking in the most beautiful place on Earth.

SCENIC DRIVES

Arches Main Park Road. Although they are not formally designated as such, the main park road and its two short spurs are scenic drives, and you can see much of the park from your car. The main road takes you through Courthouse Towers, where you can see Sheep Rock and the Three Gossips, then alongside the Great Wall and the Petrified Dunes. A drive to The Windows section takes you to Double Arch, North and South windows, and Turret Arch; you can see Skyline Arch along the roadside as you approach the campground. The road to Delicate Arch is not particularly scenic, but it allows you hiking access to one of the park's main features. Allow about two hours to drive the 36-mi round-trip, more if you explore the spurs and their features and stop at viewpoints along the way.

WHAT TO SEE

HISTORIC SITE

Wolfe Ranch. Built in 1906 out of Fremont cottonwoods, this rustic one-room cabin housed the Wolfe family after their first cabin was lost to a flash flood. In addition to the cabin you can see remains of a root cellar and a corral. Even older than these structures is the nearby Ute rock-art panel by the Delicate Arch trailhead. About 150 feet past the footbridge and before the trail starts to climb, you can see images of bighorn sheep as well as some smaller images believed to be dogs. To reach the panel, follow the narrow dirt trail along the rock escarpment until you see the interpretive sign. ⊠ *12⁹⁄₁₀ mi from the park entrance, 1²⁄₁₀ mi off the main road.*

SCENIC STOPS

Balanced Rock. One of the park's favorite sights, this rock has remained mysteriously balanced on its pedestal for who knows how long. The formation's total height is 128 feet, with the huge balanced rock rising

ARCHES IN ONE DAY

Start early, while the day is still cool, with a 3-mi round-trip hike on the **Delicate Arch Trail**. The route is strenuous but richly rewarding. Pause for a healthy snack before heading for **Landscape Arch,** the second of the park's two must-see arches. To get there you must hike through **Devils Garden,** a great spot for morning photography. If you're accustomed to hiking you might next hike out to **Double O,** a trip that is well worth the effort but that can be tough after the hike to Delicate Arch—especially in July or August. If you do hike to Double O, take your lunch with you and have a picnic in the shade of a juniper or in a rock alcove. Don't forget to pack out every scrap of paper and food. By the time you return you'll be ready to see the rest of the park by car, with some short strolls on easy paths.

In the mid- to late afternoon, drive to **Balanced Rock** for photos, then on to **The Windows.** Wander around on the easy gravel paths for more great photo ops. Depending on what time the sun is due to set, go into town for dinner before or after you drive out to Delicate Arch or the Fiery Furnace and watch the sun set the rocks on fire.

55 feet above the pedestal. A short loop (³/₁₀ mi) around the base gives you an opportunity to stretch your legs and take photographs. ⊠*9 1/5 mi from the park entrance on the main road.*

Fodor's Choice **Delicate Arch.** The familiar symbol of Arches National Park, if not for
★ the entire state of Utah, Delicate Arch is tall enough to shelter a four-story building. The arch is a remnant of an Entrada sandstone fin; the rest of the rock has eroded and now frames the La Sal Mountains in the background. You can drive a couple of miles off the main road to view the arch from a distance, or you can hike right up to it. The trail is a moderately strenuous 3-mi round-trip hike. ⊠*13 mi from the park entrance, 2⅕ mi off the main road.*

Double Arch. In The Windows section of the park, Double Arch has appeared in several Hollywood movies, including *Indiana Jones and the Last Crusade.* Less than ¼ mi from the parking lot, the spectacular rock formation can be reached in about 10 minutes. ⊠*11⁷/₁₀ mi from the park entrance on the main road.*

★ **Landscape Arch.** This natural rock opening competes with Kolob Arch at Zion for the title of largest geologic span in the world. Measuring 306 feet from base to base, it appears as a delicate ribbon of rock bending over the horizon. In 1991, a slab of rock about 60 feet long, 11 feet wide, and 4 feet thick fell from the underside, leaving it even thinner. You can reach it by walking a rolling, gravel 1⅗-mi-long trail. ⊠*Devils Garden, 18 mi from park entrance on the main road.*

Sand Dune Arch. Kids love the trail to this arch because erosion has created a giant sandbox beneath the namesake arch. While it's an easy trail, remember that sand is difficult to walk in. A cautionary note: do not climb or jump off the arch; rangers have dealt with several accidents involving people who have done so. Allow about 15 minutes to walk the ³/₁₀ mi to the arch and back to your car. The trail intersects with the Broken Arch Trail, so if you visit both arches, it's a 1½-mi round-trip. ⊠ *16 mi from the park entrance on the main road.*

Skyline Arch. A quick walk from the parking lot gives you closer views and better photos of the arch. The short trail is ⅖ mi round-trip and only takes a few minutes to travel. ⊠ *16½ mi from the park entrance on the main road.*

> ## WHAT'S AN ARCH?
>
> To be defined as an arch, a rock opening must be in a continuous wall of rock and have a minimum opening of 3 feet in any one direction. A natural bridge differs from an arch in that it is formed by water flowing beneath it.

☾ **The Windows.** Many people with limited time to spend in the park drive to this area. Here you can see a large concentration of natural windows and walk a path that winds beneath them. ⊠ *11⁷/₁₀ mi from the park entrance, 2½ mi off the main road.*

VISITOR CENTER

Arches Visitor Center. It's definitely worth stopping to see the interactive displays here; they'll make your sightseeing tour through the park more meaningful. Take time to view the 15-minute park film, *Secrets of the Red Rock,* and shop the bookstore for trail guides, books, and maps to enhance your visit. Exhibits inform you about geology, natural history, and Ancestral Puebloan presence in the Arches area. There is water in vending machines outside the center. ⊠ *At the park entrance* ☎ *435/719–2299* ⊙ *Hrs vary but generally 8 AM–5 PM daily, with extended hrs late spring through early fall.*

SPORTS & THE OUTDOORS

9

Arches National Park lies in the middle of the adventure capital of the world. Deep canyons and towering walls are everywhere you look. Slick sandstone surfaces, known locally as "slickrock" make for some of the world's best mountain biking. Thousand-foot sandstone walls draw rock climbers from across the globe. There's no better place for hiking; you can choose from shady canyons or feel like you are on top of the world as you traverse red rock fins that reach for the sky. The Colorado River runs parallel to the park, and can give you every kind of white-water adventure. Moab outfitters can set you up for any sport you may have a desire to try: mountain biking, ATVs, dirt bikes, four-wheel-drive vehicles, kayaking, climbing, and even skydiving (⇨ Outfitters & Expeditions box, Chapter 11). Within the park, it's best to stick with basics such as hiking, sightseeing, and photography. Climbers and other adventure seekers should always inquire at the visitor center about restrictions.

FLORA & FAUNA

As in any desert environment, the best time to see wildlife in Arches is early morning or evening. Summer temperatures keep most animals tucked away in cool places, though lizards crawl around all day, so if you happen to be in the right place at the right time you'll spot one of the beautiful, turquoise-necklace-collared lizards. It's more likely you'll see the Western whiptail. Mule deer, jack-rabbits, and small rodents such as pack rats are usually active in cool morning hours or near dusk. You may spot a lone coyote foraging day or night. The park protects a small herd of desert bighorns, and some of their tribe are often seen early in the morning grazing beside U.S. 191 south of the Arches entrance. If you are fortunate enough to encounter bighorn sheep, do not approach them. They have been known to charge human beings who attempt to get too close. The park's mule deer and small mammals such as chipmunks are very used to seeing people and may allow you to get close—but don't feed them.

At sunset, the rock formations in Arches glow like fire and you'll often find photographers behind their tripods waiting for the sweet light to descend upon Delicate Arch or other popular park sites. The Fiery Furnace earns its name as its narrow fins glow red just before the sun dips below the horizon. Full-moon nights are particularly dramatic in Arches as the creamy white Navajo sandstone reflects light and eerie silhouettes are created by towering fins and formations.

BICYCLING
There's outstanding mountain biking all around Arches National Park, but the park proper is not the best place to explore on two wheels. Bicycles are only allowed on established roads and since there are no shoulders, cyclists share the roadway with drivers and pedestrians gawking at the scenery. If you do want to take a spin in the park, try Willow Flats Road, the old entrance to the park. The road is about 6½-mi long one way and starts directly across from the Balanced Rock parking lot. It's a pretty ride on dirt and sand through slickrock, pinyon, and juniper country. You must stay on the road with your bicycle or you chance steep fines.

For bike rentals and expeditions, see Outfitters & Expeditions box in Chapter 11.

BIRD-WATCHING
Within the park you'll definitely see plenty of the big, black, beautiful ravens. Look for them perched on top of a picturesque juniper branch or balancing on the bald knob of a rock. The noisy black-billed magpie populates the park, as do the more melodic canyon and rock wrens. Lucky visitors will spot a red-tailed hawk and hear its distinctive call.

Serious birders will have more fun visiting the **Scott M. Matheson Wetlands Preserve** (⇨ Chapter 11) just 5 mi south of the park.

BOATING & RIVER EXPEDITIONS

Although the Colorado River runs along the border of the park, there is no boating within the park proper. You can, however, enjoy a splashy ride nearby on the Fisher Towers stretch of the river near Moab. There are plenty of fine outfitters in Moab that can set you up for expeditions *(see Outfitters & Expeditions box in Chapter 11).*

FOUR-WHEELING

With thousands of acres of nearby Bureau of Land Management lands to enjoy, it's hardly necessary to use the park's limited trails for four-wheel adventures. You can, however, go backcountry in Arches on the Willow Flats Road and the Salt Valley Road—just don't set out for this expedition without first stopping at the visitor center to learn of current conditions. The Salt Valley road is very sandy and requires special driving skills.

For guided 4X4 trips, see Outfitters & Expeditions box in Chapter 11.

HIKING

Getting out on any one of the park trails will surely cause you to fall in love with this Martian landscape. But remember, you are hiking in a desert environment. Many people succumb to heat and dehydration because they do not drink enough water. Park rangers recommend a gallon of water per day per person.

EASY ☾ **Balanced Rock Trail.** You'll want to stop at Balanced Rock for photo opportunities, so you may as well walk the easy, partially paved trail around the famous landmark. This is one of the most accessible trails in the park and is suitable for small children and folks who may have difficulty walking. The trail is only ³/₁₀ mi round-trip; you should allow 15 minutes for the walk. ⊠ *Approximately 9 mi from the park entrance.*

Broken Arch Trail. An easy walk across open grassland, this loop trail passes Broken Arch, which is also visible from the road. The arch gets its name because it appears to be cracked in the middle, but it's not really broken. The trail is 2 mi round-trip, and you should allow about an hour for the walk. ⊠ *End of Sand Dune Arch trail, ³/₁₀ mi off the main park road, 11 mi from the park entrance.*

Double Arch Trail. Near the Windows Trail is this relatively flat trail that leads you to two massive arches that make for great photo opportunities. Although only ½ mi round-trip, you get a good taste of desert flora and fauna. ⊠ *2½ mi from the main road on the Windows Section spur road.*

Park Avenue Trail. Walk under the gaze of Queen Nefertiti, a giant rock formation that some observers think has Egyptian-looking features. The nearby rock walls resemble a New York City skyline—hence the

9

name Park Avenue. The trail is fairly easy, with only a short hill to navigate. It's 2 mi round-trip, or, if you are traveling with companions, you can have one of them pick you up at the Courthouse Towers Viewpoint, making it a 1-mi trek downhill. Allow about 45 minutes for the one-way journey. ✉ *On the main road, 2 mi from the park entrance.*

Sand Dune Arch Trail. Your kids will return to the car with shoes full of sand at this giant sandbox in the desert. It's a shady, quick hike that everyone in the family will enjoy. Set aside 30 minutes for this ⅖-mi walk. ✉ *On the main road, about 15½ mi from the park entrance.*

Windows Trail. One of everyone's favorite stops in the park also gives you an opportunity to get out and enjoy the desert air. Here you'll see three giant openings in rock and walk on a trail that leads you right through the holes. Allow about an hour on this gently inclined 1-mi round-trip hike. ✉ *On the main road, 9½ mi from the park entrance.*

MODERATE
Fodor's Choice ★

Devils Garden Trail. If you want to take a longer hike in the park, head out on this network of trails, where you can see a number of arches. You will reach Tunnel and Pine Tree arches after only ⅖ mi on the gravel trail, and Landscape Arch is ⅘ mi from the trailhead. Past Landscape Arch the trail changes dramatically, increasing in difficulty with many short, steep climbs. You will encounter some heights as you inch your way across a long rock fin. The trail is marked with rock cairns, and it's always a good idea to locate the next one before moving on. Along the way to Double O Arch, 2 mi from the trailhead, you can take short detours to Navajo and Partition arches. A round-trip hike to Double O takes from two to three hours. For a longer hike, include Dark Angel and/or return to the trailhead on the primitive loop. This is a difficult route through fins with a short side trip to Private Arch. If you hike all the way to Dark Angel and return on the primitive loop, the trail is 7⅕ mi round-trip. Allow about five hours for this adventure, take plenty of water, and watch your route carefully. ✉ *18 mi from the park entrance on the main road.*

Tower Arch Trail. In a remote, seldom-visited area of the park, this trail takes you to a giant rock opening. If you look beneath the arch you will see a 1922 inscription left by Alex Ringhoffer, who "discovered" this section of the park. Reach the trail by driving to the Klondike Bluffs parking area via a dirt road that starts at the main park road across from Broken Arch. Check with park rangers for road conditions before attempting the drive. Allow from two to three hours for this hike. ✉ *24½ mi from the park entrance, 7⁷⁄₁₀ mi off the main road.*

DIFFICULT ★

Delicate Arch Trail. To see the park's most famous freestanding arch up close takes some effort. The 3-mi round-trip trail ascends a steep slick-rock slope that offers no shade—it's very hot in summer. What you find at the end of the trail is, however, worth the hard work. You can walk under the arch and take advantage of abundant photo ops, especially at sunset. In spite of its difficulty, this is a very popular trail. Allow anywhere from one to three hours for this hike, depending on your fitness level and how long you plan to linger at the arch. The trail starts at Wolf Ranch. ✉ *13 mi from the park entrance, 2⅕ mi off the main road.*

★ **Fiery Furnace Hiking.** Rangers strongly suggest taking the guided hike through this area before you set out on your own, as there is no marked trail. A hike here is a challenging but fascinating trip through rugged terrain into the heart of Arches. The trail occasionally requires the use of hands and feet to scramble up and through narrow cracks and along narrow ledges above drop-offs. To hike this area on your own you must get a permit at the visitor center ($2). If you're not familiar with the Furnace you can easily get lost and cause resource damage, so watch your step and use great caution. ✉ *Off the main park road, about 15 mi from the visitor center.*

HORSEBACK RIDING

Horseback riding is very restricted in the park. Horses are not allowed in the campground and must be fed a special diet for a period of time before taking them into the park. You should check with the National Park Service for current regulations.

For rentals and riding expeditions, see Outfitters & Expeditions box in Chapter 11.

ROCK CLIMBING

Rock climbers travel from across the country to scale the sheer red rock walls of Arches National Park and surrounding areas. Most climbing routes in the park require advanced techniques. Permits are not required, but you are responsible for knowing park regulations and restricted routes. One popular route in the park is Owl Rock in the Garden of Eden (about 10 mi from the visitor center), which ranges in difficulty from 5.8 to 5.11 on a scale that goes up to 5.13+. Many climbing routes are available in the Park Avenue area, about 2⅕ mi from the visitor center. These routes are also extremely difficult climbs. Before climbing, it's imperative that you stop at the visitor center and talk with a ranger.

For rock climbing outfitters, see Outfitters & Expeditions box in Chapter 11.

SWIMMING

There is no swimming in the park. The nearby Colorado River may be suitable for swimming in late summer or early fall, but never enter the river without a life jacket as currents can be surprisingly strong.

EDUCATIONAL OFFERINGS

PROGRAMS & TOURS

For more information on current schedules and locations of park programs, contact the visitor center (☎435/719–2299) or check the bulletin boards located throughout the park.

Campfire Program. Every evening mid-March through October, a park ranger presents a program around the campfire at Devils Garden Campground. It's a great way to learn about subjects such as moun-

GOOD READS

The park visitor center and the Moab Information Center (⇨ *Chapter 11*) are good places to find books to enhance your visit to the parks. You can also order them from **Canyonlands Natural History Association** (☎ *800/840–8978* ⊕ *www.cnha.org*).

A Naturalist's Guide to Canyon Country by David Williams and Gloria Brown is an excellent, compact field guide for both Arches and Canyonlands.

Best Easy Day Hikes: Arches and Canyonlands by Bill Schneider is a pocket-size trail guide that should boost your confidence as you hit the trails.

Canyon Country Wildflowers by Damian Fagan can help you name the colorful blossoms you see during wildflower season (spring and early summer).

Desert Solitaire—every visitor should read Edward Abbey's classic.

Exploring Canyonlands and Arches National Parks by Bill Schneider provides comprehensive advice on hiking trails, backcountry roads, and trip planning.

Hiking Guide to Arches National Park by Damian Fagan details all of the park's hiking trails.

Into the Mystery: A Driving Tour of Moab Area Rock Art by Janet Lowe offers insight on ancient Native American rock art.

Road Guide to Arches National Park by Peter Anderson has basic information about the geology and natural history in the park.

tain lions, the Colorado River, human history in Arches National Park, or the night life of animals. ⊠ *Devils Garden Campground Amphitheater, 17⁷⁄₁₀ mi from the park entrance, ½ mi off the main road* 🖭 *Free* ⊗ *Mid-Mar.–Oct., nightly at 9.*

★ **Fiery Furnace Walk.** Join a park ranger on a two- or three-hour walk through a mazelike labyrinth of rock fins and narrow sandstone canyons. You'll see arches that can't be viewed from the park road and spend time listening to the desert. You should be relatively fit and not afraid of heights if you plan to take this moderately strenuous walk. Wear sturdy hiking shoes, sunscreen, and a hat, and bring at least a quart of water. Walks into the Fiery Furnace are usually offered twice a day (hours vary) and leave from Fiery Furnace viewpoint. Tickets may be purchased for this popular activity up to seven days in advance at the visitor center. ⊠ *Fiery Furnace trailhead, about 15 mi from the visitor center off the main park road* 🖭 *$10 adults, $5 children 6–12* ⊗ *Mid-Mar.–Oct., daily.*

Guided Walks. You can really get to know Arches National Park by joining these walks with park rangers. Many of the walks explore The Windows section of the park, but they also visit other areas of the park. Topics include geology, desert plants, and the survival tactics of animals. Check at the visitor center or on park bulletin boards for times, topics, and locations. 🖭 *Free.*

Junior Ranger Program. Kids 6–12 can pick up a Junior Ranger booklet at the visitor center. It's full of activities, word games, drawings, and educational material about the park and the wildlife. To earn your Junior Ranger badge you must complete the booklet, attend a ranger program or watch the park slide program, and gather a bag of litter or bring 20 aluminum cans to be recycled. ☎*435/719–2299* *Free.*

SHOPPING

Arches Visitor Center Bookstore. Operated by Canyonlands Natural History Association, this is the place to buy maps, guidebooks, and material about the natural and cultural history of Arches National Park. ✉*At the park entrance* ☎*435/719–2299, 435/259–6003, 800/840–8978 to order books.*

NEARBY TOWNS

Moab is the major gateway to both Arches and Canyonlands national parks. It's an interesting, eclectic place to visit, especially if you're looking for fine restaurants with good wine lists, abundant shopping, art galleries, and varied lodging. Also, here you'll find the area's greatest number of sports outfitters to help you enjoy the parks. For those who want civilization and culture with their outdoor itineraries, Moab is the place to be.

The next-closest town to Arches, about 47 mi to the northwest, is **Green River.** Unlike hip Moab, this sleepy little town is more traditional and off the tourists' radar screen. It's worth a visit for the **Crystal Geyser,** which erupts for 30 minutes every 14 to 16 hours.

See Chapter 11 for more information about these and other nearby towns.

9

WHERE TO EAT

In the park itself, there are no dining facilities and no snack bars. Supermarkets, bakeries, and delis in downtown Moab will be happy to make you a sandwich to go. If you bring a packed lunch, there are several picnic areas from which to choose. *For dining recommendations in Moab see Chapter 11.*

PICNIC AREAS **Balanced Rock.** The view is the best part of this picnic spot. There are no cooking facilities or water, but there are tables. If you sit just right you might find some shade under a small juniper; otherwise, this is an exposed site. Pit toilets are nearby. ✉*Opposite the Balanced Rock parking area, 9⅕ mi from the park entrance on the main road.*

Devils Garden. There are grills, water, picnic tables, restrooms, and depending on the time of day, some shade from large junipers and rock walls. It's a good place for lunch before or after you go hiking. ✉*On the main road, 18 mi from the park entrance.*

WHERE TO STAY

Though there are no hotels or cabins in the park itself, in the surrounding area every type of lodging is available, from economy chain motels to B&Bs and high-end, high-adventure resorts. *See Chapter 11* for recommended lodgings.

The Devils Garden Campground in the park is a wonderful spot to call home for a few days, though it is often full and does not provide an RV dump station. Otherwise, the most centrally located campgrounds are in Moab and will generally provide services needed by RV travelers (⇨ *Where to Stay in Moab*).

CAMPGROUNDS & RV PARKS

★ $

Devils Garden Campground. This small campground is one of the most unusual—and gorgeous—in the national park system, and in the West, for that matter. Sites, which are tucked away into red rock outcroppings, are available on a first-come, first-served basis during the off-season, but March through October, when the campground gets full, campers are required to pre-register for a site; this can be done at the visitor center between 7:30 and 8 AM, or at the campground entrance station after 8 AM. Also March through October, up to 28 of the campsites can be reserved in advance (at least four but no more than 240 days prior) by contacting National Recreation Reservation Service (NRRS) via phone or online; there is a $9 booking fee. ⊠ *18 mi from the park entrance on the main park road* ☎ *435/719–2299, 518/885–3639 or 877/444–6777 NRRS reservations* 🖷 *435/259–4285* ⊕ *www.recreation.gov* 🛏 *52 sites* ♿ *Flush toilets, drinking water, fire grates, picnic tables* ⊟ *No credit cards.*

ARCHES ESSENTIALS

ACCESSIBILITY

Not all park facilities meet federally mandated ADA standards, but as visitation to Arches climbs, the park is making efforts to increase accessibility. Visitors with mobility impairments can access the visitor center, all restrooms throughout the park, and one campsite (#7) at the Devils Garden Campground. The Park Avenue Viewpoint is a paved path with a slight decline near the end, and both Delicate Arch and Balanced Rock viewpoints are partially hard surfaced.

ADMISSION FEES

Admission to the park is $10 per vehicle and $5 per person on foot, motorcycle, or bicycle, good for seven days. You must pay admission to Canyonlands separately. A $25 local park pass grants you admission to both the Arches and Canyonlands parks for one year.

ADMISSION HOURS

Arches National Park is open year-round, seven days a week, around the clock. It's in the Mountain time zone.

ATMS/BANKS
There are no ATMs in the park. The nearest ATM and full-service bank is in Moab.

Contacts Wells Fargo Bank (✉ *4 N. Main St., Moab*). **Zions Bank** (✉ *300 S. Main St., Moab*).

AUTOMOBILE SERVICE STATIONS
Head to Moab for fuel, oil and tire changes, and auto-repair work.

Contacts American Car Care Center/Chip's Grand Tire (✉ *312 N. Main St., Moab* ☎ *435/259–7909*). **Certified Ford Domestic Repair Service** (✉ *500 S. Main St., Moab* ☎ *435/259–6107*). **Moab Chevron** (✉ *817 S. Main, Moab* ☎ *435/259–0500*).

EMERGENCIES
Call 911 or contact a park ranger (on hand at the visitor center during operating hours). There are no first-aid stations in the park; report to the visitor center for assistance. The closest hospital is in Moab.

LOST AND FOUND
For lost-and-found, stop by the park's visitor center.

PERMITS
Permits are required for backcountry camping and for hiking without a park ranger in the Fiery Furnace. You can purchase a Fiery Furnace permit ($2 per person for adults, $1 for kids 7–12) at the visitor center.

RESTROOMS
You can find public restrooms at the visitor center, Devils Garden Campground, and Balanced Rock picnic area, as well as at the following trailheads: Delicate Arch trailhead, Delicate Arch Viewpoint, Devils Garden, Fiery Furnace, and Windows section. The only flush toilets are at the visitor center and campground; the rest are vault or pit toilets.

SHOPS & GROCERS
There is no place within the park itself to get basic groceries or camping supplies, but several stores in Moab sell groceries and supplies for camping, climbing, and hiking.

Contacts Dave's Corner Market (✉ *401 Mill Creek Dr., Moab* ☎ *435/259–6999*). **Walker Drug Co.** (✉ *290 S. Main St., Moab* ☎ *435/259–5959*).

VISITOR INFORMATION
Contacts Arches National Park (✉ *N. U.S. 191, Moab, UT 84532* ☎ *435/719–2299, 435/719–2200, 435/719–2391 for the hearing-impaired* ⊕ *www.nps.gov/arch*).

Canyonlands National Park

WELCOME TO CANYONLANDS

Colorado River

TOP REASONS TO GO

★ **Solitude:** Take time for reflection in this rarely crowded park.

★ **Radical rapids:** Experience some white-water adventure in Cataract Canyon on the Colorado River.

★ **Native American artifacts:** View rock art and Ancestral Puebloan dwellings in the park.

★ **Last Hold Out for Wilderness:** Walk, raft, or drive through some of this country's wildest, most untouched country.

★ **Bighorn sheep:** Snap a photo of them grazing along the roadway.

1 Island in the Sky. From any of the overlooks here you can see for miles and look down thousands of feet to canyon floors. Chocolate-brown canyons are capped by white rock, and deep-red monuments rise nearby.

2 Needles. Pink, orange, and red rock is layered with white rock and stands in spires and pinnacles around grassy meadows. Extravagantly red mesas and buttes interrupt the horizon, as in a picture postcard of the Old West.

3 The Maze. Only the most-adventurous visitors walk in the footsteps of Butch Cassidy in this area, for it is accessible only by four-wheel-drive vehicles.

4 Rivers. The park's waterways are as untamed and undammed as when John Wesley Powell explored them in the mid-1800s.

5 Horseshoe Canyon. This unit, separate from the main park, is just northwest of the Glen Canyon Recreation Area. The famous rock art panel "Great Gallery" is the reward at the end of a long hike.

GETTING ORIENTED

In southeastern Utah, Canyonlands National Park is divided into three distinct land districts and the river district, so it can be a little daunting to visit. Unless you have several days, you will need to choose between the Island in the Sky or the Needles districts.

Chesler Park

KEY	
🏠	Ranger Station
△	Campground
🎋	Picnic Area
🍴	Restaurant
🏨	Lodge
🚶	Trailhead
🚻	Restrooms
⚜	Scenic Viewpoint
⋯⋯	Walking/Hiking Trails
⋯⋯	Bicycle Path

Great Gallery

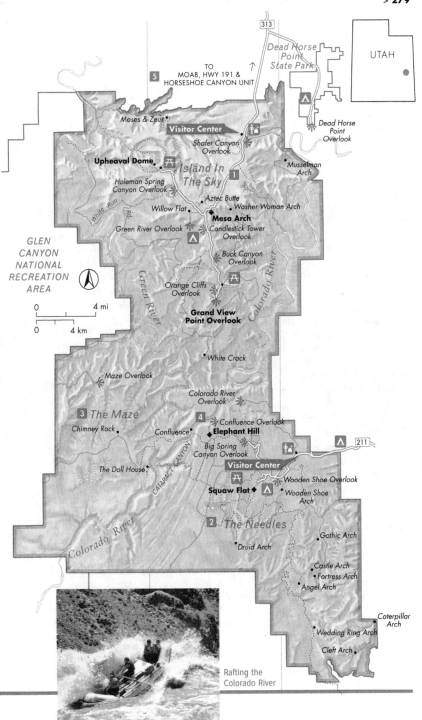

UTAH

313

Dead Horse
Point
State Park

TO
MOAB, HWY 191 &
HORSESHOE CANYON UNIT

5

Dead Horse
Point
Overlook

Moses & Zeus

Visitor Center

Shafer Canyon
Overlook

*Island
In
The Sky*

Musselman
Arch

Upheaval Dome

1

Holeman Spring
Canyon Overlook

Aztec Butte

White Rim Rd.

Willow Flat

Washer Woman Arch

Mesa Arch

Green River Overlook

Candlestick Tower
Overlook

Buck Canyon
Overlook

*GLEN
CANYON
NATIONAL
RECREATION
AREA*

Green River

Colorado River

Orange Cliffs
Overlook

**Grand View
Point Overlook**

0   4 mi

0   4 km

• White Crack

Maze Overlook

Colorado River
Overlook

3 *The Maze*

4

Confluence Overlook

Chimney Rock •

Confluence •

Elephant Hill

Big Spring
Canyon Overlook

211

10

CATARACT CANYON

The Doll House •

Visitor Center

Wooden Shoe Overlook

Colorado River

Squaw Flat ◆

Wooden Shoe
Arch

2 *The Needles*

Gothic Arch

• Druid Arch

Castle Arch
• Fortress Arch

Angel Arch

Caterpillar
Arch

Wedding Ring Arch •

Cleft Arch

Rafting the
Colorado River

CANYONLANDS PLANNER

When to Go

The busiest times of year for the park are spring and fall. Compared to most national parks, Canyonlands is seldom crowded, but in spring backpackers and four-wheelers populate the trails and roads. During Easter week, some of the four-wheel-drive trails in the park are used for Jeep Safari, an annual event drawing some 15,000 visitors to town.

The crowds thin out in summer as the thermostat approaches 100°F in July and then soars beyond that for about four weeks. It's a great time to get out on the Green or Colorado rivers as they wind through Canyonlands. October can be rainy season, but the region only receives an annual rainfall of 8 inches.

The well-kept secret is that winter is the best time in the park. Crowds are gone, roads are good, and snowcapped mountains stand in the background. Winter at Canyonlands is one of nature's most memorable shows, with red rock dusted white and low-floating clouds partially obscuring canyons and towers.

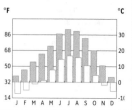

Flora & Fauna

Your chances of seeing wildlife are fairly good in Canyonlands because there are fewer people and less traffic to scare the animals away. Cool mornings and evenings are the best time to spot them, especially during the summer when the heat keeps them in cool, shady areas. Mule deer are nearly always seen along the roadway as you enter the Needles District, and you'll no doubt see jackrabbits and small rodents darting across the roadway. Approximately 250 bighorns populate the park in the Island in the Sky District, and the Maze shelters about 100 more. If you happen upon one of these regal animals, do not approach it even if it is alone, as bighorn sheep are skittish by nature and easily stressed. Also, report your sighting to a ranger.

Getting There & Around

Off U.S. 191, Canyonlands' Island in the Sky is 21 mi from Arches National Park and 32 mi from Moab on Route 313 west of U.S. 191; the Needles District is reached via Route 211, west of U.S. 191. The nearest airport is Grand County Airport, also know as Canyonlands Field (☎435/259–7419), 18 mi north of Moab. Flights are very limited. The nearest train "station" is a solitary Amtrak stop in Green River, about 60 mi northwest of Moab. For train inquiries, call Amtrak (☎800/872–7245).

Before starting a journey to any of Canyonlands' three districts, make sure your gas tank is topped off, as there are no services inside the large park. Island in the Sky is 32 mi from Moab, Needles District is 80 mi from Moab, and the Maze is more than 100 mi from Moab. The Island in the Sky road from the district entrance to Grand View Point is 12 mi, with one 5-mi spur to Upheaval Dome. The Needles scenic drive is 10 mi with two spurs about 3 mi each. Roads in the Maze, suitable only for rugged, high-clearance, four-wheel-drive vehicles, wind for hundreds of miles through the canyons. Within the parks, safety and courtesy mandate that you always park only in designated pullouts or parking areas.

By Janet
Buckingham

WHILE ARCHES LOOKS LIKE MARS, Canyonlands resembles the moon. Mushroomlike rock formations rise randomly out of the ground, twisting into all manner of shapes: spires, pinnacles, buttes, and mesas. It's a desert landscape, but it's not devoid of water or color. The Green and Colorado rivers traverse the canyons, where the rich browns, verdant greens, and fresh yellows of the pinyon-juniper forests complement the deep reds, baby pinks, bright oranges, and milky whites of the rocks. The park's dirt roads appeal to mountain bikers, and the rising rapids of Cataract Canyon challenge rafters.

SCENIC DRIVES

Island in the Sky Park Road. This 12-mi long road connects to a 5-mi side road to the Upheaval Dome area. You can enjoy many of the park's vistas by stopping at the overlooks—get out of your car for the best views. Once you get to the park, allow about two hours to explore.

Needles District Park Road. You'll feel certain that you've driven into a picture postcard as you roll along the park road in the Needles District. Red mesas and buttes rise against the horizon, blue mountain ranges interrupt the rangelands, and the colorful red and white needles stand like soldiers on the far side of grassy meadows. The drive, about 10 mi one way, takes about half an hour.

WHAT TO SEE

HISTORIC SITES

★ ☺ **Cowboy Line Camp.** The remnants here include furniture and camp gear. The artifacts are found on the **Cave Springs Trail,** which is short but requires some ladder climbing and sloping slickrock navigating. ⊠ *On Cave Springs Rd., 2 ³/₁₀ mi from the park entrance, Needles.*

Shafer Trail. This road was probably first established by ancient Native Americans, but in the early 1900s ranchers used it to drive cattle into the canyon. Originally narrow and rugged, it was upgraded during the uranium boom, when miners hauled ore by truck from the canyon floor. You can see the road's winding route down canyon walls from Shafer Canyon Overlook. Today, Shafer Trail is used by daring fourwheelers and energetic mountain bikers. It descends 1,400 feet to the White Rim and another 700 feet to the Colorado River. ⊠ *On the main road, less than 1 mi from the park entrance, Island in the Sky.*

SCENIC STOPS

★ **Grand View Point.** At the end of the main road of Island in the Sky, don't miss this 360-degree view that extends all the way to the San Juan Mountains in Colorado on a clear day. ⊠ *On the main road, 12 mi from the park entrance, Island in the Sky.*

★ **Mesa Arch.** Even though it can be crowded, you simply can't visit Island in the Sky without taking the quick ½-mi walk to Mesa Arch. The arch is above a cliff that drops nearly 1,000 feet to the canyon bottom. Views through Washerwoman Arch and surrounding buttes, spires,

10

and canyons make this a favorite photo opportunity. ✉ *On the main road, 6 mi from the park entrance, Island in the Sky.*

Pothole Point Trail. This is an especially good stop after a rainstorm, which fills the potholes with water. Stop to study the communities of tiny creatures, including fairy shrimp, that thrive in the slickrock hollows. Along the way, discover dramatic views of the Needles and Six Shooter Peak, too. The easy ⁶⁄₁₀-mi round-trip walk takes about 45 minutes. There's no shade, so wear a hat. ✉ *On the main road, about 9 mi from the park entrance, Needles.*

> **MEET ME AT SUNSET**
>
> Sunset is one of the picture-perfect times in Canyonlands, as the slanting sun shines over the vast network of canyons that stretch out below Island in the Sky. A moonlight drive to Grand View Point can also give you lasting memories as the moon drenches the white sandstone in the light. Likewise, late afternoon color in the spires and towers at the Needles District is a humbling, awe-inspiring scene.

Upheaval Dome. This colorful, mysterious crater is one of the many wonders of Island in the Sky. Some geologists believe it to be an eroded salt dome, but others have theorized that it is an eroded meteorite-impact dome. To see it, you'll have to walk a short distance to the overlook. ✉ *On Upheaval Dome Rd., 11 mi from the park entrance, Island in the Sky.*

VISITOR CENTERS

Hans Flat Ranger Station. This remote spot is nothing more than a stopping point for permits, books, and maps before you strike out into the Maze District of Canyonlands. To get here, you must drive 46 mi on a dirt road that is sometimes impassable to two-wheel-drive vehicles. There's a pit toilet, but no water, food, or services of any kind. ✉ *46 mi east of Rte. 24; 21 mi south and east of the Y-junction and Horseshoe Canyon kiosk on the dirt road, Maze* ☎ *435/259–2652* ⊙ *Daily 8–4:30.*

Island in the Sky Visitor Center. Stop and watch the orientation film and then browse the bookstore for information about the Canyonlands region. Exhibits help explain animal adaptations as well as some of the history of the park. ✉ *Past the park entrance on the main park road, Island in the Sky* ☎ *435/259–4712* ⊙ *Daily 9–4:30 with expanded hrs Mar.–Oct.*

Needles District Visitor Center. This gorgeous building that blends into the landscape is worth seeing, even if you don't need the books, trail maps, or other information available inside. ✉ *Less than 1 mi from the park entrance on the main park road, Needles* ☎ *435/259–4711* ⊙ *Daily 9–4:30 with expanded hrs Mar.–Oct.*

SPORTS & THE OUTDOORS

Canyonlands is one of the world's best destinations for adrenaline junkies. You can rock climb, mountain bike treacherous terrain, tackle world-class white-water rapids, and make your 4x4 crawl over steep cliffs along precipitous drops. Compared to other national parks, Canyonlands allows you to enjoy an amazing amount of solitude while having the adventure of a lifetime.

AIR TOURS

OUTFITTERS & EXPEDITIONS **Slickrock Air Guides.** This company's regional tours give you an eagle's-eye view of the park, and you'll walk away with new respect and understanding of the word "wilderness." ⊠ *Canyonlands Air Field (also known as Grand County Airport), N. U.S. 191, near Moab* ☎ *435/259–6216 or 866/259–1626* ⊕ *www.slickrockairguides.com.*

BICYCLING

White Rim Road. Mountain bikers all over the world like to brag that they've ridden this 112-mi road around Island in the Sky. The trail's fame is well-deserved: it traverses steep roads, broken rock, and ledges as well as long stretches that wind through the canyons and look down onto others. There's always a good chance you'll see bighorn sheep here, too. Permits are not required for day use, but if you're biking White Rim without an outfitter you'll need careful planning and backcountry reservations (make them as far in advance as possible through the reservation office, ☎ 435/259–4351). Information about permits can be found at www.nps.gov/cany. There's no water on this route. White Rim Road starts at the end of Shafer Trail near Musselman Arch. ⊹ *Off the main park road about 1 mi from the entrance, then about 11 mi on Shafer Trail; or off Potash Rd. (Rte. 279) at the Jug Handle Arch turnoff about 18 mi from U.S. 191, then about 5 mi on Shafer Trail, Island in the Sky.*

See Four-Wheeling in this chapter for more routes. For bike outfitters, see Outfitters & Expeditions box in Chapter 11.

BIRD-WATCHING

Without getting on the Colorado River, you can see a variety of wrens, including the Rock wren, Canyon wren, and Bewick's wren. Blue-gray gnatchatchers are fairly common in the summer, along with the Solitary vireo and Black-throated gray warbler and Virginia's warbler. You'll have the most fun spotting the American kestrel or peregrine falcon and watching golden and bald eagles soar overhead. The common raven is everywhere you look, as are the common magpie and a variety of jays. Once on the Colorado River, you'll stand a chance of glimpsing the elusive White-faced ibis, and you'll almost certainly see a great blue heron swooping along the water or standing regally on a sandbar.

BOATING & RIVER EXPEDITIONS

Seeing Canyonlands National Park from the river is a great and rare pleasure. Long stretches of calm water on the Green River are perfect for lazy canoe trips. In Labyrinth Canyon, north of the park boundary, and in Stillwater Canyon, in the Island in the Sky District, the river is quiet and calm and there's plenty of shoreside camping. The Island in the Sky leg of the Colorado River, from Moab to its confluence with the Green River and downstream a few more miles to Spanish Bottom, is ideal for both canoeing and for rides with an outfitter in a large, stable jet boat. If you want to take a self-guided flat-water float trip in the park you must obtain a $20 permit, which you have to request by mail or fax. Make your upstream travel arrangements with a shuttle company before you request a permit. For permits, contact the reservation office at park headquarters (☎435/259–4351).

Below Spanish Bottom, about 64 mi downstream from Moab, 49 mi from the Potash Road ramp, and 4 mi south of the confluence, the Colorado churns into the first rapids of legendary Cataract Canyon. Home of some of the best white water in the United States, this piece of river between the Maze and the Needles District rivals the Grand Canyon stretch of the Colorado River for adventure. During spring melt-off these rapids can rise to staggering heights and deliver heart-stopping excitement. The canyon cuts through the very heart of Canyonlands, where you can see this amazing wilderness area in its most pristine form. The water calms down a bit in summer but still offers enough thrills for most people. Outfitters will take you for the ride of your life in this wild canyon, where the river drops more steeply than anywhere else on the Colorado River (in ¾ mi, the river drops 39 feet). You can join an expedition lasting anywhere from one to six days, or you can purchase a $30 permit for a self-guided trip from park headquarters.

For boating outfitters and rental companies, see Outfitters & Expeditions box in Chapter 11.

FOUR-WHEELING
Nearly 200 mi of challenging backcountry roads lead to campsites, trailheads, and natural and cultural features in Canyonlands. All of the roads require high-clearance, four-wheel-drive vehicles, and many are inappropriate for inexperienced drivers. Especially before you tackle the Maze, be sure that your four-wheel-drive skills are well honed and that you are capable of making basic road and vehicle repairs. Carry at least one full-size spare tire, extra gas, extra water, a shovel, a high-lift jack, and—October through April—chains for all four tires. Double-check to see that your vehicle is in top-notch condition, for you definitely don't want to break down in the interior of the park: towing expenses can exceed $1,000. For overnight four-wheeling trips you must purchase a $30 permit, which you can reserve in advance by contacting the Backcountry Reservations Office (☎435/259–4351). Cyclists share all roads, so be aware and cautious of their presence. Vehicular traffic traveling uphill has the right-of-way. It's best to check at the visitor center for current road conditions before taking off into the backcountry. You must carry a washable, reusable toilet with you in the Maze district and carry out all waste. *For guided 4X4 trips, ⇨ see Outfitters & Expeditions box in Chapter 11.*

★ **Elephant Hill.** The Needles route is so difficult—steep grades, loose rock, and stair-step drops—that many people get out and walk. In fact you can walk it faster than you can drive it. From Elephant Hill trailhead to Devil's Kitchen it's 3 ½ mi; from the trailhead to the Confluence Overlook, it's a 16-mi round-trip and requires at least eight hours. ⊠ *Off the main park road, 7 mi from the park entrance, Needles.*

Flint Trail. This remote, rugged road is the most used road in the Maze District, but don't let that fool you into thinking it's smooth sailing. It's very technical with 2 mi of switchbacks that drop down the side of a cliff face. You reach Flint Trail from the Hans Flat Ranger Station, which is 46 mi from the closest paved road (Rte. 24 off I–70). From Hans Flat to the end of the road at the Doll House it's 41 mi, a drive that takes about seven hours one way. From Hans Flat to the Maze Overlook it's 34 mi. The Maze is not generally a destination for a day trip, so you'll have to purchase an overnight backcountry permit for $30. ⊠ *Hans Flat Ranger Station (46 mi east of Rte. 24, Maze).*

★ **White Rim Road.** Winding around and below the Island in the Sky mesa top, the dramatic 112-mi White Rim Road offers a once-in-a-lifetime driving experience. As you tackle Murphy's Hogback, Hardscrabble Hill, and more formidable obstacles, you will get some fantastic views of the park. A trip around the loop takes two to three days and you must make reservations almost a year in advance for an overnight campsite—unless you manage to snap up a no-show or cancellation. For reservation information call the Backcountry Reservation Office (☎ 435/259–4351). White Rim Road starts at the end of Shafer Trail near Musselman Arch. ⊹ *Off the main park road about 1 mi from the entrance, then about 11 mi on Shafer Trail; or off Potash Rd. (Rte. 279) at the Jug Handle Arch turnoff about 18 mi from U.S. 191, then about 5 mi on Shafer Trail; Island in the Sky.*

HIKING

Canyonlands National Park is a good place to saturate yourself in the intoxicating colors, smells, and textures of the desert. Many of the trails are long, rolling routes over slickrock and sand in landscapes dotted with juniper, pinyon, and sagebrush. Interconnecting trails in the Needles District provide excellent opportunities for weeklong backpacking excursions. The Maze trails are primarily accessed via four-wheel-drive vehicle. In the separate Horseshoe Canyon area, Horseshoe Canyon Trail takes a considerable amount of effort to reach, as it is more than 100 mi from Moab, 32 mi of which are a bumpy, and often sandy, dirt road.

10

EASY **Aztec Butte Trail.** Chances are good you'll enjoy this hike in solitude. It begins level, then climbs up a steep slope of slickrock. The highlight of the 2-mi round-trip hike is the chance to see Ancestral Puebloan granaries. ⊠ *On Upheaval Dome Rd., about 6 mi from the park entrance, Island in the Sky.*

Grand View Point Trail. If you're looking for a level walk with some of the grandest views in the world, stop at Grand View Point and wander the 2-mi trail along the cliff edge. Most people just stop at the overlook and drive on, so the trail is not as crowded as you might think. On a clear day you can see up to 100 mi to the Maze and Needles districts of the park, the confluence of the Green and Colorado rivers, and each of Utah's major laccolithic mountain ranges: the Henrys, Abajos, and La Sals. ⊠ *On the main park road, 12 mi from the park entrance, Island in the Sky.*

Fodor'sChoice ★ **Mesa Arch Trail.** By far the most popular trail in the park, this ⅔-mi loop acquaints you with desert plants and terrain. The highlight of the hike is a natural arch window perched over an 800-foot drop below. The vistas of the rest of the park are nothing short of stunning. ⊠ *6 mi from the Island in the Sky Visitor Center.*

Slickrock Trail. If you're on this trail in summer, make sure you're wearing a hat, because you won't find any shade along the 2⅖-mi round-trip trek across slickrock. This is one of the few front-country sites where you might see bighorn sheep. ⊠ *On the main park road, about 10 mi from the park entrance, Needles.*

Whale Rock Trail. If you've been hankering to walk across some of that pavement-smooth stuff they call slickrock, the hike to Whale Rock will make your feet happy. This 1-mi round-trip adventure, complete with handrails to help you make the tough 100-foot climb, takes you to the very top of the whale's back. Once you get there, you are rewarded with great views of Upheaval Dome and Trail Canyon. ⊠ *On Upheaval Dome Rd., 11 mi from the park entrance, Island in the Sky.*

MODERATE ★ ☾ **Cave Spring Trail.** One of the best, most diverse trails in the park takes you past a historic cowboy camp, prehistoric Native American petroglyphs, and great views along the way. About half of the trail is in shade, as it meanders under overhangs. Slanted, bumpy slickrock make this hike more difficult than others, and two ladders make the ⅗-mi round-trip walk even more of an adventure. Allow about 45 minutes. ⊠ *Off the main park road on Cave Springs Rd., 2 3/10 mi from the park entrance, Needles.*

DIFFICULT **Chesler Park Loop.** Chesler Park is a grassy meadow dotted with spires and enclosed by a circular wall of colorful "needles." One of Canyonlands' more popular trails leads through the area to the famous Joint Trail. The trail is 6 mi round-trip to the viewpoint. ⊠ *Elephant Hill trailhead, off the main park road, about 7 mi from the park entrance, Needles.*

★ **Horseshoe Canyon Trail.** You arrive at this detached unit of Canyonlands National Park via a washboarded, two-wheel-drive dirt road. Park at the lip of the canyon and hike 6½ mi round-trip to the Great Gallery, considered by some to be the most significant rock-art panel in North America. Ghostly life-size figures in the Barrier Canyon style populate the amazing panel. The hike is moderately strenuous, with a 750-foot descent. Allow at least six hours for the trip and take a gallon of water per person. There's no camping allowed in the canyon, although you can camp on top near the parking lot. ⊠ *32 mi east of Rte. 24, Maze.*

★ **Joint Trail.** Part of the Chesler Park Loop, this well-loved trail follows a series of deep, narrow fractures in the rock. A shady spot in summer, it will give you good views of the Needles formations for which

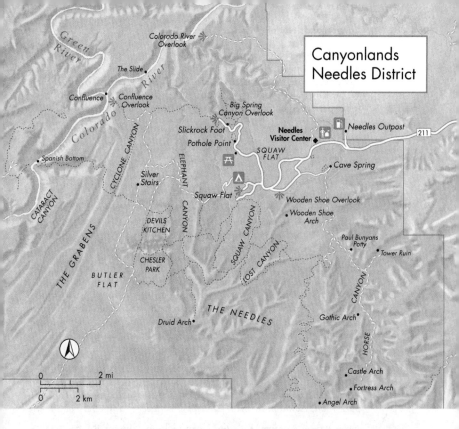

Canyonlands Needles District

Colorado River Overlook

Green River

The Slide

Colorado River

Confluence

Confluence Overlook

Spanish Bottom

CATARACT CANYON

CYCLONE CANYON

Silver Stairs

ELEPHANT CANYON

Big Spring Canyon Overlook

Slickrock Foot

Pothole Point

SQUAW FLAT

Needles Visitor Center

Needles Outpost

211

Cave Spring

Squaw Flat

DEVILS KITCHEN

CHESLER PARK

BUTLER FLAT

THE GRABENS

Wooden Shoe Overlook

Wooden Shoe Arch

SQUAW CANYON

LOST CANYON

Paul Bunyans Potty

Tower Ruin

CANYON

THE NEEDLES

Druid Arch

Gothic Arch

HORSE

Castle Arch

Fortress Arch

Angel Arch

0   2 mi

0   2 km

the district is named. The loop travels briefly along a four-wheel-drive road and is 11 mi round-trip; allow at least five hours to complete the hike. ⊠ *Elephant Hill trailhead, off the main park road, 7 mi from the park entrance, Needles.*

Syncline Loop Trail. Are you up for a long, full day of hiking? Try this 8-mi trail that circles Upheaval Dome. You not only get great views of the dome, you actually make a complete loop around its base. Stretches of the trail are rocky, rugged, and steep. ⊠ *On Upheaval Dome Rd., 11 mi from the park entrance, Island in the Sky.*

★ **Upheaval Dome Trail.** It's worth the steep hike to see this formation, which is either an eroded salt dome or a meteorite crash site. You reach the main overlook after just ½ mi, but you can double your pleasure by going on to a second overlook for a better view. The trail becomes steep and rough after the first overlook. Round-trip to the second overlook is 2 mi. ⊠ *On Upheaval Dome Rd., 11 mi from the park entrance, Island in the Sky.*

ROCK CLIMBING

Canyonlands and many of the surrounding areas draw climbers from all over the world. Permits are not required, but because of the sensitive archaeological nature of the park, it's imperative that you stop at the

10

visitor center to pick up regulations pertaining to the park's cultural resources. Popular climbing routes include Moses and Zeus towers in Taylor Canyon, and Monster Tower and Washerwoman Tower on the White Rim Road. Like most routes in Canyonlands, these climbs are for experienced climbers only.

For climbing outfitters, see Outfitters & Expeditions box in Chapter 11.

EDUCATIONAL OFFERINGS

PROGRAMS & TOURS

For more information on current schedules and locations of park programs, contact the visitor centers (☏435/259–4712 Island in the Sky, ☏435/259–4711 Needles) or check the bulletin boards throughout the park. Note that programs change periodically and may sometimes be cancelled because of limited staffing.

Campfire Program. You can enrich your visit to Canyonlands by attending a campfire program. Topics include wildlife, cultural and natural history of the park, Native American legends, cowboy history, and geology. Check with the visitor centers or on park bulletin boards for more information. ⊠ *Willow Flat Campground, Island in the Sky; Squaw Flat Campground, Needles* ☑*Free* ☉*½ hr after sunset.*

Grand View Point Overlook Talk. By attending this session you can learn something about the geology that created Canyonlands or the rich mining history of the region. Check at the visitor centers for times and locations. ⊠ *Grand View Point, 12 mi from the park entrance on the main park road, Island in the Sky* ☑*$10 per vehicle* ☉*Apr.–Oct., daily.*

Junior Ranger Program. Kids 6–12 can pick up a Junior Ranger booklet at the visitor centers. It's full of activities, word games, drawings, and educational material about the park and the wildlife. To earn the Junior Ranger badge, they must complete the booklet, attend a ranger program, or watch the park slide program, and gather a bag of litter or bring 20 aluminum cans to be recycled. ☏*435/259–4712 Island in the Sky, 435/259–4711 Needles* ☑*Free.*

NEARBY TOWNS

Moab (⇨ Chapter 11) is the major gateway to both Arches and Canyonlands national parks, with the most outfitters, shops, and lodging options of the area. A handful of communities, which are much smaller and with fewer amenities, are scattered around the Needles and Island in the Sky districts along U.S. 191.

Roughly 55 mi south of Moab is **Monticello** (⇨ Chapter 11). Convenient to the Needles District, it lies at an elevation of 7,000 feet, making it a cool summer refuge from the desert heat. In winter, it gets downright cold and sees deep snow; the Abajo Mountains, whose highest point is 11,360 feet, rise to the west of town. Monticello motels serve the steady stream of tourists who venture south of Moab, but the town offers few dining or shopping opportunities. **Blanding** (⇨ Chapter 11), 21 mi south of Monticello, prides itself on old-fashioned conservative values. By popular vote there's a ban on the sale of liquor, beer, and wine, so the town has no state liquor store and its restaurants do not serve alcoholic beverages. Blanding is a good resting point if you're traveling south from Canyonlands to Natural Bridges Natural Monument, Grand Gulch, Lake Powell, or the Navajo Nation. About 25 mi south of Blanding, tiny **Bluff** (⇨ Chapter 11) is doing its best to stay that way. It's a great place to stop if you aren't looking for many amenities but value beautiful scenery, silence, and starry nights. Bluff is the most common starting point for trips on the San Juan River, which serves as the northern boundary for the Navajo Reservation; it's also a wonderful place to overnight if you're planning a visit to Hovenweep National Monument, about 30 mi away.

WHERE TO EAT

There are no dining facilities in the park itself. Needles Outpost, just outside the entrance to the park's Needles District, offers a snack bar with hamburgers and a small grocery store for picnicking necessities. Restaurants in Monticello and Blanding offer simple meals, and most do not serve alcohol. Your best bet for a variety of dining experiences, from microbreweries to fine dining or good home cooking, is in Moab. Moab delis and bakeries also can prepare fresh-made sandwiches to go. *For dining options outside the park, see Chapter 11.*

PICNIC AREAS   **Grand View Point.** Stopping here for a picnic lunch might be one of your more memorable vacation events. It's a gorgeous spot in which to recharge your energy and stretch your legs. There are picnic tables, grills, restrooms, and a little shade, if you sit near a juniper or pinyon. ✉ *12 mi from park entrance on the main road, Island in the Sky.*

Needles District Picnic Area. The most convenient picnic spot in the Needles District is a sunny location right near the roadway. There is one picnic table, but there are no grills, restrooms, water, or other amenities. ✉ *About 5 mi from the park visitor center, Needles.*

Upheaval Dome. Charming is a word that comes to mind to describe this picnic area nestled among the pinyon and juniper trees at the trailhead. There are no real vistas here, but the location is convenient to the Syncline Loop and Upheaval Dome trails. Amenities consist of picnic tables, grills, and restrooms without running water. ✉ *11 mi from the park entrance on Upheaval Dome Rd., Island in the Sky.*

10

WHERE TO STAY

There is no lodging inside Canyonlands. The towns of Monticello and Blanding offer basic motels, both family owned and national chains. Bluff also has motels and B&Bs and offers a quiet place to stay. A wide range of lodgings is available in Moab. *For lodging recommendations outside the park, see Chapter 11.*

CAMPGROUNDS & RV PARKS

Canyonlands campgrounds are some of the most beautiful in the National Park System. At the Needles District, campers will enjoy fairly private campsites tucked against red rock walls and dotted with pinyon and juniper trees. At Island in the Sky, starry nights and spectacular vistas make the small campground an intimate treasure. Hookups are not available in either of the park's campgrounds; however, the sites are long enough to accommodate units up to 28 feet long. There are no RV dump stations in the park. Bureau of Land Management (BLM) campgrounds between Moab and Monticello take a bit of a drive to get to but the solitude and privacy may be worth it. There are fewer opportunities for camping once you are in Monticello and Blanding. The best place to camp near Bluff is Sand Island Campground, 2 mi south of town. There are no amenities, but its location right on the San Juan River makes it something quite special.

See also Chapter 11 for information about campgrounds outside the park.

⚠ **Needles Outpost.** You may need to stop here for gas, supplies, or an icy drink and good meal after hiking, and you can also camp here. This privately run campground isn't as pretty or private as the others in and near Needles, but a chat with the owners will be a guaranteed hoot. ⊠*Rte. 211 about 1½ mi inside the park entrance, Needles* ☎*435/979–4007* ⏞*23 sites* ⚑*Flush toilets, dump station, drinking water, showers, fire grates, food service, service station* ▭*AE, D, MC, V* ☾*Mid-Mar.–Oct.*

★ ⚠ **Squaw Flat Campground.** Squaw Flat is one of the best campgrounds in the National Park System. The sites are spread out in two different areas, giving each site almost unparalleled privacy. Each site has a rock wall at its back, and shade trees. The sites are filled on a first-come, first-served basis. ⊠*About 5 mi from the park entrance off the main road, Needles* ☎*435/259–7164* ⏞*25 sites* ⚑*Flush toilets, drinking water, fire pits, picnic tables* ▭*No credit cards.*

⚠ **Willow Flat Campground.** From this little campground on a mesa top, you can walk to spectacular views of the Green River. Most sites have a bit of shade from juniper trees. To get to Willow Flat you have to travel down a rough, washboarded road with tight and tricky turns. Since the drive is so difficult and only two sites are really suitable for RVs, RVers might prefer another campground. It is filled on a first-come, first-served basis only. ⊠*About 9 mi from the park entrance off the main park road, Island in the Sky* ☎*435/259–4712* ⏞*12 sites* ⚑*Pit toilets, drinking water, fire pits, picnic tables* ▭*No credit cards.*

CANYONLANDS ESSENTIALS

ACCESSIBILITY

There are currently no trails in Canyonlands that are accessible to people in wheelchairs, but Grand View Point and Buck Canyon Overlook at Island in the Sky are wheelchair accessible. The visitor centers at the Island in the Sky and Needles districts are also accessible, and the park's pit toilets are accessible with some assistance.

ADMISSION FEES

Admission is $10 per vehicle and $5 per person on foot, motorcycle, or bicycle, good for seven days. Your Canyonlands pass is good for all the park's districts. There's no entrance fee to the Maze District of Canyonlands. A $25 local park pass grants you admission to both Arches and Canyonlands for one year.

ADMISSION HOURS

Canyonlands National Park is open 24 hours a day, seven days a week, year-round. It is in the Mountain time zone.

ATMS/BANKS

The park has no ATM.

Contacts **Wells Fargo Bank** (✉ *4 N. Main St., Moab* ✉ *16 S. Main St., Monticello*). **Zions Bank** (✉ *300 S. Main St., Moab*).

AUTOMOBILE SERVICE STATIONS

Contacts **Car Care Center** (✉ *217 N. Main St., Monticello* ☎ *435/678–3705*)does repairs.**Out West Food & Fuel** (✉ *17 N. Main St., Monticello* ☎ *435/587–2555*)has fuel only, no repairs.

EMERGENCIES

In the event of a fire or a medical emergency, dial 911 or contact a park ranger. There are no first-aid stations in the park; report to the visitor center for assistance. The closest hospitals are in Moab and Monticello. To reach law enforcement, dial 911 or contact a park ranger (rangers are on hand at the visitor center during operating hours).

PERMITS

You need a permit for overnight backpacking, four-wheel-drive camping, mountain-bike camping, four-wheel-drive day use in Horse and Lavender canyons (Needles District), and river trips. You can get information on the Canyonlands reservation and permit system by visiting the park's Web site at ⊕*www.nps.gov/cany* or by calling the reservations office at ☎435/259–4351.

PUBLIC TELEPHONES

You can find public telephones at the park's visitor centers, as well as at Hans Flat Ranger Station in the Maze District. Cell-phone reception may be available in some parts of the park, but not reliably so.

RESTROOMS

In Island in the Sky, public restrooms are at the visitor center, Willow Flat Campground, Grand View Point, and Upheaval Dome trailhead. In the Needles District, you can find facilities at the visitor center, Squaw Flat Campground, and Big Spring Canyon Overlook Trail. In the Maze, the Hans Flat Ranger Station has restrooms, and at Horseshoe Canyon you can find relief at the trailhead. The only flush toilet is at the Needles Visitor Center; the rest are vault toilets.

SHOPS & GROCERS

Needles Outpost, just outside the park boundary, is the place to get basic groceries and camping supplies—but it won't likely have everything you need.

Contacts **Blue Mountain Foods** (⊠ *64 W. Central, Monticello* ☎ *435/587–2451*). **Clark's Market** (⊠ *820 S. Main, Blanding* ☎ *435/678–2721*). **Needles Outpost** (⊠ *Rte. 211 about 1½ mi inside the park entrance, Needles* ☎ *435/979–4007*).

VISITOR INFORMATION

Contacts **Canyonlands National Park** (⊠ *2282 W. Resource Blvd., Moab, UT 84532* ☎ *435/719–2313, 435/259–4351 Backcountry Reservation Office* ⊕ *www.nps.gov/cany*).

Moab & Southeastern Utah

WORD OF MOUTH

"I would not go out of my way for Monument Valley. The views are spectacular from afar. It's not a national park and doesn't have that solitude and wilderness feel. I didn't think it was worth the time to actually drive around each monument on a dusty, uninteresting road. Lake Powell is a marvel."

—travelottie

"I'd spend 3 nights in Moab—lots to see and do. Jeep trips, float trips, petroglyphs, Arches, Canyonlands, Dead Horse . . . Don't miss Moab."

—sharondi

By Janet
Buckingham

THE FIRST THING TRAVELERS TO southeastern Utah notice is the color. Red, orange, purple, pink, creamy ivory, deep chocolate, and even shades of turquoise paint the landscape. Rocks jut and tilt first one way, then another. There's no flat canvas of color in this country, and near-vertical walls stand in the way of easy route-finding. Deep canyons, carved by wild Western rivers, crisscross the area. Rocks teeter on slim columns or burst like mushrooms from the ground. Snowcapped mountains stand in the distant horizon no matter which direction you look. The sky is more often than not blue in a region that receives only about eight inches of rain a year. When thunderstorms do build, the sky turns a dramatic gunmetal gray, bringing deep orange cliffs into sharp relief.

Embroidered through the region is evidence of the people who came before modern-day rock climbers and Mormons. Rock art as old as 4,000 years is etched or painted on canyon walls. The most familiar of these ancient dwellers are the Ancestral Puebloans, popularly known as Anasazi, who occupied the area between 700 and 2,000 years ago.

In modern-day southeastern Utah, Moab has become one of the state's liveliest small towns and the gateway to Arches and Canyonlands national parks. Surrounding the town, the area's unique and colorful geology calls out to mountain bikers, who love to ride over the humps of slickrock that act like natural highways in the wilderness. Thousands more take four-wheel-drive vehicles into the backcountry to drive the challenging network of roads left from mining days. Still others flock to the shores of the Colorado River, where they set out in rafts to tackle some of the largest white-water rapids in the country. With so many things to do, Moab has become a major tourist destination in the Southwest.

EXPLORING SOUTHEASTERN UTAH

I–70 is the speedway that gets you across Utah, but to dip into southeastern Utah, you'll need to use the main artery, U.S. 191, which runs south toward the Arizona border. The only road that stretches any distance westward across the region is Route 95, which dead ends at Lake Powell. No matter which of the state roads you use to explore the area, you're in for a treat. Here the earth is red, purple, and orange. The Manti–La Sal Mountains rise out of the desert like ships. Mesas, buttes, and pinnacles interrupt the horizon in a most surprising way. But this is some of the most remote country in the United States, so services are sometimes far apart.

ABOUT THE RESTAURANTS

Since most people come to southeastern Utah to play on the rocks and rivers, casual is the *modus operandi* for dining. Whether you select an award-winning Continental restaurant or an outdoor patio grill, you can dress comfortably in shorts or jeans. Although you're in the middle of nowhere, there are some wonderful culinary surprises waiting for you, often with spectacular views as a bonus.

GREAT ITINERARIES

11

IF YOU HAVE 3 DAYS

On a short trip to Southeastern Utah, you'll be happier if you base yourself in **Moab**, a central spot for visiting both of the region's national parks, and it's nice to have a comfortable place to come back to at the end of the day. Start your whirlwind tour with a day in **Arches National Park.** You can drive the park's main road and see a few of the top sights in day; be sure to save time for at least one short hike, but at least stop at the Delicate Arch trailhead to see Wolfe Ranch and then drive to the viewpoint trail for a glimpse of the state icon. On Day 2, pack a picnic lunch and head for **Canyonlands National Park**'s Island in the Sky District. On the way, stop at Dead Horse Point State Park. Make sure you have plenty of film for this day's tour. Make time for a morning hike and drive all the way to the tip of the "island" to Grandview Point. Spend Day 3 on the Colorado River with one of Moab's many river-rafting companies. Select either a playful daily raft trip or a scenic tour via a sturdy jet boat.

IF YOU HAVE 5 DAYS

Spend your first and second days as above in the three-day tour, basing yourself in **Moab**. On the third day choose between a river expedition or traveling south to the Needles District of **Canyonlands National Park**. Upon leaving Canyonlands continue your journey south on U.S. 191 to **Blanding,** where you should make a stop at **Edge of the Cedars State Park** to learn about the ancient Native Americans who inhabited this country. Continue south to Route 95, and stop at **Natural Bridges National Monument.** If you can, make arrangements to spend the night at Fry Canyon Lodge in the heart of Cedar Mesa. On Day 4, continue on Route 95 and cross **Lake Powell** at Hite before continuing north. Camp that night at Goblin Valley State Park near **Hanksville,** or continue on to **Green River** for less rustic accommodation.

ABOUT THE HOTELS

Every type of lodging is available in southeastern Utah, from economy chain motels to B&Bs and high-end–high-adventure resorts. It's important to know when popular events are held, however, as motels and resorts can fill up weeks ahead of time during the busiest periods.

WHAT IT COSTS					
	¢	$	$$	$$$	$$$$
RESTAURANTS	under $8	$8–$12	$13–$18	$19–$25	over $25
HOTELS	under $70	$70–$110	$111–$150	$151–$200	over $200

Restaurant prices are for a main course at dinner, excluding sales tax of 7½%–8½%. Hotel prices are for two people in a standard double room in high season, excluding service charges and 11%–12¼% tax.

MOAB

In 1855, at the behest of Mormon leaders, a group of 41 men set out to establish the Elk Mountain Mission, where the city of Moab now stands. They were driven out by Indian attacks six months later, and permanent settlers did not return to the valley until the late 1870s. At first a ranching and farming community, Moab became a mining center and garnered a rich history as a boom-and-bust town. In the 1950s, Charlie Steen, a down-on-his-luck prospector, wandered into town and made a dramatic uranium strike that changed Moab's character forever. For about a decade after that, Moab was known as a wild, rough-and-tumble town filled with hard-working and hard-playing miners. It was overflowing with people living in tents and other makeshift homes, and barroom brawls were as plentiful as bars. But in 1964, when the demand for uranium decreased, the largest mine closed and thousands of workers lost their jobs. Moab's wealth and freewheeling ways disappeared as the town entered into almost two decades of economic downturn. When Moab began to embrace adventure tourism, a new boom cycle began. Today, the town has become southeastern Utah's outdoor-adventure hub.

EXPLORING MOAB

Moab's diverse population makes it a culturally fascinating place to visit. Environmentalists must learn to coexist with ranchers; prodevelopment factions come up against antigrowth forces; and Mormon church leaders struggle with values issues in a predominantly non-Mormon community.

Whatever their viewpoints, differences between residents fade briefly in early December at the festive **Electric Light Parade** (☎ 435/259–7814). Merchants, clubs, and other organizations build whimsical floats with Christmas lights for a nighttime parade down Main Street.

Each year during the Easter week **Jeep Safari** (☎ 435/259–7625), thousands of four-wheel-drive vehicles descend on Moab to tackle some of the toughest backcountry roads in America.

The **Moab Information Center,** right in the heart of town, is the best place to find information on Arches and Canyonlands national parks as well as other destinations in Utah's southeast. It has a wonderful bookstore operated by Canyonlands Natural History Association. The hours vary, but during the busiest part of the tourist season it's open until at least 7 PM, and sometimes later; in winter the center is open a few hours each morning and afternoon. ⊠ *Center and Main Sts.* ☎ *435/259–8825 or 800/635–6622* ⊕ *www.discovermoab.com* ⊙ *Mar.–Oct., daily 8–7; Nov.–Feb. hrs vary.*

For a small taste of history in the Moab area, stop by the **Museum of Moab.** Ancient and historic Native Americans are remembered in exhibits of sandals, baskets, pottery, and other artifacts. Other displays chronicle the early Spanish expeditions into the area and the history of uranium discovery and exploration. ⊠ *118 E. Center St.* ☎ *435/259–7985* ⊕ *www.moabmuseum.org* ☞ *$3* ⊙ *Apr.–Oct., weekdays 10–6, Sat. noon–6; Nov.–Mar., weekdays 10–3, Sat. noon–5.*

Scott M. Matheson Wetlands Preserve is the best place in the Moab area for bird-watching. This desert oasis is home to hundreds of species, including such treasures as the pied-billed grebe, the cinnamon teal, and the northern flicker. It's also a great place to spot beaver and muskrat playing in the water. A boardwalk winds through the preserve to a viewing shelter. Free nature walks are offered Saturday at 8 AM from March to May and from September to November. To reach the preserve, turn northwest off U.S. 191 at Kane Creek Boulevard and continue northwest approximately 2 mi. ⊠ *934 W. Kane Creek Blvd.* ☎ *435/259–4629* ⊕ *www.nature.org* ☞ *Free* ⊙ *Daily dawn–dusk.*

★ One of the finest state parks in Utah, **Dead Horse Point State Park** overlooks a sweeping oxbow of the Colorado River, some 2,000 feet below, as well as the upside-down landscapes of Canyonlands National Park. Dead Horse Point itself is a small peninsula connected to the main mesa by a narrow neck of land. As the story goes, cowboys used to drive wild horses onto the point and pen them there with a brush fence. Some were accidentally forgotten and left to perish. There's a modern visitor center and museum as well as a 21-site campground with drinking water and an overlook. ⊠ *34 mi west from Moab at end of Rte. 313* ☎ *435/259–2614, 800/322–3770 campground reservations* ⊕ *www.stateparks.utah.gov* ☞ *$10 per vehicle* ⊙ *Daily 8–6.*

Fodor'sChoice The start of one of the most scenic drives in the country is found 2 mi
★ north of Moab off U.S. 191. The **Colorado River Scenic Byway — Route 128** runs along the Colorado River northeast to I–70. First passing through a high-walled corridor, the drive eventually breaks out into Professor Valley, home of the monoliths of Fisher Towers and Castle Rock, which you may recognize from various car commercials. The byway also passes the single-lane Dewey Bridge, which was in use from 1916 to 1986. Near the end of the 44-mi drive is the tiny town of Cisco. ⊠ *Rte. 128, from Moab to Cisco.*

★ If you're interested in Native American rock art, the **Colorado River Scenic Byway — Route 279** is a perfect place to spend a couple of hours. If you start late in the afternoon, the cliffs will be glowing orange as the sun sets. Along the first part of the route you'll see signs reading "Indian Writings." Park only in designated areas to view the petroglyphs on the cliff side of the road. At the 18-mi marker you'll see Jug Handle Arch on the cliff side of the road. Allow about two hours round-trip for this Scenic Byway drive. A few miles beyond this point, the road turns to four-wheel-drive only and takes you into the Island in the Sky District of Canyonlands. Do not continue on this road unless you are in a high-clearance four-wheel-drive vehicle with a full gas tank and plenty of water. ⊠ *Rte. 279, southwest of Moab.*

SPORTS & THE OUTDOORS

Moab's towering cliffs and deep canyons can be intimidating and unreachable without the help of a guide. Fortunately, guide services are abundant in Moab, whether you are interested in a 4X4 expedition into the rugged backcountry, a river-rafting trip, a jet-boat tour on calm water, bicycle tours, rock-art tours, or a scenic air flight. It's always best to make reservations, but don't hesitate to call if you make a last-minute decision to join an expedition. Cancellations or unsold spots sometimes make it possible to jump on a tour with short notice.

FOUR-WHEELING

There are thousands of miles of four-wheel-drive roads in and around Moab. The rugged terrain, with its hair-raising ledges, steep climbs, and smooth expanses of slickrock is the perfect place for drivers to test their mettle. There are abundant trails suitable for all levels of drivers. Seasoned 4X4 drivers might tackle the daunting **Moab Rim, Elephant Hill,** or **Poison Spider Mesa.** Novice drivers will be happier touring **Long Canyon, Hurrah Pass,** or, for those not afraid of precipitous cliff edges, the famous **Shafer Trail.** All of the routes offer spectacular scenery in the vast desert lands surrounding Moab. Expect to pay around $60 for a half-day tour, $100 for a full-day trip; multiday safaris usually start at around $500. Almost all of Moab's river-running companies also offer four-wheeling excursions. *For outfitters, see the Outfitters & Expeditions box.*

GOLF

Moab Golf Course (⊠ *2705 S. East Bench Rd.* ☎ *435/259–6488*)is undoubtedly one of the most beautiful in the world. The 18-hole, par-72 course has lush greens set against a red-rock sandstone backdrop, a lovely visual combination that's been know to distract even the most focused golfer. Greens fees are $39 for 18 holes, including cart rental.

HIKING

Ramble through the desert near a year-round stream or get your muscles pumping with a hike up the side of a steep slickrock slope. Hiking is a sure way to fall in love with the high desert country, and there are plenty of hiking trails for all fitness levels. For a great view of the Moab valley and surrounding red rock country, hike up the steep **Moab Rim Trail.** For something a little less taxing, hike the shady, cool path of **Negro Bill Canyon**, which is off Route 129. At the end of the trail you'll find giant Morning Glory Arch towering over a cool pool created by a natural spring. If you want to take a stroll through the heart of Moab, hop on the **Mill Creek Parkway,** which winds along the creek from one side of town to the other. It's paved and perfect for bicycles, strollers, or joggers. For a taste of slickrock hiking that feels like the backcountry but is easy to access, try the **Corona Arch Trail,** off Route

279. You'll be rewarded with two large arches hidden from view of the highway. The Moab Information Center carries a free hiking trail guide to these and other trails. The many trails in the nearby Arches and Canyonlands national parks can get your boots moving in the right direction as well.

MOUNTAIN BIKING

Moab has earned a well-deserved reputation as the mountain-biking capital of the world, drawing riders of all ages off the pavement and onto rugged four-wheel-drive roads and trails. It's where the whole sport started and the area attracts bikers from all over the globe. One Fodor'sChoice of the many popular routes is the **Slickrock Trail,** a stunning area of steep ★ slickrock dunes a few miles east of Moab. Beginners should master the 2½-mi practice loop before attempting the longer, and very challenging, 10⅓ -mi loop. More moderate rides can be found on the **Gemini Bridges** or **Monitor and Merrimac** trails, both off U.S. 191 north of Moab. Klondike Bluffs, just north of Moab, is an excellent ride for novices. The Moab Information Center carries a free biking trail guide. Mountain bike rentals range from $38 for a good bike to $50 for a top-of-the-line workhorse. If you want to go on a guided ride, expect to pay between $120 to $135 per person for a half day, $155 to $190 for a full day, including the bike rental; you can save money by banding together with a larger group to keep the per-person rates down. Several companies offer shuttles to and from the trailheads.

For bike shops, shuttles, and tour companies, see the Outfitters & Expeditions box.

RIVER EXPEDITIONS

Fodor'sChoice On the Colorado River northeast of Arches and very near Moab, you ★ can take one of America's most scenic—yet unintimidating—river raft rides. This is the perfect place to take the family or to learn to kayak with the help of an outfitter. The river rolls by the red Fisher Towers as they rise into the sky in front of La Sal Mountains. A day trip on this stretch of the river will take you about 15 mi. Outfitters offer full- or half-day adventures here.

White-water adventures await more adventuresome rafters both upstream and down. Upriver, in narrow, winding Westwater Canyon near the Utah–Colorado border, the Colorado River cuts through the oldest exposed geologic layer on Earth. The result is craggy black granite jutting out of the water with red sandstone walls towering above. This section of the river is rocky and considered highly technical for rafters and kayakers, but it dishes out a great white-water experience in a short period of time. Most outfitters offer this trip as a one-day getaway, but you may also linger in the canyon as long as three days to complete the journey. A permit is required from the Bureau of Land Management (BLM) in Moab to run Westwater Canyon. Heart-stopping multiday trips through Cataract Canyon are for folks ready for a real adventure.

For rafting outfitters, see the Outfitters & Expeditions box.

WHERE TO EAT

★ $$–$$$$ ✕**Center Café.** This little jewel in the desert has a courtyard for outdoor dining. The mood inside is Spanish Mediterranean, made even more lovely by the fireplace. From grilled Black Angus beef tenderloin with caramelized onions and Gorgonzola, to roasted eggplant lasagna with feta cheese and Moroccan-olive marinara, there's always something on the contemporary menu to make your taste buds go "ah." Be sure to ask for the impressive wine list. ⊠*60 N. 100 West St.* ☎*435/259–4295* ⊟*D, MC, V* ⊙*Closed Dec.–Jan. No lunch.*

$–$$$$ ✕**Buck's Grill House.** For a taste of the American West, try the buffalo
Fodor'sChoice meat loaf or elk stew served at this popular dinner spot. The steaks are
★ thick and tender, and the gravies will have you licking your fingers. A selection of Southwestern entrées, including duck tamales and buffalo chorizo tacos, round out the menu. Vegetarian diners, don't despair; there are some tasty choices for you, too. A surprisingly good wine list will complement your meal. Outdoor patio dining with the trickle of a waterfall will end your day perfectly. ⊠*1393 N. U.S. 191* ☎*435/259–5201* ⊟*D, MC, V* ⊙*Closed Thanksgiving–mid-Feb. No lunch.*

$–$$ ✕**Moab Brewery.** You can always find someone to talk to about canyon country adventure, since river runners, rock climbers, and locals all hang out here. There's a wide selection of menu choices, including fresh salads, creative sandwiches, and hot soups. Try the gyros salad for a taste of the Mediterranean. Last but not least, this hot spot serves the best brew in town. ⊠*686 S. Main* ☎*435/259–6333* ⊟*AE, D, MC, V.*

¢–$$ ✕**La Hacienda.** This family-run local favorite serves good south-of-the-border meals at an equally good price. The helpings are generous and the service is friendly. And yes, you can order a margarita. ⊠*574 N. Main St.* ☎*435/259–6319* ⊟*AE, D, MC, V.*

¢–$$ ✕**Moab Diner.** For breakfast, lunch, and dinner, this is the place where old-time Moabites go. A mixture of good old-fashioned American food and Southwestern entrées gives you plenty to choose from. ⊠*189 S. Main St.* ☎*435/259–4006* ⊟*D, MC, V.*

¢–$ ✕**Eklecticafe.** This small place is easy to miss but worth searching out for one of the more creative menus in Moab. Breakfast and lunch items include a variety of burritos and wraps, scrambled tofu, Polish sausage, Indonesian satay kebabs, and many fresh, organic salads. On nice days you can take your meal outside to the large covered patio. In winter you'll want to stay inside by the wood-burning stove. ⊠*352 N. Main St.* ☎*435/259–6896* ⊟*MC, V* ⊙*No dinner.*

WHERE TO STAY

$$$$ ▥**Sorrel River Ranch.** This luxury ranch on the banks of the Colorado
Fodor'sChoice River 17 mi from Moab is the ultimate getaway. No matter which way
★ you look in a landscape studded with towering red cliffs, buttes, and spires, the vista is spectacular. Rooms are furnished with hefty log beds, tables, and chairs, along with Western art and Native American rugs. Some of the bathtubs even have views of the river and sandstone cliffs. For an extra cost, you can choose to relax in the spa with aromatherapy and a pedicure, go river rafting or mountain biking, or take an ATV out

for a spin. At the **Sorrel River Grill** ($$–$$$$), the most scenic dining experience in the Moab area, the seasonal menu changes regularly to incorporate the freshest ingredients. ⊠*Rte. 128, Box K, mile marker 17.5, 84532* ☎*435/259–4642 or 877/359–2715* 📠*435/259–3016* ⊕*www.sorrelriver.com* ⇔*32 rooms, 27 suites* ⋄*In-room: kitchen, VCR (some), Wi-Fi. In-hotel: restaurant, tennis court, pool, gym, spa, bicycles, laundry facilities, no-smoking rooms* ⊟*AE, MC, V.*

$$$–$$$$ ▣ **Gonzo Inn.** When creating this eclectic inn, the owners gave careful attention to design, color, and art. The furnishings are all decidedly contemporary, using much metal and steel, and some rooms have fireplaces. The pool, hot tub, and courtyard overlook a shady pathway that winds for 2 mi along Mill Creek. ⊠*100 W. 200 South84532* ☎*435/259–2515 or 800/791–4044* 📠*435/259–6992* ⊕*www.gonzoinn.com* ⇔*21 rooms, 22 suites* ⋄*In-room: kitchen (some), Wi-Fi. In-hotel: pool, no elevator, laundry facilities, some pets allowed, no-smoking rooms* ⊟*AE, D, MC, V* ⦿*CP.*

$$$–$$$$ ▣ **Sunflower Hill Bed and Breakfast.** Tucked away on a quiet neighborhood street, this turn-of-the-20th-century dwelling is operated by a family who ensures that their guests feel truly welcome. Antiques and farmhouse treasures, well-tended gardens, and pathways make you feel like you're in the country. The full breakfast is buffet style and features a vegetable frittata, side meats, and home-baked pastries. Outdoors there's a hot tub. ⊠*185 N. 300 East, 84532* ☎*435/259–2974 or 800/662–2786* ⊕*www.sunflowerhill.com* ⇔*9 rooms, 3 suites* ⋄*In-room: no phone, VCR (some). In-hotel: pool, no elevator, laundry facilities, public Wi-Fi, no-smoking rooms* ⊟*AE, D, MC, V* ⦿*BP.*

★ $$$ ▣ **Red Cliffs Adventure Lodge.** You can have it all at this gorgeous, classically Western lodge. The Colorado River rolls by right outside your door, and canyon walls reach for the sky in all their red glory; you can gaze at it all from your private riverfront patio. Rooms are Western in flavor, with log furniture, lots of wood, and Saltillo tile. Added attractions include an on-site winery, a movie memorabilia museum, as well as guided rafting, hiking, biking, and horseback-riding adventures into the desert. The setting is fabulous, but note that you're 14 mi from town. ⊠*Rte. 128, mile marker 14, 84532* ☎*435/259–2002 or 866/812–2002* ⊕*www.redcliffslodge.com* ⇔*79 rooms, 30 cabins, 1 suite* ⋄*In-room: kitchen, VCR, Ethernet, Wi-Fi. In-hotel: restaurant, room service, pool, gym, no elevator, laundry facilities* ⊟*AE, D, MC, V* ⦿*CP.*

$$–$$$ ▣ **Adobe Abode.** A lovely B&B near the nature preserve, this one-story inn surrounds you with solitude. When you're not out exploring, you can unwind in a picture-perfect common room with fireplace and Southwest decor. **Pro:** Relaxing in the beautifully decorated common area. **Con:** You can bicycle to town, but it's too far to walk. ⊠*778 W. Kane Creek Blvd., 84532* ☎*435/259–7716* ⊕*www.adobeabodemoab.com* ⇔*5 rooms, 1 suite* ⋄*In-room: Wi-Fi. In-hotel: no elevator, no kids under 16, no smoking* ⊟*AE, D, MC, V* ⦿*CP.*

$$–$$$ ▣ **Dream Keeper Inn.** Serenity is just a wish away at this B&B in a quiet
Fodor'sChoice   Moab neighborhood, on large, shady grounds filled with flower and
★   vegetable gardens. The rooms line a hallway in the ranch-style home,

OUTFITTERS & EXPEDITIONS

BICYCLING

Chile Pepper Bikes. For bicycle rentals, repairs, and espresso, stop here before you hit the trails. ✉ 702 S. Main St., Moab ☎ 435/259–4688 or 888/677–4688 ⊕ www.chilebikes.com. **Moab Cyclery.** You can't miss this busy place right on Main Street. Bike rentals and tours will get you rolling in canyon country. ✉ 391 S. Main St., Moab ☎ 435/259–7423 or 800/559–1978 ⊕ www.moabcyclery.com. **Poison Spider Bicycles.** This fully loaded shop is staffed by young, friendly bike experts. ✉ 497 N. Main St., Moab ☎ 435/259–7882 or 800/635–1792. **Rim Cyclery.** For full-suspension bike rentals and sales, solid advice on trails, and parts, equipment and gear, this is the oldest bike shop in town. ✉ 94 W. 100 North St., Moab ☎ 435/259–5333 or 888/304–8219 ⊕ www.rimcyclery.com. **Rim Tours.** Reliable, friendly, and professional, this outfit can take you on a great guided mountain-bike tour. Trips include Gemini Bridges, the Slickrock Trail, Klondike Bluffs, and many other locations—including the White Rim Trail in Canyonlands. ✉ 1233 S. U.S. 191, Moab ☎ 435/259–5223 or 800/626–7335 ⊕ www.rimtours.com. **Western Spirit Cycling.** This company offers fully supported, go-at-your-own-pace multiday bike tours throughout the region, including trips to the 140-mi Kokopelli Trail, which runs from Grand Junction, Colorado, to Moab. Guides versed in the geologic wonders of the area cook up meals worthy of the scenery each night. There's also the option to combine a Green River kayak trip with the three-night bike route. ✉ 478 Mill Creek Dr., Moab ☎ 435/259–8732 or 800/845–2453 ⊕ www.westernspirit.com.

FOUR-WHEELING

Coyote Land Tours. Let this company take you to backcountry where you could never wander on your own. Their big Mercedes Unimog vehicles cover some rough terrain while you sit back and enjoy the sights. ✉ 397 N. Main St., Moab ☎ 435/259–6649 ⊕ www.coyotelandtours.com. **Highpoint Hummer Tours.** This outfitter does the driving while you gawk at the scenery as you travel off-road routes in an open-air Hummer ✉ 281 N. Main St., Moab ☎ 435/259–2972 or 877/486–6833 ⊕ www.highpointhummer.com.

MULTISPORT

Adrift Adventures. This outfitter can get you out on the Colorado or Green rivers for either day-long or multiday raft trips. Adrift also offers a unique combination horseback ride and river trip, movie-set tour, rock-art tours, and other 4X4 excursions. ✉ 378 N. Main, Moab ☎ 435/259–8594 or 800/874–4483 ⊕ www.adrift.net. **Coyote Shuttle.** If you need a ride to or from your bicycle trailhead or river trip, call the Coyote. These folks also do shuttles to and from Green River for the train and bus service there. ✉ 397 N. Main, Moab ☎ 435/259–8656 ⊕ www.coyoteshuttle.com. **Moab Adventure Center.** For a short trip on the Colorado River, a Hummer tour, scenic flight, national park tour, or rubber kayak rental, contact this reputable company. Its shop also sells gear and clothing. ✉ 225 S. Main St., Moab

☏ 435/259-7019 or 866/904-1163 ⊕ www.moabadventurecenter.com.

NAVTEC. A fast little boat by this outfit gets you down the Colorado River and through Cataract Canyon in one day. They also offer trips up to five days and 4X4 trips into nearby backcountry. Raft rentals are also available. ✉ 321 N. Main St., Moab ☏ 435/259-7983 or 800/833-1278 ⊕ www.navtec.com.

OARS. This company can take you rafting on the Colorado River and four-wheeling in the parks. They also offer a calm-water ride on the Colorado. ✉ 543 N. Main St., Moab ☏ 435/259-5865 or 800/342-5938 ⊕ www.oarsutah.com.

Red Cliffs Adventure Lodge. Take a horseback ride near one of Moab's working cattle ranches for a true Western experience. The lodge also offers guided rafting, hiking, and biking trips. ✉ Milepost 14, Rte. 128, Moab ☏ 435/259-2002 or 866/812-2002 ⊕ www.redcliffs-lodge.com.

Roadrunner Shuttle. Call for a ride to the airport or for a river or bike shuttle. They'll even take you to Salt Lake City or Grand Junction, Colorado, to catch a plane. ☏ 435/259-9402 ⊕ www.roadrunnershuttle.com.

Tag-A-Long Expeditions. This company holds more permits with the National Park Service and has been taking people into the white water of Cataract Canyon and Canyonlands longer than any other outfitter in Moab. They also run four-wheel-drive expeditions into the backcountry of the park as well as calm-water excursions on the Colorado River. They are the only outfitter allowed to take you into the park via both water and 4X4. Trips run from half day to six days in length. ✉ 452 N. Main St., Moab ☏ 435/259-8946 or 800/453-3292 ⊕ www.tagalong.com.

RIVER EXPEDITIONS

Canyon Voyages Adventure Company. This friendly, professional company is the only outfit that operates a kayak school. You can rent rafts and kayaks here. Inside the booking office is a great shop that sells river gear, outdoor clothes, hats, sandals, and backpacks. ✉ 211 N. Main St., Moab ☏ 435/259-6007 or 800/733-6007 ⊕ www.canyonvoyages.com.

Holiday River Expeditions. You can rent a canoe or book a raft trip on the Green and Colorado rivers at this reliable company with decades of river experience. ✉ 1055 E. Main St., Green River ☏ 800/624-6323 ⊕ www.bikeraft.com.

Sheri Griffith Expeditions. This longtime Moab outfitter offers trips through the white water of Cataract, Westwater, and Desolation canyons. Specialty expeditions include river trips for women, writers, and families. They also offer more luxurious expeditions. ✉ 2231 S. U.S. 191, Moab ☏ 435/259-8229 or 800/332-2439 ⊕ www.griffithexp.com.

Tex's Riverways. The folks at Tex's will take very good care of you when you rent a canoe for a self-guided trip, and they can shuttle you to and from the Green or Colorado rivers. ✉ 691 N. 500 West, Moab ☏ 435/259-5101 ⊕ www.texsriverways.com.

ROCK CLIMBING

Desert Highlights. The only permitted canyoneering guide service in Arches. ✉ 50 E. Center St., Moab ☏ 435/259-4433 or 800/747-1342 ⊕ www.deserthihglights.com.

and each opens onto the pool, patio, and courtyard area, where you may want to have your morning coffee. Or, you may prefer to have breakfast in the sunny indoor dining area. Some rooms have jetted tubs. **Pros:** Located on a quiet street. You can unwind in the shade near the pool. **Cons:** You'll have to leave the kids at home (which may not be a con for some). ⊠ *191 S. 200 East, 84532* ☎*435/259–5998 or 888/230–3247* ☎*435/259–3912* ⊕*www.dreamkeeperinn.com* ➦*6 rooms* ☼*In-room: refrigerator, VCR, Wi-Fi. In-hotel: pool, no elevator, no kids under 15, no-smoking rooms* ☐*AE, D, MC, V* ⦿*BP.*

☾ **$$** 🖳**Best Western Canyonlands Inn.** The best asset of this reliably comfortable and clean motel is its ideal location in the center of downtown Moab. It's within a few footsteps of many restaurants and shops, and within easy reach of the Mill Creek Parkway foot and bicycle trail. The kids will enjoy the pool and can cool off in the bubbling water feature. ⊠ *16 S. Main St., 84532* ☎*435/259–2300 or 800/649–5191* ☎*435/259–2301* ⊕*www.canyonlandsinn.com* ➦*46 rooms, 30 suites* ☼*In-room: refrigerator, Ethernet (some), Wi-Fi (some). In-hotel: pool, gym, laundry facilities.* ☐*AE, D, MC, V* ⦿*BP.*

WHERE TO CAMP

🜄 **Big Bend.** Both RVs and tents can camp at this spot next to the Colorado River near Arches National Park. There are large cottonwoods for shade and you can hear the river rumble through the red rock canyons. ⊠*7 2/15 mi from U.S. 191 on Rte. 128* ➦*23 sites* ☼*Pit toilets.*

🜄 **Bureau of Land Management Campgrounds.** There are 342 sites at 18 different BLM campgrounds near Arches and Canyonlands national parks. Most of these are in the Moab area near Arches and Canyonlands' Island in the Sky District, along the Route 128 Colorado River corridor, on Kane Creek Road, and on Sand Flats Road. All sites are primitive, though Wind Whistle and Hatch Point do have water. Campsites go on a first-come, first-served basis. They are all open year-round. Credit cards are not accepted. ☎*435/259–6111* ⊕*www.blm. gov/utah/moab.*

★ 🜄 **Dead Horse Point State Park Campground.** A favorite of almost everyone who has ever camped here, either in RVs or tents, this mesa-top site fills up a little later in the day than the national park campgrounds. It is impressively set near the edge of a 2,000-foot cliff above the Colorado River. If you want to pay for your stay with a credit card you must do so during business hours (8–6 daily); otherwise you must pay in cash in the after-hours drop box. ☼*Flush toilets, dump station, drinking water, picnic tables, public telephone, ranger station* ➦*21 sites* ⊠*Dead Horse Point State Park, Rte. 313, 18 mi off U.S. 191 (right outside the entrance to Canyonlands National Park)* ☎*435/259–2614, 800/322–3770 reservations* ⊕*www.stateparks.utah.gov* ☐*MC, V.*

🜄**Goose Island Campground.** This area on the river road near Arches is suitable for RVs and tents. You can dip your toes in the Colorado River while you lounge under a cottonwood—but the river is dangerous, so don't swim without a life jacket. ⊠*1 2/5 mi from U.S. 191 on Rte. 128* ➦*18 sites* ☼*Pit toilets.*

🜄**Hatch Point Campground.** If it's solitude you're looking for and you're not concerned with convenience (to get here you have to drive 32 mi south of Moab on U.S. 191, then 24 mi more on a road that includes 9 mi of gravel), this out-of-the-way place might have your name on it. You're within short walks or drives of stunning overlooks into Canyonlands' Needles District. Red and white slickrock will be the view from your site and pinyon or juniper will provide your shade. There's no water November–mid-April. ⊠*24 mi west of U.S. 191 from the Canyon Rims turnoff* ⌁*10 sites* △*Pit toilets, drinking water.*

Fodor's Choice ★ △ **Moab Valley RV Resort.** Near the Colorado River, with a 360-degree view, this campground seems to get bigger and better every year. Just 2 mi from Arches National Park, it's convenient for sightseeing, river rafting, and all types of area attractions and activities. On-site you can pitch some horseshoes, perfect your putting, or soak in the hot tub. Kids and parents alike will enjoy all the playgrounds, including a giant chess- and checkerboard. The place is spotlessly clean, with everything from tent sites to cottages. ⊠*1773 N. U.S. 191, 84532* ☎*435/259–4469* ⊕*www.moabvalleyrv.com* ⌁*108 sites (62 with full hook-ups, 7 with water and electric only, 39 tent sites); 33 cabins* △*Flush toilets, full hookups, dump station, drinking water, guest laundry, showers, grills, picnic tables, electricity, public telephone, general store, play area, swimming (pool), Wi-Fi* ▤*MC, V.*

△ **Moonflower Camping Area.** A favorite of tent campers because of the quiet and solitude, these sites are all walk-in. There's a large panel of ancient Native American petroglyphs at the mouth of Moonflower Canyon. ⊠*3 mi from Hwy. 191 on Kane Creek Rd., Moab* ⌁*8 sites* △*Pit toilets.*

△ **Sand Flats Recreation Area.** The largest of the campgrounds near Arches National Park, this spot is tucked back in the slickrock near the bike trail of the same name. Juniper and pinyon provide a little shade and the La Sal Mountains loom in the distance. During certain times of the year, most notably Spring Break, this is a favorite of young folks with boom boxes, beer, and bicycles, so unless you're looking for a party atmosphere it's best to avoid this campground in March and early April. ⊠*2 mi east of Moab on Sand Flats Rd., Moab84532* ⌁*143 sites* △*Pit toilets.*

△ **Sand Island Campground.** The special charm of this campground is its proximity to the San Juan River. You'll also be surrounded by giant cottonwood trees. ⊠*3 mi west of Bluff on U.S. 191* ⌁*27 sites* △*Pit toilets, drinking water, fire grates, picnic tables.*

★ △ **Up the Creek Campground.** This neighborhood campground lies under big cottonwoods on the banks of Mill Creek. Even though you are near downtown, you'll feel like you're in the woods—the campground has walk-in tent sites only. ⊠*210 E. 300 South, 84532* ☎*435/259–6995* ⊕*www.moabupthecreek.com* ⌁*20 sites* △*Flush toilets, drinking water, showers, grills, picnic tables* ▤*MC, V* ☽*Mar.–Oct.*

△ **Wind Whistle Campground.** Close to the Needles District of Canyonlands, this small campground is tucked into a pinyon and juniper forest amid red rocks. Tight turns on the access road make this a less-than-ideal destination for RVs. There's no water November–mid-April. ⊠*6 mi west of the Canyon Rims turnoff from U.S. 191* ⌁*17 sites* △*Pit toilets, drinking water.*

NIGHTLIFE & THE ARTS

NIGHTLIFE

There's not much in the way of nightlife in Moab, but when there is, it's at the **Moab Brewery** (⊠*686 S. Main St.* ☎*435/259–6333*). Several TVs draw a crowd to the separate barroom and occasionally there's impromptu music. It's definitely a favorite of locals and tourists alike. On weekends there's live music, dancing, and karaoke at the **Rio Colorado** (⊠*2 S. 100 West St.* ☎*435/259–6666*).

THE ARTS

The Moab Arts and Recreation Center (⊠*111 E. 100 North St.* ☎*435/259–6272*)hosts art exhibits featuring local artists every other month, as well as concerts and classes in yoga, tai chi, Pilates, and dance. This historic downtown building is the hub of arts activities in Moab.

During the lively **Moab Art Walk** (☎*435/259–4446*), you can stroll the streets to browse (and purchase) original art in Moab's galleries and shops. The Art Walk takes place on the second Saturday of the month, from March through June and again from September through November.

The **Moab Arts Festival** (☎*435/259–2742* ⊕*www.moabartsfestival.org/*)happens in May, when the area's weather is at its finest. Artists from across the West gather at the Swanny City Park to show their wares, including pottery, photography, and paintings. Live music and lots of food keep everyone happy.

Moab's artists, many of whom are inspired by the dramatic landscape nearby, open their studios to show and sell their art during the annual **Moab Artists Studio Tour** (☎*435/259–6272 or 435/259–8631*), during Labor Day weekend in September.

FodorsChoice
★ September brings world-class music to red rock country with the **Moab Music Festival** (☎*435/259–7003* ⊕*www.moabmusicfest.org*). Musicians from all over the globe perform primarily classical, jazz, and traditional music in the canyons, desert, and local performance halls. The Colorado River Benefit Concert, set in a natural grotto, is a once-in-a-lifetime experience. This inspiring event is worth driving great distances to attend.

The music continues to drift across the desert in November when the **Moab Folk Music Festival** (☎*435/260–2488* ⊕*www.moabfolkfestival.com*)brings favorite folk singer–songwriters to downtown venues.

A fast-growing tradition in Moab, the **Western Stars Cowboy Poetry Gathering** (☎*435/259–6272* ⊕*www.moabwesternstars.com*) brings cowboy poets and singers to town during the February Presidents' Day holiday weekend. Besides the verse and the music, there's a dutch-oven cook-off, horse- and mule-shoeing demonstrations, traditional Western dancing and crafts, barrel racing, and art shows.

SHOPPING

11

In Moab, shopping opportunities are plentiful with art galleries, jewelry stores, and shops carrying T-shirts and souvenirs on every block. If your book shopping goes better with an espresso in your hand, try **Arches Book Company** (⊠*78 N. Main St.* ☎*435/259–0782* ⊕*www. archesbookcompany.com*), a friendly store with a full coffee bar; they stock a wide selection of titles ranging from best sellers to local authors, as well as area maps and guidebooks.**Back of Beyond Books** (⊠*83 N. Main St.* ☎*435/259–5154* ⊕*www.backofbeyondbooks.com*), a decidedly "green" bookstore, features an excellent selection of books on environmental studies, Native American cultures, Western water issues, and Western history.At **Dave's Corner Market** (⊠*401 Mill Creek Dr.* ☎*435/259–6999*), you can get most anything you might need, including some of the best cappuccino and Colombian coffee in town. The store is also the heartbeat of the local community and the place where everyone discusses local politics.

If you forgot anything for your camping, climbing, hiking, or other outdoor adventure, you can get it at **Gearheads** (⊠*471 S. Main St.* ☎*435/259–4327*), which is packed not only with essentials, but with hard-to-find things like booties and packs for your dog.**Lema Kokopelli Gallery** (⊠*70 N. Main St.* ☎*435/259–5055*)has built a reputation for fair prices on a giant selection of authentic Native American jewelry and other art.At the elegant little **Overlook Gallery** (⊠*82 E. Center* ☎*435/259–3861*)on a side street just a short walk from Main Street, you can find some great surprises in local art.

For stunning original photographs of the Arches and Canyonlands areas, visit **Tom Till Gallery** (⊠*61 N. Main St.* ☎*435/259–9808*). **Walker Drug Co.** (⊠*290 S. Main St.* ☎*435/259–5959*) has been a Moab landmark since the 1950s; this is as close as you'll get to a department store for more than 100 mi. Besides pharmacy and drugstore items, you can buy forgotten camping supplies, swimsuits, hats, sunglasses, souvenirs, and almost anything else.

SIDE TRIP FROM MOAB

LA SAL MOUNTAINS
8 mi south of Moab via U.S. 191.

Although Moab is best known for its slickrock desert, it's also the gateway to the second-highest mountain range in the state—the 12,000-foot La Sal Mountains. Long a favorite stomping ground of locals, the often snowcapped peaks have been discovered by out-of-towners as a welcome retreat from the summer heat. You can picnic in a meadow or take one of many alpine hikes.

On Old Airport Road (a left turnoff from U.S. 191) 8 mi south of Moab, the 62-mi **La Sal Mountain Loop** climbs over the laccolithic mountain range, affording some great vistas of the valley. The road enters La Sal Division of the Manti–La Sal National Forest just as the dominant red rock cliffs east of Moab begin to alternate with sagebrush and juniper flats. Passing through the cool heights of La Sal Mountains, the loop winds north through red rock country to Castle Valley and an intersection with Route 128. The road is paved, except for a couple of gravel sections, but it does have steep switchbacks, and it does become snow-packed in the winter. Check with the National Forest Service before embarking on winter driving on this road. ⊠*U.S. 191, 8 mi south of Moab* ☎*435/259–7155 or 435/637–2817* ⊕*www.fs.fed.us/r4/mantilasal* ۞*Year-round.*

Hole 'n the Rock is a 14-room, 5,000-square-foot home carved into a solid rock wall. It would be just another funky roadside attraction if it didn't represent 20 years of toil for the late owners Albert and Gladys Christensen. Road-weary children will appreciate the break, and you can pick up snacks in the trading post. ⊠*12 mi south of Moab on U.S. 191* ☎*435/686–2250* ⊕*www.theholeintherock.com* ☜*$5* ۞*June–Sept., daily 8–8; Oct.–May, daily 9–5.*

The giant roadside **Wilson Arch** makes a great photo stop. In Moab you can still find old photos of an airplane flying through this arch. No one has tried the stunt lately, probably because it's now illegal. ⊠*22 mi south of Moab on U.S. 191.*

OFF THE BEATEN PATH

Canyon Rims Recreation Area. With a few hours to spare, you can enjoy two remarkable canyon country vistas. Turn off U.S. 191 at a point centered between Moab and Monticello (about 27 mi south of Moab and 26 mi north of Monticello), and the paved Needles Overlook Road runs 22 mi west to Needles Overlook, which takes in the southern end of Canyonlands National Park. Less than 20 mi farther on a good, graded road is the Anticline Overlook, which encompasses the Colorado River, Dead Horse Point, and other locales to the north.

SPORTS & THE OUTDOORS

Once snow flies, portions of La Sal Mountain Loop road are impassable, but a well-maintained hut-to-hut system, operated by **Tag-A-Long Expeditions** (⊠*452 N. Main St., Moab* ☎*435/259–8946 or 800/453–3292* ⊕*www.tagalong.com*)makes this a wonderful place for cross-country skiing for those of moderate to expert ability. Since roads at the top of the mountain are impassable to cars in winter, you drive to the ski trail's parking lot, and then Tag-A-Long snowcats drop you and your supplies off at one of the two huts for $80. Lodging in the huts is $35 per person per night. Should you require subsequent snowcat transport, it's an additional $160 per day. At the end of your expedition, you can ski back to the mountain-top trailhead and parking lot, where you get your own vehicle for the ride back to town. Marked routes link the huts.

WHERE TO STAY

$–$$$

Mt. Peale Resort. This outlying guest ranch is at the foothills of the snowcapped La Sal Mountains. The inn features five cozy rooms with homey decor, and the four cabins each have three bedrooms. A hot tub will feel great after a day of snowshoeing (you can rent snowshoes) or cross-country skiing, and if your muscles still need a little help, an on-site massage therapist will do the trick. Hearty breakfasts (available for $8.50 per person) of multigrain waffles, fruit, and yogurt will start your day in a healthy way. ⊠*1415 East Hwy. 46, Old La Sal, 84530*

☎435/259–5505 🖷435/259–8879 ⊕*www.mtpeale.com* ➫*5 rooms,*
4 cabins ♿*In-room: no a/c, no phone, kitchen, VCR (some), no TV*
(some). In-hotel: public Wi-Fi. ▤*MC, V.*

11

SOUTHEASTERN UTAH

There is surprise around every corner, whether you explore Southeastern Utah by car, by raft, by foot, by bicycle, or in a rugged 4X4. On the trail you'll discover cactus or a lush garden of ferns created by precious springs or seeps. On the river, hawks float overhead. On the road, you'll encounter trading posts that have been selling Native American art for decades or, nearer Navajo land, you can purchase art directly from its makers. Enter these lands with a mind as open as the skies. Be a curious, willing traveler in one of the wildest regions left in America. Also be a prepared traveler. This is the area that invented the term "you can't get there from here," so plan your journey by using all or part of our suggested route. Whatever you do, don't forget your camera.

GREEN RIVER

70 mi west of the Colorado state line via I–70.

Named for the river that runs through town, Green River, Utah, and its namesake are historically important. Early Indians used the river for centuries. The Old Spanish Trail also crossed the river, and the Denver and Rio Grande Railroad bridged the river here in 1883. Some say "the green" refers to the color of the water; others claim it's the vegetation along the river bank. Another story reports that it was named after a mysterious trapper named Mr. Green. Whatever the etymology, Green River remains a sleepy little town and a nice break from some of the more "hip" tourist towns in southern Utah.

In September the fragrance of fresh cantaloupe, watermelon, and honeydew fills the air in Green River. They celebrate the harvest with **Melon Days** (☎435/564–3526 or 888/564–3600 ⊕*www.emerycounty. com*)the third weekend of September. This small-town event features a parade and fair, plenty of music, square dancing, a canoe race, and thousands of pounds of melons, which are famous in the region.

Green River State Park is a shady retreat on the shores of the Green River. Best known for its 9-hole golf course, it's also a favorite of RV campers. It is the starting point for boaters drifting through Labyrinth and Stillwater Canyons on the Green River. ✉*450 S. Green River Rd.* ☎*435/564–3633, 800/322–3770 for campground reservations* ⊕*www.stateparks.utah.gov* 🖳*$7 per vehicle* ☺*Summer, daily 6* AM–*10* PM*; winter, daily 8–5.*

The riverfront **John Wesley Powell River History Museum** gives visitors the opportunity to see what it was like to travel down the Green and Colorado rivers in the 1800s. A series of interactive displays tracks the Powell party's arduous and dangerous 1869 journey. The center also houses the River Runner's Hall of Fame, a tribute to those who have followed in Powell's wake. An art gallery reserved for works themati-cally linked to river exploration is also on-site. ⊠*1765 E. Main St.* ☎*435/564–3427* ⊕*www.jwprhm.com* 🖃*$3* ⊙*Apr.–Oct., daily 8–7; Nov.–Mar., daily 9–5.*

The **Sego Canyon Rock Art Panels** are one of the most dramatic and mysti-fying rock-art sights in the area. On the canyon walls you can see large, ghostlike rock-art figures etched by Native Americans approximately 4,000 years ago. There's also art left by the Ute Indians from the 19th-century. Distinctive for their large anthropomorphic figures, and for horses, buffalo, and shields painted with red-and-white pigment, these rare drawings are some of the finest Ute pictographs in the region. The panels are 3½ mi off I-70 on a maintained gravel road. ⊠*I-70, Exit 185, 25 mi east of Green River* ☎*435/259–6111 Bureau of Land Man-agement Office in Moab.*

OFF THE BEATEN PATH

Crystal Geyser. The geyser erupts every 14 to 16 hours for about 30 minutes. The water shoots 80 to 100 feet high. On the banks of the Green River, 10 mi south of town, you'll get a good taste of back-country on good, graded road. Mineral deposits have created a dra-matic orange terrace surrounding the eruption site. The staff at the Green River Information Center, which is in the John Wesley Powell River History Museum, can provide detailed directions and updated road conditions.

SPORTS & THE OUTDOORS

RIVER FLOAT TRIPS

Bearing little resemblance to its name, Desolation Canyon acquaints those who venture down the Green River with some of the last true American wilderness. This journey takes you through a lush, ver-dant canyon where the rapids promise more laughter than fear and trembling. It's a favorite destination of canoe paddlers, kayakers, and beginning rafters. May through September raft trips through Gray-Desolation Canyon are popular and can be arranged by outfitters in Green River. South of town the river drifts at a lazier pace through Labyrinth and Stillwater canyons, and the 68-mi stretch of river that runs south to Mineral Bottom in Canyonlands National Park is best suited to canoes and motorized boats.

For river trip outfitters, see the Outfitters & Expeditions box.

WHERE TO STAY & EAT

¢–$$ ✕**Ben's Cafe.** At the local hot spot for homemade enchiladas you can also get a good porterhouse steak. This unpretentious restaurant on Green River's main thoroughfare offers plenty of choices at reasonable prices. ⊠*115 W. Main St.* ☎*435/564–3352* 🖃*AE, D, DC, MC, V.*

★ ¢–$ ✕**Ray's Tavern.** Ray's is something of a Western legend and a favorite hangout for river runners. Stop here for great tales about working on the river as well as the coldest beer and the best all-beef hamburger in two counties. ⊠*25 S. Broadway* ☎*435/564–3511* 🖃*AE, D, MC, V.*

$–$$ 🏨**Best Western River Terrace Hotel.** The setting, on the bank of the Green River, is conducive to a good night's rest. Comfortable, updated rooms are furnished with large beds, and the premises are clean. **Pros:** River-side location is a real treat (be sure to request a river-view room). **Cons:**

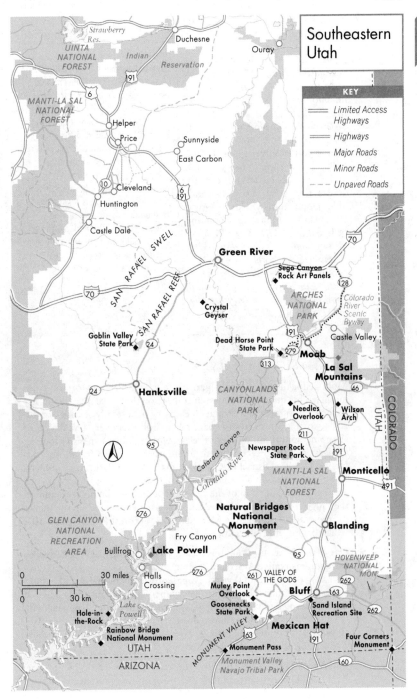

Southeastern Utah

KEY

═══ Limited Access Highways
─── Highways
┈┈┈ Major Roads
─── Minor Roads
- - - Unpaved Roads

Strawberry Res.

UINTA NATIONAL FOREST

Duchesne

Ouray

Indian Reservation

191

6

MANTI-LA SAL NATIONAL FOREST

Helper
Price

Sunnyside

East Carbon

10
Cleveland

Huntington

6
191

Castle Dale

SAN RAFAEL SWELL

SAN RAFAEL REEF

Green River

70

Sego Canyon Rock Art Panels

128

ARCHES NATIONAL PARK

Colorado River Scenic Byway

Crystal Geyser

Goblin Valley State Park

24

Dead Horse Point State Park

191

279 **Moab**

Castle Valley

La Sal Mountains

313

46

24

Hanksville

CANYONLANDS NATIONAL PARK

Needles Overlook

Wilson Arch

211

95

Cataract Canyon

Colorado River

Newspaper Rock State Park

191

MANTI-LA SAL NATIONAL FOREST

Monticello

491

GLEN CANYON NATIONAL RECREATION AREA

276

Natural Bridges National Monument

Fry Canyon

Blanding

95

HOVENWEEP NATIONAL MON.

Bullfrog

Lake Powell

0   30 miles

0   30 km

Halls Crossing

276

261 VALLEY OF THE GODS

Muley Point Overlook

Goosenecks State Park

Bluff

163

262

Sand Island Recreation Site

262

Hole-in-the-Rock

Lake Powell

Rainbow Bridge National Monument

UTAH

MONUMENT VALLEY

163

Mexican Hat

191

Four Corners Monument

ARIZONA

Monument Pass

Monument Valley Navajo Tribal Park

160

COLORADO

UTAH

Nearby dining options are limited. ⊠*1740 E. Main St., 84525* ☎*435/564–3401 or 800/528–1234* 🖷*435/564–3403* ⊕*www.bestwestern.com* 🛏*50 rooms* ⚘*In-room: Wi-Fi. In-hotel: pool, no-smoking rooms* ⊟*AE, D, DC, MC, V* ⍾⊙*BP.*

¢–$ 🛏 **Green River Comfort Inn.** Right off I–70, this reliable motel is convenient if you're only stopping for the night. The decor is modern motel, and there's a restaurant directly across the street. **Pros:** Dependable chain motel. **Cons:** Green River isn't the place for shopping or fine dining. ⊠*1975 E. Main St.* ☎*435/564–3300* 🖷*435/564–3299* ⊕*www.choicehotels.com* 🛏*54 rooms, 3 suites* ⚘*In-room: refrigerator (some), Wi-Fi. In-hotel: pool, gym, no elevator, laundry facilities* ⊟*AE, D, DC, MC, V* ⍾⊙*CP.*

> **BOOK CLIFFS**
>
> The Book Cliffs, part of an escarpment that forms a 200-mi semicircle from Green River, Utah, across the state border into Colorado, are so named because they resemble the leaves of a partially opened book. Buried in the rocks are vast deposits of coal, oil shale, and rock asphalt. Compared to other parts of Utah, this area is desolate and monochromatic, but the implacable wall is testimony to the building up and tearing down of the earth's surface. The area remains remote, with only a few dirt roads making it accessible to hunters and four-wheel-drive recreationists.

MONTICELLO

53 mi south of Moab via U.S. 191.

Monticello, the seat of San Juan County, is a mostly Mormon community. This quiet town has seen some growth in recent years, mostly in the form of new motels made necessary by a steady stream of tourists venturing south from Moab, but it still offers very few dining or shopping opportunities. Nevertheless, with several inexpensive lodging choices, it's a more convenient alternative to Moab for those visiting the Needles District of Canyonlands National Park. At 7,000 feet, Monticello provides a cool respite from the summer heat of the desert, and it's at the doorstep of the Abajo Mountains. The highest point in the range, 11,360-foot Abajo Peak, is accessed by a road that branches off the graded, 22-mi Blue Mountain Loop (Forest Service Road 105, which begins in Monticello).

★ One of the West's most famous rock-art sites, **Newspaper Rock Recreation Site** contains Native American etchings that were engraved on the rock over the course of 2,000 years. Apparently, early pioneers and explorers to the region named the site Newspaper Rock because they believed the rock, crowded with drawings, constituted a written language with which early people communicated. Archaeologists now agree the petroglyphs do not represent language. The site is northwest of Monticello. ⊠*Rte. 211, about 15 mi west of U.S. 191.*

The Abajo Loop Scenic Backway (also known as Route 285 or Forest Road 079) climbs to 9,000 feet through the mountains between

Hoodoos, Bridges & Arches

11

After a while, the fantastically eroded landscapes and formations found in southern Utah can all begin to look the same. Don't worry. It happens to everyone. A brief course in the geology of the Colorado Plateau can get your vacation back on track and clear up any confusion while you're busy making memories.

An **arch** is an opening created primarily by the ceaseless erosional powers of wind and weather. Airborne sand constantly scours cliff faces; tiny and huge chunks of stone are pried away by minuscule pockets of water as it freezes, expands, and thaws, again and again over the course of thousands or millions of years. Arches are found in all stages, from cavelike openings that don't go all the way through a stone fin to gigantic stone ribbons shaped by an erosional persistence that defies imagination.

Bridges are the product of stream or river erosion. They span what at some time was a water source powerful enough to wear away softer layers of sedimentary stone through constant force and motion. As softer stone is washed away, the harder capstone layers remain in the form of natural bridges.

The most bizarrely shaped formations have the strangest name. **Hoodoos** are chunks of rock chiseled through time into columns or pinnacles. Like all rock formations, hoodoos are constructed of layers and layers of horizontal bands. Each band or stratum has its own composition. When wind or water, particularly in the form of heavy, sporadic rainstorms, goes to work on these pillars, the eventual result is a hoodoo—an eccentric and grotesque formation usually found in the company of other hoodoos.

Monticello and Blanding. This route skirts the base of Abajo Peak and traverses 30 mi of mountainous terrain. The single-lane graded gravel or dirt road is rough and rocky. High clearance and stiff suspension are recommended. The route is impassable in winter and after rain storms. Allow at least three hours to drive this difficult but beautiful drive.

Before starting out on any trip into this rugged wilderness area, contact the **Manti–La Sal National Forest** (☎435/587–3235)to inquire about road conditions and to get further information about trails.

WHERE TO STAY & EAT

¢–$$ ✕**Homestead Steak House.** The folks here specialize in authentic Navajo fry bread and Navajo tacos. The popular—and big!—sheepherder's sandwich, is made with the fry bread and comes with your choice of beef, turkey, or ham and all the trimmings. No alcohol is served. ⊠*121 E. Center St.* ☎*435/678–3456* ▭*AE, D, MC, V.*

¢–$ ▦**Days Inn.** One of the largest properties in Monticello, this is also one of the nicest, with a heated indoor pool and a hot tub that's just what the doctor ordered for soaking adventure-weary bodies. **Pros:** Management takes good care of the reliable chain rooms. **Cons:** Sits near the highway, so might be noisy (ask for a room on the back side). ⊠*549 N. Main St., Box 759, 84535* ☎*435/587–2458* ▤*435/587–2191* ⊕*www. daysinn.com* ⬅*43 rooms* ⬪*In-room: refrigerator (some), Wi-Fi. In-hotel: pool, no elevator* ▭*AE, D, DC, MC, V* ⦾*CP.*

¢ 📺 **The Monticello Inn.** Quiet and well maintained, this motel has basic rooms, but it's a great bargain for this part of Utah. **Pros:** Clean, refurbished rooms. **Cons:** Monticello doesn't offer much in the way of dining or entertainment. ⊠ *164 E. Center (U.S. 491), 84535* 📞 *435/587–2274 or 800/657–6622* 📠 *435/587–2175* ⊕ *www.themonticelloinn.com* ➫ *26 rooms* ♿ *In-room: refrigerator, Wi-Fi* ⊟ *AE, D, MC, V.*

BLANDING

20 mi south of Monticello via U.S. 191.

Pioneers started settling along the base of the Abajo and Henry mountains near Blanding in 1897. Some of the stone buildings they raised still stand, and the town has a number of excellent museums that document the past. Thousands of ancient Pueblo ruins are scattered across the surrounding mesa top. You can't buy alcohol in this solidly Mormon town, and that includes even beer in grocery or convenience stores. Stock up in Monticello, 20 mi north on U.S. 191.

TRAIL OF THE ANCIENTS

As you head toward the southeast corner of Utah, you are not only entering the Four Corners Region of the United States, but approaching what is known as the "Trail of the Ancients." Route 95 is designated as such because it's rich with ancient Indian dwellings. Deep in the canyons of this area are petroglyphs, pictographs, and artifacts of the Ancestral Puebloan peoples. Enjoy looking but never touch, remove, or vandalize these historic sites or their artifacts; it's a federal offense to do so.

Stretch your legs while you learn about southeastern Utah in the **Blanding Visitor Center.** Maps, guidebooks, and regional books are for sale here, and it's staffed by locals who really know the area. You'll see it right on the highway. ⊠ *12 N. Grayson Pkwy.* 📞 *435/678–3662* ⊕ *www.blandingutah.org* 🕐 *Apr.–Sept., Mon.–Sat. 8–8; Oct.–Mar., Mon.–Sat. 8–6.*

One of the nation's foremost museums dedicated to the Ancestral Puebloan Indians is at **Edge of the Cedars State Park.** The museum displays pots, baskets, spear points, and the only known metal implements from the Anasazi era in Utah. Behind the museum, you can visit an actual Anasazi ruin. ⊠ *660 W. 400 North St.* 📞 *435/678–2238* ⊕ *www.stateparks.utah.gov* 💲 *$6 per vehicle* 🕐 *May–Sept., daily 9–6; Oct.–Apr., daily 9–5.*

🔅 Road-weary travelers, especially children, will enjoy a stop at the **Dinosaur Museum,** the private collection of a family of working paleontologists. Skeletons, fossil logs, and footprints from all over the world are all on display. Hallways hold a collection of movie posters featuring Godzilla and other dinosaurlike monsters dating back to the 1930s. ⊠ *754 S. 200 West St.* 📞 *435/678–3454* ⊕ *www.dinosaur-museum. org* 💲 *$2* 🕐 *Apr.–Oct., Mon.–Sat. 9–5.*

**OFF THE
BEATEN
PATH**

Hovenweep National Monument. For anyone with an abiding interest in the ancient Anasazi Indians, now called Ancestral Puebloans, a visit to this archaeological site is a must. Along a remote stretch of the Utah–Colorado border southeast of Blanding, Hovenweep features several unusual tower structures that may have been used for astronomical observations. A ½-mi walking tour, or a more rigorous 1½-mi hike into the canyon, allows you to see the ancient dwellings. A 32-site campground is available for overnighters in tents or small vehicles. ✉ *28 mi east of U.S. 191 on Rte. 262* ☎ *970/562–4282* ⊕ *www.nps.gov/hove* 🎟 *$6* ☼ *Daily 8 AM–sunset.*

BLUFF

25 mi south of Blanding via U.S. 191.

Bluff, settled in 1880, is one of southeastern Utah's oldest towns. Mormon pioneers built a ranching empire that made the town at one time the richest per capita in the state. Although this early period of affluence has passed, several historic Victorian-style homes remain and can be seen on a short walking tour of the town. Pick up the free brochure "Historic Bluff by Bicycle and on Foot" at any business in town, and then take a walk through the era it describes. Most of the original homes from the 1880 town-site of Bluff City are part of the Bluff Historic District. In a dozen or so blocks are 42 historic structures, most built between about 1890 and 1905. On a windswept hill above town, gravestones bear the names of many of the town's first families.

Bluff is something of a supply point for residents of the Navajo Indian Nation, the largest Native American reservation, which lies just beyond the San Juan River. Bluff is a quiet place that has deliberately avoided the development that many nearby towns pursued. The San Juan River corridor and nearby canyons are rich with Native American rock art, dwellings, and other archaeological sites.

In September you can see traditional Ute ceremonial dances at the **Bear Dance** (☎ *435/678–3397*), sponsored by the White Mesa Ute Council in a three-day celebration held Labor Day weekend.

Hot-air balloon enthusiasts gather for the **Bluff International Balloon Festival** (☎ *435/672–2303*)each January. Colorful balloons take to the skies over the San Juan River and nearby Valley of the Gods.

Three miles southwest of Bluff, the **Sand Island Recreation Site** has a large panel of Ancestral Puebloan rock art. The panel includes several large images of Kokopelli, the mischief maker from Pueblo Indian lore. ✉ *About 3 mi west of Bluff on U.S. 191* ☎ *435/587–1500 Monticello BLM office.*

**OFF THE
BEATEN
PATH**

Four Corners Monument. This marker represents the only place in the country where four states—Utah, Arizona, New Mexico, and Colorado—meet. Administered by the Navajo Nation, Four Corners offers not only a geography lesson but also a great opportunity to buy Native American jewelry and other traditional crafts directly from Navajo artisans. Bring cash, as credit cards and checks may not be accepted, particularly when buying from roadside displays or other impromptu marketplaces. To reach the monument, head south from Bluff on U.S. 191 for about 35 mi, to its junction with U.S. 160. (The U.S. 191– U.S. 160 junction is south of the Utah–Arizona border in the Navajo Nation.) Drive east on U.S. 160 for about 30 mi. At this point, U.S. 160 curves north to the monument site.

SPORTS & THE OUTDOORS

RIVER EXPEDITIONS While somewhat calmer than the Colorado, the San Juan River offers some truly exceptional scenery and abundant opportunities to visit archaeological sites. It can be run in two sections: from Bluff to Mexican Hat, and from Mexican Hat to Lake Powell. Near Bluff (3 mi southwest on U.S. 191), the Sand Island Recreation Site is the launch site for most river trips. You'll find a primitive campground there. Permits from the Bureau of Land Management are required for floating on the San Juan River. For permits, contact the **Bureau of Land Management, Monticello Field Office** (*San Juan Resource Area, Box 7, Monticello, 84535* ☎*435/587–1544* ⊕*www.blm.gov/ut*).

Wild River Expeditions (✉*101 Main St.* ☎*435/672–2244 or 800/422– 7654* ⊕*www.riversandruins.com*)can take you out on the San Juan River on one- to eight-day float trips. This reliable outfitter is known for educational trips, which emphasize the geology, natural history, and archaeological wonders of the San Juan and its canyons.

WHERE TO STAY & EAT

$$–$$$ ✗**Cow Canyon Trading Post.** Tiny but absolutely charming, this restaurant next to a classic trading post serves three dinner entrées daily. Meals are creative and diverse, with a touch of ethnic flair. Menu selections include a meat or vegetarian main with soup and salad. You can enjoy beer or wine with your meal. ✉*U.S. 191 and Rte. 163* ☎*435/672– 2208* ▤*AE, D, MC, V* ⊗*Closed Nov.–Mar. No lunch.*

$ ▥**Desert Rose Inn and Cabins.** Bluff's largest motel is truly a rose in the
Fodor'sChoice desert. It's an attractive log-cabin-style structure with a front porch that
★ gives it a nostalgic touch, and all rooms are spacious and clean with uncommonly large bathrooms. The cabins have small refrigerators and microwaves. **Pros:** Beautiful motel with comfortable rooms. **Cons:** Has no particular historic charm. ✉*701 W. Main St. (U.S. 191), 84512* ☎*435/672–2303 or 888/475–7673* ▤*435/672–2217* ⊕*www.desertroseinn.com* ➳*30 rooms, 6 cabins* ♿*In-room: refrigerator (some), Wi-Fi. In-hotel: no elevator, laundry facilities* ▤*AE, D, MC, V.*

¢–$ ▥**Recapture Lodge.** Known for its friendliness, this older but popular and regionally famous inn runs guided tours into the surrounding canyon country and presents nightly slide shows about local geology, art, and history. The plain motel rooms offered at good prices book up fast, so call ahead for reservations. **Pros:** Quiet lodge set on shady grounds, welcoming owners. **Cons:** Older property with small rooms and basic amenities. ✉*220 E. Main St. (U.S. 191), Box 309, 84512* ☎*435/672–2281* ▤*435/672–2284* ⊕*www.recapturelodge.com* ➳*26 rooms* ♿*In-room: kitchen (some), Wi-Fi. In-hotel: pool, no elevator, laundry facilities* ▤*AE, D, MC, V.*

SHOPPING

Comb Ridge Trading Post (✉*680 S. U.S. 191* ☎*435/672–2415*)is an absolute gem of a trading post right on the highway. Here you will find arts and crafts by local Navajo artisans as well as a few well-chosen collectibles.

EN ROUTE

A red fairyland of slender spires and buttes, the **Valley of the Gods** is a smaller version of Monument Valley (⇨ below). Approximately 12 mi west of Bluff, you can take a pretty private drive through this relatively unvisited area on the 17-mi long Forest Road 242, which winds through the area and brings you back to Route 163 via Route 261.

MEXICAN HAT

20 mi southwest of Bluff via U.S. 163.

Tiny Mexican Hat lies on the north bank of the San Juan River. Named for a nearby rock formation, which you can't miss on the way into town, Mexican Hat is a jumping-off point for visiting two geological wonders: Utah's Goosenecks and Arizona's Monument Valley. Magnificent Monument Valley, stretching to the south into Arizona, is home to many generations of Navajo farmers but is most recognizable from old Westerns.

From the overlook in **Goosenecks State Park** (✉*Rte. 316, off Rte. 261, 10 mi northwest of Mexican Hat*)you can peer down upon what geologists claim is the best example of an "entrenched meander" in the world. The river's serpentine course resembles the necks of geese in spectacular 1,000-foot-deep chasms. Although the Goosenecks of the San Juan River is a state park, no facilities other than pit toilets are provided, and no fee is charged.

★ The soaring red buttes, eroded mesas, deep canyons, and naturally sculpted rock formations of **Monument Valley Navajo Tribal Park** are an easy 21 mi drive south of Mexican Hat on U.S. 163 across Navajo land. Monument Valley is a small part of the nearly 16-million acre Navajo Reservation and is sacred to the Navajo Nation, or Diné (pronounced din-*eh,* which means "the people"), as they refer to themselves. For generations, the Navajo have grown crops and herded sheep in Monument Valley, considered to be one of the most scenic and mesmerizing destinations in the Navajo Nation. Director John Ford made this amazing land of buttes, towering rock formations, and mesas popular when he filmed *Stagecoach* here in 1938. The 30,000-acre Monument Valley Navajo Tribal Park lies within Monument Valley. A 17-mi self-guided driving tour on a dirt road (there's only one road, so you can't get lost) passes the memorable **Mittens** and **Totem Pole** formations, among others. Drive slowly, and be sure to walk (15 minutes round-trip) from North Window around the end of Cly Butte for the views. The park has a 99-site campground, which closes from early October through April. Be sure to call ahead for road conditions in winter. The Monument Valley **visitor center** holds a small crafts shop and exhibits devoted to ancient and modern Native American history. Most of the independent

11

Where the West Was Filmed

Were it not for Hollywood—with a little help from Harry Goulding—Monument Valley might have remained a quiet, hidden enclave of the Navajo Nation. Goulding urged John Ford to help bring the beauty of Monument Valley to the attention of the American public. Ford began in 1938 with his classic movie *Stagecoach*, and the film notoriety never ended. Ford subsequently filmed *My Darling Clementine*, *War Party*, and *She Wore a Yellow Ribbon* during the 1940s. Then came *Billy the Kid*, *Kit Carson*, *Fort Apache*, *How the West Was Won*, *The Living Desert*, *The Searchers*, and *Cheyenne Autumn*. And those were just the John Ford Westerns.

The area is as popular a film location today as it was in the 1940s and '50s, when Americans (and Hollywood) were just learning about it. Monument Valley is frequently seen as a

backdrop for automobile and other commercials. Dozens more films have been shot in the area, including a few classics (and nonclassics): *2001: A Space Odyssey*, *Easy Rider*, *The Moviemakers*, *National Lampoon's Vacation*, *Back to the Future Part III*, *Forrest Gump*, *Pontiac Moon*, *Waiting to Exhale*, and *Windtalkers*.

While many people associate Monument Valley with filmmaking or as a home to the Navajo Nation, others cannot think about the area without remembering Harry Goulding and his wife Mike, who established the trading post there in 1923. The Gouldings offered crucial trading services to the Navajos for more than half a century. Today, Goulding's Trading Post is on the National Register of Historic Places and still provides lodging, meals, and other services to tourists who visit the area.

guided tours here use enclosed vans, charge about $20 for 2½ hours, and will usually approach you in the parking lot; you can find about a dozen approved Navajo Native American guides in the center. They will escort you to places that you are not allowed to visit on your own. Bring your camera (and extra batteries) to capture this surreal landscape that constantly changes with the rising and setting sun. ⊠ *Visitor center, off U.S. 163, 21 mi south of Mexican Hat, Monument Valley* 🕭 *Box 2520, Window Rock, 86515* ☎ *435/727-3353 park visitor center, 928/871-6647 Navajo Parks & Recreation Dept.* ⊕ *www.navajonationparks.org* 🖃 *$5* ☉ *Visitor center May–Sept., daily 7–7; Oct.–Apr., daily 8–5.*

OFF THE BEATEN PATH

Moki Dugway. Route 261 takes you to the Moki Dugway, a road that was bulldozed out of a cliff during the uranium boom. It's been improved since it was originally built, but its steep grade and tight switchbacks still provide thrills sufficient for most drivers. From the top of the cliff you're rewarded with outrageous views south over the Navajo Reservation with Monument Valley visible over 20 mi away. This drive is not recommended for vehicles over 20 feet in length. ⊠ *Rte. 261, 9 mi north of Rte. 163.*

Muley Point Overlook. Five miles beyond the Moki Dugway turnoff on Route 263 brings you to the Muley Point Overlook, which has a panoramic view of the Goosenecks of the San Juan River and Monument

Valley. It's also 1,000 feet higher in elevation than the Goosenecks overlook further south.

WHERE TO STAY

$$$ 　☷ **Goulding's Lodge.** With spectacular views of Monument Valley from each room's private balcony, this motel often serves as headquarters for film crews. The lodge has handsome stucco buildings and all the rooms have balconies, coffeemakers, and hair dryers. The on-premises Stagecoach restaurant ($–$$$) serves the area favorite, a Navajo taco, or you can eat traditional American entrées; breakfasts are particularly good. Goulding's also conducts custom-guided tours of Monument Valley and provides Navajo guides into the backcountry. The lodge is 2 mi off U.S. 163, at the Monument Valley Tribal Park turnoff. **Pros:** This place is truly a slice of American history. And the views! **Cons:** It's miles from anything in any direction. ⊠ *Off U.S. 163, about 25 mi southwest of Mexican Hat, Box 360001, Monument Valley, 84536* 🕾 *435/727–3231* 🖷 *435/727–3344* ⊕ *www.gouldings.com* ⤳ *77 rooms* ⚲ *In-room: refrigerator, DVD (some), VCR (some), Wi-Fi. In-hotel: restaurant, pool, no elevator, laundry facilities* ▤ *AE, D, DC, MC, V.*

$ 　☷ **San Juan Inn & Trading Post.** This spot is a well-known take-out point for white-water runners on the San Juan, a river that vacationing sleuths will recognize as the setting of many of Tony Hillerman's Jim Chee mystery novels. The motel's Southwestern-style, rustic rooms overlooking the river at Mexican Hat are clean and well maintained. Diners can watch the river flow by at the Old Bridge Grill ($–$$), which serves great grilled steaks and juicy hamburgers. Fresh trout and inexpensive Navajo dishes add variety to the menu. **Pros:** The location on a bluff overlooking the San Juan River. **Cons:** There's not much to do in Mexican Hat itself besides watching the river roll by. ⊠ *U.S. 163* 🕾 *Box 310276, 84531* 🕾 *435/683–2220* 🖷 *435/683–2210* ⊕ *www. sanjuaninn.net* ⤳ *39 rooms* ⚲ *In-hotel: restaurant, gym, laundry facilities* ▤ *AE, D, DC, MC, V.*

NIGHTLIFE & THE ARTS

If you find yourself at Goulding's Lodge in the evening, take in the **Earth Spirit Show,** a sound-and-sight show produced by photographer Ric Ergenbright. Admission to this show is free if you have purchased a Goulding's guided trip through Monument Valley; otherwise, tickets are $2.

SHOPPING

You can't leave Monument Valley without stopping at the historic **Goulding's Trading Post** (⊠ *Off U.S. 163, about 25 mi southwest of Mexican Hat, Monument Valley* 🕾 *435/727–3231*). The store started in a tent in 1923 and the rest, as they say, is history. The trading post has a reputation for selling only authentic Native American art.

NATURAL BRIDGES NATIONAL MONUMENT

33 mi north of Mexican Hat via Rtes. 261 and 275; 38 mi west of Blanding via Rtes. 95 and 275.

Nowhere but in Natural Bridges National Monument are three large river-carved bridges found so close together. When Elliot McClure, an early visitor, drove through the park in 1931, using the term "road" to describe the route into the Natural Bridges area was being generous. It's said the road was so bad that his car literally fell apart on the journey: First his headlights fell off. Next, his doors dropped off. Finally, his bumpers worked loose, and the radiator broke away.

Today a trip to see the three stone bridges is far less hazardous. All roads are paved, and a scenic 9-mi drive takes you to stops that over-look Sipapu, Owachomo, and Kachina bridges. Sipapu is the second-largest natural bridge in the world. Kachina is the most massive in the park. It was named for pictographs near its base that resemble katsina dolls. At 106-feet high and 9-feet thick, Owachomo Bridge is the small-est of the three. You'll need an hour or two to drive to overlooks of the natural bridges and remains of an Ancestral Puebloan structure, but if you have more time, you can also hike to each of the bridges on the uncrowded trails that are fragrant with the smell of sage. Sipapu and Kachina are fairly strenuous, with steep trails dropping into the canyon. Owachomo is an easy walk. The scientists among you should be sure to stop by the monument's array of solar panels, once the larg-est in the world; the solar energy helps keep Natural Bridges National Monument clean and quiet. ⊠ *Rte. 275, off Rte. 95* ☎ *435/692–1234* ⊕ *www.nps.gov/nabr* ⊠ *$6 per vehicle* ⊙ *Daily 8* AM*–sunset.*

LAKE POWELL

50 mi west of Natural Bridges National Monument (to Hall's Cross-ing) via Rte. 276.

Lake Powell, 185 mi long with 2,000 mi of shoreline—longer than America's Pacific coast—is the heart of the huge 1,255,400-acre Glen Canyon National Recreation Area. Created by the barrier of Glen Can-yon Dam—a 710-foot wall of concrete in the Colorado River—Lake Powell took 17 years to fill. The second-largest man-made lake in the nation, Lake Powell extends through terrain so rugged it was the last major area of the United States to be mapped. It's ringed by red cliffs that twist off into 96 major canyons and countless inlets (most acces-sible only by boat) with huge, red-sandstone buttes randomly jutting from the sapphire waters. You could spend 30 years exploring the lake and still not experience everything there is to see. The Sierra Club has started a movement to drain the lake to restore water-filled Glen Can-yon, which some believe was more spectacular than the Grand Canyon, but the lake is likely to be around for years to come, regardless of the final outcome of this plan.

The most popular thing to do at Lake Powell is rent a houseboat and chug leisurely across the lake, exploring coves and inlets. You'll have plenty of company, however, since thousands of people visit the lake during spring, summer, and fall. Fast motorboats, Jet Skis, and sailboats all share the lake. It's a popular spot for bass fishing, but you'll need a Utah fishing license from one of the marinas. Remember also that the lake extends into Arizona and if your voyage takes you across the state line, you'll need a fishing license that covers the southern end of the lake. Unless you love crowds and parties, it's best to avoid visiting during Memorial Day or Labor Day weekends. Because of drought conditions in the West, the level of water in Lake Powell has dropped significantly leading to the closure of boat ramps and marinas. It is important to check with the National Park Service for current water levels, closures, and other weather-related conditions.

Guided day tours are available for those who don't want to rent a boat. A popular full-day or half-day excursion sets out from the Bullfrog and Hall's Crossing marinas to **Rainbow Bridge,** the largest natural bridge in the world, and this 290-foot-high, 275-foot-wide span is a breathtaking sight. The main National Park Service visitor center is at Bullfrog Marina; there's a gas station, campground, general store, and boat docks at the marina. ⊠*Bullfrog visitor center, Rte. 276* ☎*435/684–7400* ⊕*www.nps.gov/glca* ☒*$15 per vehicle* ☉*Hrs. vary; call for times.*

Hall's Crossing Marina is the eastern terminus of the **Lake Powell Ferry.** You and your car can float across a 3-mi stretch of the lake to the Bullfrog Basin Marina, from which it's an hour's drive north to rejoin Route 95. Ferries run seven days a week and depart on the even hour from Hall's Crossing and on the odd hour from Bullfrog. ⊠*Hall's Crossing Marina, Rte. 276* ☎*435/684–7000* ☒*$20 per car* ☉*Mid-May–mid-Sept., daily 8–7; mid-Sept.–Oct. and mid-Apr.–mid-May, daily 8–5; Nov.–mid-Apr., two trips per day (call for times).*

SPORTS & THE OUTDOORS

Boating and fishing are the major sports at Lake Powell. Conveniently, all powerboat rentals and tours are conducted by the same company, a division of Aramark called **Lake Powell Resorts & Marinas** (⊠*Bullfrog Marina* ⬡*Box 56909, Phoenix, 85079* ☎*800/528–6154* ⊕*www. lakepowell.com*). Daylong tours go to Rainbow Bridge, and there's also a Canyon Explorer tour that goes into some of the more interesting canyons. The company also rents houseboats, which are a popular option on Lake Powell.

WHERE TO STAY

$$ 🏨**Defiance House Lodge.** At the Bullfrog marina, this cliff-top lodge has comfortable and clean rooms, but the real draw is the view. An onsite restaurant also serves three meals a day. Families can take advantage of the three-bedroom units with full kitchens. ⬡*Bullfrog Marina, Box 4055, Lake Powell, 84533* ☎*435/684–2233 or 800/528–6154* 📠*435/684–3114* ⊕*www.lakepowell.com* ⬠*48 rooms, 8 suites* ⬡*In-hotel: restaurant, public Wi-Fi, some pets allowed (fee)* ⊟*AE, D, MC, V.*

HANKSVILLE

95 mi northwest of Natural Bridges National Monument via Rte. 95.

In its early years, Hanksville was the closest settlement to Robbers Roost country, a hangout for Butch Cassidy and his crew of outlaws, the Wild Bunch. Today it's a good place to gas up and grab a burger.

All of the landscape in this part of the country is strange and surreal, but **Goblin Valley State Park** takes the cake as the weirdest of all. As the name implies, the area is filled with hundreds of gnomelike rock formations. Colored in a dramatic orange hue, the goblins especially delight children. Short, easy trails wind through the goblins, and there's a small, but dusty, campground with modern restrooms and showers. ⊠ *Rte. 24, 12 mi north of Hanksville* ☎ *435/564-3633* ⊕ *www.state parks.utah.gov* ⊠ *$7 per vehicle* ⊙ *Daily 8–sunset.*

WHERE TO EAT

¢ ✕**Stan's Burger Shack.** This is the traditional pit stop along the route between Lake Powell and Capitol Reef. Great burgers, fries, and shakes—and the only homemade onion rings you'll find for miles and miles—can fill your belly. ⊠ *140 S. Rte. 95* ☎ *435/542-3330* ▭ *AE, D, MC, V.*

SOUTHEASTERN UTAH ESSENTIALS

AIR TRAVEL

The nearest large airport to southeastern Utah is Walker Field Airport in Grand Junction, Colorado, 110 mi from Moab. It's served by Allegiant Air, American Eagle, Great Lakes Aviation, Sky West, United Express, and US Airways. Great Lakes Aviation also offers air service from Denver into Moab's Canyonlands Air Field.

Information Canyonlands Air Field (⊠ *1 Airport Rd., Moab* ☎ *435/259-0566*). **Walker Field Airport** (⊠ *Grand Junction, CO* ☎ *970/244-9100* ⊕ *www.walker-field.com*).

BUS TRAVEL

The only bus service in this part of Utah goes to Green River.

Information Greyhound Lines (☎ *801/355-9579 or 800/231-2222* ⊕ *www.greyhound.com*).

CAR RENTAL

Avis and Budget have outlets at Walker Field Airport in Grand Junction, Colorado. Thrifty has an outlet in Moab.

Contacts Avis (⊠ *Walker Field, Grand Junction, CO* ☎ *970/244-9170* ⊕ *www.avis.com*). **Budget** (⊠ *Walker Field, Grand Junction, CO* ☎ *970/244-9155* ⊕ *www.budget.com*). **Thrifty** (⊠ *1 Airport Rd., Moab* ☎ *435/259-7317* ⊕ *www.thrifty.com*).

CAR TRAVEL

To reach southeastern Utah from Salt Lake City, take I–15 to U.S. 6 and then U.S. 191 south. Take I–70 or U.S. 491 from Colorado and the east. Take U.S. 191 from either Wyoming or Arizona. Most roads are well-maintained two-lane highways. Be sure your car is in good working order, as there are long stretches of empty road between towns, and keep the gas tank topped off.

Information **Utah Highway Patrol** (☎ *435/965–4684* ⊕ *www.highwaypatrol. utah.gov*). **Utah State Road Conditions** (☎ *511 toll-free within Utah*).

EMERGENCIES

Ambulance or Police **Emergencies** (☎ *911*).

24-Hour Medical Care **Allen Memorial Hospital** (✉ *719 W. 4th North St., Moab* ☎ *435/259–7191*). **Blanding Medical Center** (✉ *930 N. 400 West St., Blanding* ☎ *435/678–3434*). **Green River Medical Center** (✉ *305 W. Main St., Green River* ☎ *435/564–3434*). **San Juan County Hospital** (✉ *364 W. 1st North St., Monticello* ☎ *435/587–2116*).

LODGING

Some of the best values in Moab are condominiums. Moab Lodging and Central Reservations, a very professional firm, handles reservations for these units and dozens of other motels, condos, and B&Bs in all price ranges in southeastern Utah.

Information **Moab Lodging and Central Reservations** (☎ *435/259–5125, 800/505–5343, or 800/748–4386* 🖶 *435/259–6079* ⊕ *www.moabutahlodging. com*).

CAMPING Camping opportunities are abundant and gloriously beautiful throughout southeastern Utah. The area around Moab not only offers camping within the nearby national parks, but up and down the Colorado River corridor. Green River State Park is a favorite shady campground on the banks of the Green River. Lake Powell offers miles of shoreline as well as developed campgrounds. For cooler climes in the summer months, try La Sal Mountains near Moab. There are 342 sites at 18 different Bureau of Land Management campgrounds near Arches and Canyonlands national parks. Most of these are in the Moab area, near Arches and Canyonlands' Island in the Sky District, along Route 128's Colorado River corridor, on Kane Creek Road, and on Sand Flats Road. All sites are primitive and, except for Wind Whistle and Hatch Point, have no water. Campsites are available only on a first-come, first-served basis. The BLM's Moab Field Office can give you a complete listing of campsites in the area. The Moab Information Center has information on Bureau of Land Management, National Forest Service, and National Park Service campgrounds in nearby areas. The Moab or Monticello Ranger District offices of the Manti–La Sal National Forest can give you information on Forest Service campgrounds in their respective areas.

Information **Bureau of Land Management Moab Office** (☎ *435/259–6111* ⊕ *www.blm.gov*). **Manti–La Sal National Forest** (☎ *435/259–7155 Moab Ranger District, 435/587–2041 Monticello Ranger District* ⊕ *www.fs.fed.us/r4/mantilasal*). **Moab Information Center** (☎ *435/259–8825* ⊕ *www.discovermoab.com*).

VISITOR INFORMATION

Information **Arches National Park** (✉ N. U.S. 191, Moab, 84532 ☎ 435/719–2299 or 435/259–2200 ⊕ www.nps.gov/arch). **Blanding Chamber of Commerce** (🖂 Box 792, Blanding, 84511 ☎ 435/678–2539 ⊕ www.blandingutah.org). **Blanding Visitor Center** (✉ 12 N. Grayson, Blanding, 84511 ☎ 435/678–3662 ⊕ www.blandingutah.org). **BLM Grand Resource Area** (🖂 Box M, Moab, 84532 ☎ 435/259–8193 ⊕ www.ut.blm.gov). **Business Owners of Bluff** (⊕ www.bluffutah.org).**Canyonlands National Park** (✉ 2282 W. Resource Blvd., Moab, 84532 ☎ 435/719–2313, 435/259–4351 Backcountry Reservation Office ⊕ www.nps.gov/cany).**Grand County Travel Council** (✉ 125 E. Center St., Moab, 84532 ☎ 435/259–1370, 435/259–8825, or 800/635–6622 ⊕ www.discovermoab.com). **Green River Information Center** (✉ 885 E. Main St., Green River, 84525 ☎ 435/564–3427). **San Juan County Community Development and Visitor Services** ✉ 117 S. Main St., Box 490, Monticello, 84535 ☎ 435/587–3235 or 800/574–4386 ⊕ www.southeastutah.com.

Utah
Essentials

PLANNING TOOLS, EXPERT INSIGHT, GREAT CONTACTS

There are planners and there are those who, excuse the pun, fly by the seat of their pants. We happily place ourselves among the planners. Our writers and editors try to anticipate all the issues you may face before and during any journey, and then they do their research. This section is the product of their efforts. Use it to get excited about your trip to Utah, to inform your travel planning, or to guide you on the road should the seat of your pants start to feel threadbare.

GETTING STARTED

We're really proud of our Web site: Fodors.com is a great place to begin any journey. Scan Travel Wire for suggested itineraries, travel deals, restaurant and hotel openings, and other up-to-the-minute info. Check out Booking to research prices and book plane tickets, hotel rooms, rental cars, and vacation packages. Head to Talk for on-the-ground pointers from travelers who frequent our message boards. You can also link to loads of other travel-related resources.

▮ RESOURCES

ONLINE TRAVEL TOOLS
Safety Transportation Security Administration (TSA; ⊕www.tsa.gov)

Time Zones Timeanddate.com (⊕www.timeanddate.com/worldclock)can help you figure out the correct time anywhere.

Weather Accuweather.com (⊕www.accuweather.com).**Weather.com** (⊕www.weather.com)is the Web site for the Weather Channel.

Other Resources CIA World Factbook (⊕www.odci.gov/cia/publications/factbook/index.html)has profiles of every country in the world. It's a good source if you need some quick facts and figures.

VISITOR INFORMATION
Contacts Utah Office of Tourism (✉Council Hall, Capitol Hill, 300 N. State St., Salt Lake City, 84114 ☎801/538–1030, 800/200–1160, 800/882–4386 📠801/538–1399 ⊕www.utah.com).

▮ THINGS TO CONSIDER

GEAR
Informality reigns here; jeans, sport shirts, and T-shirts fit in almost everywhere, for both men and women. The few restaurants and performing-arts events where dressier outfits are required, usually in resorts and larger cities, are the exception.

If you plan to spend much time outdoors, and certainly if you go in winter, choose clothing appropriate for cold and wet weather. Cotton clothing, including denim—although fine on warm, dry days—can be uncomfortable when it gets wet and when the weather's cold. A better choice is clothing made of wool or any of a number of new synthetics that provide warmth without bulk and maintain their insulating properties even when wet.

In summer you'll want shorts during the day. But because early morning and night can be cold, and high passes windy, pack a sweater and a light jacket, and perhaps also a wool cap and gloves. Try layering—a T-shirt under another shirt under a jacket—and peel off layers as you go. For walks and hikes, you'll need sturdy footwear. To take you into the wilds, boots should have thick soles and plenty of ankle support; if your shoes are new and you plan to spend much time on the trail, break them in at home. Bring a day pack for short hikes, along with a canteen or water bottle, and don't forget rain gear, a hat, sunscreen, and insect repellent.

In winter, prepare for subfreezing temperatures with good boots, warm socks and liners, thermal underwear, a well-insulated jacket, and a warm hat and mittens. Dress in layers so you can add or remove clothes as the temperatures fluctuate.

If you attend dances and other events at Native American reservations, dress conservatively—skirts or long pants for women, long pants for men—or you may be asked to leave.

Trip Insurance Resources

INSURANCE COMPARISON SITES		
Insure My Trip.com	800/487–4722	www.insuremytrip.com.
Square Mouth.com	727/490–5803 or 800/240–036	www.squaremouth.com.
COMPREHENSIVE TRAVEL INSURERS		
Access America	800/729–6021	www.accessamerica.com.
CSA Travel Protection	800/873–9855	www.csatravelprotection.com.
HTH Worldwide	610/254–8700 or 888/243–2358	www.hthworldwide.com.
Travelex Insurance	800/228–9792	www.travelex-insurance.com.
Travel Guard International	715/345–0505 or 800/826–4919	www.travelguard.com.
Travel Insured International	800/243–3174	www.travelinsured.com.
MEDICAL-ONLY INSURERS		
International Medical Group	800/628–4664	www.imglobal.com.
International SOS		www.internationalsos.com.
Wallach & Company	540/687–3166 or 800/237–6615	www.wallach.com.

When traveling to mountain areas, remember that sunglasses and a sun hat are essential at high altitudes, even in winter; the thinner atmosphere requires sunscreen with a greater SPF than you might need at lower elevations. Bring moisturizer even if you don't normally use it. Utah's dry climate can be hard on your skin.

TRIP INSURANCE
What kind of coverage do you honestly need? Do you even need trip insurance at all? Take a deep breath and read on.

We believe that comprehensive trip insurance is especially valuable if you're booking a very expensive or complicated trip (particularly to an isolated region) or if you're booking far in advance. Who knows what could happen six months down the road? But whether or not you get insurance has more to do with how comfortable you are assuming all that risk yourself.

Comprehensive travel policies typically cover trip-cancellation and interruption, letting you cancel or cut your trip short because of a personal emergency, illness, or, in some cases, acts of terrorism in your destination. Such policies also cover evacuation and medical care. Some also cover you for trip delays because of bad weather or mechanical problems as well as for lost or delayed baggage. Another type of coverage to look for is financial default—that is, when your trip is disrupted because a tour operator, airline, or cruise line goes out of business. Generally you must buy this when you book your trip or shortly thereafter, and it's only available to you if your operator isn't on a list of excluded companies.

If you're going abroad, consider buying medical-only coverage at the very least. Neither Medicare nor some private insurers cover medical expenses anywhere outside of the United States (including time aboard a cruise ship, even if it leaves from a U.S. port). Medical-only policies typically reimburse you for medical care (excluding that related to pre-existing conditions) and hospitalization abroad, and provide for evacuation. You still have to pay the bills and await reimbursement from the insurer, though.

Expect comprehensive travel insurance policies to cost about 4% to 7% or 8% of the total price of your trip (it's more like 8%–12% if you're over age 70). A medical-only policy may or may not be cheaper than a comprehensive policy. Always read the fine print of your policy to make sure that you are covered for the risks that are of most concern to you. Compare several policies to make sure you're getting the best price and range of coverage available.

BOOKING YOUR TRIP

Unless your cousin is a travel agent, you're probably among the millions of people who make most of their travel arrangements online.

But have you ever wondered just what the differences are between an online travel agent (a Web site through which you make reservations instead of going directly to the airline, hotel, or car-rental company), a discounter (a firm that does a high volume of business with a hotel chain or airline and accordingly gets good prices), a wholesaler (one that makes cheap reservations in bulk and then re-sells them to people like you), and an aggregator (one that compares all the offerings so you don't have to)?

Is it truly better to book directly on an airline or hotel Web site? And when does a real live travel agent come in handy?

▮ ONLINE

You really have to shop around. A travel wholesaler such as Hotels.com or Hotel-Club.net can be a source of good rates, as can discounters such as Hotwire or Priceline, particularly if you can bid for your hotel room or airfare. Indeed, such sites sometimes have deals that are unavailable elsewhere. They do, however, tend to work only with hotel chains (which makes them just plain useless for getting hotel reservations outside of major cities) or big airlines (so that often leaves out upstarts like jetBlue and some foreign carriers like Air India).

Also, with discounters and wholesalers you must generally prepay, and everything is nonrefundable. And before you fork over the dough, be sure to check the terms and conditions, so you know what a given company will do for you if there's a problem and what you'll have to deal with on your own.

▮ **TIP→** To be absolutely sure everything was processed correctly, confirm reservations made through online travel agents, discounters, and wholesalers directly with your hotel before leaving home.

Booking engines like Expedia, Travelocity, and Orbitz are actually travel agents, albeit high-volume, online ones. And airline travel packagers like American Airlines Vacations and Virgin Vacations—well, they're travel agents, too. But they may still not work with all the world's hotels.

An aggregator site will search many sites and pull the best prices for airfares, hotels, and rental cars from them. Most aggregators compare the major travel-booking sites such as Expedia, Travelocity, and Orbitz; some also look at airline Web sites, though rarely the sites of smaller budget airlines. Some aggregators also compare other travel products, including complex packages—a good thing, as you can sometimes get the best overall deal by booking an air-and-hotel package.

▮ WITH A TRAVEL AGENT

If you use an agent—brick-and-mortar or virtual—you'll pay a fee for the service. And know that the service you get from some online agents isn't comprehensive. For example Expedia and Travelocity don't search for prices on budget airlines like jetBlue, Southwest, or small foreign carriers. That said, some agents (online or not) *do* have access to fares that are difficult to find otherwise, and the savings can more than make up for any surcharge.

A knowledgeable brick-and-mortar travel agent can be a godsend if you're booking a cruise, a package trip that's not available to you directly, an air pass, or a complicated itinerary including several overseas flights. What's more, travel agents that specialize in a destination

Online Booking Resources

AGGREGATORS

Kayak	www.kayak.com	looks at cruises and vacation packages.
Mobissimo	www.mobissimo.com	examines airfare, hotels, cars, and tons of activities.
Qixo	www.qixo.com	compares cruises, vacation packages, and even travel insurance.
Sidestep	www.sidestep.com	compares vacation packages and lists travel deals and some activities.
Travelgrove	www.travelgrove.com	compares cruises and vacation packages and lets you search by themes.

BOOKING ENGINES

Cheap Tickets	www.cheaptickets.com	discounter.
Expedia	www.expedia.com	large online agency that charges a booking fee for airline tickets.
Hotwire	www.hotwire.com	discounter.
lastminute.com	www.lastminute.com	specializes in last-minute travel; the main site is for the U.K., but it has a link to a U.S. site.
Luxury Link	www.luxurylink.com	has auctions (surprisingly good deals) as well as offers on the high-end side of travel.
Onetravel.com	www.onetravel.com	discounter for hotels, car rentals, airfares, and packages.
Orbitz	www.orbitz.com	charges a booking fee for airline tickets, but gives a clear breakdown of fees and taxes before you book.
Priceline.com	www.priceline.com	discounter that also allows bidding.
Travel.com	www.travel.com	allows you to compare its rates with those of other booking engines.
Travelocity	www.travelocity.com	charges a booking fee for airline tickets, but promises good problem resolution.

ONLINE ACCOMMODATIONS

Hotelbook.com	www.hotelbook.com	focuses on independent hotels worldwide.
Hotel Club	www.hotelclub.net	good for major cities and some resort areas.
Hotels.com big	www.hotels.com	Expedia-owned wholesaler that offers rooms in hotels all over the world.
Quikbook	www.quikbook.com	offers "pay when you stay" reservations that allow you to settle your bill when you check out, not when you book; best for trips to U.S. and Canadian cities.

OTHER RESOURCES

Bidding For Travel	www.biddingfortravel.com	good place to figure out what you can get and for how much before you start bidding on, say, Priceline.

may have exclusive access to certain deals and insider information on things such as charter flights. Agents who specialize in types of travelers (senior citizens, gays and lesbians, naturists) or types of trips (cruises, luxury travel, safaris) can also be invaluable.

■ TIP➜ Remember that Expedia, Traveloc-ity, and Orbitz are travel agents, not just booking engines. To resolve any problems with a reservation made through these com-panies, contact them first.

Agent Resources American Society of Travel Agents (☎703/739–2782 ⊕www. travelsense.org).

Utah Travel Agents Morris Murdock Travel (✉240 E. Morris Ave., Salt Lake City, UT 84115 ☎800/395–2608 ⊕www.morrismur dock.com).

Utah Adventures (✉728 W. 100 South St., Ste. 3, Heber City, UT 84032 ☎435/657–2800 or 888/881–1120 ⊕www.utadventures.com).

▌ ACCOMMODATIONS

Chain motels are everywhere. Other than that, accommodations are varied. The resort towns along the Wasatch Front—especially Park City and Snowbird—cater to the wealthy jet set and there are posh resorts in Deer Valley and pampering spas at Green Valley or Red Mountain. Salt Lake City has hotels in every price range. National chains like Best Western, Super 8, and Motel 6 are dependable in Utah and are sometimes the best beds in town. The gateway towns to the national parks usually have a large range of accommo-dations. There are also more bed-and-breakfasts, as international tourists often prefer to meet the locals at such places. Independent motels can also be found all over the state. Look for guest ranches if you're trying to find an authentic cowboy experience. They often require a one-week stay, and the cost is all-inclusive. During the busy summer season from Memo-rial Day to Labor Day, it's a good idea

to book hotels and bed-and-breakfasts in advance. Some motels and resorts have off-season rates. Take advantage of these since hiking is best in the south in cool weather and the mountains are beautiful even without snow.

The lodgings we list are the cream of the crop in each price category. We always list the facilities that are available—but we don't specify whether they cost extra: When pricing accommodations, always ask what's included and what costs extra. Most hotels and other lodg-ings require you to give your credit-card details before they will confirm your res-ervation. If you don't feel comfortable e-mailing this information, ask if you can fax it (some places even prefer faxes). However you book, get confirmation in writing and have a copy of it handy when you check in.

Be sure you understand the hotel's can-cellation policy. Some places allow you to cancel without any kind of penalty—even if you prepaid to secure a discounted rate—if you cancel at least 24 hours in advance. Others require you to cancel a week in advance or penalize you the cost of one night. Small inns and B&Bs are most likely to require you to cancel far in advance. Most hotels allow children under a certain age to stay in their par-ents' room at no extra charge, but others charge for them as extra adults; find out the cutoff age for discounts.

■ TIP➜ Assume that hotels operate on the European Plan (EP, no meals) unless we specify that they use the Breakfast Plan (BP, with full breakfast), Continental Plan (CP, Continental breakfast), Full American Plan (FAP, all meals), Modified American Plan (MAP, breakfast and dinner) or are all-inclu-sive (AI, all meals and most activities).

General Information Utah Hotel & Lodg-ing Association (✉Box 176, Roy, UT 84067 ☎801/359–0104 ⊕www.uhla.org).

BED & BREAKFASTS

Charm is the long suit of these establishments, which generally occupy a restored older building with some historical or architectural significance. They're generally small, with fewer than 20 rooms. Breakfast is usually included in the rates. Call ahead to determine the extent of ADA compliance; most B&Bs do not have elevators, for instance.

Reservation Services **BB Getaways** (⊕www.bbgetaways.com). **Bed & Breakfast. com** (☎512/322–2710 or 800/462–2632 ⊕www.bedandbreakfast.com)also sends out an online newsletter.**Bed and Breakfast Inns of Utah** (⌂Box 3071, Park City84060 ⊕www. bbiu.org). **Bed & Breakfast Inns Online** (☎615/868–1946 or 800/215–7365 ⊕www. bbonline.com). **BnB Finder.com** (☎212/432–7693 or 888/547–8226 ⊕www.bnbfinder.com).

GUEST RANCHES

If the thought of sitting around a campfire after a hard day on the range makes your heart beat faster, consider playing dude on a guest ranch. These range from wilderness-rimmed working ranches that accept guests and encourage them to pitch in with chores and other ranch activities to luxurious resorts on the fringes of a small city, with an upscale clientele, swimming pools, tennis courts, and a lively roster of horse-related activities such as breakfast rides, moonlight rides, and all-day trail rides. Rafting, fishing, tubing, and other activities are usually available; at working ranches, you even may be able to participate in a cattle roundup. In winter, cross-country skiing and snowshoeing keep you busy. Lodgings can run the gamut from charmingly rustic cabins to the kind of deluxe quarters you expect at a first-class hotel. Meals may be fancy or plain but hearty. Many ranches have packages and children's and off-season rates.

Information **The Dude Ranchers' Association** (⌂Box 2307, Cody, WY82414 ☎866/399–2339 ⊕www.duderanch. org).

HOSTELS

Hostels offer bare-bones lodging at low, low prices—often in shared dorm rooms with shared baths—to people of all ages, though the primary market is young travelers, especially students. Most hostels serve breakfast; dinner and/or shared cooking facilities may also be available. In some hostels you aren't allowed to be in your room during the day, and there may be a curfew at night. Nevertheless, hostels provide a sense of community, with public rooms where travelers often gather to share stories. Many hostels are affiliated with Hostelling International (HI), an umbrella group of hostel associations with some 4,000 member properties in more than 60 countries. Other hostels are completely independent and may be nothing more than a really cheap hotel.

Membership in any HI association, open to travelers of all ages, allows you to stay in HI-affiliated hostels at member rates. One-year membership is about $28 for adults. Rates in dorm-style rooms run about $15–$25 per bed per night; private rooms are more, but are still generally well under $100 a night. Members have priority if the hostel is full; they're also eligible for discounts around the world, even on rail and bus travel in some countries.

Hostelling through Utah is an inexpensive way to see the mountains and the desert. Utah has several, generally in Salt Lake City or outdoorsy meccas such as Moab.

In Utah, most hostels are geared to the student–backpacker crowd. Some have camping facilities with access to an indoor kitchen and bath. In some 4,500 locations in more than 70 countries around the world, Hostelling International (HI), the umbrella group for a number of national youth-hostel associations, offers single-sex, dorm-style beds and, at many hostels, rooms for couples and family accommodations. HI is also an especially helpful organization for road cyclists.

Information **Hostelling International—USA**
(☎301/495–1240 ⊕www.hiusa.org).**Hostels.
com** (⊕www.hostels.com). **The Avenues Hostel** (☎801/359–3855 ⊕www.saltlakehostel.
com).

HOTELS

Most Salt Lake City hotels cater to business travelers with such facilities as restaurants, cocktail lounges, Internet,
swimming pools, exercise equipment, and
meeting rooms. Room rates usually reflect
the range of amenities available. Most
other Utah towns and cities also have less
expensive hotels that are clean and comfortable but have fewer facilities. A popular accommodations trend is the all-suite
hotel, which gives you more room for the
money; examples include Courtyard by
Marriott and Embassy Suites. In resort
towns, hotels are decidedly more deluxe,
with every imaginable amenity in every
imaginable price range; rural areas generally have simple, and sometimes rustic,
accommodations.

Many properties have special weekend
rates, sometimes up to 50% off regular
prices. However, these deals are usually not extended during peak summer
months, when hotels are normally full.
The same discounts generally hold true
for resort town hotels in the off-seasons.

All hotels listed have private bath unless
otherwise noted.

RESORTS

Ski towns throughout Utah such as Deer
Valley, Sundance, and Brian Head, are
home to dozens of resorts in all price
ranges; the activities lacking in any individual property are usually in the town
itself—in summer as well as winter. Off
the slopes, there are both wonderful rustic and luxurious resorts bordering the
national parks: Zion Ponderosa Ranch
Resort near Zion, Sorrel River Ranch and
Red Cliffs Lodge near Arches.

▌ AIRLINE TICKETS

Most domestic airline tickets are electronic; international tickets may be either
electronic or paper. With an e-ticket the
only thing you receive is an e-mailed
receipt citing your itinerary and reservation and ticket numbers.

The greatest advantage of an e-ticket
is that if you lose your receipt, you can
simply print out another copy or ask the
airline to do it for you at check-in. You
usually pay a surcharge (up to $50) to get
a paper ticket, if you can get one at all.

The sole advantage of a paper ticket is that
it may be easier to endorse over to another
airline if your flight is canceled and the airline with which you booked can't accommodate you on another flight.

The least expensive airfares to Utah are
often priced for round-trip travel and
must usually be purchased in advance.
Airlines generally allow you to change
your return date for a fee; most low-fare
tickets, however, are nonrefundable. If
you don't mind some driving, check into
flying into Las Vegas rather than Salt
Lake City, especially if you're traveling
to southern Utah. Fares to Las Vegas are
often cheaper.

▌ RENTAL CARS

When you reserve a car, ask about cancellation penalties, taxes, drop-off charges
(if you're planning to pick up the car in
one city and leave it in another), and surcharges (for being under or over a certain
age, for additional drivers, or for driving
across state or country borders or beyond
a specific distance from your point of
rental). All these things can add substantially to your costs. Request car seats and
extras such as GPS when you book.

Rates are sometimes—but not always—
better if you book in advance or reserve
through a rental agency's Web site. There
are other reasons to book ahead, though:

Car Rental Resources

AUTOMOBILE ASSOCIATIONS		
American Automobile Association (AAA)	315/797–5000	www.aaa.com; most contact with the organization is through state and regional members.
National Automobile Club	650/294–7000	www.thenac.com; membership is open to California residents only.
LOCAL AGENCIES		
Rugged Rentals	800/977–9111	www.ruggedrental.com.
MAJOR AGENCIES		
Alamo	800/462–5266	www.alamo.com.
Avis	800/331–1212	www.avis.com.
Budget	800/527–0700	www.budget.com.
Hertz	800/654–3131	www.hertz.com.
National Car Rental	800/227–7368	www.nationalcar.com.

for popular destinations, during busy times of the year, or to ensure that you get certain types of cars (vans, SUVs, exotic sports cars).

■TIP➜ **Make sure that a confirmed reservation guarantees you a car. Agencies sometimes overbook, particularly for busy weekends and holiday periods.**

You can rent an economy car with air-conditioning, an automatic transmission, and unlimited mileage in Salt Lake City for about $30 a day and $150 a week. This does not include tax on car rentals, which is 16.35% in Salt Lake City. If you're planning to do any skiing, biking, four-wheeling, or towing, check into renting an SUV, van, or pickup from a local company like Rugged Rentals, which specializes in outdoor vehicles and provides supplemental insurance as part of the rental charge. For around $60 per day or $300 per week (plus taxes and other fees), you can rent a relatively new SUV or van with bike rack, ski rack, or towing equipment included.

Renting a car in Las Vegas can be less expensive than renting one in Salt Lake City, especially if you're visiting south-ern Utah. The driving time between Las Vegas and Salt Lake City is 7 to 9 hours, but it's only a 2- to 3-hour trip from Las Vegas to Zion National Park.

In Utah you must be 21 and have a valid driver's license to rent a car; most companies also require a major credit card. If you're over 65, check the rental company's policy on overage drivers. You may pay extra for child seats (but shop around; some companies don't charge extra for this), which are compulsory for children under five, and for additional drivers. Non-U.S. residents will need a reservation voucher, a passport, a driver's license, and a travel policy that covers each driver, in order to pick up a car.

CAR-RENTAL INSURANCE

Everyone who rents a car wonders whether the insurance that the rental companies offer is worth the expense. No one—including us—has a simple answer. It all depends on how much regular insurance you have, how comfortable you are with risk, and whether or not money is an issue.

If you own a car and carry comprehensive car insurance for both collision and liability, your personal auto insurance will probably cover a rental, but read your policy's fine print to be sure. If you don't have auto insurance, then you should probably buy the collision- or loss-damage waiver (CDW or LDW) from the rental company. This eliminates your liability for damage to the car.

Some credit cards offer CDW coverage, but it's usually supplemental to your own insurance and rarely covers SUVs, minivans, luxury models, and the like. If your coverage is secondary, you may still be liable for loss-of-use costs from the car-rental company (again, read the fine print). But no credit-card insurance is valid unless you use that card for *all* transactions, from reserving to paying the final bill.

■TIP➔ Diners Club offers primary CDW coverage on all rentals reserved and paid for with the card. This means that Diners Club's company—not your own car insurance—pays in case of an accident. It *doesn't* mean that your car-insurance company won't raise your rates once it discovers you had an accident.

You may also be offered supplemental liability coverage; the car-rental company is required to carry a minimal level of liability coverage insuring all renters, but it's rarely enough to cover claims in a really serious accident if you're at fault. Your own auto-insurance policy will protect you if you own a car; if you don't, you have to decide whether you are willing to take the risk.

U.S. rental companies sell CDWs and LDWs for about $15 to $25 a day; supplemental liability is usually more than $10 a day. The car-rental company may offer you all sorts of other policies, but they're rarely worth the cost. Personal accident insurance, which is basic hospitalization coverage, is an especially egregious rip-off if you already have health insurance.

■TIP➔ You can decline the insurance from the rental company and purchase it through a third-party provider such as Travel Guard (www.travelguard.com)—$9 per day for $35,000 of coverage. That's sometimes just under half the price of the CDW offered by some car-rental companies.

Some states, including Nevada, have capped the price of the CDW and LDW.

■ GUIDED TOURS

Guided tours are a good option when you don't want to do it all yourself. You travel along with a group (sometimes large, sometimes small), stay in prebooked hotels, eat with your fellow travelers (the cost of meals sometimes included in the price of your tour, sometimes not), and follow a schedule.

But not all guided tours are an if-it's-Tuesday-this-must-be-Belgium experience. A knowledgeable guide can take you places that you might never discover on your own, and you may be pushed to see more than you would have otherwise. Tours aren't for everyone, but they can be just the thing for trips to places where making travel arrangements is difficult or time-consuming (particularly when you don't speak the language).

Whenever you book a guided tour, find out what's included and what isn't. A "land-only" tour includes all your travel (by bus, in most cases) in the destination, but not necessarily your flights to and from or even within it. Also, in most cases prices in tour brochures don't include fees and taxes. And remember that you'll be expected to tip your guide (in cash) at the end of the tour.

Utah Adventures and Utah Tours both offer a variety of packages that run the gamut of Utah sports and activities.

Recommended Companies Adventure Vacation (☎865/558-3595 ⊕www. adventurevacation.com). **Utah Adventures** (☎888/881-1120 ⊕www.utadventures.com).

Utah Tours (☎800/961–7375 ⊕www.
utahtours.net).

SPECIAL-INTEREST TOURS

BIKING

Utah offers a wide range of topography and scenery to satisfy cyclists of all styles. Moab for years has been heralded as a mecca for mountain bikers, but fat-tire lovers pedal all corners and all elevations of the state. Hard-core road cyclists, including pros in training, challenge themselves by climbing the grueling canyons to the east of Salt Lake City. But there are plenty of roads for the less gonzo rider to explore, and biking is an excellent way for a family to bond while getting some exercise.

■ TIP→ **Most airlines accommodate bikes as luggage, provided they're dismantled and boxed.**

Contacts **Bicycle Adventures** (☎800/443–6060 ⊕www.bicycleadventures.com).**Escape Adventures** (☎800/596–2953 ⊕www.escapeadventures.com). **Utah Tours** (☎800/961–7375 ⊕www.utahtours.net). **Western Spirit** (☎800/845–2453 ⊕www.westernspirit.com).

FISHING

Located close to Salt Lake City, the Provo and Logan rivers are world-class trout fishing rivers that attract anglers from around the globe. In some parts of the Provo, it is said that there are upwards of 7,500 trout per square mile.

Contacts **Four Seasons Fly Fishers** (☎435/657–2010 or 800/498–5440 ⊕www.utahflyfish.com).

GOLF

In the sunny, dry southwestern corner of Utah, the proliferation of golf courses in the St. George area may be at least partly responsible for the region's burgeoning population. You can find variety in terrain, scenery, and level of difficulty.

Contacts **Red Rock Golf Trail** (☎888/345–5551 ⊕www.redrockgolftrail.com). **Utah Adventures** (☎888/881–1120 ⊕www.utadventures.com). **Utahfairways.com** (☎435/668–4888 ⊕www.utahfairways.com).

SKIING

If ever an outdoor activity was synonymous with Utah, skiing is it. The bulk of the state's resorts, known for the fluffy powder that falls on average 500 to 600 inches or more a year, are within a comfortable drive from the Salt Lake airport.

Contacts **Alta Vacation** (☎800/220–7067 ⊕www.altavacations.net). **Ski the Rockies** (☎800/291–2588 ⊕www.skitherockies.com). **Snow Ventures** (☎800/845–7157 ⊕www.snowventures.com).

TRANSPORTATION

Salt Lake City is Utah's major air gateway, although if southern Utah is your primary destination, Las Vegas is a convenient and often less-expensive alternative. Once on land, a car or other vehicle is your best bet for getting around. Most of the state's population is concentrated along the narrow corridor from Ogden south to Provo, by way of Salt Lake City, so it doesn't take long to get away from it all and find yourself on the open road. Much of Utah is comprised of wide-open vistas and empty asphalt.

Outside of the Salt Lake City and Park City areas, much of what draws most people to Utah is in the southern part of the state. I-15 is the main north-south thoroughfare, branching off to U.S. 6 toward Moab and to Arches and Canyonlands National Parks in the southeast, passing west of Capitol Reef National Park in the south-central, and continuing all the way to the St. George area for Zion and Bryce National Parks in the southwest.

TRAVEL TIMES FROM SALT LAKE CITY	BY CAR
To	
Park City	40 min
Zion National Park	4 ¾ hours
Bryce National Park	4 ¼ hours
Arches National Park & Moab	4 hours
Canyonlands National Park	4 ¼ hours
Capitol Reef National Park	3 ¾ hours

■TIP→ Ask the local tourist board about hotel and local transportation packages that include tickets to major museum exhibits or other special events.

■ BY AIR

Salt Lake City is approximately 16 hours from Sydney, 12 hours from London, 3 hours from Dallas, 5 hours from New York, 4 hours from Chicago, 3¾ hours from Los Angeles, and 1½ from Las Vegas.

If you're traveling during snow season, allow extra time for the drive to the airport, as weather conditions can slow you down. If you'll be checking skis, arrive even earlier. Smoking policies vary from carrier to carrier. Most airlines prohibit smoking on all of their flights; others allow smoking only on certain routes or certain departures. Ask your carrier about its policy. Smoking on airplane flights within the United States is prohibited.

■TIP→ If you travel frequently, look into the TSA's Registered Traveler program. The program, which is still being tested in several U.S. airports, is designed to cut down on gridlock at security checkpoints by allowing prescreened travelers to pass quickly through kiosks that scan an iris and/or a fingerprint. How sci-fi is that?

Airlines & Airports Airline and Airport Links.com (⊕ www.airlineandairportlinks.com)has links to many of the world's airlines and airports.

Airline Security Issues Transportation Security Administration (⊕ www.tsa.gov)has answers for almost every question that might come up.

AIRPORTS

The major gateway to Utah is Salt Lake City International Airport. Flights to smaller, regional, or resort-town airports generally connect through this hub. A convenient gateway to southern Utah, particularly Zion and Bryce Canyon national parks, is McCarran International Airport in Las Vegas.

■TIP→ Long layovers don't have to be only about sitting around or shopping. These days they can be about burning off vacation calories. Check out www.airportgyms.com for lists of health clubs that are in or near many U.S. and Canadian airports.

Airport Information McCarran International Airport (LAS) (☎702/261–5211 ⊕www. mccarran.com).Salt Lake City International Airport (SLC) (☎801/575–2400 ⊕www. slcairport.com).

GROUND TRANSPORTATION

You can get to and from the Salt Lake City airport by taxi, bus, or hotel shuttle. Public transportation information counters are located near baggage claim in all terminals, or at the front desk at hotels. If you're in downtown Salt Lake City, your best bet is to call ahead for a taxi.

Contacts City Cab Company (☎801/363–8400). Utah Transit Authority (UTA) (☎801/743–3882 or 888/743–3882 ⊕www. rideuta.com). Ute Cab Company (☎801/359–7788). Yellow Cab (☎801/521–2100).

FLIGHTS

Salt Lake City has a large international airport, so you'll be able to fly here from anywhere, though you may have to connect somewhere else first. The airport is a major hub for Delta Airlines and is also served by discount airlines, including Southwest and jetBlue, which often have incredibly good prices but not as many flights in and out. If you're flying in from somewhere other than the United States, you'll likely connect in Los Angeles or San Francisco if you're coming from Australia or New Zealand, or a major airport in the East, such as Detroit or New York, if you're traveling from Europe. Occasionally in winter you may be delayed by a major snowstorm, but those generally affect the mountain areas, not the airport. If you're heading to southern Utah, you will probably find it more convenient to fly into Las Vegas, which has more flights and is often a cheaper destination. Connecting flights

to smaller airports throughout Utah are available most frequently from either Salt Lake or Las Vegas, though it's often just as easy (and cheaper) to drive. During ski season some of the major resort towns have increased service, and direct flights may be available.

Airline Contacts American Airlines (☎800/433–7300 ⊕www.aa.com). Continental Airlines (☎800/523–3273 for U.S. and Mexico reservations, 800/231–0856 for international reservations ⊕www.continental. com). Delta Airlines (☎800/221–1212 for U.S. reservations, 800/241–4141 for international reservations ⊕www.delta.com). Frontier (☎800/432–1359 ⊕www.frontierairlines.com). jetBlue (☎800/538–2583 ⊕www.jetblue. com). Northwest Airlines (☎800/225–2525 ⊕www.nwa.com). SkyWest (☎800/453–9417 ⊕www.skywest.com). Southwest Airlines (☎800/435–9792 ⊕www.southwest.com). United Airlines (☎800/864–8331 for U.S. reservations, 800/538–2929 for international reservations ⊕www.united.com). USAirways (☎800/428–4322 for U.S. and Canada reservations, 800/622–1015 for international reservations ⊕www.usairways.com).

■ BY BUS

Greyhound Lines runs several buses each day to Salt Lake's terminal. The company also serves Provo, Ogden, Tremonton, Green River, Logan, Brigham City, Cedar City, and St. George.

Bus Information Greyhound Lines (✉300 S. 600 West St., Salt Lake City ☎801/355–9579 or 800/231–2222 ⊕www.greyhound.com).

■ BY CAR

You'll need a car in Utah. Public transportation exists, but caters to commuters, not tourists. You'll seldom be bored driving. Scenery ranges from snow-capped mountains to endless stretches of desert with strange rock formations and intense color. There are more national parks here than in any other state except Alaska and

California, although their interiors are not always accessible by car.

Before setting out on any driving trip, it's important to make sure your vehicle is in top condition. It is best to have a complete tune-up. At the least, you should check the following: lights, including brake lights, backup lights, and emergency lights; tires, including the spare; oil; engine coolant; windshield-washer fluid; windshield-wiper blades; and brakes. For emergencies, take along flares or reflector triangles, jumper cables, an empty gas can, a fire extinguisher, a flashlight, a plastic tarp, blankets, water, and coins or a calling card for phone calls (cell phones don't always work in high mountain areas).

GASOLINE
In major cities throughout Utah, gas prices are roughly similar to the rest of the continental United States; in rural and resort towns, prices are considerably higher. In urban areas, stations are plentiful, and most stay open late (some are open 24 hours). In rural areas, stations are less frequent, and hours are more limited, particularly on Sunday; you can sometimes drive more than 100 mi on back roads without finding gas. It's best to always keep your tank at least half full.

PARKING
Parking is generally easy to find, except in the larger downtowns, such as Salt Lake City, particularly on weekend nights. Many parking garages offer free visitor parking, typically for one or two hours. Meters are usually free for two hours at a stretch on Saturday and all day on Sunday.

ROAD CONDITIONS
Utah has some of the most spectacular vistas—and challenging driving—in the world. Roads range from multilane blacktop to narrow dirt roads; from twisting switchbacks bordered by guardrails to primitive backcountry paths so narrow that you must back up to the edge of a steep cliff to make a turn. Scenic routes and lookout points are clearly marked, enabling you to slow down and pull over to take in the views. You'll find highways and the national parks crowded in summer, and almost deserted (and occasionally impassable) in winter.

In many locations, particularly in the burgeoning Salt Lake valley and St. George areas, there always seems to be road construction underway, which slows traffic. Check road conditions before you set out, and allow a little extra time when traveling in these busier regions.

One of the more unpleasant sights along the highway are roadkills—animals struck by vehicles. Deer, elk, and even bears may try to get to the other side of a road just as you come along, so watch out for wildlife on the highways. Exercise caution, not only to save an animal's life, but also to avoid possible extensive damage to your car.

Road Conditions In Utah (☎511 ⊕commuterlink.utah.gov).

ROADSIDE EMERGENCIES
Throughout Utah, call 911 for any travel emergency, such as an accident or a serious health concern. For automotive breakdowns, 911 is not appropriate. Instead, find a local directory and dial a towing service. When out on the open highway, call the non-emergency central administration phone number of the Utah Highway Patrol for assistance.

Emergency Services Utah Highway Patrol (☎801/965-4518 ⊕highwaypatrol.utah.gov).

RULES OF THE ROAD
Utah law requires seat belts for drivers and all passengers in vehicles so equipped. Always strap children under age 5 into approved child-safety seats. Helmets are required for motorcyclists and passengers under the age of 18.

You may turn right at a red light after stopping if there is no sign stating otherwise and no oncoming traffic. Right turns on red are prohibited in some areas, but these are signed accordingly. When in doubt, wait for the green.

SPEED LIMITS
The speed limit on U.S. interstates is 75 mph in rural areas and 65 mph in urban zones. But watch out. "Rural areas" are determined by census boundaries and sometimes make little sense. Increased speeds are allowed only where clearly posted. Transition zones from one speed limit to the next are indicated with pavement markings and signs. Fines are doubled for speeding in work zones and school zones.

WINTER & DESERT DRIVING
Modern highways make mountain driving safe and generally trouble free even in cold weather. Although winter driving can occasionally present some real challenges, road maintenance is good and plowing is prompt. However, in mountain areas, tire chains, studs, or snow tires are essential. If you're planning to drive into high elevations, be sure to check the weather forecast and call for road conditions beforehand. Even main highways can close. Be prepared for stormy weather: carry an emergency kit containing warm clothes, a flashlight, some food and water, and blankets. It's also good to carry a cell phone, but be aware that the mountains can disrupt service. If you do get stalled by deep snow, do not leave your car. Wait for help, running the engine only if needed, and remember that assistance is never far away. Winter weather isn't confined to winter in the high country (it's been known to snow on July 4), so be prepared year-round. Keep your tank full of gas and remember water, even in winter. Always tell someone, even if it's the hotel clerk or gas station attendant, where you're going and when you expect to return.

Desert driving can be dangerous winter or summer. Always carry water, even in winter. You'll encounter extreme conditions in remote areas with drifting snow and/or sand and little chance of anyone driving by to help. Never leave children or pets in a car—summer temperatures climb quickly over 100°F.

▌ BY TRAIN

Amtrak connects Utah to both coasts and many major American cities, with trains that stop in Salt Lake City, Ogden, Provo, Helper, Green River, and St. George.

Information **Amtrak** (☎800/872–7245 ⊕www.amtrak.com).

SCENIC TRAIN TRIPS
On the Heber Valley Historic Railroad in Utah, you can catch the *Heber Creeper,* a turn-of-the-20th-century steam engine train that rides the rails from Heber City across Heber Valley, alongside Deer Creek Reservoir, down Provo Canyon to Vivian Park. Depending on the time of year, you can catch the Comedy Murder Mystery Train, the Polar Express, the Cowboy Poetry Train, or special holiday rides.

Information **Heber Valley Historic Railroad** (✉450 S. 600 West St., Heber City84032 ☎435/654–5601 ⊕www.hebervalleyrr.org).

ON THE GROUND

▌BUSINESS SERVICES & FACILITIES

There are about 20 FedEx Kinko's Office and Print centers located throughout the greater Salt Lake area. Call or visit their Web site to find the location nearest you.

Contacts **FedEx Kinko's** (☎800/254-6567 ⊕www.fedex.com/us/officeprint/main/).

▌COMMUNICATIONS

INTERNET

Most major chain hotels and many smaller motels throughout Utah now offer Wi-Fi or other Internet access at no cost to guests. Many coffee shops provide Wi-Fi free of charge (although it's a little harder to find in southern Utah), as do most libraries, which also provide computers with Internet access. There's also free Wi-Fi along Main Street in downtown Salt Lake City.

Contacts **Cybercafes** (⊕www.cybercafes. com)lists over 4,000 Internet cafés worldwide.

▌EATING OUT

Dining in Utah is generally casual. Menus are becoming more varied, but you can nearly always order a hamburger or a steak. There are a growing number of fine restaurants in Salt Lake and Park City, and good places are cropping up in various other areas. Also look for good dining in Springdale, Moab, and Torrey. Seek out colorful diners along the secondary highways like U.S. 89; they usually serve up meat and potatoes along with the local flavor of each community. Authentic ethnic food is easy to find in Salt Lake City but generally not available elsewhere. Dinner hours are from 6 PM to 9 PM. Outside the large cities and resort towns in the high seasons, many restaurants close by 10 PM. The restaurants we

list are the cream of the crop in each price category.

MEALS & MEALTIMES

Although you can find all types of cuisine in the major cities and resort towns of Utah, be sure to try native dishes like trout, elk, and buffalo (the latter two have less fat than beef and are just as tasty); organic fruits and vegetables are also readily available especially in finer establishments in Salt Lake City and Park City. Southwestern food is popular, and you'll find several restaurants that specialize in it or show Southwestern influences in menu selections. Thai cuisine and sushi are both gaining in popularity (and quality) in the Salt Lake area.

Unless otherwise noted, the restaurants listed in this guide are open daily for lunch and dinner.

PAYING

Credit cards are widely accepted, though not always at restaurants located in rural areas.

RESERVATIONS & DRESS

We mention dress only when men are required to wear a jacket or a jacket and tie—which is almost never in casual Utah. Even at nice resorts, dress is usually casual, and in summer you're welcome nearly everywhere in your shorts, T-shirt, and hiking shoes.

Contacts **OpenTable** (⊕www.opentable. com).**DinnerBroker** (⊕www.dinnerbroker. com).

WINES, BEER & SPIRITS

Despite what you've heard, it's not hard to get a drink in Utah, though you must be 21 to purchase or consume alcohol. The key is knowing what kind of place you're in according to Utah liquor laws. There are three types of places you can get a drink: a private club, a restaurant with a liquor license, and a brewpub, beer bar, or tavern.

A private club is a bar that sells just about any kind of liquor you can imagine, usually along with at least appetizers if not a full menu. The trick here is that you must either buy a membership (usually $4 for a three-week membership) or be a guest of someone who already has a membership. There may be a cover charge if a popular band is in town.

Many restaurants have liquor licenses, which allow them to serve you liquor—or at least wine—with a meal. You can simply sit down and order your food and drink from a server. Some restaurants—generally those that cater to families—have decided that it's too much trouble to deal with the State Liquor Commission and have opted not to carry a liquor license. If you're set on having a drink with your meal, check before you go.

At brewpubs, beer bars, and taverns, you can get beer, beer, more beer, and, generally, wine coolers. There are several brewpubs with their own beers on tap—try St. Provo Girl and Polygamy Porter to get a taste of the local drinking humor. You don't need a membership, and there's generally no cover charge unless a hot band is playing. Many brewpubs also have a liquor license that allows the sale of wine and spirits—only in the dining room, not at the bar.

If you're staying in a nicer hotel, your "membership" to the hotel bar will be included in your accommodation fees. Most hotel restaurants carry a liquor license, and you'll be able to get your own drinks from the minibar in your room.

To buy your own liquor (other than beer with 3.2% alcohol), you'll have to go to a state liquor store. There are 17 liquor stores throughout Salt Lake City and others throughout the state. They are closed on Sunday, Election Day, and holidays. It's best not to take your own wine or other liquor to a restaurant—lots of regulations cover brown bagging.

▌ MONEY

Hotel prices in Salt Lake City run the gamut, but on the average prices are a bit lower than in most major cities. You can pay $100–$350 a night for a room in a major business hotel, though some "value" hotel rooms go for $50–$75, and budget motels are also readily available. Weekend packages at city hotels can cut prices in half (but may not be available in peak winter or summer seasons). As a rule, costs outside cities are lower, except in the deluxe resorts, where costs can be double those anywhere else in the state. Look for senior and kids' discounts at many attractions.

Prices throughout this guide are given for adults. Substantially reduced fees are almost always available for children, students, and senior citizens.

CREDIT CARDS

Throughout this guide, the following abbreviations are used: **AE**, American Express; **D**, Discover; **DC**, Diners Club; **MC**, MasterCard; and **V**, Visa.

It's a good idea to inform your credit-card company before you travel, especially if you're going abroad and don't travel internationally very often. Otherwise, the credit-card company might put a hold on your card owing to unusual activity—not a good thing halfway through your trip. Record all your credit-card numbers—as well as the phone numbers to call if your cards are lost or stolen—in a safe place, so you're prepared should something go wrong. Both MasterCard and Visa have general numbers you can call (collect if you're abroad) if your card is lost, but you're better off calling the number of your issuing bank, since MasterCard and Visa usually just transfer you to your bank; your bank's number is usually printed on your card.

Some small-town restaurants may not accept credit cards, but otherwise plastic is readily accepted at dining, lodging, shopping, and other facilities throughout the state. Minimum purchase amounts may apply.

Reporting Lost Cards American Express (☎800/528–4800 in the U.S. or 336/393–1111 collect from abroad ⊕www.american-express.com). **Diners Club** (☎800/234–6377 in the U.S. or 303/799–1504 collect from abroad ⊕www.dinersclub.com). **Discover** (☎800/347–2683 in the U.S. or 801/902–3100 collect from abroad ⊕www.discovercard.com). **MasterCard** (☎800/627–8372 in the U.S. or 636/722–7111 collect from abroad ⊕www.mastercard.com). **Visa** (☎800/847–2911 in the U.S. or 410/581–9994 collect from abroad ⊕www.visa.com).

▌ SAFETY

All those strenuous activities in high altitudes can be fun but dangerous. Utah is full of wide-open, lonely spaces. Though you may enjoy the freedom, openness, and solitude, it's always best to tell someone—the hotel desk clerk, the ski rental person—where you're going. Cell phones don't always work in the backcountry, and even a general idea of where you are can help rescuers find you quickly. Regardless of the outdoor activity or your level of skill, safety must come first. Remember: know your limits.

Many trails are at high altitudes, where oxygen is thinner. They're also frequently desolate. Hikers and bikers should carry emergency supplies in their backpacks. Proper equipment includes a flashlight,

a compass, waterproof matches, a first-aid kit, a knife, and a light plastic tarp for shelter. Backcountry skiers should add a repair kit, a blanket, an avalanche beacon, and a lightweight shovel to their lists. Always bring extra food and a canteen of water as dehydration is a common occurrence at high altitudes. Never drink from streams or lakes, unless you boil the water first or purify it with tablets. Giardia, an intestinal parasite, may be present.

Always check the condition of roads and trails, and get the latest weather reports before setting out. In summer take precautions against heat stroke or exhaustion by resting frequently in shaded areas; in winter take precautions against hypothermia by layering clothing. Ultimately, proper planning, common sense, and good physical conditioning are the strongest guards against the elements.

You may feel dizzy and weak and find yourself breathing heavily—signs that the thin mountain air isn't giving you your accustomed dose of oxygen. Take it easy and rest often for a few days until you're acclimatized. Throughout your stay drink plenty of water and watch your alcohol consumption. If you experience severe headaches and nausea, see a doctor. It is easy—especially in Utah, where highways climb to 9,000 feet and higher—to go too high too fast. The remedy for altitude-related discomfort is to go down quickly, into heavier air. Other altitude-related problems include dehydration and overexposure to the sun due to the thin air.

Flash floods can strike at any time and any place with little or no warning. The danger in mountainous terrain intensifies when distant rains are channeled into gullies and ravines, turning a quiet streamside campsite or wash into a rampaging torrent in seconds; similarly, desert terrain can become dangerous when heavy rains fall on land that is unable to absorb the water and thus floods quickly. Check weather reports before heading into the backcountry and be prepared to head for higher ground if the weather turns severe.

One of the most wonderful parts of Utah is the abundant wildlife. And while a herd of grazing elk or a bighorn sheep high on a hillside is most certainly a Kodak moment, an encounter with a bear or mountain lion is not. To avoid such an unpleasant situation while hiking, make plenty of noise, keep dogs on a leash, and small children between adults. While camping, be sure to store all food, utensils, and clothing with food odors far away from your tent, preferably high in a tree (also far from your tent). If you do come across a bear or big cat, do not run. For bears, back away quietly; for lions, make yourself look as big as possible. In either case, be prepared to fend off the animal with loud noises, rocks, sticks, etc. And, like the saying goes, do not feed the bears—or any wild animals, whether they're dangerous or not.

When in any park, give all animals their space and never attempt to feed any of them. If you want to take a photograph, use a long lens and keep your distance. This is particularly important for winter visitors. Approaching an animal can cause stress and affect its ability to survive the sometimes brutal climate. In all cases remember that the animals have the right-of-way; this is their home, you are the visitor.

▌ TAXES

Sales tax is 4.65% in Utah. Most areas have additional local sales and lodging taxes, which can be quite significant. For example, in Salt Lake City, the combined sales tax is 6.80%. Utah sales tax applies to everything, including food.

▌ TIME

Utah is in the Mountain Time Zone. Mountain time is two hours earlier than Eastern time and one hour later than Pacific time.

It is one hour earlier than Chicago, seven hours earlier than London, and 17 hours earlier than Sydney. In summer, Utah observes Daylight Savings Time.

▌ TIPPING

Utahns are notoriously stingy tippers, so don't ask a local what to tip. It is customary to tip 15% at restaurants; 18%–20% in resort towns is increasingly the norm. For coat checks and bellmen, $1 per coat or bag is the minimum. Taxi drivers expect 10% to 15%, depending on where you are. In resort towns, ski technicians, sandwich makers, coffee baristas, and the like also appreciate tips.

TIPPING GUIDELINES FOR UTAH	
Bartender	$1 to $5 per round of drinks, depending on the number of drinks
Bellhop	$1 to $5 per bag, depending on the level of the hotel
Hotel Concierge	$5 or more, if he or she performs a service for you
Hotel Doorman	$1–$2 if he helps you get a cab
Hotel Maid	1$–$3 a day (either daily or at the end of your stay, in cash)
Hotel Room-Service Waiter	$1 to $2 per delivery, even if a service charge has been added
Porter at Airport or Train Station	$1 per bag
Skycap at Airport	$1 to $3 per bag checked
Taxi Driver	15%–20%, but round up the fare to the next dollar amount
Tour Guide	10% of the cost of the tour
Valet Parking Attendant	$1–$2, but only when you get your car
Waiter	15%–20%, with 20% being the norm at high-end restaurants; nothing additional if a service charge is added to the bill

INDEX

W

PHOTO CREDITS

7, *Sylvain Grandadam/age fotostock.* 8, *Seb Rogers/Alamy.* 9 (right), *Jacom Stephens/Avid Creative, Inc./iStockphoto.* 10, *NPS.* 11 (left), *Rollie Rodriguez/Alamy.* 11 (right), *SuperStock/age fotostock.* 14, *True North Images/age fotostock.* 15 (left), *Mark D. Maziarz/age fotostock.* 15 (right), *Raymond Forbes/age fotostock.* 16, *Jean Du Boisberranger/age fotostock.* 17 (left), *Mark Gibson/Alamy.* 17 (right), *Daniel Kourey/iStockphoto.* 18, *imagebroker/Alamy.* 19 (left), *Avid Creative, Inc./iStockphoto.* 19 (right), *Larry Hansen/iStockphoto.* 22, *Arco Images/Alamy.* 23 (left), *Ron Yue/Alamy.* 23 (right), *David Underwood.* **Chapter 5: Capitol Reef National Park:** 178 (top left and bottom), *Frank Jensen/ Utah Office of Tourism.* 178 (top right), *Jacom Stephens/Avid Creative, Inc./iStockphoto.* **Chapter 9: Arches National Park:** 262 (all), *NPS.* **Chapter 10: Canyonlands National Park:** 278 (all), *NPS.*

ABOUT OUR WRITERS

Writer **John Blodgett** has moved to Utah three times since 1996. He's explored almost every corner of the Beehive State but has a particular passion for the south. It was in these silent canyons and wide-open lands of sage brush and juniper that John discovered a new muse. He also became a much better skier schussing Utah's famous powder. He has written for *Utah Business, Digital IQ, Salt Lake Magazine, Utah Homes & Garden, Salt Lake City Weekly,* and *Catalyst;* and is a former magazine editor, newspaper reporter, and photojournalist. He updated the Salt Lake City, Southwestern Utah, Bryce, and Zion chapters for this book.

Janet Buckingham has been writing and living in Moab, Utah, since 1991 when she gave up city life to make the desert her home. A seasoned contributor to Fodor's guidebooks, Janet has written several books on the national parks and the Moab area including *Into the Mystery: A Driving Guide to Moab Area Rock Art.* She is also the author of an audio tour to Arches National Park. Her column "Life and Times in Moab," ran for eight years in *Moab Happenings,* and she was a winner of a Utah Press Association Award for feature writing. Janet's poetry appears in numerous anthologies including *Glyphs I* and *III.*

Jane Gendron stopped in Park City on what was meant to be a cross-country trek and never left. Like any good resort worker, she dabbled in everything from waiting tables to heading up public relations for a non-profit organization before abandoning the office for her under-used skis, loyal golden retriever, neglected husband, and smiling baby boy (not necessarily in that order). She's written for *Park City Magazine, Wasatch Journal, Utah Business, Las Vegas Life,* and *Estates West* magazines as well as for arts and eco-friendly clients.

Jenie Skoy is a freelance travel writer and former magazine editor who lives in a studio perched above City Creek canyon in Salt Lake City. She's writes for *Sunset* and *USAToday.* An avid road-tripper, she's explored many parts of the west, including Northern Utah where she learned the art of fly-fishing and leaf-kicking while hiking ankle-deep in autumn leaves on Logan Canyon's trails. She's infatuated with Southern Utah and enjoys rock-climbing, petroglyph gazing, listening to wind in the junipers, and inhaling the after-rain smell of sage.

Raised in the Rocky Mountains, **Lucia Stewart** continues to write and work from where her heart is. Currently an editor for *NewWest.Net,* an online magazine covering the dynamically changing Rockies region, Lucia also works as a freelance writer and conference coordinator in the area and beyond. Updating the Dinosaurland and Eastern Utah chapter for this edition took her to places she didn't think she'd visit after high school in Utah, but she found they're still just as magical.

Freelance writer **Jonathan Stumpf** spent two years living in Missoula, Montana and recently relocated to Seattle. A member of the Outdoor Writers Association of America, he contributes to *Skiing, National Ski Areas Association Journal,* and the *Missoula Independent,* among other publications. He recently completed a large multimedia project about the arctic grayling in Montana's Big Hole River. When not writing about his misadventures chasing fish across the West, he can be found seeking local music in clubs around the region.

Fodor's

Utah Maps

SALT LAKE CITY & ZION NAT'L PARK

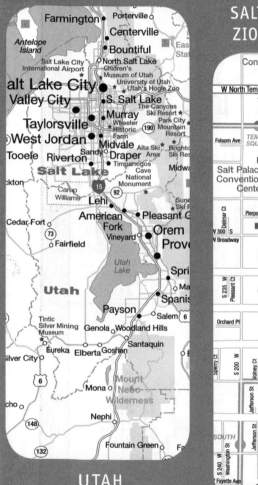

UTAH

MAPS.com

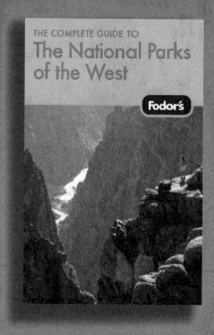